Embodied Liturgy

Embodied Liturgy

Lessons in Christian Ritual

Frank C. Senn

Fortress Press
Minneapolis

EMBODIED LITURGY

Lessons in Christian Ritual

Cover design: Alisha Lofgren

Library of Congress Cataloging-in-Publication Data

Print ISBN: 978-1-4514-9627-7

eBook ISBN: 978-1-5064-0846-0

The paper used in this publication meets the minimum requirements of American
National Standard for Information Sciences — Permanence of Paper for Printed
Library Materials, ANSI Z329.48-1984.

Manufactured in the U.S.A.

This book was produced using Pressbooks.com, and PDF rendering was done by
PrinceXML.

Dedicated to Danny Salim,
the students and staff
of the Faculty of Performing Arts
of Satya Wacana Christian University,
Salatiga, Central Java, Indonesia,
and the pastors
who accompanied me
on this experimental and experiential journey
into liturgical embodiment.
May they continue to glorify God in their bodies.

Contents

Introduction: Return to the Body

This book originated in a course I taught at Satya Wacana Christian University in Salatiga, Central Java, Indonesia, in June 2014. I was invited to offer an intensive course in liturgy by Danny Salim, dean of the Faculty of Performing Arts, to undergraduate church music students; he also invited pastors to attend the course. One reason for my retirement from parish ministry at the end of June 2013 (at the age of seventy) was to be available for just these kinds of invitations. So I said yes.

Since this was a department of performing arts rather than theology, I decided to teach the course from the perspective of the body engaged in liturgy and worship, since performing artists use their bodies to communicate. Musicians use their bodies to sing or play instruments. Dancers and actors use their bodies to tell stories or to communicate emotion. Likewise, pastors need to be more mindful of the use of their bodies in their leadership roles in the liturgy. Physically present before the assembly or congregation, they move from one location to another in the worship space. They use gestures and postures. They read Scripture, preach sermons, offer prayers, and administer sacraments. Sometimes they chant or lead singing; sometimes they touch people with the laying on of hands. Worship leaders are constantly using their bodies in a public and visible way. As such, they need to be comfortable with their bodily presence. Discomfort shows, calling attention to itself in ways that distract from the people's worship. Lack of a sense of bodily presence includes self-conscious actions, awkward gestures, sloppy postures, and slovenly dress.

With the body as a primary focus, I prepared a course that included basic introductory material on liturgy. In order of appearance the chapters in this book address liturgical theology, daily prayer offices, liturgical calendar, sacraments and sacramental theology, vestments, ritual studies, words and eucharistic meals, fasting and feasting, penitential rites and festivals, rites of passage, inculturation, architecture and art, music, drama, and performance theory. Some of these topics are covered in my *Introduction to Christian Liturgy*, and I will make reference to that book for greater detail on those topics.[1] On other topics, however, I go well beyond that introduction as we explore the role of the body in liturgy, worship, and devotion.

As far as possible, this course was taught from the perspective of the body. I had never before taught a liturgy course from this perspective, but by what other means do we worship God than with our bodies? Unfortunately, many Protestants seem to have forgotten this reality. I believe that the renewal of worship requires a return to the body as the vehicle of worship.

The course was attended by church music students in the Faculty (Department) of Performing Arts of Satya Wacana Christian University, Indonesian pastors from throughout Indonesia (Java, Sumatra, Borneo), and auditors from the performing arts faculty. I had never before taught such a spectrum of students at different levels in one classroom. Moreover, translators recruited from the Faculties of Performing Arts, Language, and Theology were present in each class session. I had never taught a course that required simultaneous translation. I was honored that the rector of the university, Dr. John A. Titaley, formally inaugurated the course to make it an official offering of Satya Wacana Christian University.

Because of the need for simultaneous translation the lectures all had to be written in advance. This process gave me a literary product to expand upon for this book. The class was held three hours a day

---

1. Frank C. Senn, *Introduction to Christian Liturgy* (Minneapolis: Fortress Press, 2012).

for ten days an hour and a half before lunch and another hour and a half after lunch—which explains the parts A and B for each chapter. I edited the lectures to remove classroom directions, to address them to a more general and global audience, and to elaborate on some ideas that I discussed extemporaneously in the classroom. Wanting to be as comprehensive as possible, I added lessons on youth rites (baptism of infants and youth, confirmation and affirmation of baptism), healing rites (churching of women, ministry to the sick, exorcism), and marriage and burial rites, which I did not cover in the course for lack of time (although I touched on some of these practices in passing). Since these lessons originated as classroom lectures, there were questions. I have gathered some of the questions that I recalled at the end of the book. I do not recall any questions after the last session on liturgical performance, but the students and the pastors expressed appreciation for that particular lecture. They said it helped them to appreciate other traditions. By way of conclusion, chapter 12, part B is a greatly expanded version of my closing remarks. The actual last afternoon session was devoted to individual oral exams in which the dean and a translator were present. I asked the students to share with me three ideas from three different lectures that they found interesting and wanted to apply to their work in the church.

I'm grateful that Fortress Press is willing to enable me to share the course through the wider means of this book because I think it will be of interest to many Christians today as we strive to regain a sense of ourselves as bodily creatures with a calling to worship and serve God.

The Body in Worship

The most fundamental thing we can say about ourselves is that we are creatures of the earth. It is an article of faith that among all the creatures of the earth it is human beings who bear the image of God. We are God's representatives in the world. We are also the priests of the world who offer the world to God in a sacrifice of love and praise. We serve these functions by means of our bodily selves. Public worship, which is what liturgy is, is a sensuous experience that involves speaking and hearing, touching and tasting, seeing and doing, motion and emotion. We cannot participate in liturgical worship apart from the body, and we do so through a variety of movements and postures as well as a script. As we have come to recognize in recent years, worship is more than words. Yet amazingly, few people have given much thought to these basic realities.

In recent and not-so-recent years (in fact, from the beginning of my active ministry in 1969), a concerted effort has been made to make worship more relevant to people where they are. The Constitution on the Sacred Liturgy (*Sacrosanctum concilium*) of the Second Vatican Council, promulgated in 1963 by Pope Paul VI, calls for more active participation of the people in their liturgy. There is no way for worship to be more relevant to people where they are or to foster their active participation than by engaging them bodily in liturgical rites. The more the senses and postures are used in worship, the more we can individually and collectively connect with what is happening in the liturgy and, in my experience, sense the presence of God. Worship that is focused only on music and preaching, as much of contemporary Protestant worship is, will be sensuously deficient, no matter how loud the music or how engaging the oration, because it doesn't offer sufficient visual, olfactory, taste, and tactile stimulation. Worship in which the worshipers are primarily seated is kinesthetically deficient because the body likes to be up and about—especially young bodies. As parents have known for years, little bodies don't like being hemmed in by wooden benches, and there's no reason they have to be. Nor do they need to be dismissed from the worshiping assembly so that the adults can worship in peace. We need a better understanding of the liturgical assembly as a congregation of the whole people of God, which is comprised of all ages.

The "body" has been treated as a metaphor as well as a physical object. In fact, as Mark Johnson and George Lakoff demonstrate, much of our experience of the physical world, including those experiences that impact our bodies, are conceptualized by use of metaphors.[2] Throughout this book, we will pay attention to some of these metaphorical uses of the term "body", such as the eucharistic body, the ecclesial body, and the cultural body, but I would advise against becoming so metaphorical that we lose our connection to actual bodies. For example, the eucharistic body of Christ is (or should be) actual food that literally feeds the physical body (no matter how minimally), entering into the chemistry of our physical bodies to be broken down either for use or elimination (sorry, but it's true). This meal builds up the church as an assembly (*ekklesia*) of many actual bodies. The "body of Christ" is more than a metaphor for the church; it has a physical reality in the physical bodies of its members who constitute the assembly. The cultural body is concretely expressed in how we engage bodily in public rituals, how we interact bodily with one another, how the body is portrayed in visual presentations, and how the body is used physically to make music, dance, and perform plays.

As a graduate student at Oxford University in the summer term of 1968, I studied the seventeenth-century English metaphysical poets and discovered the Anglican divine, mystic, and poet Thomas Traherne (1637-74), whose work has been known only since the beginning of the twentieth century. Living on the cusp of the Enlightenment (he was a contemporary of Thomas Hobbes and John Locke), Traherne delighted in the world of nature and the human body within the natural world. In a poem entitled *The Person*, he writes:

> The Naked Things
>   Are most Sublime, and Brightest shew,
>   When they alone are seen:
>   Mens Hands then Angels Wings
>   Are truer Wealth even here below:
>   For those but seem
> Their Worth they then do best reveal,
> When we all Metaphores remove,
>   For Metaphores conceal,
>   And only Vapours prove.
> They best are Blazond when we see

---

2. George Lakoff and Mark Johnson, *Metaphors We Live By* (Chicago: University of Chicago Press, 1980).

The Anatomie,
Survey the Skin, cut up the Flesh, the Veins
  Unfold: The Glory there remains.
The Muscles, Fibres, Arteries and Bones
Are better far then Crowns and precious Stones.[3]

As I deal with the body in worship I want to explore the actual body that God created to serve him. I have scoured liturgical and paraliturgical rites to find ways in which the body is actually engaged in ritual acts. The images scattered throughout this book include some of the more unusual uses of the body in worship as well as cultural portrayals of Christ's body, as discussed in the chapters that follow.

In my particular case, there is an autobiographical facet to the idea of a "return to the body." My "return to the body" came about when I underwent surgery for colon cancer in August 2006 and then received chemotherapy for most of a year. The chemo protocol was devastating to my normal functioning, and I gave up trying to live and work as if nothing were happening to my body and as if what was happening to my body didn't affect my mind. I began to pay attention to everything that was happening to my body. I also found myself mentally reviewing my life in my body during long afternoon rest periods on the sofa. I began to remember how much I used my body when I was a youth performing in the elementary school boys' gymnastics show, in children's operettas, and in piano recitals. I conducted the high school orchestra in the national anthem in school assemblies, took part in native American dancing in Boy Scout summer camp, and climbed mountains and canoed lakes in the Adirondacks of upstate New York. I reflected on how my use of my body diminished as I grew older and how I increasingly utilized only my mind in my academic and pastoral work. But I also considered how my boyhood experiences of public performance contributed to my sense of ease as a leader of public ritual. In addition, my spiritual and religious development in late adolescence helped me find more ways to use my body, particularly my senses and postures, in worship. This explains my early

3. Thomas Traherne, *Centuries, Poems and Thanksgivings*, ed. H. M. Margoliouth (Oxford: Oxford University Press, 1958), II, 24-25.

interest in ritual and liturgical action. In a sense, my early interests got sidetracked as I became involved in the work of liturgical revision in the 1970s, which was primarily text-centered. In practice as a parish pastor, however, I never forgot the importance of choreography in the liturgy or how liturgical ministers were presenting themselves bodily to the worshipers. We have not given as much attention to these aspects of liturgical leadership as we should have. Therefore I welcome this opportunity to return to the body as a primary liturgical focus.

As I rebounded from the effects of chemotherapy I also needed to rehabilitate my body through exercise. In an active older adults class at the YMCA I discovered yoga, and as I explored this practice, combined with massage therapy, I learned more about my body than I ever knew before. As I prepared this course, I thought about how helpful it would be if the participants were also able to get more in touch with their own bodies. We cannot talk about "embodiment" of liturgy and worship without actually getting into our bodies. Besides, I thought the undergraduates could use some "stretch time" in the course of a three-hour class—and it wouldn't hurt the pastors either.

An Apology for Yoga

For this reason, as I prepared the lectures, I asked Dean Salim about the propriety of engaging the students in some yogic exercises as a way of getting them to give new attention to the use of their bodies. Danny was OK with this and even gave us the recital hall for our classroom so that we could spread out our bodies on the stage. But he advised that I should say something about the use of yoga because some of the students might have heard sermons telling them to stay away from it. Wariness about yoga would not be unusual with Asian Christians, who associate yoga with Hinduism or Buddhism. Moreover, yoga does not yet flourish in Indonesia except among expatriates and tourists in Bali, perhaps because it is a mostly Muslim country. So in my first class session I gave a personal statement regarding my interest in recovering an experience of embodiment through the practice of yoga, as well as a thumbnail sketch of the history of yoga.

As a pastor and theologian I was well aware that some Christian leaders admonish Christians to stay away from yoga because of its roots in Eastern religions. As an orthodox Christian I didn't want to get into much less espouse something that is contrary to Christian beliefs. At the same time there are Hindus in India and America dedicated to "taking back yoga" from its Western and entrepreneurial appropriations and claiming it as a unique Hindu practice. Aware of these concerns, I began a study of the yoga traditions and discovered there are many.[4] As a historian I took a long view of yoga through the millennia and came to understand that yoga represents ancient wisdom about the body, which is rooted in ancient Indian culture. Yoga itself is not a religion; it is about bringing mind and body together. (The word "yoga" means "yoke".) But it has been used in religions. It was systematized in Hinduism (especially Brahmanism) for use in devotion to Hindu gods like Krishna. Yoga was also a discipline used by the Jains to cultivate moral perfection. It was transformed by Buddhism into a spirituality that aided one on the path to enlightenment. There was actually a Muslim embrace of yoga in the Mughal Empire in India in the late sixteenth century. Yoga was used in Tantra, which was a revolt against orthodox Brahmanism, that regarded the body and daily life as a source of reality and flourished among all segments of the population in medieval India, and in Buddhism as well as Hinduism.[5] Tantra views the body as a microcosm of the macrocosm (the universe) and as the location (embodiment) of the Divine, especially the divine feminine. While Tantra became largely an esoteric practice, it contributed to the development of Hatha yoga, which is the most commonly practiced form of yoga in the world today.

Yoga fell on hard times between the end of the Middle Ages and the modern period in India. It was renewed in the early twentieth century under the influence of the Northern European body culture movement,

4. See Georg Feuerstein, *The Yoga Tradition: Its History, Literature, Philosophy, and Practice* (Prescott, AZ: Hohm, 2008).
5. See Mircea Eliade, *Yoga: Immortality and Freedom*, trans. Willard R. Trask, with a new introduction by David Gordon White (Princeton: Princeton University Press, 2009) and David Gordon White, *Kiss of the Yogini: "Tantric Sex" in its South Asian Contexts* (Chicago and London: University of Chicago Press, 2003).

including German calisthenics and Scandinavian gymnastics, which was brought to India during the British Raj.[6] The YMCA generally promoted healthy minds, bodies, and spirits based on the Christian value of healthy living as part of its mission; this was also the case in the Indian YMCA. Indians were looked down upon by British administrators as unfit and unhealthy people. As part of emerging Indian nationalism, gurus like T. Krishnamacharya in southern India and Swami Sivananda in northern India took this criticism seriously and tapped into the physical postures (*asanas*) of Hatha Yoga—a tradition going back to the fifteenth century (although *asanas* had not been widely practiced except as an aid to meditation)—, blending it with Western approaches. As a result, Krishnamacharya, who is regarded as the father of modern yoga, produced a more gymnastic style of yoga not unlike the gymnastics promoted in the Indian YMCA. Students of Krishnamacharya, particularly B. K. S. Iyengar and K. Pattabhi Jois, also promoted this revitalized Hatha postural yoga in the West. I think a case can be made that the postural yoga practiced by many people around the world today has at least some Christian influence on its development through the values of having fit and healthy bodies, as promoted by the YMCA in India. In the meantime, all kinds of new yoga practices are being developed, such as hot yoga and acro yoga, and yoga has become a truly global phenomenon.

Modern yoga has become mostly an exercise regimen for health-conscious modern people. Even in modern India yoga is valued as much for its health benefits as for its metaphysics.[7] The yoga most Westerners experience is largely shorn of its religious and spiritual dimensions except as allied with New Age spirituality. I don't think it is necessarily a good thing for yoga to lose some of its spiritual and metaphysical aspects. I am interested in more of a dialogue between yoga's classical spiritual traditions and its modern physiological and psychological applications. Thankfully, I found a yoga teacher in

---

6. See Mark Singleton, *Yoga Body: The Origins of Modern Posture Practice* (Oxford University Press, 2010).
7. See Joseph A. Alter, *Yoga in Modern India: The Body between Science and Philosophy* (Princeton: Princeton University Press, 2004).

Nicholas Beem at Grateful Yoga in Evanston, Illinois, who engages in just that kind of dialogue in his teaching.

I built some yogic exercises into some of the sessions of this course. It was pretty simple yoga, consisting of introductory samples. The directions for doing these exercises appear in this book in italics if readers want to do the exercises individually or in a group. In a group situation, someone could read the directions (very slowly) while the group follows them. Those who practice yoga regularly could simply make a list of the *asana* sequences (as is often done in private practice), place it within sight, and go through the poses. I want to note that I am not a yoga teacher; I am simply relating the experience of my own practice. That said, my yoga teacher, Nick Beem, offered mini-courses in yoga cosmology and metaphysics, I received tutorials in tantric practice from the respected Chicago yoga teacher Per Erez, I participated in a weekend workshop given by nationally-known yoga teacher Rod Stryker on "Tantra: Awakening the Sacred Channel", and I participated in a week-long course on "The Embodied History of Yoga" at the Kripalu Center for Yoga and Health in Stockbridge, MA taught by Professor David Gordon White and Yoganand Michael Carroll in August 2015. I acknowledge here the assistance of my teachers Nick and Lela Beem (co-owners of Grateful Yoga, Evanston, Illinois) in shaping the sequences and finessing the directions for the yoga exercises included in this book.

A New Interdisciplinary Interest in Embodiment

As I prepared these lectures and then beefed them up after my return from Indonesia, I delved even more deeply into the human body in its various aspects. I was amazed at how much interest there has been in the human body throughout all fields of intellectual inquiry in recent years. I touch on some of these disciplines in this book, beginning with anatomy and biochemistry, but also including philosophy and phenomenology, environmental science and cosmology, incarnational and sacramental theology, ritual studies, cultural studies, architecture, art, music, dance, and drama.

The body is fundamental to human existence. We can ignore neither the biology of the body nor the body's location in the natural world. Our environment also has an effect on the body (as well as an affect in certain seasons). We cannot ignore the physical functions of the body, such as eating, drinking, sleeping, having sex, and dying. Liturgy accounts for all of these somatic—functions a fact that has been underexplored by liturgists.

We also cannot ignore the impact on the body of the belief systems of the societies in which we live—a reality that has been underexplored by theologians. How we function in life is determined to a great extent by religious beliefs and cultural mores. Belief systems that influence bodily behavior vary from unarticulated assumptions derived from the cultures in which we live to ritualized practices and explicit doctrines. Beliefs and values shape the body in many ways, from the stylization of external appearance (including clothing and ornamentation, or no clothing) to the structuring of bodily actions and comportment (including essential practices like eating and fasting) and to inner modes of affect (moods that are felt somatically and that may be cultivated in contrasting liturgical seasons like Lent and Easter). Beliefs about the human body may be systematized in a theology of the body. I found myself studying the teachings of Tantra Yoga while at the same time working through Pope John Paul II's theology of the body. Both are expressions of an incarnational theology and spirituality. They see divinity and the experience of divinity related to the body.

This book deals with embodied liturgy, but the uses of the body in liturgies, paraliturgical devotions, and other rituals are not confined to established ecclesiastical (that is, social) norms; they also include expressions of faith and commitment that are individualistic or even antagonistic to the liturgical mainstream, such as we see in flagellant processions or Mardi Gras parades. More than a mere instrument to be used in the worship of God, the body is also a site and weapon of protest, as we see in art and theater both sacred and profane.

Taking all of this and more into account, attempting to write about the human body, even just in its liturgical use, turned out to be a huge undertaking. But then liturgy is also a comprehensive reality because it expresses, as I have written elsewhere, nothing less than a worldview.[8] Many have come to see that not only is liturgy connected with the whole of life but it also forms us in a cosmology.[9]

The Cultural Body

I was privileged to engage in these reflections on the body while living for several weeks in a southeastern Asian social setting, which afforded me an opportunity to compare and contrast the body in my North American cultural context with the less Westernized and predominantly Muslim cultural context of Java—at least in the streets and shops if not as much in the church and university. Among the most evident differences are the five-times daily call to prayer over loudspeakers in the mosques (beginning at 4:15 a.m.), the girls wearing head scarves (even in a Christian university that welcomes Muslim students), and the omnipresence of motorcycles.

Body language is important in all cultures and differs from one culture to another. I experienced the custom of a child greeting an elder (a respected person in the community, a teacher, parents, grandparents, and so on) by taking the elder's offered hand and lightly touching their forehead with it. Equals shake hands softly and then lightly touch their chests afterwards. Only the right hand should be used to pass and receive things. When calling someone over, it is customary to wave one's fingers downwards, not toward oneself. Similarly, when pointing at something or someone, the index finger should never be used. In Java, people commonly use their thumbs instead.

There's no better way to more directly experience how a culture treats the body than to get an indigenous massage. After a period of long air travel, with all of its attendant tensions (thirty hours from Chicago to Yogyakarta), getting a massage is a good idea regardless, and in Indonesia massages are very inexpensive. There was a spa above

8. See Frank C. Senn, *New Creation: A Liturgical Worldview* (Minneapolis: Fortress Press, 2000).
9. See Gordon W. Lathrop, *Holy Ground: A Liturgical Cosmology* (Minneapolis: Fortress Press, 2003).

the room where I was staying in Salatiga, and I used its services several times during my stay. The traditional Javanese massage is offered in a curtained enclosure like a hut and (I am told) is one of the more vigorous of the Asian massages. The powerful strokes of the Javanese massage—which uses all parts of the hand, including the knuckles and sometimes the knees, with the massage therapist on top of the person receiving the massage can be jarring. The purpose is to purge the toxic air ("winds") from the body that causes congestion and flu-like illnesses. Considering the amount of open-air burning of trash I experienced in Indonesia, I can understand why such a purge would be beneficial. I enjoyed comparing the Javanese massage with other massages I have received, especially other Asian massages. By getting massages in other cultural contexts, one can learn a great deal about one's own body, in addition to how the body is regarded in another culture.

An Ecumenical Approach

I hope it will be obvious that this book is written from an ecumenical perspective. The students and pastors in my course were predominantly from the Reformed tradition (the Dutch Reformed Church was established in the former Dutch East Indies that became Indonesia). I do not withhold my Lutheran commitments, especially on the sacraments, but my approach reflects the perspective of an author who has studied the whole of the Christian liturgical tradition, both East and West. I believe that in this ecumenical era and age of globalization the entire Christian tradition is available to us. I also know that liturgical ideas in this book will be used selectively, according to denominational beliefs, parish practices, and pastoral need. Readers may select from this feast what seems most delicious to them. It does not hurt to sample some new dishes.

Autobiographical Elements

Autobiographical elements have crept into this book, more so than in any of my other writings. In "retirement" I suppose one engages in greater reflection on one's life and career. I also shared aspects of my life experiences with the students in Indonesia as a way for them to get to know their "foreign" teacher better. So stories of my boyhood experiences of rituals at summer camp, my religious experience of the Eucharist as a youth, my bout with cancer, and even a massage experience in Singapore, shared with my class, are left in the book. If nothing else, these autobiographical references let the reader know of my existential investment in this project.

Acknowledgments

I express my gratitude to Satya Wacana Christian University for sponsoring my trip to Indonesia and hosting me with such attention to hospitality. Satya Wacana (Sanskrit for "Truth of the Word") is a private Christian University founded in 1956 by nine congregations and synods. It is currently owned by eighteen Protestant congregations and synods in Java and throughout Indonesia, mostly in the Reformed tradition.

My thanks to Danny Salim, dean of the Faculty of Performing Arts, for inviting me to Satya Wacana, arranging for my lectures, and personally overseeing the hospitality for my stay in Indonesia; to Yosi Nur Mahardika, the student assistant who made my stay in Salatiga more comfortable by bringing me pharmaceuticals needed to keep my body functioning properly and for seeing to the classroom needs; to the faculty members and students who took me to dinner on many evenings; to Nick and Lela Beem for encouraging me as an amateur to introduce yoga practices in a place where yoga is not yet well established; to Franklin Ishida and the Division for Global Mission of the Evangelical Lutheran Church in America for providing a travel grant to assist with the airfare, just as they did the previous summer when I taught in Singapore; and to Fortress Press for taking on this project, as well as to Michael Gibson for working with me on the editing.

Namaste!
Frank C. Senn
Evanston, Illinois
Lent 2016

Figure 1. Participants in the Embodied Liturgy course in the Faculty of Performing Arts of Satya Wacana Christian University in Salatiga, Central Java, Indonesia. Dean Danny Salim is standing to the right of the author. *Satya Wacana* is Sanskrit and means "truth of the word." This photo was taken on the last Friday after lunch. Unfortunately, several pastors who participated in the course had departed to get back to their congregations.

1

———

Bodies and Liturgy

A. Bodies Created to Worship God

This is an introductory journey in liturgy. As such, we will cover many of the basics of liturgics and the repertoire of liturgical rites. However, our journey will proceed, as far as possible, from the perspective of the human body engaged in acts of worship. The premise is that we have nothing else with which to worship God than our bodily selves. This is something that should be self-evident, but worship as a bodily act hasn't been given a great deal of attention. Most of us, especially Westerners, think of ourselves as minds with a body attached. Our religion, too, is primarily a matter of thought and feeling rather than bodily actions. In fact, we tend to look down on those whose religion is just "going through the motions," forgetting that we must start somewhere—such as getting out of bed on Sunday morning to go to church. In a time when more and more people in Western societies get out of bed on Sunday morning to go jogging or biking or to take their kids to soccer practice because they generally find worship boring and unengaging, perhaps we need to give some attention to the role of the body in worship.

Many of us need to begin giving some attention to the body. Unless we are athletes or singers or make our living by using our bodies, we don't pay a lot of attention to our bodies until we are sick. This is what happened to me. After an adult lifetime of not giving much attention to my body, my need to focus on my body hit me squarely in the solar plexus when I was diagnosed with colon cancer in 2006. After having some of my colon surgically removed and spending nearly a year on chemotherapy, I became attentive to every little thing happening to my body, both during chemotherapy and in the rehabilitation that followed. I began practicing yoga at the age of sixty-five. It did wonders for my flexibility, overall strength, sense of balance, and ability to concentrate. I think we can learn a lot about our bodies and our lives from yoga practice. An ancient Indian form of wisdom that is validated by many strains of modern Western science (e.g., anatomy, neuroscience, and psychology) needs to be given respectful attention if we want to understand more about mind-body relationships.

The Human Body

With these introductory remarks out of the way, let me begin by going back to the beginning—back to the creation story from Gen. 2. The ground was dry, "but a stream would rise up from the earth, and water the whole face of the ground—then the Lord God formed man of dust from the ground, and breathed into his nostrils the breath of life; and man became a living being" (2:6-7, NRSV).

We are creatures of the earth. That's the most fundamental thing that can be said about human beings, even in Genesis. We are living, breathing bodies composed of the earth's chemical elements. It was necessary to water the ground before we could be fashioned by our Creator from the dirt. The Lord God needed to make clay. Moreover, without water no life form as we know it is possible. Water makes up 70-85 percent of our physical being. Put another way, the human body is a container that collects and stores H_2O. Therefore, it isn't surprising that most of a human body's mass is oxygen. Carbon, the basic unit for organic molecules, comes in second. Ninety-nine percent of the mass of the human body is made up of just six elements: oxygen, carbon, hydrogen, nitrogen, calcium, and phosphorus. Body composition may also be analyzed in terms of molecular type: water, protein, connective tissue, fats (or lipids), apatite (in bones), carbohydrates (such as glycogen and glucose), and DNA. In terms of tissue type, the body may be broken down into water, fat, muscle, bone, and so on. In terms of cell type, the body contains hundreds of different types of cells, but notably, the largest *number* of cells contained in a human body (though not the largest mass of cells) consists not of human cells but of bacterial cells residing in the human gastrointestinal tract. Our bodies host other living organisms—some good, some bad. The body operates with ten different but interrelated systems: skeletal, muscular, cardiovascular, digestive, endocrine (glands), nervous, respiratory, immune/lymphatic, reproductive (different in men and women), and integumentary (skin, hair, nails, and exocrine glands). What's more, we have five sense organs by which we receive information from outside of ourselves: hearing, seeing, smelling, tasting, and touching.

The reader probably did not expect a study on liturgy to begin with a lesson in biochemistry and anatomy. But I want to emphasize that human beings are physical bodies; that's how God created us. There is nothing in the story of the creation of the human that suggests that man (Adam) is composed of body and soul. Rather, the human being is a living body. Yahweh breathed into Adam "the breath of life" (*nishmat chaim*), and Adam became "a living being" (*nefesh chaim*). Life springs directly from God as the Lord God breathes into the lifeless human body he has shaped from the ground and the ground water that rose up in the desert just before man's creation. We receive God's spirit (*ruach*) as our animating energy. We are connected with God through the breath, and we are intended to be in communion/communication with God.

Mind Over Matter

If our purpose on the earth is to take care of the garden of the Lord and serve God, we have nothing other than our bodies with which to serve and worship God. The aposle Paul says as much when he writes to the Romans, "Present your bodies as a living sacrifice, holy and acceptable to God, which is your spiritual worship" (Rom. 12:1, NRSV). Yet we Christians (Catholic as well as Protestant) are heirs of a post-Reformation rationalism that teaches we worship God primarily with our minds. Our worship continues to be affected by this rationalism. We gather in buildings arranged like classrooms, with all of the benches facing in one direction. We come to attention when the bell rings and listen to a speaker expounding texts.

Western philosophy, at least since René Descartes, has focused primarily on only one part of the body: the mind. Descartes's philosophic method rejects all probable knowledge and trusts only what can be completely known without being doubted. Since the only thing Decartes could be absolutely certain of was that he was able to think, he concluded, *Cogito ergo sum*—"I think, therefore I am"—in his 1641 *Meditations on First Philosophy*. Thinking is a conscious act that involves a formal process, like mathematics. Mathematics can be certain, like the act of consciously thinking. Following Galileo before him, Descartes helped to lay the foundation for the construction of the objective or "disinterested" sciences, which have yielded much of the knowledge and many of the technologies that are commonplace today in Western culture and in all of the places to which it is imported. The chemical table of the elements, immunization vaccines, automobiles, computers, and close-up images of the planet are all things we have come to depend upon and take for granted. They emerged from the bold approach of experimentation developed by the objective sciences.

Yet these sciences consistently overlook our ordinary, everyday experience of the world around us, which is necessarily subjective, necessarily relative to our own place in the range of things, and necessarily related to our own particular desires, tastes, and concerns. At least through environmental and psychological sciences we are learning again that human life and the world's life are intertwined. We are bodies in the world, and we are affected by what happens in nature, whether it is day or night and whether there is sunlight or rain, heat or cold. We recognize that even the scientist cannot make himself or herself as value-free as he or she would like to think. The scientist is also affected by the environment in which he lives and the needs and conditions of her own body.

Phenomenology and the Embodied Mind

The philosophy of phenomenology, first taught by Edmund Husserl in the first half of the twentieth century, moved away from the mathematically-based sciences (founded by Galileo and Descartes) in an effort to describe as nearly as possible the way in which the world makes itself known to our awareness—that is, the way we experience things through our senses. Husserl was followed by Maurice Merleau-Ponty, who writes, "All my knowledge of the world, even my scientific knowledge, is gained from my own particular point of view, or from some experience of the world without which the symbols of science would be meaningless."[1]

The physical body came to play an important role in the philosophies of Husserl and Merleau-Ponty. For Husserl the "self" is a transcendent ego separated from the phenomena that it studies, including the body. But for Merleau-Ponty the self is the body. Husserl would say, "I have a body" (implying a disconnection from the body), while Merleau-Ponty would say, "I am a body" (this body is me). Moreover, Merleau-Ponty taught that the body is fundamental to all experience. The body is not a stationary phenomenon; it takes a stand in the world by always being in motion (even if only breathing). When sitting in a concert or lecture hall or sports stadium, I turn my head or move my entire body to get a better view. When I extend an arm and wave a hand to get the attention of a friend, I am doing more than flexing a set of muscles; I am projecting myself toward someone else. By moving my body, I cause the world to exist for me. Therefore the body is more than a collection of physical systems; it is how I express myself and communicate with others, including God.

1. Maurice Merleau-Ponty, *Phenomenology of Perception*, trans. Colin Smith (London: Routledge & Kegan Paul, 1962), viii.

The philosopher David Abram writes in *The Spell of the Sensuous*:

This breathing body, as it experiences and inhabits the world, is very different from that objectified body diagrammed in physiology textbooks, with its separate "systems" (the circulatory system, the digestive system, the respiratory system, etc.) laid bare on each page. The body I speak of is very different from the body we have been taught to see and even to feel, very different, finally, from that complex machine whose broken parts or struck systems are diagnosed by our medical doctors and "repaired" by our medical technologies. Underneath the anatomized and mechanical body that we have learned to conceive, prior indeed to all our conceptions, dwells the body as it actually experiences things, this poised and animate power that initiates all our projects and suffers all our passions.[2]

Gone here is the Cartesian separation of mind and body. There is no difference between mind and body; the mind is part of the body.

In recent philosophy, an embodied mind thesis has emerged in which the nature of the human mind is largely determined by the human body. Philosophers, psychologists, and cognitive scientists argue that all aspects of knowing, including reason, are shaped by aspects of the body. The aspects of the body that shape the mind include the motor system, the perceptual system, the body's interactions with the environment, and even the ontological assumptions about the world that are built into the body and the brain. In terms of cognitive science, George Lakoff and Mark Johnson take as axioms three major findings:

The mind is inherently embodied.
Thought is mostly unconscious.
Abstract concepts are largely metaphorical.[3]

When taken together and considered in detail, Lakoff and Johnson find these conclusions from the science of the mind at odds with most of Western philosophy, especially with the influence of Descartes over the last three centuries. Descartes concluded that thinking is what

---

2. David Abram, *The Spell of the Sensuous* (New York: Vintage Books, 1996), 45-46.
3. See especially George Lukoff and Mark Johnson, *Philosophy in the Flesh: The Embodied Mind and Its Challenges to Western Thought* (New York: Basic Books, 1999), 3.

makes us human and distinct from the rest of the animal creation. Man is *Homo sapiens*. What's more, thinking is disembodied because it transcends our physical bodies. But as Lakoff and Johnson write in their magisterial work, *Philosophy in the Flesh*:

> Reason is not disembodied, as the [philosophic] tradition has largely held, but arises from the nature of our brains, bodies, and bodily experience. This is not just the innocuous and obvious claim that we need a body to reason; rather, it is the striking claim that the very structure of reason itself comes from the details of our embodiment. The same neural and cognitive mechanisms that allow us to perceive and move around also create our perceptual system and modes of reason.[4]

Hence, reason is not a function of a disembodied mind. It is shaped by the peculiarities and particularities of our human bodies. What we think about things is conditioned by how our bodies have developed and by what our bodies have experienced. These hidden thought processes are largely unconscious (depth psychology digs out these unconscious thoughts). And while Descartes might have rejected the use of the imagination in reason, he was not averse to using metaphor since he regarded thinking as a process of "enlightenment"—that is, shedding light on a subject.

If the mind is not disembodied but part of the body, how do we reach the mind through the body? The pioneering body worker, Deanne Juhan, author of the classic bodywork manual, *Job's Body*, expresses it this way in an online article entitled, "Reaching the Mind with Touch: Touch as Language in the Body's Landscape of Perception." One reaches the brain with all of its stored memories by touching the skin. After all, the nervous system runs through the entire body. Moreover, writes Juhan,

> 'Mind' is vastly more extensive than 'brain.' Mind involves the whole of our landscape, and all of the internal and external ecological processes that are fused into those mysteries and miracles that we call life and consciousness. We are moved by all levels of our feelings, ideas and beliefs, our current assessments, needs and intentions, and by all of the countless processes that underlie them.[5]

4. Ibid., 4.

"Mind" is the intelligence that resides in the body. The physical body has its own intelligence. As a former piano student I know that fingers can sometimes have a mind of their own. Sometimes they follow the path they have learned on the keyboard when the brain goes blank. Athletes also experience motor memory when they make instantaneous decisions on the sports field without thinking about what they need to do with the ball that suddenly comes into their possession. For these reasons, both physical therapists and yoga teachers have begun talking about the intelligence of different parts of the body.

Theologically, if God is going to transform our minds (conversion) he must do so through the body. This is the role and the impact of the sacraments on the body. God relates to us by impacting our bodies through earthly means that become means of grace, particularly Holy Bath (baptism) and Holy Meal (Communion). In response, we relate to God by using our bodies in the worship of God.

Theology of the Body

But more than that, our bodies are connected to the cosmos. Realizing this was the great contribution of Tantra to the yoga tradition. Most of the yoga traditions in India viewed the body as what Georg Feuerstein calls "a breeding ground for *karma* and an automatic hindrance to enlightenment."[6] Tantra, on the other hand, does not view the world or the body as mere illusion, but as a manifestation of Reality. Feuerstein wrote,

> If the world is real, the body must be real as well. If the world is in essence divine, so must be the body. If we must honor the world as a creation or an aspect of the divine Power (*Shakti*), we must likewise honor the body. The body is a piece of the world and . . . the world is a piece of the body.[7]

---

5. Deane Juhan, "Reaching the Mind with Touch: Touch as Language in the Body's Landscape of Perception," *Job's Body*, October 12, 2010, http://www.jobsbody.com/pages/articles/reachingthemind.html.
6. See Georg Feuerstein, *Tantra: The Path of Ecstasy* (Boston: Shambhala, 1998), 53.
7. *Ibid.*, 53.

In a similar way, the late Pope John Paul II, as a student of philosophy, was influenced by phenomenology, and in his catecheses on the theology of the body he took as a fundamental principle, "I don't *have* a body, I *am* a body." That is, we must relate to God, to others, and to the world through our bodies. But more than that, Pope John Paul II viewed the body as a sacrament, a visible sign of God in the world. "The body, and only the body, is capable of making visible what is invisible: the spiritual and divine. It has been created to transfer into the visible reality of the world the mystery hidden from eternity in God, and thus to be a sign of it" (Address on February 20, 1980).[8]

All the fullness of God dwelled in the body of the human Jesus. St. Athanasius says in his apologetic treatise *On the Incarnation*, "He manifested Himself by means of a body in order that we might perceive the mind of the unseen Father."[9] The ways Christ manifested the mind of the Father in his body, as listed by Athanasius, include his birth and death, resurrection and ascension—the work of Christ enumerated in the Nicene Creed.

In Christian baptism we receive the Spirit of the Father and the Son. We are bodily incorporated into, made members of, the body of Christ in the world, and our bodies, individually and collectively, are hosts to the Holy Spirit. As the apostle Paul says, "Do you not know that your body is a temple of the Holy Spirit within you, which you have from God, and that you are not your own? For you were bought with a price; therefore glorify God in your body" (1 Cor. 6:19-20, NRSV).

Body Scan

If we are our bodies, part of getting in touch with ourselves is getting in touch with our bodies. If we are going to worship God with our bodies—if we are to present our bodies as a living sacrifice—we should know what we are to present. To get to know the body better, I invite you to do a body scan meditation. This is an exercise in learning how

---

8. John Paul II, *Man and Woman He Created Them: A Theology of the Body*, trans. Michael Waldstein (Boston: Pauline Books and Media, 2006), 203.

9. Athanasius, *On the Incarnation*, trans. Penelope Lawson (Crestwood, NY: St. Vladimir's Seminary Press, 1953), 93.

9

to sense, with keener awareness, the body as a whole and also the specific parts of the body. It does so by inviting you to concentrate on different parts of the body, one part at a time. Holding your focus on each part, you will use your mind to quietly sense what is going on in that part of your body. Perhaps this meditation is also a way to reintroduce yourself to parts of your body you haven't paid attention to in a while. (Perhaps someone could read this meditation slowly while you experience it.)

Sit comfortably in a chair or on the floor on a low cushion with legs crossed (remove your shoes) and with your spine straight, your head on top of your spine, your hands on your knees with your palms open, and your eyes closed. Alternately, you may lie on the floor with legs and arms extended at a slight angle, feet falling limp toward the floor, palms facing up, and eyes closed. Note anatomically that open palms will subtly rotate your shoulders back, which will open your chest and also lengthen your spine. (This is savasana or "corpse pose," which is used as the final relaxation in yoga sequences.) Take a long deep breath through your nostrils, then breathe it out through your mouth like a big sigh (my yoga teacher calls this the "falling-out breath"). Do it several times. Then rest in the natural flow of your breath and allow your whole body to relax and your mind to begin to settle.

Bring your attention to the top of your head, and without looking for anything in particular, feel the sensations there. Then let your attention move down to the back of your head, to either side of your head, to your ears, your forehead, eyes, nose, cheeks, mouth, and jaw. Be as slow and thorough as you like. Notice any sensations in these areas. Be aware of the brain inside your skull sending messages to the rest of the body through the nervous system.

As you continue the scan, be careful not to open your eyes; they will direct your attention to something outside the body. Instead, connect directly with sensations by feeling the body from within the body. In certain parts of the body, it is common to feel numbness or to not perceive noticeable sensations. Let your attention remain in those areas for a few moments in a relaxed and easy way. You may find that as your attention deepens, you become increasingly aware of sensations. Images or thoughts will naturally arise.

Notice them passing through and gently return your attention to the sensations. If you become distracted you can always return to the breath. Release all ideas about what you think you should experience and simply experience your physical aliveness exactly as it is.

With a relaxed, open awareness, begin a gradual and thorough scan of the rest of your body. Bring your attention to the area of your neck and throat, noticing without judgment whatever sensations you feel. Then let your attention move to your shoulders and slowly down your arms and to your hands, feeling the sensations and aliveness there. Feel each finger from the inside, as well as the palms and the backs of the hands. Notice tingling, pulsing, pressure, warmth, or cold. Slowly move on to explore the sensations in your chest. Be aware of your heart sending oxygen throughout your body by means of blood flowing through your arteries as pumped by the heart. Then allow your awareness to move into your upper back and shoulder blades, then down into the middle and lower back and around to the abdomen. Consider the stomach and digestive track breaking down energy for use in the body and sending it on to be expelled from the body.

Continue to let awareness sweep down the body. Feel the sensations that arise in your hips, buttocks, and genitals. Move slowly down through the legs, feeling them from within, then through the feet and toes. Feel the sensations of contact, pressure, and temperature in the places where your body touches the chair or the floor.

Now expand your attention to include your entire body in a comprehensive way. Be aware of the body as a field of changing sensations. Can you sense the subtle energy field that gives life to every cell, every organ in your body? Is there anything in your experience that is solid and unmoving? Is there any center or boundary to the field of sensation? Our bodies have been shaped by our life experiences, by the way we use them in our daily work, by diseases we have undergone, and by our habits (for example, slouching over computer keyboards). As you rest in awareness of your whole body, if particular sensations (such as pains or tensions) call to your attention, attend to them but don't try to manage or manipulate your experience; don't grasp or push anything away. Simply open your mind to the dance of sensations as they move around your body. Feel your life from the inside out.

After you've spent some time feeling these sensations, open your eyes and return your attention to the outside world. Now focus on your senses, which allow you to receive information from the outside world. There are phenomena all around you, even in this room. Be present to those things. What are you hearing now? Seeing? Smelling? Tasting? Touching? After you have taken some time to absorb the information about your surroundings your senses are receiving, take another "falling out breath" and return slowly to your sitting position.

Using the Senses and Postures in Worship

Now turn your attention to your most recent worship experiences.

What was there to *hear* in worship? (Was there music, both instrumental and singing? Scripture read aloud? A sermon? Prayers?)

What was there to *see*? (Consider the worship space and the people in it. What about symbols, art, or banners?)

What was there to *smell*? (Perhaps the aroma of fresh bread and wine? Odors from the building? Burning candles? Incense?)

What was there to *taste*? (Bread and wine? Refreshments after the service?)

What was there to *touch*? (The worship book? Other people, through handshakes or hugs? Money placed into the offering basket? Receiving the bread in your hand? Taking the cup?)

By the knowledge we have acquired through our sense perceptions, we take into our bodies (and minds) what the liturgy offers, including the knowledge of God. In book 10 of his *Confessions*, St. Augustine refers to his "knowledge" of God and confesses that when he loves God, "it is true that I love a light of a certain kind, a voice, a perfume, a food, an embrace...".[10] Augustine's God is multisensual. Martin Luther reportedly said that God has given us five senses with which to worship him, and it would be sheer ingratitude to use less.

---

10. Saint Augustine, *Confessions*, translated with an Introduction by R. S. Pine-Coffin (Baltimore: Penguin Books, 1961), 211.

We need a stretch after sitting with such concentration. Again, perhaps someone could read this to you slowly while you practice it.

Stand up gradually. Plant your feet hip distance apart and parallel to each other, toes pointing forward, arms hanging at your side with the palms facing toward your thighs. Build upward with the spine as straight as possible. Draw your belly in and curl your tailbone under. Draw your shoulders back, but keep them relaxed. Lift your sternum and broaden your chest. Lift your head up so that it's resting on top of the spine, chin down, neck lengthened. Let breath flow in and out evenly. You are now in what is called the "mountain pose" or tadasana in yoga. It's a good position to learn if you spend a lot of time standing in public as a worship leader. It can be a relaxing stance.

Now stretch your arms overhead and bring your hands together as in prayer while you breathe in. Exhale but leave your arms in place and don't lose your height. Inhale and stretch higher. Inhale and exhale a few more times to attain greater height. Now inhale and bend your torso to the right, extending your left arm past your ears while your right arm drops alongside your right leg. Push your hips to the left to gain a greater stretch on the left side. Now exhale and come back to the center with your arms overhead. Inhale and bend your torso to the left, extending your right arm past your ears while your left arm drops alongside your left leg. Push your hips to the right. Exhale and come back to the center with your arms still overhead. Now twist your upper body to the right without altering your feet and legs or losing your height. Then bring your body back to the center and twist to the left. Return to the center. Do this a few times, making sure that every time you are in the center you inhale and stretch up further. With your arms overhead, bend backward. Moving your arms into a swan dive, fold your torso forward toward the floor, your head hanging down. Bounce your torso gently several times until your hands reach toward the floor. Now slide your hands up your legs to your knees and bring your torso parallel to the floor, with your spine straight ahead. Lift your chest and head; this is called "monkey pose." Now come to a full stand with your hands in prayer position on your chest. (Note: you don't want to stand up immediately from an inversion because the blood has gone to your head and you'll get dizzy.)

Let us now reflect on how we put our bodies into the act of worship.

How do we respond to what we have received? Think back to your most recent worship experiences (different traditions have different practices).

Did you stand? If so, for what reasons? (To sing songs of praise? For prayer? To receive Communion?)

Did you sit? When? (To hear readings and the sermon? To receive Communion?)

Did you kneel? Why? (For prayers of confession? To receive Communion?)

Did you walk? When? (In processions? To receive Communion?)

Did you turn your body? Why? (To face the cross in the procession? To greet your neighbor?)

Did you do anything with your hands? If so, what? (Did you lift your hands during praise or prayer? Did you fold them in prayer or use them to receive the Communion elements?)

Did you bow? For what purpose? (To reverence the cross, altar, or reserved sacrament? To honor the name of Jesus or the Holy Trinity?)

Did you prostrate yourself? This position is unlikely to be practiced outside of the Eastern Orthodox Church. Similar forms of prostration are also used in Muslim, Hindu, and Buddhist worship. After all, there are only so many ways to position the body. The Greek New Testament word *proskynesis* is often translated "to worship." More specifically, it means "to adore" or literally "to prostrate oneself." In the New Testament Jesus is worshiped in this sense by the wise men from the East who brought gifts to honor the Christ child, by the blind man who received his sight, by the Samaritan leper who was healed and returned to Jesus to give thanks, by the apostles who encountered the risen Lord (Matt. 28:9, 17; Luke 24:52), and by the twenty-four elders around the throne of God and the Lamb (Rev. 4:10). This type of prostration—falling on one's face—is not just an expression of an interior disposition of worship; it *is* worship.

In yoga, prostration is called the "child pose" or the "devotional pose." I invite you to try it.

Kneel on the floor in "table pose"—on your hands and knees, with your knees positioned about as wide as your hips. Breathe in. As you exhale move your buttocks back and sit between your legs. Lay your torso down between your thighs with your forehead resting on the floor. Stretch your arms in front of you with your palms down on the floor, which will give you a good stretch. Pull the shoulder blades wide across your back. To come up, first lengthen the front torso and then, with an inhalation, lift from the tailbone as it presses down and into the pelvis.

There is a slight variation of this pose called the God pose or crown pose in which you rise up on your knees (buttocks in the air) with the crown of your head on the floor. In this version you rest on your elbows with your hands folded in front of you. This is very much like Eastern Orthodox prostration.

The process of scanning the use of our body in worship should demonstrate to what extent worship—and liturgy, as we shall presently define it—is an embodied experience. Christian liturgy impacts the body from the day of our baptism until the day of our funeral. The unseen spiritual realities of the sacraments (or mysteries, as the Eastern Church calls them) express themselves through the physicality of the ritual. The manner in which the body expresses itself liturgically makes the essence of the liturgy bodily visible just as the essence of God for us became bodily visible in the Word made flesh in Jesus. What we are to see in Jesus is what the liturgy primarily celebrates: the paschal mystery of his death and resurrection.

The ancient church fathers commented on the bodily gestures and ritualistic motions of worship because those acts bear spiritual meaning. Postures, gestures, vestments, the layout of physical space in church buildings, and the choreographic positions taken for various liturgical actions are not arbitrary or superfluous. For the ancients, these aspects took on a symbolic significance as the physical expressions of spiritual realities. They understood liturgy as an enactment of the heavenly reality. The "physicality" of ritual practices that took place within the sacred spaces affected the body in perceptible ways; Christians could see and feel their spiritual endeavors. One of the tasks of the deacons was to tell people what postures to assume: "Let us stand in awe. Let us be attentive. Let us bow the head. Let us bend the knee [*Flectamus genua*]." Worship leaders still tell people when to stand, sit, or kneel.

God created us as bodies, and we use our bodies to worship God. As Pope John Paul II affirms in his theology of the body, we don't *have* bodies; we *are* bodies. We have nothing more or less with which to worship God than our bodies. Christian worship is an incarnational—an "in the body"—experience. We worship the God who in Christ dwelt among us in the flesh and whose Spirit not only gives the breath of life to our mortal bodies but will also raise them up on the last day by breathing into them once again the "breath of life" (*nishmat chaim*), as in Ezekiel's vision of the dry bones (Ezek. 37: 1–14).

Body and Soul

Some of the church fathers, taking instruction from Greek philosophy, speculated about the soul—called the *psyche* (from which we get the word *psychology*)—as an inseparable aspect of the human self. The soul could also be called our personality, our defining characteristics. But in Christian thought the soul is inseparable from the body. Ssince we experience what the body experiences, so does the soul. The character of the soul—of ourself—can be shaped by the traumas that the body experiences, including that part of the body known as the mind. It is not surprising that, especially in the West, a doctrine of purgatory arose out of concern for the need for the soul to be purified before it—before we—stand before God. Christians believe that we will be raised up with a glorified body and a purified soul to worship God forever. Some contemporary Catholic theologians have suggested that when we are raised up body and soul, the soul is purified by the brilliant light of Christ.

The Deuteronomist emphasizes worshiping the Lord our God with all our heart, mind, soul, and strength. While we worship the Lord with the mind, and the mind is part of the body, it is not the whole part. Protestant worship emphasizes *hearing* the word of God, but we receive information through all five of our senses, not just through hearing. Christian worship gives us things to see, smell, touch, and taste. Tertullian of Carthage gives a wonderful description of the liturgical body in his treatise *On the Resurrection of the Dead.* "The body is washed so that the soul may be cleansed; the body is anointed so that the soul may be consecrated; the body is overshadowed by the laying on of hands so that the soul may be enlightened by the Holy Spirit; the body is fed with the body and blood of Christ so that that soul may be nourished by God."[11] The way to the soul is through the body, just as Christ healed the body to minister to the whole person. Christian liturgy must be a bodily activity. Christian worship must be an embodied experience. Christian spirituality must account for the everyday mundane realities of our physical lives in our relationship with the God who "became flesh and dwelt among us" (John 1:14).

Figure 2. This woman is doing a prostration before an icon in a Ukrainian Orthodox Church. In the deepest prostration the head touches the floor and the hands are extended forward and clasped in prayer. Prostration looks very much like yoga child pose.

11. Tertullian, *De resurrection mortuorum* 8; cited in Anscar J. Chupungco, *What, Then, Is Liturgy? Musings and Memoir* (Collegeville, MN: Liturgical Press, 2010), 45.

B. What Is Christian Liturgy?

Thus far we have looked at the body employed in worship. Now we need to understand what liturgy is.

What Is Liturgy?

I have entitled this book "Embodied Liturgy," not "embodied worship." "Liturgy" is not a term much used in the Reformed tradition. Actually, it has become a commonly-used term in the Western Churches only from the influence of the liturgical movement in the twentieth century, although it is used in the Eastern Churches. Perhaps we capture some of what "liturgy" means with the English word "service." The English word "worship" suggests the honor we show to God. (English judges are addressed as "your worship"; American judges are addressed as "your honor".) The word used for worship in Indonesia is the Sanskrit term *bhakti*. *Bhakti* was one of the "yogas" Krishna introduced to Arjuna in the *Bhagavad Gita*. *Bhakti* is the devotional service performed by the devotee to his or her deity; it was what Arjuna should render to Arjuna. It is the devotional service Christians render to Christ. The direction of worship is thus from the worshiper to God. But "liturgy" is more multi-directional and multi-dimensional than worship.

Very briefly to explain the origins of the term, in the ancient Greek city-states *leitourgia* was a form of public service—public works that citizens undertook for their community. This might have included building a bridge or a sewer or erecting an image of the patron deity. When the apostle Paul gathered funds from the congregations in Macedonia and Greece for the relief of the poor in Jerusalem (see 2 Corinthians 8-9), he was doing a liturgy. He referred to himself as a "liturgist" (*leitourgos*). In some ancient Greek city-states the work of the citizen assemblies (*ekklesiae*) was a liturgical work, a form of communal public service. In this way *leitourgia* was also associated with *ekklesia*, the assembly called out of the world to do the work of the world in a more disinterested way.

But the term *leitourgia* was also used in the Greek Bible (Old Testament Septuagint translations as well as New Testament) to designate cultic service, such as the priestly work performed by Zechariah, the father of John the Baptist, or Christ in the heavenly sanctuary (in the Letter to the Hebrews). The term is used in Acts 13:2 to designate the assembly for worship. In the Christian tradition the word *liturgy* has been used most often to designate an order of public worship.

Liturgy includes worship, which is the service we render to God, but liturgy is more than worship understood in that way. It includes the service that God renders to his people through designated ministers in the preaching of the word and the administration of the sacraments (the divine liturgy). It includes ritual acts that Christians perform with one another in the presence of God, such as greetings and other interactions. When we think of music used in liturgy, for example, we find hymns addressed to God that express praise and adoration, thanksgiving, and supplication; but there are also songs that we address to one another as means of encouragement or comfort. Liturgy is a public work performed out of the world, but also before the world.

Every religion and every Christian denomination that practices some kind of public assembly of believers has a liturgy. Liturgy is what the faith community does when it comes together in the presence of God and of one another, out of the world and yet before the world. It can be as elaborate as the Orthodox Byzantine Rite or as simple as a Quaker meeting. It can be as ceremoniously prescribed as *The Book of Common Prayer* or as free-form as a Pentecostal celebration. Briefly put, if a public event is meant to initiate an encounter with God, who comes to us through means of grace (such as word and sacrament), and if the community of faith responds to God (with prayer, praise, and thanksgiving), and if the event allows for interaction in the assembly (such as gathering and greeting each other), then the event is a liturgy.

So liturgy is more but also less than worship. It is more in that it includes elements of rite that are directed to the people as well as to God; it is less in that it is done in public, whereas worship can

19

also be done in private (although a holistic spirituality suggests that there ought to be some correlation between the worship that occurs in the gathered church's liturgy and the devotions practiced at home or in small groups). Hence liturgy is the vehicle by which the life and mission of the church is celebrated and the public worship of God is offered. It is the vehicle by which God addresses his people through the proclamation of the word and the administration of the sacraments instituted by Christ. Liturgy is the public service of the people of God, but it is also the work of God (*opus Deo*) in word and sacrament. Through these means of grace God in Christ reconciles the world to himself. Doing the liturgy thus forms us in our relationship with the God whom we serve.

What Is Trinity?

I need to be more theologically specific here. Which God are we serving? For Christians the God we serve is the Holy Trinity.[12] The incarnational faith of Christianity requires a doctrine of trinity (three-in-one) if Christ is true God as well as true man and is bonded to the Father by the Spirit the Father sends. The so-called Athanasian Creed hammers home the idea that "The Father is God, the Son is God, the Holy Spirit is One; yet there are not three gods but One who is God."

The term *incarnation* comes from the Latin *in carnis*, which literally means "in the flesh." John 1:1 states, "The Word [*Logos* = mind, communication] of God became flesh and dwelt among us." Divinity was enfleshed, embodied, in a historical human being, Jesus of Nazareth. Ancient Christianity fought over the divinity and humanity in Jesus and settled on the formula that he was "true God and true man." In the gospel stories of the baptism of Jesus, the voice from heaven designated him as "beloved Son." Jesus taught his disciples to call this God "Abba, Father." The Spirit appeared over the baptismal

---

12. A pastor in the course asked for a book about the Trinity in the liturgy. I recommended two: Edward J. Kilmartin, *Christian Liturgy: Theology and Practice*, vol. 1, *Systematic Theology of Liturgy* (New York: Sheed and Ward, 1988) and Maxwell E. Johnson, *Praying and Believing in Early Christianity* (Collegeville, MN: Liturgical Press, 2013).

scene in the form of a dove, serving as the bond between the Father and the Son (see Matt. 3:13-17; Mark 1:9-11; Luke 3:21-22).

What Is Trinitarian Worship?

The God named Father, Son, and Holy Spirit is the God Christians are brought into a relationship with when they are baptized in that name. Therefore the liturgy that forms us in a relationship with God the Holy Trinity must be Trinitarian. In many contemporary services today, worship is not just Christocentric (as Christian worship has been since the first century), but also Christomonist (directed to and referencing Christ alone). The songs and the prayers sometimes add up to unitarianism of the second person of the Trinity. It's all about Jesus or Jesus and me. But it doesn't have to be that way. While there are thousands of contemporary worship songs, my impression is that they are most often chosen because of the mood they project (such as boisterous joy or quiet intimacy) rather than for their doctrinal content. I suspect that the lack of attention to doctrinal content is caused by the fact that leadership in worship is handed over to musicians who may lack formal theological education. In so doing, the pastors abdicate their oversight of worship. But whether the liturgy is so-called traditional or so-called contemporary (these are false choices), choices must be made. Attention must be given to the theological spread of the hymns and songs we sing.

On the other end of the spectrum we experience, especially in North America (but perhaps also in other parts of the world), worship that has become so inclusive in its God language that the names of the Father and even the Son are suppressed in favor of generic references to deity. In some of the new denominational worship books it is possible to avoid any use of the name of the Father other than in the Creed (be it the Apostles', the Nicene, or the Athanasian) and the Lord's Prayer. However, the Creed is sometimes omitted along with the confession of sins because pastors think that referring to "sin" and confessing a specific faith" will offend people. I've been to services in which we prayed to the "Holy One" or the "Compassionate One." I don't know who that god is. Any god worth having will surely be holy and compassionate. But our God, like the God of Israel, has graciously given us a name that we can use to call on him in prayer, praise, and thanksgiving. That name is placed on us in Holy Baptism—Father, Son, and Holy Spirit—and we invoke it ever thereafter.

What Is a Personal God?

The God we encounter in the liturgy is a personal God. That doesn't mean God belongs to me or is customized for my needs, like my personal computer. The word *person* in theology comes from the Latin *persona*, which means "role," as in *personae dramatis*, "roles in the drama." Because our God is Trinity, we do not really encounter the person of God, we encounter three persons: Father, Son, and Holy Spirit. In the oldest prayer formularies Christians prayed *to* the Father *through* the Son *in* the Holy Spirit. That is, they prayed to God the Father through the mediation of God the Son in the power of God the Holy Spirit.[13]

When the Arian heresy, which taught that the Son is subordinate to the Father, came along in the fourth century the Eastern Orthodox Church changed the terminating formula of prayers to something like, "We send up glory and honor and praise and worship to you, Father, Son, and Holy Spirit, now and always and unto the ages of ages." Also In order to counter Arian influence, the Western Catholic Church retained the reference to the mediation of Christ but expanded the termination of prayers to cover the whole Trinity: "through your Son, Jesus Christ our Lord, who lives and reigns with you in the unity of the Holy Spirit, ever one God, world without end" (as we used to say in older English-language prayer books).

A Personal Relationship with the Trinitarian God

It is not enough to have a personal relationship, in this sense of role, only with Jesus. Jesus intended us to have a personal relationship with

13. See Chupungco, *What, Then, Is Liturgy?*, chap. 3.

the God he called "Abba, Father," and taught his disciples to pray to "Our Father in heaven." In fact, Christians address God as "Father" only because this is the name Jesus taught us to use. That God might have a thousand names is irrelevant to our prayer life. Early Christian sources indicate that Christians prayed the Our Father three times a day when the forum bell rang at 9:00 a.m., noon, and 3:00 p.m. They also prayed the Our Father upon arising in the morning and before retiring at night—five times in all (just like the later Muslim prayer to Allah five times a day). Eucharistic prayers at Holy Communion were traditionally prayed to the Father through the mediation of the Son. We see this in the eucharistic prefaces, in which we say something like "It is indeed right and salutary that we should at all times and in all places offer thanks and praise to you, O Lord, holy Father, through Christ our Lord." Obviously, the name "Father" partakes of the qualities of the human father, though the term should not be identified with a human father. One might say that God the Father is *like* a human father, or even like a human mother, but one cannot pray to God the Father and Mother, like some ancient gnostics did, because God is not the mother of Jesus Christ. That role has been given to another. The God of Israel is the Abba of Jesus and is our Abba because we have been adopted as brothers and sisters of Christ. If we want a better understanding of the character of the Father of our Lord Jesus Christ, we can turn to the parables of Jesus, which show the true nature of God the Father. In particular, the parable of the prodigal son, which the great German preacher Helmut Thielicke said might better be called the parable of the waiting father, is instructive.

Ancient Western prayer books terminated prayers to the Father with "through Christ our Lord." Christ is the sacrament of the Father: "The Word became flesh and lived among us" (John 1:14 ESV). Christ humanized God. Colossians 1:15 (NRSV) calls him "the image [*ikon*] of the invisible God." And John 14:9 (NRSV) says, "Whoever has seen me has seen the Father." But it is not because of the incarnation that we pray to the Father through Christ; it is because of Christ's ascension. The crucified and risen Christ ascended into heaven. While the ascension may be the orphan among the articles of faith, a great deal of important theology hangs on the ascension of Christ. Christ's ascension to "the right hand of God the Father" (Nicene Creed) means that he is in a position of clout (influence) to mediate on behalf of his brothers and sisters on earth. That's why all Christian prayer should be offered "through Jesus Christ our Lord." As 1 Tim. 2:5 (NRSV) puts it, "For there is one God; there is also one mediator between God and humankind, Christ Jesus, himself human, who gave himself as a ransom for all." The reference here to "one God" means that the mediator is no less than God himself, and the idea of sacrifice—"the ransom for all," by which we are redeemed from sin, death, and the devil—is also brought into Christ's mediation. In the Letter to the Hebrews Christ's once-for-all atoning sacrifice is taken directly into the heavenly sanctuary. Christ's redemption and mediation are divine acts; not just any human being could accomplish them, no matter how holy the person. Everything is brought to the Father through the Son, including the ransoming or redemption of God's people and their earthly needs. As we pray to the Father, so our prayers are offered "through Jesus Christ our Lord."

I said above that Christian liturgy is Christocentric. Its main elements are the reading of the Scriptures and the celebration of the Lord's Supper. These two acts have belonged together since the earliest days of the church. Christ speaks to us in the reading of Scripture, especially the Gospels. Christ is present in the bread and cup, which are proclaimed and received as his body and blood, according to his word. Christ is present in the ministers who serve in his stead. Indeed, Christ is present wherever two or three gather in his name, according to his promise (Matt. 18:20).[14]

We pray to the Father, through the Son, but "in the unity of the Holy Spirit." There has been some debate about what "the unity of the Holy Spirit" means. The phrase seems to remove the Holy Spirit from the mediating work of Christ before the Father. I think that the

14. These four aspects of Christ's presence in the liturgy are laid out in the Constitution on the Sacred Liturgy (*Sacrosanctum concilium*), sec. 7, promulgated by the Second Vatican Council on December 4, 1963. See the Vatican Website, http://www.vatican.va/archive/hist_councils/ ii_vatican_council/documents/vat-ii_const_19631204_sacrosanctum-concilium_en.html.

Holy Spirit is the energy of God working in and through the church, uniting us to God. As the apostle Paul says in Romans 8, when we pray "Abba, Father," the Spirit of God is in touch with our spirit; and when we don't know "how to pray as we ought . . . the Spirit intercedes with sighs too deep for words" (Rom. 8:26, NRSV). The Holy Spirit is God reaching into human beings. We receive the Holy Spirit in Holy Baptism and in ordination through prayer and the laying on of hands. The Spirit creates the church and empowers its mission, and we make decisions in the life and mission of the church that seem "good to the Holy Spirit and to us," as the apostles affirm in Acts 15:28. Thus, within the Trinitarian liturgy we develop a relationship with each person of the Holy Trinity.

The Body of God and Our Bodies

I want to consider three other aspects of the Trinity before I conclude this lesson—aspects that relate to the theme of embodiment. First, Jesus the Christ, Son of God, true man as well as true God, ascended bodily into heaven. His body was not left behind; it was not left in the grave, and the risen Christ is not wandering around bodily on the earth. But neither did Jesus cease to have a body when he went to heaven. As one who is truly human, Christ has a body just like we do, and if he ascended into heaven his body is also in heaven.[15] Because Christ is also the Son of God and the second person of the Trinity, his body has also been taken into the Godhead. In Christ, therefore, God has a body.

Embodiment has been taken into God. Therefore even in our relationship with our Trinitarian God, it is a matter of one body relating to other bodies—God's body in Christ relating to our bodies. Christ is present spiritually where two or three are gathered in his name (see Matt. 18:20), but he is present physically in the sacrament when he binds himself to bread and wine and says, Here you may find me. The Eucharist as the real presence of Christ is simply

---

15. See N. T. Wright, *Surprised by Hope: Rethinking Heaven, the Resurrection, and the Mission of the Church* (New York: Harper Collins, 2008), 109-17.

25

incomprehensible without Christ's ascension into heaven. The human nature of Christ is circumscribed by time and place and is now in heaven, but in Martin Luther's view it shares the omnipresence of the divine nature (this is called the *communicatio idiomata*, "the sharing of attributes") and is therefore present in the bread and wine on the earthly altar for the assembly, according to Christ's word. When medieval Christians referred to the Eucharist as "God's body," they were not wrong.

Second, the Holy Spirit is the person of God who is constantly in touch with our bodies. We receive the gift of the Holy Spirit in baptism, and our bodies become temples of the Holy Spirit. "Do you not know that your body is a temple of the Holy Spirit within you, which you have from God?" (1 Cor. 6:19, NRSV). The Spirit given to us in Holy Baptism animates our physical bodies and makes them available for the service of God. The Spirit is received through outward expressions such as the laying on of hands and the anointing of the body. These Spirit-actions are already a part of the post-baptismal ceremonies, and they are essential elements in the rites of confirmation, ordination, and healing. This Spirit is "the Spirit of our Lord and of his resurrection," as a eucharistic prayer in the *Lutheran Book of Worship* puts it. The Holy Spirit is not an entity separate from the Father and the Son. The Spirit is the Spirit of the risen and glorified Lord, who will also raise our mortal bodies in the resurrection of the dead. The Holy Spirit does not connect only with our minds or with some putative "spiritual life." The Spirit is all about the body.

Third, the doctrine of the Trinity is embodied in the culture of Christendom in numerous subtle ways that may elude Christians today or Westerners who are alienated from the church, from the Christian faith, and therefore from their own cultural heritage. The best way to consider the cultural legacy of the Trinity is to think in terms of threes. The Sunday after Pentecost became Trinity Sunday in the medieval Western church, and the season "after Trinity" was also divided into three. The second trimester began with Michaelmas (the feast of St. Michael and All Angels) on September 29, and the Michaelmas period designated the opening of the fall session of law courts and schools in Great Britain. The final trimester was Kingdomtide, beginning with All Saints' Day on November 1 (actually the Eve of All Saints—Halloween) and ending at the First Sunday in Advent. In a way the tripartite Trinity season reflected the three articles of the Creed: creation (summer and natural growth), redemption (harvest and apocalyptic battle), and sanctification (commemoration of the faithful departed and resurrection of the dead). Time and history were conceived as Trinitarian. The Cistercian abbot Joachim of Flores devised a scheme dividing history into the dispensation of the Father (Old Testament), the dispensation of the Son (New Testament and the early church), and the dispensation of the Holy Spirit (which began, in his view, toward the end of the twelfth century). This scheme has captivated Western philosophy.[16] For the philosopher Georg Wilhelm Friedrich Hegel, logic itself became a tripartite progression from thesis to antithesis to synthesis. Gothic architecture often provided three entrances in the front facades of church buildings and three panels in stained-glass window configurations. Triple meter became a feature of Western music, especially dance music. For his part, J. S. Bach was a master of theological symbolism. The organ Prelude and Fugue in E-flat Major (St. Anne) has three flats in its key signature, and the prelude is divided into three sections. In addition, there are countless other artistic and musical expressions of trinity. Culturally, westerners are Trinitarians whether they believe in God the Holy Trinity or not. They are formed by the institutions and expressions of their culture to think in Trinitarian terms. But Christian liturgy, which is also a cultural form, is and must be Trinitarian because the Holy Trinity is the God who is the object of Christian worship.

Yoga Sequence

Let us conclude with a bodily devotion to the Holy Trinity. This is the half-sun salutation, which uses positions we practiced above. Assume the standing

---

16. See Karl Löwith, *Meaning in History* (Chicago: University of Chicago Press, 1949).

(mountain) pose. Extend the arms overhead, "Glory"; backward bend, "to the Father"; forward fold to the earth, "and to the Son"; monkey pose, "and to the Holy Spirit"; stand, hands in prayer position over heart, "Amen."

Do this salutation three times. Like Orthodox Christians, you could make the sign of the cross over your entire body as you bow down to the ground.

2

———

Earthly Bodies, Earthly Means

A. Days and Seasons

The most fundamental thing that can be said about human beings is that we are earthly creatures. The second creation story in Genesis 2, the Yahwist narrative, describes how God created the man (Adam) from the watered ground of the earth and breathed into him the breath of life. The first creation story in Genesis, the priestly account, adds that we were created, both male and female, in the "image of God" (Gen. 1:26). We are God's creatures, but we are also God's idols, that is, God's representatives, to the rest of the earthly creation. Because of sin—our willful disobedience of God's word—the divine image was effaced, and we became disconnected from God, from each other, and from the creation itself. God works hard to reconnect us with himself and to keep us connected by using earthly cycles and materials, which serve as means of God's grace for us.

In this chapter, I will consider how humans are a part of the created order. Like other creatures we need to eat and sleep and procreate to ensure the survival of our species. Like other creatures we are affected by the created order: the alternation of day and night, the change in the seasons, and changes in climate. Our biological rhythms are affected by the alternation of darkness and light, days and nights getting longer or shorter as the seasons change, days getting warmer or colder as the earth tilts, and the passage of time until we return to the earth from which we were created. I will also consider how we are sustained and strengthened in our relationship with God, and therefore with others, through created means that serve as signs of God's presence and actions for us.

Let us begin with our relationship to God as expressed in units of time: the day, the week, the year, and a lifetime.

The Day

> In the beginning God created the heavens and the earth. The earth was without form and void, and darkness was upon the face of the deep; and the Spirit of God was moving over the face of the waters. And God said, "Let there be light"; and there was light. And God saw that the light was good; and God separated the light from the darkness. God called the light Day, and the darkness he called Night. And there was evening and there was morning, one day. (Gen. 1:1-5, NRSV)

As we have become more technologically advanced, we have compensated for the limitations nature places on us. Electricity allows us to extend the light into times of darkness. We needn't stop work when night falls; rather, we can work through the night. Heating and cooling systems allow us to live and thrive in once-forbidding places, although we're also aware that the excessive use of various forms of energy that allow us to transcend natural conditions has an impact on the Earth's climate, on our environment, and therefore on our living conditions.

These changing conditions take their toll on economic costs and human lives, reminding us that we ignore natural rhythms and powers at our peril. Those in the field of chronobiology study the body's circadian rhythm, which is the internal clock that regulates a variety of biological processes according to an approximate twenty-four-hour period. Most of a person's body systems demonstrate circadian variations. The body systems with the most prominent circadian variations are the sleep-wake cycle, the temperature regulation system, and the endocrine system. Ignoring the body's circadian rhythm can cause sleeplessness and obesity, which comes from eating at odd times, among other conditions.[1]

Ignoring our natural rhythms also plays a role in keeping us disconnected from our Creator. For example, the sunset and sunrise no longer serve as reminders to turn to God in thanksgiving at the close of the day and to praise God in the morning for the gift of another day.

The opening chapter of Genesis—in which light and darkness, evening and morning, are created even before there are lights to govern the day and night—indicates the liturgical purpose of the priestly author. The liturgical day begins in the evening, not the morning. The night can still be a scary time for humans, whether on the streets of cities or in country places. As a child I was taught the prayer, "Now I lay me down to sleep, I pray the Lord my soul to keep. If I should die before I wake, I pray the Lord my soul to take." It might strike us today as odd to instill the fear of death into children, but they will think about death with or without our help. There was a time when parents gave their children words with which to confront their fears. In the darkness we forcibly encounter our isolation and vulnerability. In the darkness we feel ourselves being drawn down into the earth. We pray to God for protection during the night: "He who keeps Israel will neither slumber nor sleep" (Ps. 121:4, NRSV). We proclaim at the beginning of the Order of Vespers or Evening Prayer the words of John 1:5 (NRSV): "The light shines in the darkness, and the darkness did not overcome it." "Jesus Christ is the light of the world. The light no darkness can overcome."[2]

Because the liturgical day begins at sunset, night does not fall out of the picture. Before the advent of electricity people went to bed when it became dark. In winter, this meant they sometimes stayed in bed for a long time (although near the equator the hours of light and darkness are about equal and don't fluctuate very much). What's more,

---

1. Jay C. Dunlap, Jennifer J. Loros, Patricia J. DeCoursey, eds., *Chronobiology: Biological Timekeeping* (Sunderland, MA: Sinauer, 2004).
2. *Lutheran Book of Worship* (Minneapolis: Augsburg Publishing House, 1978), 141.

people sometimes had two sleeps on long winter nights and woke up during the night. This time of nocturnal mystery could be used for restoking the fire, having sex, or receiving divine visitations. Perhaps this was the time when dreams were remembered and the voices of conscience or angels made an impression that was later acted upon. Early Christians arose to have a nocturnal prayer vigil. This is the origin of the matins service in monastic communities, which is prayed between midnight and 3:00 a.m. The great festivals of Christmas, Easter, and Pentecost were observed with night vigils that culminated in the midnight Mass or Eucharist.

But then, as Philip Pfatteicher writes, "At last the rosy fingers of dawn begin to push back the cover of night, and sunrise comes with light and the fulfillment of the night of watching."[3] We awake from the world of dreams into the knowledge of reality. The rising sun, for those with the eyes of faith to see it, proclaims also the rising Sun of righteousness—the one who rose from death in triumph. Zechariah's song makes this connection as it sings:

> In the tender compassion of our God
> the dawn from on high shall break upon us,
> to shine on those who dwell in darkness and the shadow of death,
> and to guide our feet into the way of peace. (Luke 1:78-80)[4]

Ambrose of Milan, in his hymn to Christ, *Splendor paternae gloriae* ("O splendor of God's glory bright"), says:

> Morn in her rosy car is borne;
> Let him come forth, our perfect morn,
> The Word in God the Father one,
> The Father perfect in the Son.[5]

The masculine sun of Roman mythology (Mercury pulling the orb of the sun across the sky in his chariot) becomes the image of Christ

---

3. Philip H. Pfatteicher, *Liturgical Spirituality* (Valley Forge, PA: Trinity Press International, 1997), 35.
4. Lutheran Book of Worship, 135.
5. *Service Book and Hymnal* (Minneapolis: Augsburg Publishing House, 1958), Hymn 206, st. 6.

the Son of God and Sun of righteousness. This Sun fulfills the ancient prophecy from Isaiah:

The sun shall no longer be
    your light by day,
nor for brightness shall the moon
    give light to you by night;
but the Lord will be your everlasting light,
    and your God will be your glory. (Isa. 60:19 NRSV)

Early on Christians, like the Jews before them, saw significance in the pivotal times of sunset and sunrise, which embrace the extremes of human experience: darkness and light, death and life. Patterns of death and resurrection are woven into our experience of evening and morning, and thereby into daily prayer.

Daily morning and evening prayer is a way of linking us to both the continuity of life in this world and the promise of eternity. Daily prayer keeps us connected with God in our fears and in our hopes as we pray in the evening for peace and in the morning for grace. In this way, time is sanctified.

The passage of time is meant to be a time of praise and prayer. As we awaken we sing the words of the psalm, "O Lord, open my lips, and my mouth shall declare your praise" (Ps. 51:15)[6]. We may also sing words from Ps. 63:1 (LBW), "O God, you are my God; eagerly I seek you," or Ps. 103:1 (LBW), "Bless the Lord, O my soul, / and all that is within me, bless his holy name." As we come to the end of the day we sing the words of Ps. 141:2, "Let my prayer rise before you as incense; / the lifting up of my hands as the evening sacrifice."[7] As we go to bed at the end of the day we sing the words of Ps. 4:8 (LBW), "I lie down in peace, at once I fall asleep, / for only you, Lord, make me dwell in safety." During the day Christians prayed stanzas of the lengthy Psalm 119, which is a series of meditations on the law of the Lord. The psalms are at the heart of the daily prayer services (called "offices" because they were official) of the church.

6. Lutheran Book of Worship, 131.
7. Ibid., 145.

The daily prayer offices developed in the fourth century.[8] They served to sanctify the time of the day, particularly the pivotal times of evening and morning. These services were celebrated in the great basilicas or cathedral of antiquity and included psalmody, brief readings, gospel canticles, and supplicatory prayers (often in litany form). They were construed as a spiritual equivalent to the morning and evening sacrifices in the Jewish temple, which already existed in the worship of the emerging synagogue liturgies. When Christian daily prayer went public in the fourth century, the same connection was made. The Psalter, which had been compiled as the hymnal of the Second Temple, became the principal songbook of the church and was used primarily in the daily prayer services. Thus both Christianity and Judaism are spiritual descendants of the Jewish tabernacle and temple.[9]

Christian monasticism was also developing during this time. Lay Christians who found the church becoming too worldly withdrew into solitary places to contemplate God as a way to take a stand against the world. The monks engaged in "ceaseless prayer" by means of continuous recitation or chanting of psalms and continuous reading of biblical books. At first they followed the times of prayer they had followed in their households: at evening, midnight, and morning, in addition to saying the Lord's Prayer three times during the day at the ringing of the forum bell at the third, sixth, and ninth hours. The monks also added a bedtime prayer (Compline). Based on the verse from Ps. 119:164 (LBW), "Seven times a day do I praise you," the monasteries developed seven prayer offices: Vespers at sundown, Compline before retiring, Matins/Vigil during the night, Lauds at daybreak, and the three interval hours of Terce (9:00 a.m.), Sext (Noon), and None (3:00 p.m.). The Benedictine Rule added Prime after breakfast, which was followed by a meeting of the community to study the Rule and make work assignments. Thus in Western monasticism there are eight canonical prayer offices, which are also called the Liturgy of the Hours (or simply the Hours).

8. See Frank C. Senn, *Introduction to Christian Liturgy* (Minneapolis: Fortress Press, 2012), 75-96.
9. See Margaret Barker, *Temple Themes in Christian Worship* (New York: T&T Clark, 2007).

The complicated history of the prayer offices shows a blending of the styles of the cathedral and monastic offices as the bishops of the church turned to monastic communities in the cities to provide leadership in the prayer offices when the pastoral work of the cathedral clergy became more demanding. As a result, the prayer offices acquired a more monastic character as they became the preserve of monks and clergy. But at least Sunday Vespers remained popular throughout the Middle Ages. The Lutheran Reformation made an effort to reclaim the daily prayer offices as forms of congregational liturgies to replace the daily Masses by blending Matins / Lauds and Vespers / Compline. Forms of Matins and Vespers based on the Benedictine Office have retained their place in Lutheran worship books even if they aren't used daily. Archbishop Thomas Cranmer took the same approach with the Book of Common Prayer (1549, 1552). Daily Morning Prayer and Evensong have been most successfully maintained to this day in the Anglican tradition, especially in cathedral and collegiate schools in which there are choirs to provide choral leadership. While the Lutheran practice is to sing the Benedictus or the Te Deum Laudamus at Matins and the Magnificat or Nunc Dimittis at Vespers, in the Anglican office both canticles are sung at both offices.

Even if the daily public prayers of the church cannot be maintained in every congregation, Christians can still remain connected with God by praying in the morning and before retiring at night; during these times one can recite the Apostles' Creed, the Lord's Prayer, and a morning or evening prayer, such as those provided in Martin Luther's *Small Catechism*. Christians can also revive the custom of saying the Lord's Prayer at 9:00 a.m., Noon, and 3:00 p.m. wherever they are.

The Week

Returning to the first creation story in Gen. 1:1–2:4a, we see that the days of creation progress to the seventh day, on which God rested. One may argue that the entire purpose of this priestly creation account was to establish the divine institution of the Sabbath, which played a defining role in the religious identity of the Jewish people.

35

Remembering the Sabbath day and sanctifying it through worship is a tenet built into the Decalogue. The Sabbath commandment ensures a more extended periodic rest for our bodies than what we daily receive. Work is a consequence of sin, but in his grace God does not intend us to work until we drop. To ensure this precept, the whole community is to cease from work. Work animals are also to receive a periodic rest (Exod. 20:8; Deut. 5:12-14).

This tension can be seen in the Gospels with regard to Jesus' observance or nonobservance of the Sabbath day. He performed healing and other acts on the Sabbath, which the Pharisees considered contrary to the law. He responded to their accusations by asserting, "the Sabbath is made for man, not man for the Sabbath" (Mark 2:27, NRSV).

The early Christians may have initially observed the seventh day Sabbath, but increasingly they met on the first day of the week to commemorate Jesus' resurrection.[10] Some of the early church fathers, especially Clement and Origen in Alexandria, called the "day of the Sun" (Sunday) the eighth day, signifying that the resurrection happens outside of natural history.

Sunday can be considered "the eighth day" only in relation to the seventh day, the Sabbath. Christians did not think they were observing the Sabbath when they worshiped on Sunday. Indeed, regarding Sunday as an eschatological day of resurrection depends on it *not* being the Sabbath. In the first several centuries it was the first day of the week in the Roman world, as well as a day of work. But in 321 the Emperor Constantine appealed to both Sun worshipers and Christ worshipers by declaring Sunday a day of rest in the Roman Empire. Thereafter Sabbath ideas were applied to Sunday. In the societies of Christendom Sunday was strictly observed as a Sabbath day. While secularization continues to break down Sabbath laws in the Western world, Jesus' humanitarian approach to the Sabbath suggests that a periodic day of rest is needed. In religiously pluralistic Western societies the weekend includes three Sabbaths: Friday for Muslims,

---

10. See Senn, *Introduction to Christian Liturgy*, 97-99.

Saturday for Jews, and Sunday for Christians. Theologically the Sabbath is the seventh day, but Christians gather for weekly eucharistic worship on the Lord's Day, which was regarded as the eighth day (the eschatological day) in the ancient church.

The Year

Having considered the day and the week, let's turn next to how God stays connected with us through the seasons of the year. Genesis 1:14 (NRSV) says, "And God said, 'Let there be lights in the dome of the sky to separate the day from the night; and let them be for signs and for seasons and for days and years." Like sunset and sunrise, the turning of the seasons—the solstices and equinoxes—are imbued with symbolic significance. We are not allowed to take for granted that the world turns. Rituals observed at the spring equinox, summer solstice, autumn equinox, and winter solstice are well known in human societies. The Bible, however, tries to force the circle of the seasons into linear historical time. Israel turned the agricultural festivals of Unleavened Bread, Weeks (the spring harvest), and Booths (the autumn harvest) into the historical commemorations of the exodus from Egypt, the giving of the Law on Sinai, and the wilderness journey respectively.

As the calendar of festivals and commemorations developed in Christianity, these occasions were intended to be used to celebrate events in the life of Christ.[11] Since the nativity of Christ came to be celebrated in proximity to the winter solstice in the Mediterranean world and as the passion and resurrection of Christ were celebrated in proximity to the spring equinox as well as to the Jewish Passover, it was difficult to keep the natural symbols of the season out of Christian observances.

In point of fact, the principal Christian festivals *are* related to nature. The death and resurrection of Christ occurred at Passover time. This was in the spring of the year, at the first full moon after the spring equinox. Christians determined that the Passover of Christ from death

11. Ibid., 99-101.

to life fulfills not only the Passover of the Jews, but also their exodus from Egypt through the Red Sea and their transition from slavery to freedom is fulfilled in Holy Baptism; therefore Christ's resurrection should be celebrated after the beginning of the Jewish Passover festival.

Since the resurrection of Christ occurred on the first day of the week, the "day of the Sun" in the Roman world, it was celebrated weekly on Sunday. Therefore it was argued that an annual Christian celebration of the Pascha of Christ (as it is called in many languages, including Indonesian) should also be on a Sunday. Just as every Sunday is a little Pascha, so Pascha or Easter (as it is called in English, using a Germanic word for spring) is always on the Sunday after the full moon following the spring equinox. In deference to the Christians of Asia Minor who wanted to celebrate the annual Pascha on the actual Jewish Pesach (the fourteenth/fifteenth day of Nisan), the Council of Nicaea settled this disagreement by adding that the celebration of the Christian Pascha should always be observed. Calendrical discrepancies between the Eastern and Western churches are due to the fact that the Eastern and Western Churches operate on two different calendars (Julian and Gregorian).

Christmas, the nativity of Christ (called "Natal" in Indonesian), is also related to Pascha. The Jews believe that the world was created in the spring of the year at Passover time. Christians reasoned that the new creation also began at Passover time, with the invasion of the divine Word into the human flesh of the Virgin Mary. In the calendar this became the Feast of the Annunciation. But as Christians were increasingly separated from rabbinic authorities, who calculated the times of the Jewish festivals, they settled on a given date in proximity to the Passover and the equinox: March 25 in the Roman calendar and April 6 in the Egyptian calendar. Nine months later brings us to December 25 and January 6 as the dates on which to celebrate the Nativity of Christ. Of course, this placed the Nativity at the time of the winter solstice in the Mediterranean world. At first December 25 was observed in Rome and January 6 in Spain and in the East. Observing both Christmas and Epiphany gives us the twelve days of Christmas.

As Christian traditions are carried from their places of origin to new lands with different climates, the issues of natural and cultural adaptation become important. In the southern hemisphere Christmas occurs at the summer solstice rather than the winter solstice, and Easter occurs at the autumnal equinox rather than at the spring equinox. In the lands near the equator the variations in the seasons are not very pronounced. While the great festivals of Christ possess a theological content that should override the natural symbols of the seasons, it is not possible to ignore the effect of these seasons on our lives. So, natural symbols and culturally appropriate practices will be developed in the southern hemisphere. Still, it is disheartening to see winter solstice symbols such as Santa Claus (based on the Nordic god of ice and snow) continuing to be used in places where there is no ice and snow and to be taken as a symbol of Christianity.

The Christian calendar developed around the celebrations of Christ's death, resurrection, and nativity. Easter, like Passover in the Jewish calendar, became an octave of octaves (seven weeks is equal to forty-nine days) plus an eighth day (which makes fifty days), thus giving us a Christian feast of Pentecost that celebrates the outpouring of the Holy Spirit on the chosen disciples. The development of Christian initiation practices led to a forty-day period of preparation for baptism at Easter, which is marked by fasting and penitence. In Latin this is simply called "the Forty Days" (*Quadragesima*). In English it came to be called Lent, from the Anglo-Saxon word referring to the lengthening of the days in springtime.

In Western Europe the Nativity of Christ was preceded by a time of preparation that was also roughly six weeks or forty days; this season came to be known as Advent. By the tenth century the six-week Western European Advent (with its themes of the ministry of John the Baptist and the last judgment) merged with the two-week Roman preparation for Christmas (with its theme of annunciation to Mary); the resulting compromise was the four-week Advent. The themes of

Advent on the four Sundays now include the second coming of Christ, the ministry of John the Baptist, and the annunciation to Mary and Joseph.

The rest of the year is known as "ordinary time." The word *ordinary* in this sense refers to ordinals or numbers. This is because they were historically counted as Sundays after the Epiphany or after Pentecost (or Trinity).[12]

Other days commemorating the life of Christ, the saints and martyrs, and the events in the history of the church filled out the calendars of the Eastern and Western churches. Calendars, as most of us know from personal experience, abhor a vacuum. As the blank spaces are quickly filled in, it is necessary from time to time to do some pruning. Because our astronomical calculations are not absolutely perfect, it is also necessary to fix our solar and lunar calendars every several hundred years. Thus, in the sixteenth century the Julian calendar was replaced with the Gregorian calendar in much of the Western world (in Great Britain and certain other Protestant countries in Western Europe this didn't happen until the eighteenth century).

Pilgrimage

In morning and evening prayer we find the themes of life, death, and resurrection, and in the pivotal festivals of the liturgical year we celebrate the life, death, and resurrection of Christ. In the same way, as the seasons and the years come and go, we are reminded of the transitory nature of human life in an ever-changing world. Gabriel Marcel calls human beings *Homo Viator*—human transients.[13] We have lost sight of our transitory place on the earth, perhaps as we have lost the habit of walking. I don't mean walking as a matter of physical exercise but walking as a way of life. Walking was once a way of life that was shared by merchants, traveling artisans, bards, mendicant friars, and pilgrims. The Christian way of life has been described as a life of

12. Ibid., 101-4.
13. Gabriel Marcel, *Homo Viator: Introduction to a Metaphysics of Hope*, trans. Emma Craufurd (Chicago: Regnery, 1951).

pilgrimage. We are a people on the way. One doesn't get the same feel from flying. Our feet are not planted on *terra firma*, reminding us of our connection to the earth and our eventual return to it—ashes to ashes, dust to dust.

From at least the fourth century Christian life was marked by pilgrimage and processions. Accompanied by psalms and litanies, processions became an important aspect of Christian liturgy, which was not static or confined to a place. Liturgy involves movement from one location to another. According to St. Augustine of Hippo, the whole of Christian life is a pilgrimage as we make our way through the city of man to the eternal city of God.

Pilgrimage processions were accompanied by the responsorial singing of psalms (a cantor or choir singing verses, to which the congregation responds by singing a repeated refrain or antiphon) and litanies (a deacon singing petitions and the congregation responding with a short acclamation such as "Lord, have mercy" [*Kyrie eleison*]). Short responses to the prayers by the congregation made it possible for people to sing and walk at the same time.

Every gathering for worship involved pilgrimage, not to a distant land but to the local church. In ancient Rome the pope made his way with his entourage from his residence at St. John Lateran to the station church where the liturgy was being celebrated that day. Psalms and litanies were sung as they processed through the city.[14] When the pope arrived at the church he was greeted by singers (the *Schola Cantorum*), as well as the local clergy and dignitaries. The pilgrimage procession continued into the church building with psalmody and litanies—the Introit with *Gloria Patri* and the Kyrie. When the pope was at his throne behind the altar he intoned the opening hymn of praise, *Gloria in Excelsis Deo*. The liturgy of the Word followed, beginning with the greeting and prayer of the day. There was a similar pilgrimage procession into the Great Church in Constantinople, as we see in the Byzantine Liturgy.

Pilgrimage is known and practiced in all the religions of the world.

14. Aidan Kavanagh, *On Liturgical Theology* (New York: Pueblo, 1984), 64-65.

In the early twenty-first century the number of people of all faiths making pilgrimages continues to rise, with thirty-nine of the most popular sites receiving an estimated two hundred million visitors every year. Muslims make pilgrimages to Mecca. Jews visit the land of Israel. Christians also visit Israel, having designated it as the Holy Land. One of the most popular Christian pilgrimage sites from the Middle Ages is Santiago de Campostella in Spain, which involves an arduous trek across the Pyrenees. Millions of people continue to make that trek today. Interestingly, there is a growing awareness within the major faith organizations that fulfilling the spiritual obligations of pilgrimage may conflict with the spiritual obligation to care for the natural world. Pilgrims need to leave a positive footprint in the places where they walk, which means cooperating with municipal authorities to minimize the environmental impact of their spiritual walks.

Thus, within the cycles of the day, the seasons, and the year Christian life is given a goal and a direction: we are drawn by God to our eternal home. Life is not a cycle of endless repetitions but rather a pilgrimage in which we make our way through this world to the life of the world to come. The church graveyard is only a temporary resting place where we await the archangel's trumpet that shall awaken and raise the dead. The pilgrimage character of Christian life reminds us that "we have here no abiding city."

The Orthodox theologian Alexander Schmemann reminds us that "the journey of the Church into the dimension of the kingdom" begins when Christians leave home on a weekly pilgrimage to the place of assembly to constitute the church in the doing of the Divine Liturgy.[15] The kingdom of God is present where Christ is present in word and sacrament, in ministers and people. We make our way to the place of assembly to constitute the church every Lord's day, festival, and day of devotion. The entrance rite of the liturgy enacts this passage from the world into the kingdom of God with its assorted elements of rite, including confession of sins and forgiveness, praise, and supplication.

15. Alexander Schmemann, *For the Life of the World: Sacraments and Orthodoxy* (St. Vladimir's Seminary Press, 1973), 26.

Yoga Sequence: Experiencing Time and Death

In this sequence of poses we will experience in our bodies the succession of days until we come to our final day and draw our last breath. We will begin in a standing pose and by a series of movements bring our bodies down to the floor, suggestive of our daily movement from activity to rest. After taking our rest we will raise our bodies up (it can sometimes be a struggle) to a new day of activities.

Take a couple of falling-out breaths.

Stand up in mountain pose. Inhale and lift your arms over your head. Bring your arms down as you exhale. With another breath bring your arms overhead again, lift your chest, and raise your body up higher. Do this several times to attain greater height. Now do monkey pose, bringing your hands to your knees and keeping your spine straight. Go back up to standing pose with arms extended overhead. Now do forward fold with bent knees. Bounce your body downward several times with knees bent as necessary to stretch your hands to the floor. With your hands on the floor, walk your feet back and lift your buttocks into the air, making an inverted V shape (this pose is called downward dog). Then lower your buttocks and hold your body straight like a plank with your arms under your shoulders (this is called plank pose). Then drop your knees to the floor and lower your whole body to the floor. This sequence of poses moves you from a standing position to the floor, enacting our descent into rest at the end of the day. Cradle your head in your arms and take your rest. If your head is turned in one direction, turn it in the other direction after a few minutes, just as we often turn from side to side in bed.

Are you ready for another day? Lift up your torso into cobra pose. Place your hands on the floor next to your ribs and lift your chest. Press down on the tops of your feet and your pelvis but keep your knees off the floor. Lower your chest back to the floor. Now with arms under your shoulders press your whole torso upward into full cobra. Lift your buttocks into downward dog. Then walk your feet forward and stand, with your hands in prayer position in front of your chest. This sequence can be repeated to experience the succession of days.

We are ready for final relaxation, which occurs at the end of every yoga session. This enables the body to absorb what it has done. Lay on your back.

Extend your legs into a V and let your feet flop sideways. Let your arms lay at a slight angle from your body, your palms facing upward (which rolls back your shoulders and opens your chest). Breathe in and out several times, and then breathe normally.

This is savasana, or corpse pose. When we reach final relaxation there is nothing more to prove or to be done. So it is when we die.

Figure 3. "The Seven Sacraments" is an altar triptych painted by the Dutch artist Rogier can der Weyden and his workshop between 1145 and 1450. It depicts the seven sacraments of the medieval Catholic Church. On the left panel are baptism, confirmation, and confession. On the right panel are ordination, marriage, and the last rites (extreme unction). The central panel is dominated by a crucifix in the foreground, with the Eucharist in the background. Angels hover over each sacrament with scrolls and vestments that match each sacrament according to color, from white for baptism to black for the last rites.

B. Means of Grace

> Now Moses was keeping the flock of his father-in-law, Jethro, the priest of Mid'ian; and he led his flock to the west side of the wilderness, and came to Horeb, the mountain of God. And the angel of the Lord appeared to him in a flame of fire out of the midst of a bush; and he looked, and lo, the bush was burning, yet it was not consumed. And Moses said, "I will turn aside and see this great sight, why the bush is not burnt." When the Lord saw that he turned aside to see, God called to him out of the bush, "Moses, Moses!" And he said, "Here am I." Then he said, "Do not come near; put off your shoes from your feet, for the place on which you are standing is holy ground." And he said, "I am the God of your father, the God of Abraham, the God of Isaac, and the God of Jacob." Moses hid his face, for he was afraid to look at God. (Exod. 3:1-6 NRSV)

God works through the creation itself to remain connected with his human creatures. God also works through created means to stay connected with us because sinful human creatures cannot bear the fullness of God's holiness. When God wanted to get Moses's attention, he did so through a bush that burned but was not consumed. The burning bush was a means through which God worked—a means of grace. Moses encountered God through many means during his tenure as leader of the people of Israel, serving as their intermediary with God. Yet even Moses, a sinful human being, never beheld God face to face, for no sinner can see God's face and live. Moses was only allowed to get a momentary peek of God's backside (Exod. 33:17-23).

The people of Israel depended on means of grace. They were led by the pillar of cloud by day and the pillar of fire by night. They were followed through the wilderness by a water-spouting rock. When they grumbled and were bitten by snakes, they were directed to look at a bronze serpent on a pole in order to be healed. They related to God through a sacrificial system of burnt animal offerings that were instituted by God and through which they could both express their adoration and thanksgiving and petition forgiveness and well-being. The sacrifices functioned as what we Christians call sacraments—sacred signs. We believe that Christ himself instituted sacraments that make use of earthly elements—the water of baptism and the bread and wine of Holy Communion. But other earthly elements were also used in rites of Christian initiation, such as salt and oil and candles. The Lenten season is framed by physical elements called "sacramentals"—ashes and palms. In fact, they are related to each other in that the palms of Palm Sunday are burned the following year to become the ashes of Ash Wednesday.

Many of the created means that God gave human beings early on appeared to be meaningless at the time they were given. Only later did God reveal the meaning of the practices. For example, God commanded that the Israelites offer up incense during worship. "Aaron shall burn on it sweet incense every morning; when he tends the lamps, he shall burn incense on it. And when Aaron lights the lamps at twilight, he shall burn incense on it, a perpetual incense before the Lord throughout your generations" (Exod. 30:7-8, NRSV). Very strict rules were given concerning what incense could be burnt and who was allowed to burn the incense (only the priests were allowed). Not until hundreds of years later did God mention that incense represents the people's prayers to God—"Let my prayer rise before You as incense, / the lifting up of my hands as the evening sacrifice" (Ps. 141:2, LBW)—an image that is replicated in the book of Revelation with the twenty-four elders holding "bowls full of incense, which are the prayers of the saints" (Rev. 5:8, NRSV). Incense made a comeback in Christian worship in the fourth century with the development of the daily morning and evening prayer offices, which were meant to replicate the daily sacrifices in the temple.

Even more significantly, the animal sacrifices that God commanded the Israelites to offer are fulfilled in Christ. The only reason Christians do not continue the sacrifices instituted by God, apart from the fact that the temple was destroyed and the Aaronic priesthood scattered, is that Christ himself fulfilled the sacrifices. He is the fulfillment of the Passover. "For our paschal lamb, Christ, has been sacrificed. Therefore, let us celebrate the festival"—but in a new way—"not with the old yeast, the yeast of malice and evil, but with the unleavened bread of sincerity and truth" (1 Cor. 5:7-8, NRSV). Likewise, the death of Christ on the cross has become the atoning sacrifice that replaces the old atonement sacrifice of Yom Kippur.

The New Testament sheds new light on what is prefigured in the Old Testament. In order to better understand the death of Christ as a sacrifice, one must understand the sacrificial system in the Old Testament and be able to see those sacrifices, which were instituted by God, as a means of grace for Israel.

How are we to understand the relationship between these earthly signs and the worship of the living God? As a college student I read Mircea Eliade's *The Sacred and the Profane*, which greatly influenced my thought. Eliade was a Romanian Orthodox Christian who taught comparative religion at the University of Chicago for many years. He was interested in the survival of religious instincts in modern man. Eliade suggests that the religious attitude—that is, the attitude of worship—is not merely a primitive response in the face of reality but a permanent attitude of reverence when confronted by a manifestation of the sacred, which he calls a "hierophany." We don't make something sacred; the sacred shows itself to us. We don't worship a tree or a stone; we venerate them because they manifest something entirely other than what we experience in our daily lives—the sacred. "By manifesting the sacred, any object becomes *something else*, yet it continues to remain *itself*, for it continues to participate in its surrounding cosmic milieu."[16] The tree or stone does not cease to be a tree or a stone, and neither are they changed into something different from any other tree or stone; but they are particular means by which a supernatural reality is revealed. Consequently, I saw how Eliade's premise applies to sacramental theology. The bread and wine remain bread and wine, but by the power of the word of Christ the bread and wine manifest what the word proclaims: the body and blood of Christ.

It is important to note here the classic understanding of sacrament in Western Christian theology. The idea comes from St. Augustine of Hippo, who says, "The Word comes to the element; and so there is a

16. Mircea Eliade, *The Sacred and the Profane: The Nature of Religion*, trans. Willard Trask (New York: Harper & Row, 1961), 12 (Italics in the original).

sacrament, that is, a sort of visible word."[17] Augustine is saying that manifestations of God come to us through some element, some piece of the natural world—even if the appearance seems unnatural, such as the burning bush. God's speaking is attached to the earthly element and not heard apart from it.

God's word to us comes as a bath or a meal or a gesture. The church fathers were not in the habit of counting how many visible words there are, as later medieval and Reformation theology was wont to do. Augustine himself variously referred to the following as *sacramenta*: baptism, Eucharist, the sign of the cross, salt and other signs used in the catechumenate, exorcisms, penance, the laying on of hands, reconciliation, the great fast (Lent), the annual celebration of Christ's resurrection (Easter), the octave of Easter, spiritual songs, the Lord's Prayer, and so on. What these have in common is spiritual value and external visibility.

Western medieval theology reduced the number of sacraments to seven: baptism, Eucharist, penance, confirmation, ordination, marriage, and extreme unction. Seven was considered the number of completion, so in total these seven sacraments embodied the complete spectrum of the ways in which God deals with us. But what about all those other means that Augustine and other church fathers regarded as *sacramenta*, or "sacred signs?" Medieval theology calls them "sacramentals," intending by this term to mean something less than sacraments that nevertheless provide an occasion for a "gracing encounter" with Christ. They *point* to a reality rather than *effect* a reality. Some examples of sacramentals (in addition to palms and ashes) include the use of holy water that is used to bless oneself when entering or exiting a church building and rings that are blessed at a wedding. Holy water points to the reality of baptism, which effects forgiveness of sins, new life, and salvation. The wedding rings point to the reality of the marriage. Sacramentals thus relate to the church's sacraments; they prepare for and flow from the celebration of those

---

17. Augustine, *In Johannem* 80; cited in Robert W. Jenson, *Visible Words: The Interpretation and Practice of Christian Sacramentds* (Philadelphia: Fortress Press, 1978), 3.

primary sacraments. Thus, the sign of the cross, which was originally given to catechumens as they began their journey toward baptism, relates to baptism and is used at the invocation of the name of the Trinity to ward off evil and to seal blessings.

Reformation theology reduced the medieval sacraments to two or three: baptism, Eucharist, and sometimes absolution. The other so-called sacraments of the medieval church were simply called rites of the church. This designation has been a source of confusion because *rite* also refers to an order of actions and texts. Hence, the sacrament of baptism is performed in a baptismal rite. It would be better to say that among the various rites of the church, two or three are regarded as sacraments or means of grace in Reformation theology.

As Robert Jenson points out in *Visible Words*, Reformation theology contrasts "visible" not with "invisible" (as Augustine did) but with "audible."[18] The "visible words" are the things we see; the "audible word" is what we hear. Based on the apostle Paul's statement that "faith comes from what is heard" (Rom. 10:17, NRSV), the audible word of preaching acquired a higher place than the visible words of the sacraments in the Reformation churches. But we need to remember that preachers are also visible. The word of Christ is spoken through the earthly bodies of prophets, apostles, and preachers and is applied to an earthly element that becomes a means of grace, a sacrament. This particular bread and wine become the bearers of the body and blood of Christ—and not just any bread and wine—because the word of Christ is proclaimed in connection with their specific use.

Reformation theology also drew upon an understanding of law and gospel to help nail down its definition of sacrament. The Word of God is both law and gospel. In connection with the sacraments, the law is the word of command, and the gospel is the word of promise. Thus, Christ commands that baptism be performed—"Go and make disciples of all nations, baptizing them in the name of the Father and of the Son and of the Holy Spirit" (Matt. 28:19, NRSV), and Christ promises that

18. Robert W. Jenson, *Visible Words: The Interpretation and Practice of Christian Sacraments* (Philadelphia: Fortress Press, 1978), 4-5.

if baptism is performed "the one who believes and is baptized will be saved" (Mark 16:16). Likewise, there is a command of Christ to continue celebrating the meal he has instituted—"Do this in remembrance of me" (Luke 22:19, NRSV)—and there is a promise of Christ if the meal is celebrated—"This is my blood of the covenant, which is poured out for many for the forgiveness of sins" (Matt. 26:28). There is also a clear command of Christ to forgive sins: "If you forgive the sins of any, they are forgiven them; if you retain the sins of any, they are retained" (John 20:23). Only holy absolution, or the "office of the keys" in the Lutheran Church (see Matt. 16:19), lacks a material sign, unless one includes the laying on of hands in blessing.

In addition to the word of command and promise, Reformation theology requires a material sign—a "visible word"—to make a sacrament. The earthly sign is the most irreplaceable part of the sacrament. All sorts of words may surround baptism, but if there is no water for washing there is no sacrament. All sorts of words may surround the celebration of the Lord's Supper, but if there is no bread and wine there is no sacrament.

By means of water and bread and wine, the gospel spoken in the mode of the bath and the supper is an embodied word that is applied to and ingested by bodies designed to receive these visible words. Our bodies need to be renewed and nourished through bathing and dining. In human societies these acts of bathing and dining also have social contexts.

The Social Setting of Sacraments

We see this in meals. Even with our modern hectic schedules, families try to eat together, although it sometimes requires going out to a restaurant rather than cooking at home. Meals are a means of bonding. My wife and I made a point of dining with each other every Friday night in order to reconnect with each other after a week of busy schedules. Extended families share meals at their reunions. In fact, a meal is often the reason for a gathering, such as on holidays. An engaged couple hosts a dinner to meet and get acquainted with their future parents-in-law, and eating and drinking are important aspects of weddings and funerals. In all of these examples the object of the meal is bonding. Hospitality is the means by which the purpose of the meal is accomplished, but the meal is not about hospitality. It is usually about establishing or renewing relationships.

We will see that the earliest Christian Eucharists were celebrated in the context of an actual meal. But whether an actual meal or a sacramental meal with only the bread and wine, the Eucharist has served as a means of communion, of bonding with Christ and with one another in the body of Christ, the church. In fact, the Eucharistic fellowship (*koinonia*) has established church fellowship. Churches are in fellowship with one another if they are can share Holy Communion.

We don't much experience the social context of bathing today, not even in families. When I was a boy the Saturday night bath in preparation for Sunday church was a family activity. We each took our turn in the bathtub, with mother and father hoping enough hot water would be left when their turn came. The advent of showers in family homes made bathing a more individual activity. During my boyhood in the 1950s a public health interest in cleanliness was promoted throughout the public schools in the United States. In my elementary school, children were called out of their classrooms for a "shower" period, provided that the parents agreed; boys and girls went to separate gymnasium locker rooms to take showers together. High school boys used to shower and take swimming classes naked, and swimming and showering were also done naked at the YMCA. I think the previous generations of boys were less shy about their bodies than boys today simply because we spent so much time being naked with our schoolmates.

We don't experience communal bathing today in America, but community bathing used to be a part of world cultures and is still practiced in some countries. Finns, Swedes, and Russians sit in saunas together and may jump into the cold waters of a lake after their bodies have been heated up. The spa culture is popular in Japan and South Korea. In the Korean spas (called "Jjimjilbangs") it's common to see fathers and sons in the men's pool areas and mothers and daughters in the women's pool areas (and sometimes even friends) giving body scrubs to one another, naked and in public. Bonding, philosophic discussion, and even business transactions take place in saunas and hot pools, as was undoubtedly the case in ancient Greco-Roman public baths. There's something about sitting naked with family, friends, and associates that fosters honesty in discussions, as well as deeper relationships. We will see that candidates for Holy Baptism in the early church were baptized naked, although modesty was preserved by baptizing men and women separately.

Christian sacramental liturgy originally related to these acts of communal bathing and dining in the ancient world. God used the earthly elements of water, oil, bread, and wine in the social acts of bathing and dining as sacramental means of grace for his people. The communal aspect of baptism and Holy Communion has been diminished with the loss of communal bathing and dining. In the next several chapters, we will explore this idea further.

3

Naked Bodies, Clothed Bodies

A. Naked before the Lord

We are earthly creatures. Our Creator connects with us through earthly means that become means of grace: the sacraments. These means are applied to our bodies—water for washing, oil for sealing and healing, bread and wine for nourishing and enlivening, hands for affirming and forgiving. In an effort to connect or reconnect with us, to change us or renew us, God makes an impact on our bodies. There is no other way for God to connect with us except through our bodies. As we established in chapter 1, our minds are part of our bodies. But God impacts more than our minds.

In this chapter we consider how God impacts us bodily and how we stand before God—naked as we come into the world and then clothed in the garments God provides. This is already the case with our primal parents in the Book of Genesis, Adam and Eve. They were naked in the Garden until they ate the forbidden fruit and discerned that they were naked and, as an expression of their guilt, covered themselves with fig leaves. Later God made clothing of animal skins for them for protection when they were evicted from the Garden of Paradise and also to provide for social modesty in the new situation of "knowledge" gained from the act of disobediently eating of the forbidden fruit.

There are significant moments of being naked before God in the Bible: when Jacob wrestled with the angel at Peniel and received the name "Israel" (one who struggles with God) (Gen. 32:22-32—wrestling in the ancient world was done in the nude); when David did a victory dance before the Ark of the Covenant when he brought it up to Jerusalem, his new capital of a unified Israel, wearing only a linen apron (2 Sam. 6:1-6); when Jesus was nailed to the cross (Roman crucifixions didn't include a modest loin cloth); and when Jesus rose from the dead (in John 20:6-7 Simon Peter saw the linens in which Jesus' body had been wrapped lying in the tomb). These are moments of great significance in salvation history.

There are moments when nakedness has symbolic importance. In the Passion story in the Gospel of Mark a young man who had been at the baths witnessed the commotion at the arrest of Jesus and dropped his linen cloth to avoid being captured and ran off naked into the night (Mark 14:51-52). Presumably this is the same "young man," now wearing a white robe, who greets the myrrh-bearing women at the tomb on the morning of "the third day" with the announcement, "He has been raised; he is not here" (Mark 16:6, NRSV). When the risen Jesus appeared on the shore of the Sea of Galilee, Simon Peter, who had been naked for work (probably wearing a loin cloth), put on clothes and swam ashore to be with Jesus (John 21:7). We encounter the Lord not just with our minds but in our bodies, and our bodies play a significant role in that meeting.

Part A of this chapter discusses rites in which God deals directly with our bodies, especially circumcision and baptism. These rites of initiation also involve incorporation into a social group. All rites of initiation make an impact on the body so that one may speak of being "reborn" or even receiving a "new body." Indeed, the epitome of a new body is the resurrected body. Rites were established in which the body was stripped: men tore their clothing in penitence, mourning their sins; candidates for baptism went naked into the waters.

In part B we consider how God clothes us in special ways to signify our incorporation into the community of the people of God and to signify the priestly and pastoral leadership of persons set aside to serve God's people by administering the means of grace. God took an interest in clothing when he made animal skins to cover Adam and Eve. God also gave a great deal of thought to the vestments of the high priest of the old covenant. In the liturgies of the church, special clothing continues to take on an important role as well.

Circumcision

Let us begin with circumcision, which in Judaism is usually performed on infants eight days after their birth but is also carried out on adults as a way of incorporating them into the religion of Israel.

Mircea Eliade notes that circumcision is probably the most widely practiced rite of initiation in the world; it is so widespread as to be practically universal.[1] While in Judaism and often in Islam it is performed on infants, circumcision is more commonly performed as a rite of passage from adolescence to adulthood. The passage from childhood to adulthood usually occurs at puberty when the body is undergoing many changes very quickly. The rites of initiation in traditional societies draw attention to these bodily changes, including the sexual implications of these changes. Therefore societies often focus on the sexual organs.

The circumcision ceremony is held for both boys and girls who are judged to be ready for the rite. While male circumcision is considered normal around the world, female circumcision or clitoridectomy is also performed, though it is considered by many people today to be inhumane. For example, in the Masai society in Kenya this initiation is performed shortly after puberty on both boys and girls. In response to the rising challenges of the twenty-first century in the Masai society, many young Masai women no longer undergo circumcision. However,

---

1. Mircea Eliade, *Rites and Symbols of Initiation: The Mysteries of Birth and Rebirth* (New York: Harper & Row, 1958), 21ff.

young men are still eager to be circumcised and become warriors. As such, they assume the responsibility of security for their territory.

Undoubtedly, circumcision is a painful operation for young men. In traditional societies—for example, among the Australian Aborigines—the tribal elder in charge of the circumcision sits on top of the boy's chest facing his penis. He pulls up the foreskin and twists it so it can be cut off. Two men take turns cutting away the foreskin with knives that they've imbued with magical qualities. The boy bites down on a boomerang as the operation takes place. A few months later a second rite, subincision, will be made on the underside of his penis, thereafter requiring him to squat to urinate, like a woman.

The practice of circumcision seems utterly barbaric to many Westerners today. But what many of us often miss in studying these "primitive" rites is that they are performed as part of a sacred worldview. They are not performed for hygienic reasons (a defense that has been largely discredited) but as a rite of initiation into the society. As Eliade notes, "The majority of initiatory ordeals more or less clearly imply a ritual death followed by resurrection or a new birth."[2] The initiate will die to his or her former self and emerge after the ordeal as another person—in the case of adolescent rites, as an adult. In traditional societies, circumcision is regarded as a sacred act performed by the deities themselves through human agents. In the case of the Australian subincision, it may be to imitate the deities, who are bisexual. In a similar way, Christians speak of baptism as God's work through human hands and as identification with Christ in his death and resurrection (Romans 6).

Understanding circumcision as a widespread rite of initiation provides a context in which to view the institution of the rite of circumcision among the people of Abraham.

This is my covenant, which you shall keep, between me and you and your descendants after you: Every male among you shall be circumcised. You shall be circumcised in the flesh of your foreskins, and it shall be a sign of the covenant between me and you. He that is eight days old among you

2. Ibid., xii.

shall be circumcised; every male throughout your generations, whether born in your house, or bought with your money from any foreigner who is not of your offspring, both he that is born in your house and he that is bought with your money, shall be circumcised. So shall my covenant be in your flesh an everlasting covenant. Any uncircumcised male who is not circumcised in the flesh of his foreskin shall be cut off from his people; he has broken my covenant. (Gen. 17:10–14 NRSV)

Circumcision may be the most invasive way God could have chosen to stay connected with his people. As part of his covenant with God, Abram was commanded to circumcise his foreskin. Moreover, this seemingly barbaric ritual was to be applied to every male child who is eight days old and to everyone brought into the families of Israel by birth or adoption. Every covenant contained a clause concerning the witness to the covenant—that is, a perpetual reminder that the covenant existed. For example, the covenant between Jacob and Laban was witnessed by a stone marker (Gen. 31:46–48). In Abram's case, God asked that Abraham and all his male descendants who entered into the covenant bear the reminder of the covenant in their flesh.

Why would God choose to make this cutting of the foreskin on the penis the sign of the covenant? As instituted in Genesis it remains purely arbitrary; no reason for the ritual is given.[3] Only centuries later did God reveal what circumcision represents. Though circumcision was performed on the outward flesh, it represented the acceptance of the covenant in the mind as well, including the willingness to obey the laws within the covenant. In the words of Moses, the people were to purge the sin of disobedience from their lives and become obedient to the laws of God. "And the Lord your God will circumcise your heart and the heart of your descendants, so that you will love the Lord your God with all your heart and with all your soul, in order that you may live" (Deut. 30:6, NRSV).

Drawing on this spiritual understanding of circumcision in Deuteronomy centuries later, the apostle Paul tells the Roman Christians, "Circumcision is indeed of value if you obey the law; but

---

3. For a theological discussion of circumcision see R. R. Reno, *Genesis*, Brazos Theological Commentary on the Bible (Grand Rapids: Brazos, 2010), 175–80.

if you break the law, your circumcision has become uncircumcision" (Rom. 2:25, NRSV). The physical act of circumcision needed to correspond with the actual obedience that God required. Therefore Paul draws the following conclusion: "If an uncircumcised man keeps the righteous requirements of the law, will not his uncircumcision be counted as circumcision?" (Rom. 2:26, NRSV). He even redefines a Jew as one who is circumcised inwardly by doing what the covenant requires—obeying God.

Baptism

Circumcising the foreskin is not a part of God's covenant with Christians. "Was anyone called while circumcised? Let him not become uncircumcised. Was anyone called while uncircumcised? Let him not be circumcised. Circumcision is nothing and uncircumcision is nothing, but keeping the commandments of God is what matters" (1 Cor. 7:18–19, NRSV). Nevertheless, Christians have been given a physical witness that represents what circumcision represented— a witness to the acceptance of God's covenant. As Paul writes to the Colossians, "In him also you were circumcised with a circumcision made without hands, by putting off the body of the flesh in the circumcision of Christ; when you were buried with him in baptism, you were also raised with him through faith in the power of God, who raised him from the dead" (Col. 2:11–12, NRSV).

Baptism is often viewed as the Christian equivalent of circumcision. As a result of this act God connects with us through the body—the body stripped naked, bathed, and reclothed. Baptism, which Paul also understood as a crucifixion of the old self and a burial with Christ, made an impact on the body.

Candidates for baptism were enrolled as catechumens, which means those who would hear the word of God. An ancient church order known as *The Apostolic Tradition*, which is attributed to Hippolytus of Rome, gives us the rites for receiving a seeker as a catechumen, the practices of the catechumenate, and the preparation of the candidates for baptism. The Sahidic version gives this instruction.

Let those who will receive baptism fast on the day of preparation of the Sabbath [Saturday]. On the Sabbath, when those who will receive baptism gather in one place under the direction of the bishop, let them all be commanded to pray and to bend their knees. And when he has laid his hand on them, let him exorcise every foreign spirit, that they may flee from them and not return to them ever again. And when he has finished exorcising, let him blow into them. And when he has sealed their foreheads and their ears and nostrils, let him raise them up.[4]

In some ancient orders spit is applied to the ears of the catechumens to open them to hear the word of God, just as Jesus used spit to open the ears of the deaf man. Throughout the time of the catechumenate, hands were laid on the heads of the catechumens in exorcism and blessing when they were dismissed from the assembly after the liturgy of the word, which came to be called the liturgy of the catechumens, and before the liturgy of the meal or Eucharist, which came to be called the liturgy of the faithful because only the baptized could receive Holy Communion.

The rite of baptism in the ancient church required a stripping and a reclothing—literally as well as figuratively. This practice was not strange in a culture of public baths, such as existed in the Roman world. Peter Brown writes that "nudity and sexual shame were questions of social status: the way people felt about being naked, or seeing others naked, depended to a large extent on their social situation. Thus, at the top of society, nudity in the public baths expressed the utter ease of the well-to-do, moving without a trace of sexual shame in front of their inferiors."[5]

Candidates for baptism removed all of their clothing before having their bodies oiled and then going down into the font for immersion (not necessarily submersion). Emerging from the water their bodies may have been oiled again (diverse practices exist in the ancient church orders). Finally, they were clothed in a new white garment (*alba*) to signify that they had put on Christ.

---

4. *The Apostolic Tradition: A Commentary*, trans. Paul F. Bradshaw, Maxwell E. Johnson, and L. Edward Phillips (Minneapolis: Fortress Press, 2002), 106.
5. Peter Brown, *The Rise of Western Christendom: Triumph and Diversity A.D. 200–1000*, 2nd ed. (Oxford: Blackwell, 2003), 66.

The earliest description of this process of Christian initiation is recorded in the *Apostolic Tradition*, which is mentioned above. The Liturgy of Baptism (Sahidic text) required men, women, and children to remove all clothing, including all foreign objects such as jewelry and hair fasteners:

> And at the hour when the cock crows, let the water be prayed over first. Let the water be drawn into the pool or flow down into it. And let it be thus if there is no exigency. But if there is an exigency that persists and is urgent, use the water that you will find. And let them strip naked. And first baptize the small children. And each one who is able to speak for themselves, let them speak. But those not able to speak for themselves, let their parents or another one belonging to their family speak for them. Afterward, baptize the grown men, and finally, the women, loosening their hair and laying aside the jewelry of gold and silver that they are wearing. Let no one take any foreign thing down into the water with them.[6]

Imitating Jesus, who was baptized in the Jordan River, Christians have sometimes performed baptisms in streams and other natural bodies of water. Beginning in the fourth century, urban basilicas included baptisteries, which were like bathhouses attached to the church buildings with fonts or pools deep enough for adults to be standing at least waist deep in water. The pools were sometimes octagonal (suggesting the eschatological eighth day) and sometimes in the shape of a cross. Steps led down into the water, and steps ascended from the water on the other side. In Milan candidates undressed in side chambers off the baptistery.[7] Because of the nudity of the candidates, baptisms were not performed in the public assembly. With another nod to modesty, the ancient church orders specified that female deacons baptized the women and children while male deacons, presbyters, and sometimes even the bishop baptized the men. It is likely that ministers also went into the font naked to baptize the candidates. Why would a

---

6. *The Apostolic Tradition: A Commentary*, trans. Paul F. Bradshaw, Maxwell E. Johnson, and L. Edward Phillips (Minneapolis: Fortress Press, 2002), 112.

7. Garry Wills, *Font of Life: Ambrose, Augustine, and the Mystery of Baptism* (Oxford: Oxford University Press, 2012) gives a description of the archaeological reconstruction of the baptistery in Ambrose's cathedral in Milan.

patrician bishop like Ambrose, used to being naked in the public baths, ruin his splendid Pascha vestments by wearing them into the pool?

Every ritual act of baptism received commentary by the bishops in their catecheses or teachings on the sacraments after Easter. I cite Cyril of Jerusalem from his *Mystagogic Catecheses*, or "teachings on the mysteries" (sacraments are called "mysteries" in Greek):

> Upon entering you took off your clothing, and this symbolized your stripping off of "the old nature with its practices." Stripped naked, in this too you were imitating Christ naked on the cross, who in his darkness "disarmed the principalities and powers" and on the wood of the cross publicly "triumphed over them." Since hostile powers lurked in your limbs, you can no longer wear your former clothing; I do not of course refer to visible apparel but to "your old nature which is corrupt through deceitful lusts." I pray that the soul which has once thrown off that old nature may never resume it, but rather speak the words of Christ's bride in the Song of Songs: "I had put off my garment; how could I put it on?" This was a remarkable occasion, for you stood naked in the sight of all and you were not ashamed. You truly mirrored our first-created parent Adam, who stood naked in Paradise and was not ashamed.[8]

The idea that the candidates for baptism went into the water naked and were not ashamed may be a social statement as well as a theological one. Baptism is a leveling sacrament in which Jews and gentiles, men and women, slaves and free are treated equally. The lower classes had no more to be ashamed of than the upper classes, who walked around the public baths naked.

The bodies that went into the pool were first oiled in the fashion of the Roman baths. Cyril also comments on this:

> Next, after removing your garments you were rubbed with exorcised oil from the hair of your head to your toes, and so you became sharers in Jesus Christ, who is the cultivated olive tree. For you have been separated from the wild olive tree and grafted on the cultivated tree, and given a share in the richness of the true olive. The exorcised oil, then, symbolized your partaking of Christ's richness; it is the token which drives away every trace of the enemy's power. Just as the breath of the saints and the invocation of God's name burn like a fierce flame and drive out devils,

---

8. Quoted in Edward J. Yarnold, *The Awe-Inspiring Rites of Initiation*, 2nd ed. (Collegeville, MN: Liturgical Press, 1994), 76–77.

likewise the exorcised oil, through invocation of God and through prayer, is invested with such power as not merely to cleanse all traces of sin with its fire, but also to pursue all the invisible powers of the wicked one out of our persons.[9]

The tracing of a cross on the forehead with oil, as is done today, is a pretty minimal remnant of the rubdown with oil that Cyril describes. I can imagine a practice much more like receiving an Indian oil massage (abhyanga) in which an abundance of oil is rubbed into the whole body.

Thus the body was stripped naked, rubbed with oil, and immersed in the water. Immersion implies being in the water. The mode of baptism varied and could have involved submersion under the water or simply the pouring of water over the head. However, it was always done three times, with the candidate confessing faith in the Father, the Son, and the Holy Spirit.

Cyril's *Catecheses* moves beyond what happens to the individual body to discuss the interplay of bodies in the church. Throughout his homilies, he is clear that the body of the faithful is responsible for initiates—"We are the doorkeepers. We let you in."[10]—but that they are also eager to welcome individuals into the body. In other words, Cyril stresses the idea that belief cannot be cultivated apart from the context of the community of faith.

Finally, Cyril's *Catecheses* illustrates the close relationship that exists between ritual actions and the narratives that they embody. For example, Maxwell Johnson is clear that Cyril's baptism in the inner chamber (stripping, anointing, immersion, vesting) intentionally reenacts the "saving events themselves," the very events that constituted and called the church into being.[11] The fact that Cyril gave lectures explicating the meanings of the rituals after they were experienced testifies that belief can be reified and strengthened as the story of what the baptized experienced is retold within the framework

---

9. Ibid.
10. Ibid.
11. Maxwell E. Johnson, *The Rites of Christian Initiation: Their Evolution and Interpretation* (Collegeville, MN: Liturgical Press, 1999), 93–97.

of the biblical narrative. The words are joined to the ritual actions as part of the process of inculcating faith.

Even so, we should be wary of relying too heavily on the words of explanation. I think that modern people, influenced by the Western dualism that separates the mind and body, have difficulty accepting the fact that God works on and through our bodies, especially directly, as these ancient rites of Christian initiation demonstrate. We think about God appealing to our minds in order to change them or to our souls in order to sanctify them. We don't think about God dealing directly with us in a bodily way. But there is no way for God to get to our minds or our souls except through our bodies. Neither our minds nor our souls are disembodied. The words of interpretation are secondary to the primary act of the rituals performed on the body.

The Body as Limitation and Liberation

There has always been a human tendency to regard the body as a limitation that must somehow be transcended in order to attain spiritual liberation. This is evident especially in gnostic religions and spiritualities. For example, in Hindu and Jainist asceticism holy men (*sadhus*) lived in the caves and forests of the northern Indian Himalayas and went about in a state of near or total nakedness even when begging food from or bestowing blessings on surrounding villagers. They exposed the body, renouncing clothing and shelter, not as a way of glorifying the body but as a way of splitting the soul from the body. The vessels of life, including the body, were regarded as the encasement of our inner, unchanging core. The intention of yogic practice was to overcome or transcend the outer plane, which was characterized by dualistic thought and perception, and to merge it with an undifferentiated, unified plane of being. They did not accept the body as it is or intend to improve it in the way that modern yoga teaches. Sadhus gave attention to the body in order to not give attention to it.

The concept of the body as a barrier to spiritual freedom manifested itself in Christian asceticism at nearly the same time as the development of baptismal practices in the early church and is evident in the rigors and austerities of holy men and women, beginning with the desert fathers and the first monks. But if the Christian ascetics, like St. Jerome, prayed and meditated naked in the desert, it was also to be exposed to God without any barriers, as God created him.

In Christian cultures both East and West, a general desire to achieve spiritual freedom through mortification of the flesh persisted for a long period of time, most notably in the hermitage, the cloisters, and the hair shirts of medieval Christians. While some of that asceticism has abated today, there still remains the feeling of guilt and shame about the human body, particularly since the body has become almost synonymous with sexuality. Sexuality, in the view of Augustine, is the biological means by which the sin of the first parents was transmitted to their descendant. In Christian cultures, the message of the basic goodness of God's creation, including the goodness of the human body and of sexuality, became clouded.

Civilization in Christian Europe seemed to favor the development of intellectual powers over physical ones—of mind over matter—and eventually the body was totally covered. It was believed that the natural instincts of the barbarian needed to be subdued in Christian civilization in order to live chaste lives. As Christian missionaries fanned out into lands previously unknown to Europeans, they required their native converts to put on clothes. People in the non-Western world who lived in warmer climes and went about in a state of semi- or total nudity were no exception.

In modern times there has been a reaction and we have gloried in athleticism and physical training and glamorized sexuality for commercial purposes. But this does not mean that we have achieved a state of balance between the physical and the spiritual; it means that we have overreacted. We have lost the Greek ideal of the healthy mind in the healthy body. The ancient Greeks not only exercised in naked in their gymnasiums, but they also engaged in philosophical discussions even in the gyms and baths.

The early Christian church reflected contemporary attitudes towards nakedness, which was considered acceptable in some contexts, such as working outdoors. In ancient Egypt and elsewhere in the Middle East men usually wore only a loincloth when going about their daily work. I cited the example, in John 21:7, of Simon Peter working naked while fishing from a boat but then getting dressed in order to meet Christ. As we have seen, ancient Christian baptisms were performed on nude candidates, and ancient Christian art depicts nude baptisms, even the baptism of Jesus by John the Baptist in the River Jordan.

At the time of the Renaissance, artists like Michelangelo and Caravaggio recaptured the beauty of the human form. Pictures of nudes were painted on the walls and ceilings of Catholic churches—most famously in the Sistine Chapel in the Vatican. In the mural of "The Last Judgment" that Michelangelo painted on the wall above the altar of the Sistine Chapel, all the hundreds of figures, including Christ the Judge, are naked. (Do we think we will rise from the dead fully clothed?) But this glorification of the naked body was short-lived and there was a puritan reaction, not only in Protestant iconoclasm (which was really more against the images of the saints than against nude bodies) but also in later Catholic liturgical art. Michelangelo sculpted a figure of a naked Christ rising from the tomb, but a seventeenth-century pope had the genitals draped. In paintings and sculptures of Christ on the cross the "private parts" had to be covered with a loin cloth. In the liturgical movement of the twentieth century the naked body of Christ on the cross was often replaced with the figure of a risen and reigning Christ (*Christus Rex*) wearing priestly robes and hovering over the cross rather than being fixed onto it. This was not so much revulsion at our Lord's nakedness as replacing the crucified Savior with the risen Lord as a central liturgical symbol.

Naked before the Lord

Nevertheless, our crucified Savior was raised up on a public pole, naked before God and the world—the New Adam exposed in a radical act of obedience to God, without shame. The crucified Christ is a model of how we stand in our bodies before the Lord who created us. In *Love and*

Responsibility, Pope John Paul II expresses the Roman Catholic Church's attitude to the exposure of the human body in the following way:

> The human body can remain nude and uncovered and preserve intact its splendor and its beauty . . . Nakedness as such is not to be equated with physical shamelessness . . . Immodesty is present only when nakedness plays a negative role with regard to the value of the person . . . The human body is not in itself shameful . . . Shamelessness (just like shame and modesty) is a function of the interior of a person.[12]

I deal with the issue of shame and clothing the body in the second part of this lesson, but here I want to affirm that the human body was created good. In the ancient interpretations of the baptismal rites the church fathers saw nakedness as a symbol of the return to the primordial blessedness bestowed on the baptized. As one comes naked into the world through the waters of the birth canal, so one comes naked into the new creation in the waters of baptism. And, as Michelangelo clearly portrayed in his mural of "The Last Judgment" in the Sistine Chapel, we shall be resurrected in the state of nakedness.

I have tried to use the word "naked" rather than "nude" when referring to our state of undress before the Lord. Dorian Sagan suggests that there is a difference between nakedness and nudity.

> Nakedness is pretty straightforward. It is exposure, What you see is what you get.
>
> The allure of nudity is subtler. What is concealed is equal to or greater than what is revealed. What you see is not what you get.
>
> Partial revelation triggers temptation, seduction, the dance of desire. This is the principle of nudity. Even if what is revealed is the naked body, there is more than meets your eye. Nakedness, although seemingly so close to nudity, is in a way its opposite. Nakedness is our natural state, but it may show too much too soon, more than we want to see, destroying desire.[13]

This is why throughout this book I have tried to use the concept of nakedness when referring to our situation before God, our status of

12. Karol Wojtyla (Pope John Paul II), *Love and Responsibility*, trans. H. T. Willetts (San Francisco: Ignatius, 1993), 79–80.
13. Doran Sagan, *Sex* in *Sex/Death* (two books in one) (White River Junction, VT: Chelsea Green Publishing Company, 2009), 7.

holiness. Nudity, I think, is appropriate for works of art since the very nature of art is to conceal as well as reveal. Yet the concepts sometimes merge. Michelangelo paints all nude figures in "The Last Judgment" to show humankind rising naked in the resurrection.

Baptism invites nakedness, not nudity. There are probably no cultures in the world today where totally naked baptism of adults would be acceptable. However, in Greek Orthodox churches adult candidates sometimes wear underwear or bathing suits for their immersion in the font, basin, or pool, and babies are typically baptized naked. The baptism of naked babies is slowly becoming more acceptable in more churches; it was once common practice.

I have seen photos of adults baptized in immersion fonts (aboveground) or pools (underground) entering the water wearing their baptismal clothing, including the liturgical alb. But the point of the rites of initiation is to shed the old life, which is symbolized by the old clothing. The candidate renounces sin, Satan, and the devil's "pomps" (honors) while facing west and then turns east to profess adherence to Christ. Going into the water, he or she confesses belief in God the Father, Son, and Holy Spirit and is submersed or has water poured over the body three times, coming up from the water as a new person, which is symbolized by putting on the new baptismal clothing. The baptismal garment should be reserved for after the baptism. With baptismal fonts or pools in the open assembly rather than in semi-secluded baptisteries, candidates must wear some type of covering—perhaps some special garment can be devised just for the purpose of going into the water. But the new clothing, especially the alb, should be put on after the baptism, just as a baby's baptismal dress is put on after the baptism. While this will require time (and a place) to change clothing before continuing with the rite, this can be done while other candidates are being baptized. In the meantime, the congregation can be devotionally occupied with a hymn or psalm or litany that is sung as the newly baptized emerge from the changing room and are led to the altar for the concluding rites, which include the laying on of hands for invocation of the Holy Spirit and anointing of the forehead for the sealing of the Holy Spirit. These Spirit-infusing and Spirit-sealing gestures can be regarded as certification by the bishop or the pastor before the assembly of the baptisms that have been performed in the semi-privacy of the baptistery. The newly baptized are then welcomed into the inner fellowship of the church in Holy Communion.

Being Comfortable in Our Skin

God is acting on our bodies in the sacrament of Holy Baptism no matter how it is performed. Some part of the body gets wet, even if only the head, and oil may be applied, again perhaps only on the forehead in the shape of a cross. Likewise, God works on the body through the laying on of hands in the rite of confirmation and the application of oil in the ministry of healing. Of course, one receives food and drink into one's body in Holy Communion. In addition, one processes to the communion station to receive the sacrament.

It would be very good for children to witness ministrations of the church on the body so that they know that God deals with them bodily and not only mentally. They are very aware of their bodies, which are often growing faster than they can process the implications of that fact. They need tactile ways of relating to one another. Up to a certain age they're happy to be hugged by their parents. Children are often touching one another. In the American culture we begin to discourage that by word or example by the time children begin attending school. But I took note of school boys, and even young men, in Singapore walking down the street with arms around one another's shoulders or waists. I saw more touching of one another by Southeast Asian and Indian boys and men than I'm used to seeing in America.

A form of touch we all experience in the liturgy is at the greeting of peace. St. Paul concluded several of his letters with commands for the Christians to whom he was writing to greet one another with a holy kiss (Rom. 16:16, 1 Cor. 16:20, 2 Cor. 13:2, 1 Thess. 5:26; see also 1 Pet. 5:14). Michael Philip Penn has surveyed the instances of kissing in Greco-Roman societies. Since much of this kissing occurred in an erotic context, Christians leaders were careful to manage ritual kissing between Christians on the basis of kissing among family members and friends. He suggested that "The Greco-Roman greeting kiss clearly influenced early Christian use of the kiss as a rite of inclusion and all five New Testament references to the ritual kiss speak of it as a greeting. Early Christians also used the implications of refusing a kiss to help fashion the ritual kiss into a rite of exclusion."[14] In *The Apostolic Tradition* catechumens are excluded from the greeting of peace "because their kiss is not yet pure" (Arabic version).[15] However, after their baptismal and anointing the newly-baptized are greeted by the bishop with a kiss. The mouth-to-mouth kiss of peace continued to be practiced in the ancient church. In the Middle Ages it became an embrace with a bussing on the cheeks, at least among the clergy at a solemn high mass. It fell out among the lay people. Today the greeting of peace has been restored in the liturgies of many churches, but the gesture accompanying the greeting of peace is usually a handshake or perhaps an embrace.

Massage as a Rite of Initiation and Healing

A form of touch many people experience is massage. Some people think of massage as a luxury or as therapy for athletes or those who put a let of stress and strain on their bodies. But given the pressures of living and working in modern society and the increase in stress-related illnesses, massage is becoming more of an integral part of ordinary life. It plays a role in preventative health maintenance as well as in treatment of bodily injuries. Massage aids in circulation and in detoxification. But most of all, massage is about touch. Touch is the first of the senses to develop in babies. It enables us to have a relationship beyond our own periphery. Becoming a healthy human being requires the loving touch of parents, and development may be

14. Michael Philip Penn, *Kissing Christians: Ritual and Community in the Late Ancient Church* (Philadelphia: University of Pennsylvania Press, 2005), 13-14.
15. Bradshaw, Johnson, Phillips, *The Apostolic Tradition*, 100.

inhibited when touch is denied. The need for touch continues throughout our lives.

I experienced the power of touch when I received a massage at an Asian spa in Singapore. Upon my arrival in Singapore, my body was full of tension. I had just retired from forty years of active parish ministry and had just completed the process of closing out my pastoral ministry of twenty-three years in Immanuel Lutheran Church in Evanston, Illinois, saying my goodbyes and moving my office from the church to my home while also preparing material for workshops, public lectures, and a seminary course in Singapore. My flight from Chicago was long, and a few days after my arrival I sought out an Asian men's spa (Singapore is known for shopping, dining, and massage). I was greeted by a young Asian masseur who removed my shoes, brought me a fruit drink, and showed me the massage menu. After I chose a fusion acupressure and oil massage that I thought would both work out kinks and provide relaxation, the masseur led me to a curtained cubicle and, after I undressed, to a shower. He did a great job on both parts of the massage. I was amazed that his hands and arms (as well as his knees when he was on top of me) could so strongly apply pressure and then so gently apply and rub in the oil. I was draped for the acupressure part of the massage because oil was not used, but then I was undraped for oil aromatherapy. The masseur only wore his briefs. I was used to this nakedness from receiving a body scrub in a Korean spa near my home in which the client is totally naked and the masseur wears only briefs. But I was totally unprepared for what the young Asian masseur did at the end of the massage. He said, "You need to relax." With that he laid his naked torso over mine in a kind of profound embrace that lasted for what seemed like several minutes. Of course I immediately tensed up, but as he lay still on top of me I did relax and found his hug deeply peaceful. Afterwards he wiped off the excess oil and led me back to the shower. When I returned he had prepared a tray of green tea, which we sipped while sitting on the massage table. I paid him and gave him a good tip as he walked me to the door. The whole experience was characterized by hospitality and graciousness.

This massage made a profound impression on me. On later reflection I thought about its initiatory qualities. I was welcomed with gracious hospitality. I went through the "ordeal" of the acupressure massage (it was strong!), and then my covering was removed for the oil massage (an anointing). The embrace of his hug functioned as a kiss of peace. I was then led to the water, which was followed by the "communion" of the tea and his company. I regarded the experience as a rite of initiation into my retirement, which was officially beginning in those days, leading me to a new birth. I felt prepared to do in Singapore exactly what I hoped I might be doing in my retirement ministry.

I have since come to see an initiatory quality in all massage: it transforms a hurting body into a renewed body. This renewal comes through touch. In fact, massage is all about touch. Massage therapists know that the stimulation of the skin through touch is as necessary to us as water, food, or oxygen. Without adequate stimulation of the skin through touch, we languish. Infants sufficiently deprived of touch perish, regardless of being fed and sheltered. We also need to be touched by God.

Experiencing God in My Body

As a youth I needed a more tangible way to connect with God than through the mind alone, which is what I experienced in my confirmation and first Holy Communion at the age of thirteen, going on fourteen. In the rite of confirmation the pastor laid his hands on my head as he asked God the Father, for Jesus' sake, to strengthen in me the Holy Spirit, given in baptism.

In my first Holy Communion after my confirmation I experienced the strange consistency of the communion wafer in my mouth and the astringency of the communion wine going down my esophagus and into my stomach. I heard the words, "the body of Christ, given for you. The blood of Christ, shed for you." I remembered the teaching of the catechism—that the most important thing about the sacrament is believing that the body and blood of Christ are "given and shed for you for the forgiveness of sins." I felt physically forgiven of whatever real or imagined adolescent sins I had committed as I consumed the wine, "cleansed by the blood of the lamb of God who takes away the sins of the world." I also felt connected with my fellow communicants in the sharing of this holy meal. This was probably the most significant religious experience in my early life. Perhaps as a result, Holy Communion (or the Eucharist) became important to me throughout the rest of my life—the subject of academic study and pastoral focus. God touched me through the sacrament of the altar, which impacted my body internally.

I learned to respond to God's touch by worshiping God with my body; I learned to use all of my senses as well as bodily gestures and postures, including some that weren't practiced in my home congregation. I found that crossing myself and bowing or kneeling gave me a more immediate sense of God's presence. I had to be self-conscious about what I was doing, and the gesture or posture reminded me of why I was doing it. I was worshiping God with my body and it brought meaning to mind.

Marks on the Body

Many people today receive tattoos on their bodies. Tattoos can also be viewed as a way to worship God with one's body. In some countries tattooing is an adolescent rite of passage. Today young people all across America and around the world get tattoos, and I'm amazed by how many have the cross or even the face of Jesus tattooed on their bodies.

Tattoo actually comes from a Polynesian word, and such markings have been found in cultures around the world for several millennia. In the ancient Mediterranean world they were known by the Greek term *stigma* (plural, *stigmata*), a word that in contemporary times carries the negative connotations of the original. A stigma was an indelible mark on the body painfully applied with needles or brands that showed the downgraded social status of the person; slaves and criminals were distinguished in this way. Certain Christians adopted the stigma as a way of showing their commitment to be a "slave to God." Persecuted

Coptic Christians in Egypt tattooed crosses on their inner arms as a sign of faithfulness. Some Ethiopian Christians even today have a cross tattooed on their forehead to profess their faith. For almost two millennia, tattoos have visually and bodily marked the faith of Christians.

On Ash Wednesday the sign of the cross is applied to our foreheads with ashes and the words "Remember that you are dust, and to dust you shall return." Being marked on Ash Wednesday is like receiving a temporary tattoo. The ashes remind us that the body, which came naked into the world, will depart from the world, just as the sign of the cross reminds us of the hope that these mortal bodies will be raised from the dead.

We will not enter eternity without a body. It will be a glorified body, like Christ's body after his resurrection, but it will still be a body. Apparently, it will retain the needs of the body since Christ ate and drank with his disciples after his resurrection.

The Subtle Body

Is it possible to experience the body as more than a biological machine without ignoring the physicality of our bodily existence? The yoga tradition, especially Tantra, recognizes a subtle body that interacts with the physical body. It is called the "subtle body" because it provides us with a reference system of the connections between the physical and spiritual aspects of ourselves.[16]

16. See Georg Feuerstein, *The Yoga Tradition* (Prescott, AR: Hohm, 2008), 350–57.

Figure 306. Seven Lotus Centers of the Kundalini

Figure 4. A diagram of the yoga subtle body with its *nadis* and chakras.

The subtle body focuses on lines called *nadis*, which are invisible to the eye, that are like the meridians in Chinese medicine used in acupuncture. The *nadi* that moves up the central axis of the body from the perineum to the crown of the head is called the *sushumna*. Two other lines (*nadis*), the *ida* and *pingala*, spiral along the *sushumna*. The *ida* represents the lunar or female side of the human (the left side) and governs the downward flow of energy. It relates to the parasympathetic nervous system. The *pingala* nadi represents the solar or masculine side of the human and governs the upward flow of energy. It relates to the sympathetic nervous system. The object of Hatha yoga practice is to bring these opposites together—the lunar and solar energies producing a calm mind and an energetic body.

Between the intersecting *nadis* are seven energetic centers or vortices called "*chakras.*" Located along the *sushumna* at the perineum, sacrum, solar plexus, heart, throat, in the middle of the forehead (third eye), and at the crown of the head (actually above the head and therefore out of the body), they are regarded as the main receivers and distributors of the vital energy moving throughout the physical body.

Coiled at the base of the perineum, yogis imagined the *kundalini,* a sleeping serpent identified with the goddess Shakti. The *kundalini* represents creative energy. The object of yoga practices with the breath (*pranayama*), postures (*asanas*), and chanting (*mantras*) is to arouse the *kundalini* and send energy up through the *chakras* to the crown of the head, where consciousness, identified with the god Shiva, resides. The object of tantric yoga is to bring about the union of consciousness and energy, at which juncture enlightenment—the elimination of all duality—occurs.

The seven *chakras* play a vital role in the process of enlightenment. They are interrelated, and a blockage at one can impact the others. The three lower chakras are regarded as relating to our physical selves and deal psychologically with issues of security and survival (root area), creativity and sexuality (genital area), and confidence and self-definition (abdominal area). The upper three are regarded as relating to our spiritual selves and deal psychologically with communication and self-expression (throat), imagination and intuition (third eye), and knowledge and enlightenment (the crown of the head). The heart chakra deals psychologically with issues of love and devotion and provides the balance between our physical and spiritual selves.

There are whole dimensions of the subtle body that I haven't mentioned. Ideas about the subtle body came out of centuries of observation of experiences concerning how the body and mind interconnect. The chakra system is one way of mapping the emotional energy centers of our bodies. They cannot be medically observed, although their location and actions correspond to our endocrine system. You do not have to "believe" in the existence of the subtle body to practice yoga. It may even be more beneficial to practice without preconceived ideas. Yoga is an experiential science.

A Yoga Sequence: The Three Lower Chakras and the Heart Chakra

The chakras may serve as a means of organizing a yoga sequence. What follows is the sequence I arranged for my class at Satya Wacana. This exercise focuses first on the three lower chakras, which relate to our most incarnational or embodied selves: our basic physiological needs—concern for security, desire for belonging, and identity. These issues are addressed in this lesson in terms of nakedness and initiation. To access or activate the root chakra (*maladhara*), standing poses will promote qualities of groundedness and stability. For the sacral chakra (*sradhishthana*) we will move to the belly and experience both comfort and grasping (maybe even gasping!). For the solar plexus chakra (*manipura*) we will lie on the back and do abdominal poses, which will stimulate digestive fire in the belly. We will do bridge pose to elevate both the pelvis and the abdomen. Then we will focus on the heart chakra (*anahata*), the center of *bhakti*—of love, devotion, and worship. We will do poses that open the heart, of which bridge will serve as a transition to a more powerful pose. We will then subside and I conclude with *savasana*.

As usual, begin with several falling-out breaths. You will also need to warm up if you have been sitting. Stand in mountain pose (tadasana) with your hands folded in front of your heart. I find mountain pose to be very centering. It helps to get the body in balance before you make other movements. Make sure your feet are parallel with each other and not at an angle. Feel your feet and legs grounded into the floor and then inhale as you stretch with your arms overhead.

Mountain pose roots us to the earth. So do other standing poses, such as warrior 1 (virabhadrasana).[17] *We will use this pose to tune into the root chakra. Lift your left foot and place it behind your right foot at a forty-five degree angle, with your torso facing the right leg. Inhale as you lift your arms overhead and bend your right leg so that your knee is over your ankle. Hold the pose. Exhale as you straighten the right leg, lower your arms, and turn your torso around to face the opposite direction. Inhale as you raise your arms overhead and bend your left leg so that your knee is over your foot, turning the back foot at a forty-five degree angle. Hold the pose. Do you notice any sensations, emotions, or thoughts as you hold the pose?*

Figure 5. The author is leading the Embodied Liturgy class in warrior 1 pose (*virabhadrasana*).

17. There are five warrior poses: 1, 2, 3, humble warrior, and reverse warrior. The warrior poses remind us of the warrior yogis—naked armies of ascetics who served as mercenaries to Indian rulers. Some of the naked ascetics (*naga sadhus*) still carry sticks and get into jousting matches. See Sondra L. Hausner, *Wandering with Sadhus: Asceticism in the Hindu Himalayas* (Bloomington: Indiana University Press, 2007).

Exhale as you bring your arms to the floor and step back into downward dog. Then lower your pelvis to plank pose, shoulders over your wrists. Lower down on your belly for locust pose (shalabhasana). We will use this pose to activate the sacral chakra. As you inhale extend your arms off the floor (to the side like wings or forward along your ears for a stronger pose) and extend your legs behind but lifted off the floor. Exhale and lower your limbs. Raise your arms and legs again, resting on your belly and breathing in and out. Then lower your limbs down to the floor. Did you notice any sensations, emotions, or thoughts as you held the pose?

Roll over on your back. With arms at your side (perhaps slightly under your buttocks), lift your feet in the air and then lower them down without touching the ground. You may also lower and raise one leg at a time. Do this five times for both legs. This will light a fire in your belly.

Next, bring your knees to your chest and place your feet on the floor in front of your buttocks. Place your arms alongside your torso and lift your pelvis off the floor. This is bridge pose, which we use to activate the solar plexus chakra. Clasp your hands under your raised buttocks to bring your shoulders together and move your feet closer to your buttocks. Push up higher as you inhale and hold the pose. Do you notice any sensations, emotions, or thoughts while in this pose?

In bridge pose now extend your arms overhead (on the floor) as you raise your pelvis. From here you may choose a backbend that you are able to do. You could remain in the extended bridge pose (easiest option).Or, from extended bridge pose you might push up with your hands (palms on the floor) into wheel pose (the most difficult option)or roll forward and come up on your knees and do camel pose (ushtrasana)(medium difficulty) or roll forward and on your stomach do cobra (bhujangasana) (less difficult option). Do you notice any sensations, emotions, or thought while in this pose?For a final stretch we will do a supine twist. Bring your knees to your chest. Extend your arms to each side in the shape of a T. Inhale and extend your knees to your right side toward your armpit while you turn your head to the left, trying to keep your navel as much in the center as possible. Exhale and bring your knees to the center. Inhale and extend your knees to your left side toward your armpit while you turn your head to the right, trying to keep your navel as much in the center as possible.

Exhale and bring your knees back to the center. Extend your legs and prepare for final savasana, in which you will absorb what you have done.

Figure 6a. An infant is baptized in a Russian Orthodox Church.

B. God Clothes the Body

Then the eyes of both were opened, and they knew that they were naked; and they sewed fig leaves together and made loincloths for themselves. They heard the sound of the Lord God walking in the garden at the time of the evening breeze, and the man and his wife hid themselves from the presence of the Lord God among the trees of the garden. But the Lord God called to the man, and said to him, "Where are you?" He said, "I heard the sound of you in the garden, and I was afraid, because I was naked; and I hid myself." He said, "Who told you that you were naked? Have you eaten from the tree of which I commanded you not to eat?" . . . And the Lord God made garments of skins for the man and for his wife, and clothed them. (Gen. 3:7-11, 21, NRSV)

We come into the world naked, but as we enter the world of human society we are clothed. The kind of clothing we wear is culturally conditioned. We wear clothing because the primal man and woman transgressed the limits the Lord God placed on them—a practice we continue. Adam and Eve ate of the tree of the knowledge of good and evil and came to know things about themselves of which they were previously innocent. One might even say that a new condition came into the world that did not exist before. Adam and Eve realized that they were naked, and they were ashamed. They tried to hide from God so that their nakedness was not exposed.

The Experience of Shame

The nakedness of which Adam and Ever were ashamed revolves around the genital area, not the whole body. Shame is a complex experience in the sense that it distances us from one another—the man and woman from each other and humanity from God. The shame experienced by the man and the woman in the presence of God is the knowledge that they disobeyed the word of God, which is manifested in their awareness of their bodily nakedness. We transgress the limits, and then we are dissatisfied with ourselves. This often involves dissatisfaction with our bodies, because our bodies are ourselves.

Especially in Western culture, this sense of shame is experienced in the fear that our bodies don't measure up to our expectations of how our bodies compare with the ideal bodies presented in the media or our concern that others view us with disapproval because we are too fat or too skinny or have the wrong pigmentation. Body shame, which manifests itself in the form of self-objectification, has been linked to eating disorders, unhealthy sexual practices, the rise in cosmetic surgery, diminished mental performance at school, diminished athletic performance, anxiety and depression, and sedentary lifestyles. *These impairments occur among all ethnicities and ages.* Today, body shame is a condition most often treated with therapy.

The primal shame is a rejection of the fact that we were created by God without a need for shame, as we see in Gen. 2:15: "The man and his wife were both naked and were not ashamed" —now we are ashamed, contrary to God's intention for us.

While punishment is prescribed because of the transgression of the boundary God established, the situation is not lacking in grace. God creates clothing to cover the man and the woman. He works with us in our fallen condition by providing the means to conceal our need for shame.

This situation of experiencing nakedness and being clothed is replicated in the celebration of Holy Baptism. As Cyril of Jerusalem says in his *Catecheses* to the newly baptized that was quoted in Part A, "This was a remarkable occasion, for you stood naked in the sight of all and you were not ashamed. You truly mirrored our first-created parent Adam, who stood naked in Paradise and was not ashamed."[18] But even the newly baptized are not left in the state of primal nudity; they are vested. It became a time-honored aspect of the post-baptismal ceremonies to confer a baptismal garment on the newly baptized. In the case of infant candidates this was often a baptismal dress. The words of the apostle Paul, "All who are *baptized*, have put on Christ" Gal. 3:27, NRSV, emphasis added) have been applied to the post-baptismal vesting. I have experienced congregations singing the verse "You have put on Christ" during the presentation of the garment. With adult candidates in Roman Catholic, Lutheran, and Anglican practice the vestment presented is often an alb, the white tunic that is worn by liturgical ministers, from acolytes to celebrants. When candidates have gone into the pool, it is necessary to provide time for them to dry off and put on their new white garment. The symbolism of "taking off" and "putting on" needs to be recovered in our baptismal practice. It would not be appropriate for someone to be baptized in the alb, even in terms of practicality. They will then be in a dripping wet garment for the rest of the liturgy.

In the ancient church, the week of Pascha was called the week of white robes. The newly baptized attended services every day of that week and listened to sermons preached by the bishops on the meaning of the sacramental rites they had just experienced at the Easter Vigil—the mystagogical catecheses. At the end of the liturgy on the

---

18. Yarnold, *The Awe-Inspiring Rites of Initiation*, 77.

Sunday after Pascha, they removed their white robes—but even this received commentary by the bishops. Augustine of Hippo admonishes them to be watchful, lest in putting off their baptismal garments they should permit the slower process to begin which is putting off the Christ-like person, whom they have just put on.[19]

God's Vestment Designs

This brings us to the matter of vestments. The Lord God gives explicit directions on making the vestments for the priests and the high priest in Exodus 28. The entire section in Exodus concerning the construction of the tabernacle is fascinating. It is as if God is creating a new creation in the wilderness in the midst of the old creation. The concentrated point of holiness resides in the holy of holies, which contains the Ark of the Covenant, and it radiates out into the adjacent chambers and outer courtyards. However, it does not extend indefinitely; the area of holiness is marked by the fence around the tabernacle. The priests who enter the holy area where sacrifices are offered, and especially the high priest who enters the holy of holies, must be suitably attired—all the way down to his underwear.

Men did not always wear underwear in those days, though they might have worn loincloths when they were working. Certainly, there was always the risk of the genitals being exposed, but the priests' genitals were to be covered. Exodus doesn't explain why, but speculation ranges from avoiding untoward thoughts among the worshipers if they should happen to see the priests' private parts through the linen fabric to the idea that the high priest cannot approach God from a position of strength with his genitals showing since Yahweh is Israel's alpha male. From another perspective, the high priest also represents God. Exposing his nudity would be tantamount to exposing God's. In any event, the high priest is covered with layers of cloth, symbolic breast pieces, and headgear.

19. See Ferdinand van der Meer, *Augustine the Bishop*, trans. B. Battershaw and G. R. Lamb (London: Sheed & Ward, 1961), 381.

Christian Liturgical Vestments

The early Christian community had no priesthood like that of Israel. If Jewish or pagan priests joined the church they were granted no special status. The church had charismatic leaders—the apostles, prophets, and teachers. As it settled into history and social responsibility, the community chose ministers. By the second century there emerged a threefold order of ministers that included overseers (bishops), elders (presbyters), and assistants (deacons). At first there were no special vestments for the church's ministers, but after Christianity was given legal status as a recognized religion in the Roman Empire, the bishops of the church were given the status of magistrates; they could try cases (the bishops' courts were regarded to be above reproach), and Roman protocol required that the insignia of office be granted to them. This explains the origin of the stole often worn today by ordained pastors.

In all other settings, the clergy wore the dress of Roman gentlemen—tunic and topcoat. In the Western church this became the alb and chasuble. Sometimes a ceremonial cape, which came to be called a cope, was worn for processions. The clergy of so-called liturgical churches continue to wear these garments as vestments. Vestments relate the church of today to its origins. Worn by leaders in world religions, vestments are almost always the clothing worn at the time of the founding, whether those leaders are Tibetan Buddhist monks or Iranian imams or Christian ministers. When I stand before the congregation on Sundays in alb, stole, and chasuble, I look like a Roman gentleman from the early centuries of Christianity. These vestments are especially important when presiding at the eucharistic meal, the Lord's Supper. The Eucharist is not casual dining. It is served by those who are attired to reverently handle holy things. Assisting as well as presiding ministers should be vested because vestments cover the person (and personality) of the minister in order to emphasize the office of the ministry. In fact, vestments promote both uniformity and distinctions: uniformity in office and distinctions among the offices. The pastor is distinguished from assisting ministers or acolytes by wearing additional vestments, such as the stole and chasuble, just like the high priest in Israel's tabernacle and later in the temple wore vestments in addition to the normal priestly attire.

Not all Christians were comfortable with the development of special clothes for the worship leaders. It looked like too much pomp. But in fact, some of the practices of the Roman or Byzantine court influenced Christian liturgical practice. Talk about pomp. Consider the situation Moses confronted when he came down from Mt. Sinai and found the people worshiping the golden calf. There was certainly plenty of pomp as the Israelites danced around the golden calf. Understandably, the historic renunciations required at baptism were of the devil and all of his works and pomps. Away with the devil's pomp; the Lord wants his own pomp—and deserves it. *Worship* means "ascribing worth." As the hymns in the book of Revelation say, "You are worthy, our Lord and God, to receive glory and honor and power" (Rev. 4:11, NRSV). "Worthy is the Lamb that was slaughtered to receive power and wealth and wisdom and might and honor and glory and blessing" (Rev. 5:12, NRSV).

Even so, a critical perspective must be brought to the consideration of vestments. I cannot here trace in detail the entire ecclesiastical and political history of vestments. But I would briefly note that at various times in Christian history vestments were provided or prohibited by political authorities. Constantine and subsequent Roman emperors gave to the bishops the insignia of the court to show their new status in Roman society (the origin of the stole and other items that have since passed out of usage). The alb was the basic tunic given to all the baptized at their baptism. The chasuble in its Eastern and Western styles was simply the topcoat of a Roman gentleman, and patrons provided the bishops, presbyters, and deacons with robes (dalmatics from Dalmatia for the deacons), as befitting their public function. These were kept in a sacristy closet as "Sunday best" to be worn in the liturgy, but not on the street. On the streets clergy wore a long coat called a cassock.

During the Middle Ages, a tug-of-war commenced between popes and kings over who would present the pallium to an archbishop—a conflict called the "investiture controversy." At the time of the Reformation, the English Prayer Book, authorized by Parliament, prohibited chasubles, which were associated with the sacrifice of the Mass, but allowed copes since Anglicans loved processions. The Puritans would have no "popish rags," not even a "comely surplice." All such garments were abolished in the Commonwealth. Likewise, the Reformed tradition abolished all vestments. However, the black clergy gown, which was also worn as street wear by scholars and professional people, became a vestment when it was worn for worship, along the tabs that signified authority (which were also worn by magistrates and jurists).

During the Enlightenment vestments passed out of use among all Protestants, except for the preaching gown, and even that was shed by many American Protestant ministers who found it difficult to carry vestments with them when they ministered to scattered settlements on the frontier. Even in the Catholic Church vestments became more minimal. Surplices became waist length rather than ankle length, and chasubles were called "fiddlebacks" because so much material was cut away in the back and the front.

In the nineteenth century, interest arose among the romantics to recover the lost vestments. The Gothic Revival, which aimed to reclaim suitable attire for liturgical ministers who were performing restored rites in reconstructed late medieval church buildings, may have been successful because of the Industrial Revolution, against which they were rebelling. The new vestments, which were restored to gothic length, could be mass-produced by machine in sweat shops instead of being sewn by hand in cloisters. But because shoddy materials that did not correctly display medieval folds were the result, some purists, out of a sense of ritual correctness and moral scruples, returned to making individual vestments by hand, although at a higher price. However, let us remember that vestments are fundamentally garments, not costumes. They are to be worn for special events, and therefore "off the rack" will not do. I'm proud that the hands of a church member lovingly crafted all the vestments worn at Immanuel Lutheran Church in Evanston, Illinois, where I served as pastor for twenty-three years. I'm proud that good material was used and that the same material was used to create altar paraments and other hangings.

The vestments are sacred garments. They derive their sacrality from the nature of the events for which they are worn. Since these events—the proclamation of the word and the celebration of the sacraments—are not trivial, neither can the garments worn by the liturgical ministers be trivial. Shoddy vestments amount to a visual statement; they communicate that the act in which they are used is less than it purports to be. This act is nothing less than the worship of the Creator of all things through his Son Jesus Christ in the Holy Spirit.

What is at stake in terms of liturgical vestments is the sense that worship is both sober in attitude and splendid in scope. The vestments worn for such worship must be equally sober and splendid. Sobriety means that vestments are not billboards advertising ecclesiastical programs or ideological causes. The vestments themselves are symbols. They don't need to be decorated with more symbols. A cross on each side of the stole as well as a decorative band down the front and back of the chasuble is sufficient. Vestments also contribute to the splendor of the liturgy. For this reason they are made of good quality natural material like lamb's wool or silk and may be decorated with bands of brocade or gold—or with nothing. Vestments should model simplicity and splendor simultaneously. They should not be ostentatious, but they should be worthy. In a sense, vestments that meet such criteria are a model of the Christian life. In fact, the juxtaposition of these qualities can be the focus of an extended meditation.

Dressing Up for Worship

There has been a tendency in the Western world to dress more casually for social events, including attending worship. When I was a youth we always wore our "Sunday best" to go to church. In fact, getting dressed for church became a family ritual and probably put us in mind that we were going to a special event in a special place. Dressing our bodies for church in our suits and dresses and polished shoes became a way of preparing our minds for worship. Today many churches allow and even promote casualness in attire as a way of helping people to feel more comfortable about attending worship. But I think this can have adverse consequences.

In this chapter we have seen that nakedness is associated with initiation and penitence; candidates for baptism in the ancient church went into the fonts naked and penitents ripped their garments and sat in sackcloth and ashes. Being clothed is associated with inclusion and forgiveness; the newly baptized put on a new white garment when they were led into the eucharistic banquet hall and penitents who were to be forgiven and reconciled washed and dressed for their re-incorporation into the eucharistic fellowship. Guests in Jesus' parable of the wedding feast were given wedding garments to wear; that's why the king was surprised that someone got in without a wedding garment (Matt. 22:1-14). In the parable of the prodigal son the father's forgiveness of his son is signified by hosting a banquet in his honor and putting the robe of sonship on him (Luke 15:11-32).

We do get dressed up for banquets and special events and I think we ought to reconsider the tendency to dress casual for worship, especially Sunday worship. Sunday is the Lord's Day, the day of resurrection and new creation, and the liturgy of the Lord's Day is the Eucharist, the Lord's Supper. It is the eschatological eighth day on which we celebrate the eschatological meal, the heavenly banquet, at which Christ comes again in his sacramental presence. We should give some thought to how we appear in the presence of our Lord and Savior, our Ruler and our Judge.

Meditation

Simplicity and dignity can be cultivated in meditation. Though they are seemingly opposites, the union of opposites is what yoga aims to accomplish. The word *yoga* means "to yoke." Classical yoga or the eight-limbed path (*ashtanga*) was originally all about meditation. It grew from a codification of yogic core principles in the *Yoga Sutras* of Patanjali, a yogi who lived around AD 200. The goal of Patanjali's *Sutras* is to center and ground, to make present and aware. It is to create an inner climate of receptivity through a process of (1) resisting natural human desires (*yama*), (2) cleansing the body (*niyama*), (3) stilling the body in physical postures (*asanas*), (4) controlling breathing (*pranayama*), (5) withdrawing the senses from worldly distraction (*pratyahara*), (6) concentrating by fixing on one point (*dharana*), (7) prolonging concentration through meditation (*dhyana*), and (8) contemplating one's life—for example, in relation to God (*samadhi*).[20]

Postures (*asanas*), which have become the dominant feature of modern yoga, were only one of the eight limbs. Their purpose was simply to stabilize the body for meditation. Yoga *asanas* were originally seats used for comfort in meditation (*asana* means "seat"). The most essential or fundamental *asana* is lotus pose (*padasana*), which is simple and dignified. In the diagram of the subtle body in part A of this chapter, the figure sits in full lotus position. In full lotus the feet are placed on the opposite thighs so that the knees touch the ground (few people can achieve this position, even after years of practice). In half lotus one foot is placed on the opposite thigh. I should note that it is important to change feet positions periodically. An alternative is to sit with legs folded.

One should sit on a cushion so that the knees are below the hips. In order to sit up straight, place your hands on your knees with palms open. This helps to rotate your shoulders back and open your chest. Palms may also be placed open in your lap. Close your eyes. Relax your jaw. Make adjustments until the right alignment and balance are achieved. Begin breathing in and out evenly (for example, four counts in, four counts out), and if your mind wanders during meditation return your focus to the breath. The breath itself may be a focus of meditation, and the Christian will connect the life-giving breath (prana) with the Holy Spirit (ruach, pneuma, spiritus, life-giving breath of God).

20. Patanjali, *Yoga: Discipline of Freedom—The Yoga Sutra Attributed to Patanjali*, trans. Barbara Stoler Miller (New York: Bantam Books, 1998), 52.

Bring your attention to what you are doing at this moment (dharana). You are sitting in a dignified position and simply breathing (dhyana). You are meditating on dignity and simplicity in your body. This moment might lead you to insight (samadhi).

Figure 6b. The baptism of Clovis, king of the Frank, in Reims in 411, by the Master of St. Giles. Franco-Flemish c. 1500.

4

———

Ritual and Play

A. Ritual: What It Does and How It Works

Human beings engage in rituals. We also engage in ritualization. That is, we act out both our values and what we believe in a ritual act. In fact, ritual and ritualization are instinctive because they are brain-generated activities. We are wired to ritualize; the signals are emitted from the brain stem, which is also called the reptilian brain.

Though some religious groups, including some Christian traditions, don't care much for ritual, they can't avoid ritual as long as they are human beings. Neuropsychological research has been investigating the neurobiological underpinnings of religiosity for several decades, and the results shed new insight on the roots of religious belief (e.g., myths) and the rituals by which these beliefs or myths are acted out. In "The Neurobiology of Myth and Ritual," a central chapter of *The Spectrum of Ritual*,[1] Eugene d'Aquili and Charles Laughlin outline a basic position

---

1. Eugene d'Aquili and Charles D. Laughlin, Jr., "The Neurobiology of Myth and Ritual," in Eugene d'Aquili, Charles D. Laughlin, Jr., and J. McManus, *The Spectrum of Ritual* (New York: Columbia University Press, 1979), 152-82.

that has been elaborated upon in other places, especially the 1999 book by d'Aquili and Andrew Newberg, *The Mystical Mind*.[2]

Briefly, the d'Aquili/Laughlin article asserts that ritual accomplishes two important biological feats. First, it coordinates the neural systems and functions of ritual participants to allow for group action. Ritual behavior for most species seems to be a way of overcoming social distance between individuals so that they can coordinate their activity in a way that helps the species survive. Mating rituals are the most obvious example, but ritual activity before coordinated group attacks or hunts is also common. Wolf packs go through ceremonial tail-wagging sessions and group howls, and ritual aggression among primates establishes social order and rank for possible battle. The second biological achievement of ritual is its effect on cognitive development or socialization within the individual organism. It teaches the younger members of the species what is important and how to behave.

Religion and religious rituals are intimately intertwined with the human brain, and the two phenomena also influence one another. Religion, it seems, can be studied as a biological phenomenon, although whether or not it should be studied in this way is up for debate. The study of ritual and the body is not new, however. The study of ritual and the brain allows for an even deeper analysis of how and why humans are religious and why they are ritualizers.

Researchers have shown that any type of ritual, whether or not it is religious, results in a state of pleasure and even a sense of disengagement from the ordinary aspects of life. Ritual activity is defined as a behavior or sequence of behaviors that is "structured or patterned" and "[recurs] in the same or nearly same form with some regularity."[3] That is, rituals are "repeated actions" that humans draw upon in particular situations. The nervous system activity responsible for this emotional state is similar in animals exposed to "repetitive

2. Eugene d'Aquili and Andrew B. Newberg, *The Mystical Mind: Probing the Biology of Religious Experience* (Minneapolis: Fortress Press, 1999).
3. Eugene G. D'Aquili, "The Myth-Ritual Complex: A Biogenetic Structural Analysis," in *Zygon: Journal of Religion & Science* 18, no. 3 (September 1983): 261.

rhythmic stimuli," which in humans often presents itself as ritual activity.[4]

Thus, ritual can be understood both biologically and theologically. In terms of biology, our brains, and therefore our bodies, have similar reactions to states of meditation and prayer regardless of the ritual. This begs the question of the universality of rituals—that is, why they are so similar in different religions. Human beings devise similar rituals as they respond to similar situations, such as threats or overcoming threats. Examining this concept from a neurological point of view provides scientific evidence in support of this idea. Theologically, we need to consider the proposition that if God created us with a capacity to ritualize then God will connect with us through ritual.

We have discussed how God works through natural cycles and uses earthly means on our bodies to stay connected with us. Now we will consider how God works through rituals, since the use of earthly means applied to human bodies requires ritual actions. Our discussions thus far come together in the following reading from the book of Numbers:

> From Mount Hor they set out by the way to the Red Sea, to go around the land of Edom; and the people became impatient on the way. And the people spoke against God and against Moses, "Why have you brought us up out of Egypt to die in the wilderness? For there is no food and no water, and we loathe this worthless food." Then the Lord sent fiery serpents among the people, and they bit the people, so that many people of Israel died. And the people came to Moses, and said, "We have sinned, for we have spoken against the Lord and against you; pray to the Lord, that he take away the serpents from us." So Moses prayed for the people. And the Lord said to Moses, "Make a fiery serpent, and set it on a pole; and every one who is bitten, when he sees it, shall live." So Moses made a bronze serpent, and set it on a pole; and if a serpent bit any man, he would look at the bronze serpent and live. (Num. 21:4-9, NRSCV)

When the people of Israel, wandering through the wilderness on their way to the Promised Land, complained and rebelled for a seventh time, God attacked them with poisonous serpents. This demonstrates the involvement of nature. The snakes bit the complainers and some

4. Ibid., 262.

died. That's God working through bodies. The antidote was a bronze serpent placed on a pole. The bronze serpent was a means of grace, a sacramental object. The people had to look at the bronze serpent whenever they were bitten in order to live. That's a ritual. It was a simple ritual—look at the snake—but God worked through this ritual to effect healing. Rituals accomplish something.

Learning Rituals at Scout Camp and Church

Rituals are repetitive actions, and because they are repeated they are formative. They form us into the values of the community that performs the rituals. Korean Presbyterian liturgist Hwarang Moon argues that while this is undoubtedly true for people of any age, it is especially true for children. Children, and the cognitively-challenged, easily learn ritual patterns.[5]

When I was a youth I was a Boy Scout. At summer camp we had flag ceremonies. We gathered in full uniform on the parade ground in the morning to raise the flag and again in the evening to lower the flag. A small cannon was shot off toward the lake in salute. The daily flag ceremony formed me into valuing love of country just as the weekly liturgy at church was forming me into a devoted follower of Jesus Christ.

I should make a distinction here between ritual and ceremony. The ritual is the basic action; ceremonies are the ways in which the ritual is done. The basic ritual was to raise and lower the flag with all due respect as a symbol of the nation. The ceremonies were the particular ways in which the ritual was carried out. The same distinction applies to rituals in the church. It is a ritual to celebrate Holy Communion, and the core elements of taking bread and wine, giving thanks over them, distributing them, and eating and drinking are the ceremonies—the particular ways in which communion is served.

Rituals are *performed*, which should not be taken for granted. The

---

5. See Hwarang Moon, *Engraved Upon the Heart: Children, the Cognitively Challenged, and Liturgy's Influence on Faith Formation.* (Eugene, OR: Wipf and Stock, 2015). Moon also demonstrates John Calvin's interest in ritual as a means of faith formation.

issue of performance has become very important in ritual theory because the deliberate, self-conscious doing of highly symbolic actions is the key to ritual. The characteristic element of public rituals, including liturgy, is that they are performed. While this may seem like an obvious fact, sometimes the obvious is overlooked. If the ritual is not performed, the reality it enacts does not exist. The reality of the nation requires that the flag be planted or raised. When explorers arrived in a new land they took possession of it for their country by planting their country's flag in it. Likewise, the presence of the body and blood of Christ requires that bread and wine be consecrated. As the anthropologist Roy Rappaport writes, "The relationship of the act of performance to that which is being performed—that it brings it into being—cannot help but specify as well the relationship of the performer to that which he is performing. He is not merely transmitting messages he finds encoded in the liturgy. He is participating in—that is, becoming part of—the order to which his own body and breath give life."[6] Our bodily performance validates the reality that the ritual encodes.

The flag ceremony, like a liturgy, was a formal event. It was formal in the sense that a prescribed form or order was followed. There was a script to be followed in the flag ceremony. The person who was giving the orders learned the script and did not deviate from it. The ceremony was invariable, just like liturgy tends to be. In fact, invariance is often taken to be the primary definition of ritual. However, variants may be built into the ritual, such as occasional ceremonies, changes due to the calendar, or the propers of the liturgical year. The flag ceremony was also formal in the sense that it was not to be performed casually; the troops were expected to stand at attention.

Like liturgy in the church, the flag ceremony conveyed a sense of tradition. We were doing something that others had done long before us. In fact, our identity with our predecessors came from continuing to do what they had done. As Catherine Bell says in her book *Ritual:*

---

6. Roy Rappaport, *Ritual and Religion in the Making of Humanity* (Cambridge: Cambridge University Press, 1999), 118.

Perspectives and Dimensions, "A ritual that evokes no connection with any tradition is apt to be found anomalous, inauthentic, or unsatisfying by most people."[7]

A ceremony with sacred significance must be framed. It was not acceptable for the Boy Scout troops to just casually walk to the parade grounds and hang around the perimeter watching the flag being raised or lowered. They marched as units from their troop campsites and formed in the places that had been assigned to them. They also marched as units from the flagpole to the mess hall. In a similar way, liturgy is framed with entrance and exit processions of the ministers.

The script for the flag ceremony included more than words; it also required certain actions to be performed. In fact, the whole focus of the flag ceremony was the action of raising or lowering the flag. These actions had to be rehearsed in advance so that they could be done in a way that gave due reverence to the flag. Care needed to be taken in the performance of this act because the flag is a sacramental representation of our nation, just as the bread and wine are a sacramental representation of Christ and must be handled reverently. Sacred signs are not "mere symbols."

Those who executed roles in the flag ceremony had to be conscious of the fact that they were performing highly symbolic actions in public. They had to know what they were doing, practice their part until they could do it perfectly, and then perform their part as flawlessly as possible. It would not do to get the ropes tangled, leaving the flag halfway up or down the pole. When folding the flag, the flag bearers had to make sure that they started the fold correctly; otherwise they would be fussing clumsily with an important symbolic object and trying the patience of the participants. This sometimes happened, of course, and the natural tendency of youths to giggle at the foibles of their peers had to be suppressed. To drop the flag or even let a part of it touch the ground was considered a sacrilege, much like dropping the host or spilling the wine in the Eucharist. Just as there is a correct way

---

7. Catherine Bell, *Ritual: Perspectives and Dimensions* (New York: Oxford University Press, 1997), 145.

to fold and carry the flag, there are appropriate ways for ministers to move around the chancel and handle holy things.

Furthermore, music was played at the flag ceremony (trumpet calls), just as the liturgy of the church includes music. The music wasn't incidental to the ceremony but an integral part. It contributed to the solemnity of the event. The same may be said about the role of music in the liturgy. One doesn't play whatever he or she wants; the music must be appropriate to the occasion and its purpose. A basic purpose of ritual music is to support the ritual.

An inspection of the troops was a part of the evening assembly at the flagpole. Someone from the camp staff, whose ages ranged from sixteen through adults, was designated every evening to inspect the troops. No matter the age, the person inspecting the troops was to be treated with respect by the senior patrol leader who stood in front of his troop. The staff member might be a boy only slightly older than the boys being inspected, but the senior patrol leader saluted him. The young staffer performed a serious role and could not fall out of character as if he were only "pretending" to be an inspecting officer. He *was* that officer. On some occasions I was that officer. It was an office to be carried out that transcended who I was as a person, just as the church's ministers have roles to carry out by virtue of their ordination to the ministry of the word and the sacraments.

Following the flag ceremonies the troops moved to the dining hall for breakfast or dinner. A ritual order also applied to meals in the dining hall. Designated waiters arrived early to set the tables and prepare to bring food from the counter to the table. When the troops entered the hall they all stood at their places until grace was said and they were invited to be seated. Hats were removed upon entering the hall (the Boy Scout soldier-type hats could be folded over the belt when not being worn). Food was served family style, and Scouts did not begin eating until everyone was served. At the end of the meal everyone helped to gather the plates and utensils, but only the waiters could take them to the counter. After the meal there were usually songs, skits, and announcements. While Scouts at summer camp may not have followed the table etiquette observed in their homes—dining was undoubtedly more casual at a table of young boys—some table manners were observed. Table etiquette conveys symbolic messages about the social importance of eating and gives social significance to how one eats. The table is a distinct ceremonial arena, and dining is demarcated from other forms of social activity, whether at Boy Scout camp, the family table, or the church's Eucharist. Food handling as well as eating and drinking are important ritual elements, and the way in which these actions are done conveys important messages about the nature of the dining that is taking place.

Rites of Initiation

Some rituals that belong to the entire community involve actions that are applied to particular members of the community, such as rites of initiation. At Boy Scout camp we were initiated into a camping fraternity called the Order of the Arrow with a ceremony that included dressing in Native American costumes and dancing around a huge fire. The use of Native American ceremonies intended to affirm that Native Americans were models for how we should relate to the natural environment. In order to be tapped out for this fraternity all of the boys who were not members of the Order of the Arrow had to process to the fire bowl with bare right shoulders, placing a hand on the shoulder of the boy in front of them and maintaining strict silence. This showed that they were available for the ordeal of initiation into the fraternity. The huge bonfire was at the center of the ceremony, and boys who were members of the Order dressed as "Indians" (Native Americans); they came into the arena and danced around the fire and then went running in all directions to tap out the boys who had been elected by their troop to go through the ordeal (the candidates were pointed out by their Scoutmasters, who stood behind them). The "tapping" was sometimes expressed by literally lifting the candidate off the ground and carrying or dragging him down to the fire pit. Those who were tapped out for initiation went through an ordeal of silence, slept in the open fields, and worked hard on projects during the day, in addition to keeping a twenty-four hour fast. Absolute obedience to the ordeal master was required. If one passed the ordeal the boy was inducted into the Order of the Arrow in a public ceremony that involved another bonfire and more Native American dancing.

The British anthropologist Victor Turner (1920–83) proposes that undergoing such an initiation ordeal together forges a bond of brotherhood (he calls it "communitas") that could be a source of renewal for the whole society. That's what rites of initiation do: they forge a bond among those who go through them that becomes a source of renewal for the whole social group. He calls the ordeal a "liminal" or "threshold experience." A liminal experience occurs in the transition betwixt and between one social status and another.

In his book *The Ritual Process,*[8] Turner draws upon the theory of Arnold Van Gennep in *The Rites of Passage,*[9] who compares rites of passage to going on a journey. The three stages of rites of passage are leave-taking, transition (the liminal or threshold state), and incorporation. We experience all kinds of rites of passage in our social lives: adolescent transitions from childhood to adulthood (which may be longer or shorter depending on the nature of the society), job training or military boot camp, getting married, and so on. Among the most highly developed rites of passage are rites of initiation, particularly among archaic peoples such as the Ndembu tribe, which was studied by Turner.

Mircea Eliade comments in *Rites and Symbols of Initiation* that traditionally the boys learned the lore of the spirit world and the girls learned the lore of the natural world.[10] In some archaic tribes boys were initiated by being separated from their mothers. The ceremony involved sitting in a circle around a fire with their mothers sitting behind them, covered with a blanket. The men approached from the bush making a lot of noise and often wearing masks. The men grabbed

8. Victor Turner, *The Ritual Process: Structure and Anti-Structure* (Chicago: Aldine, 1969).

9. Arnold van Gennep, *The Rites of Passage*, trans. Monika B. Vizedom and Gabrielle L. Caffee (Chicago: University of Chicago Press, 1960).

10. Mircea Eliade, *Rites and Symbols of Initiation: the Mysteries of Birth and Rebirth*, trans. Willard R. Trask (New York: Harper & Row, 1958), 47.

the boys and carried them off to a prepared place of initiation where the boys were made to lie on the ground covered with sticks. The ceremony was a ritual of death and burial, with their old lives as children being buried. The boys then underwent an ordeal, the length of which varied. They were also taught various skills and initiated into the mysteries of sex and cosmology. Either during this ordeal or at its close a rite would be performed on their bodies: circumcision, knocking out a tooth, or branding. Finally, they were incorporated into the fellowship of men and shared a meal.

The initiation of girls in archaic societies was different. It was done individually at the outset of menstruation, which biologically marked a break with childhood. The girl was separated from society, sequestered in a dark place, and taught the culture of the tribe by the older women. The girl learned ritual songs and dances as well as the skills needed by women, such as sowing and planting, spinning and weaving. At the end of her period of instruction the girl went through a ritual bath and was dressed and presented to society as a woman ready for marriage and family. During periods of initiation, rituals are performed on the body and usually involve some degree of nudity. Various stages in the ritual process often entail divestiture, nakedness, and investiture in special garments, or sometimes the individual is presented with a special insignia.

Eliade points out that initiation into adult status most importantly involved acquiring a sense of sexual identity.[11] Hence, novices might be dressed in the clothing of the opposite sex or be sent naked into the bush. The undifferentiated sexuality of childhood is left behind; in the rite of initiation the children are born again into a new status as adult men or women who are ready and available to bear responsibilities in the social group.

Turner also applies his theories of liminality and communitas to Christian rites of initiation as well as to going through a novitiate in a religious order like the Franciscans. Rites of Christian initiation in the ancient church orders included enrollment in the catechumenate

11. Ibid., 26.

and a period of preparation for baptism that could last three years or even a lifetime. *The Apostolic Tradition* attributed to Hippolytus of Rome mentions certain professions that catechumens would be required to give up in order to become a Christian. For example, artisans and craftsmen who made idols or objects used in pagan worship had to give up their business. The same was true for pimps and prostitutes and magicians. The catechumens engaged in acts of ministry, and as the time of their actual baptism approached they engaged in fasting, almsgiving, and prayer (with members of the congregation joining them in these disciplines in a gesture of support and encouragement). The season of Lent originated from this rite of initiation, which replicated Jesus' time of trial and temptation during his forty days of fasting in the wilderness after his baptism. The catechumenate, like military boot camp, was a liminal period in which the catechumens moved from one status to another, developing the bonds of communitas in the process.

The final ordeal of the liminal stage in Christian initiation was the water bath itself. In the previous chapter I discussed how the candidates in ancient Christian baptismal rites removed their old clothes, had their bodies oiled, and stepped down into the font naked. The ritual was about leaving the old world behind as one shed clothing in order to become a new creation in Christ, symbolized by putting on the new white garment—the robe of righteousness. Sometimes in archaic initiation rites the initiates were painted white, the shade of ghosts, to show their resurrection into a new world. After putting on their white robes the newly baptized were led into the assembly hall where the whole church (*ekklesia*) was gathered for rites of incorporation. Performed by the bishop, these rites included the laying on of hands, offering their gifts of bread and wine along with the faithful, and receiving Holy Communion for the first time. The eucharistic fellowship is the fellowship of the church and is therefore the goal of Christian initiation.

The purpose of the ordeal for boys in archaic societies was to develop in them a sense of dependability. In hunting parties and in tribal warfare, men depended on each other for their lives; they needed to be certain that their brothers would not turn and run in the face of danger. So, too, the liturgy of baptism included a rite of renunciation of Satan and adhesion to Christ. Especially in times of persecution, fellow believers needed to be dependable. This is why apostasy was regarded as an unforgiveable sin.

From ancient times baptism included a ritual for the renunciation of evil known as the *apotaxis* ("stand apart from") and, in some cases, a ritual for pledging personal allegiance to Christ known as the *syntaxis* ("stand with"). Tertullian mentions the renunciation of "the devil and his pomp and his angels" at baptism. Later, in the fourth century, Cyril of Jerusalem speaks of a threefold act of renunciation while the candidates face west, the symbolic "direction" of darkness and evil, followed by a Trinitarian confession of faith made while facing east, the direction of the rising sun, or Christ. Thus, with their bodies the candidates indicated renunciation of one reality (facing the west) and commitment to another reality (facing the east). The Syrian *Apostolic Constitutions* (ca. 380) likewise mentions a threefold renunciation that is followed by an explicit act of adhesion in which the candidates associate themselves with Christ before making the threefold confession of faith with the triple effusion of or submersion in water. The newly baptized emerges from the font and is vested in a new white robe.

Undressing and dressing are powerful symbolic actions that indicate this change from one status to another. We recall the story of the young Francis of Assisi shedding the expensive clothes his father had bought for him and standing naked in front of his father and his associates to renounce wealth and take on the charism of poverty. Because clothing signifies worldly status, Francis thereafter wore a beggar's robe. Francis's ritual action was not a formal ritual; it was improvisational theater. But it drew on the time-honored ritual of changing clothing to signify a change of status.

The Personal Body and the Social Body

If we want to understand how ritual works, and how liturgy as a species of ritual works, we must begin with the body because the body maps our access to God and our relationships with others in society. Access to God requires divesting ourselves of our old way of life and investing or reclothing ourselves—both actually and figuratively—in our new life in Christ. Nakedness and covering play an important role in our encounter with God. Moses was instructed to remove his sandals when God spoke to him out of the burning bush because he was standing on holy ground. The priests who served in the temple were required to wear special vestments in the presence of God. Mourning or penance entailed tearing one's garments. Celebrating included putting on festive garments.

Anthropologist Mary Douglas demonstrates in *Natural Symbols*[12] that our attitudes toward social structure and social control (what she calls "group" and "grid") shape our sense of the body's boundaries. Our use of our bodies is socially determined. In a tight social group with a loose grid (relaxed rules) like the family, the boundaries of the body are loose. For example, one can walk around the house in a state of undress that wouldn't do in public society. A more loosely bound group, such as the civic community, has a tighter grid or rules of conduct, so the boundaries of the use of the body will be tighter. We present ourselves differently in public than we do in our families.

What Mary Douglas means by grid is the set of rules by which we relate to one another. These rules can be tighter or looser. The group dimension describes how strongly people are bonded together. At one end there are distinct and separated individuals, perhaps with a common reason to be together though with looser sense of connection, like a civic community or even a large congregation. This is a loose group. At the other end of the spectrum, people have a connected sense of identity, relating more deeply and personally to one another. They

12. Mary Douglas, *Natural Symbols: Explorations in Cosmology* (New York: Vintage Books, 1973).

103

spend more time together and have stable relationships. This is a tight group, like a family or a small congregation.

Mary Douglas applies her thesis of grid and group to religious groups. She suggests that a ritualistic religion will flourish if the group is loosely bound but the grid (the rule of social conduct) is tightly controlled. Think about the Roman Catholic Church, which embraces wide swaths of populations in large congregations but traditionally has strict laws governing the celebration of its liturgical rites. Bodily expression is certainly encouraged, but it is prescribed. Everyone stands and makes the sign of the cross at the same time. On the other hand, a tightly bound group with a loosely controlled grid allows conditions for what Douglas calls "effervescence" to flourish. Think about Pentecostal assemblies in which social relations within the group are very tight but the rules of conduct are relaxed. This allows members of a Pentecostal Assembly to express themselves bodily during worship in a more individual way, such as shouting out, waving their hands, speaking in tongues, laying hands on other worshipers in acts of healing or exorcism, and so on. A tight group with a tight grid consists of intimate relationships among the members but strict control of bodily behavior, like in a fundamentalist sect. A loose group with a loose grid can be seen in the Orthodox liturgy, with people coming and going, doing various things on their own during the liturgy—such as kissing icons, lighting candles, prostrating themselves in adoration and praise—and then coming together at pivotal moments like the reading of the Gospel and the distribution of Holy Communion. Of course, these grid-group relationships can be tweaked in other ways. I'll leave it to you to figure out where your church body is situated in the spectrum of relationships between group and grid.

I have referred to Mary Douglas's theory because I think it provides a plausible explanation of how the social body constrains or liberates our bodily behavior. It suggests that the freedom to be relaxed and informal in our bodily interactions is as socially conditioned as restrictions placed on the body that make our interactions stiff and formal.

I want to point out one other consideration. Rituals break the customary rules of bodily behavior by giving us permission to do things in public that we wouldn't do in private. Two examples from my youth come to mind. I wore an animal costume in a children's operetta. While I wouldn't have been caught dead wearing that costume even among my friends, I was content to wear it on stage. Another experience entailed dancing around a bonfire in a loincloth in the Boy Scout Native American ceremony I described in detail above. I was a skinny teenager and was otherwise self-conscious about my body, but I willingly participated in this ritual.

Playacting is another situation that gives a person permission to be less inhibited with his or her body. I had an interesting experience with a couple of fourteen- and fifteen-year-old boys when doing a play based on the biblical story of Joseph and his brothers. The fourteen-year-old boy playing Joseph had to change costumes several times—from his coat of many colors to the loincloth of an Egyptian slave and then to the skirt, collar, and headdress of an Egyptian official. He took in stride his semi-nakedness on the stage when wearing only a loincloth (we tried to be pretty authentic in wrapping the long strip of cloth around his groin). His mother was surprised by his willingness to appear in public in this way because she said he never walked around in the house in a state of undress. He must have sensed that the theater gave him permission to do in public what he wouldn't do in private. On the other hand, a boy who was a star swimmer and appeared before many spectators at swimming meets in swimming briefs resisted dressing as Pharaoh, for which he had to wear a skirt, collar, and headdress, with his torso exposed. The costume lady pointed out to him that that he swims in public competitions in front of hundreds of spectators wearing only briefs. "But that's swimming," he said. "This is church." He had a strong sense of the place and what was considered appropriate attire in church. He finally consented to wear the skirt and collar when I explained to him that actors as well as athletes use their bodies in public and that in both venues the usual rules of social conduct don't apply. While the perceptions of both boys were correct, confusion arose as a result of doing theater in the church.

One of the commonalities that theater and liturgy share is the capacity to take us out of the realm of ordinary life. Both can require costumes and use stage props. Both may employ singing, including to one another (like in an opera or musical). Sometimes the participants touch each another—for example, when Potiphar's wife grabs Joseph and rips off his loincloth (an action that supposedly took place offstage as she chased Joseph out of the room) or when people shake hands in greeting, even with strangers. Liturgy has a dramatic character that can't be denied. When the Lord's Supper is celebrated, the priest or minister plays Jesus as host (as in the upper room on the night of Jesus's betrayal), and the communicants play the disciples. The hope is that in the liturgy we are enacting a drama of the way the world should be—the way that God intended it to be from the beginning and the way it is being restored in the kingdom of God.

A Yoga Sequence: The Sun Salutation

I spoke of the act of confessing our faith in baptism. We should do a yoga sequence that expresses an act of commitment and adoration to deity—the full sun salutation (*Surya Namaskara*)—which is one of the most frequently practiced *vinyasa* or flowing sequences in yoga. This sequence originated in ancient Indian worship of the solar deity Surya and might have been a daily ritual of devotion. Like Ambrose, who applied the image of the Roman sun deity Mercury to Christ in his hymn "O Splendor of the Father's Light," we can use this sequence to hail the Sun/Son of righteousness. In our bodily devotion to the Holy Trinity, we did a half-sun salutation, but in doing the full sun salutation we can enact the entire Gloria Patri.

The following diagram shows the twelve positions of the sun salutation. Typically, one inhales on an upward movement and exhales on a downward movement.

Figure 7. The twelve poses of the sun salutation (*Surya Namaskara*).

Take a falling-out breath. Let's begin with some warm-up moves. Get on your hands and knees in table pose. Raise your spine into a cat stretch and then move back into child pose with arms outstretched. Move back and forth between these two poses several times. Inhale as you move into table pose; exhale as you move into child pose. Move from child pose to downward-facing dog.

Step forward to mountain pose, hands folded over your heart (position 1). Bring your arms overhead and do a backbend (2). Exhale and do a standing forward bend to your feet (3). Inhale and lunge your left leg back while the right leg is bent and your hands are on the floor on either side of your right foot (4). Retain your breath and extend your legs back into plank or downward-facing dog pose (5). Exhale and lower to your belly (6). Inhale and brace your arms on the floor to lift your chest and pelvis into cobra or the upward-facing dog (7). Exhale and raise your buttocks into the air for downward-facing dog (8). Inhale and lunge your left leg forward with your right leg extended and both hands on the floor on either side of your left foot (9). Exhale and move into forward fold (10). Inhale, stand, and raise your arms over your head into a backward bend (11). Exhale and bring your hands back into prayer position over your heart, standing in mountain pose (12).

Repeat the entire sequence but change the order of the legs in the lunges. Also add the Gloria Patri—either in your mind or chanted aloud.

Mountain pose—Glory
Backbend—to the Father
Forward fold—and to the Son
Lunge—and to the Holy Spirit;
Plank or downward-facing dog—
To the belly—as it was
Upward-facing dog—in the beginning
Downward-facing dog—is now
Lunge—and will be
Forward fold—forever.
Backbend—Alleluia.
Mountain pose in prayer position—Amen.

Now that you have the hang of the sun (Son) salutation with the Gloria Patri, repeat it two more times. You need to repeat it twice more rather than once to give each leg equal treatment. This also allows you to do an adoration for each person of the Holy Trinity.

Note: As a vinyasa, the sun salutation should flow gracefully from one pose to the next. However, it may be necessary to practice moving back and forth between poses until the sequence has been mastered, just as a musician plays a difficult passage over and over until the progression is mastered and committed to the motor memory of the fingers.

Figure 8. Adult baptisms in an Orthodox church in Guatemala. Notice the cross-shaped pool and the simple white garments covering the candidates before they enter the water. This is a model of what adults can wear for baptism. After baptism they could put on an alb or their new baptismal clothing. Baptism in the Orthodox Church is by submersion, for both infants and adults. The sponsors of the candidates stand in the well opposite the priest and deacon.

B. Fantasy and Play

We have considered the body when it is engaged in formal public rituals. Now let us consider the body when it is engaged in play, which can also be a social activity. Play seems to be a part of the biological makeup of animals, including humans. We are amused to watch our cats and dogs, as well as other higher mammals—such as apes, bears, and dolphins—play. Human beings play. Children play freely but often seriously as they construct or act out their own visions of reality. They may play house with dolls and toy furniture, or they may build houses and entire villages. They may act out their fantasies as characters they've read about in books or seen in movies. When I was a boy I often played cowboys and Indians, pirates, or soldiers with my friends. In early adolescence we played war games with certain rules, such as "steal the flag." We also played sports on our own without adult supervision, like softball or flag football. Today adults organize children's sports activities from an early age so that the rules are imposed by the adults rather than figured out by the children through trial and error. Adults also play games, but the role of fantasy is diminished unless it is realized in very large group activities like historical reenactments. Adults also play sports, board games, cards, charades, and other social games.

All of these play activities have been studied by biologists, zoologists, psychologists, anthropologists, and sociologists. Each discipline has its own "take" on the meaning of play. Even if we put all of these studies together, I suspect that play would still be something of a mystery, defying analysis. The Dutch historian and philosopher Johan Huizinga (1872–1945) suggests that one aspect of play—"fun"—resists all analysis. Why do we want to have fun? He notes that not all languages have a word equivalent to the English word *fun*.[13] In his view, studying play as a cultural phenomenon begins where biology and psychology leave off.

Huizinga may have been influenced in his study of "human play" by the Catholic liturgist, Romano Guardini (1885–1968). Guardini was born in Verona, Italy, but his family moved to Mainz when he was one year old, and he lived in Germany for the rest of his life. He was ordained a Catholic priest and studied and taught philosophy at leading German universities, such as Berlin. He was relieved of that position by the Nazis in 1935 because of his emphasis on the Jewishness of Jesus. In 1945 Guardini was appointed professor in the Faculty of Philosophy at the University of Tübingen and resumed lecturing on the philosophy of religion. In 1948 he became professor at the University of Munich, where he remained until retiring for health reasons in 1962. Guardini's books often serve as powerful studies of traditional themes

13. Johan Huizinga, *Homo Ludens: A Study of the Play Element in Culture* (Boston: Beacon, 1955).

in light of present-day challenges or examinations of current problems as approached from the Christian, and especially Catholic, tradition. His first major work, *Vom Geist der Liturgie* (*The Spirit of the Liturgy*), which was published during the First World War, was probably his most influential—particularly on the Liturgical Movement in Germany and by extension on the liturgical reforms of the Second Vatican Council. Pope Paul VI offered to make him a cardinal in 1965, but he declined.

In his book Guardini teaches that liturgy is a communal rather than an individual activity drawing upon symbols that arise from actual and particular spiritual conditions that enjoy widespread currency and become universally significant. In the chapter "The Liturgy as Play" Guardini says that liturgy is "useless but significant (*zwecklos aber doch sinnvoll*)," which is an important insight into the nature of liturgy as worship. Liturgy is something we do out of devotion to God, not because of what we can get out of it. Guardini goes on to compare liturgy to play, though he specifies free play rather than rule-regulated games. He writes: "The liturgy wishes to teach but not by means of an artificial system of aim-conscious educational influences; it simply creates an entire spiritual world in which the soul can live according to the requirements of its nature. The liturgy is to purposeful spiritual exercises as play in the open fields is related to the gymnasium in which every game aims at a calculated effect."[14]

What can we say about liturgy as play? What are the characteristics of the free play to which Guardini refers?[15]

First, free play is a voluntary activity. We can't order someone to engage in free play. Free play is something added to the routines of life and may therefore be regarded as superfluous. The need for free play is urgent only to the extent that we have a need for enjoyment. Free play is done during our free time and can therefore be regarded

---

14. Romano Guardini, *The Church and the Catholic and the Spirit of the Liturgy,* trans. Ada Lane (New York: Sheed & Ward, 1953), 177.

15. In what follows I loosely follow the ideas of Johan Huizinga about play in "Nature and Significance of Play as a Cultural Phenomenon," *Ritual, Play, and Performance: Readings in the Social Sciences/ Theatre,* ed. Richard Schechner and Mady Schuman (New York: Seabury, 1976), 46–65.

as a leisure activity. In the past, Catholics had an obligation to attend Sunday Mass and other days of devotion, and they confessed to the priest if they missed Sunday Mass. Today both the sense of obligation and the need to confess have waned. Catholics miss attending church just like Protestants do. Unfortunately, when people are told that something is in the area of freedom, they take it to mean that they are free from having to do it. The Protestant reformers learned this soon enough, and Luther used to complain about how people abused their new freedom in the gospel. In its concern for church discipline, the Reformed tradition soon reverted back to a kind of canon law and required church attendance. But for most of us today, worship by and large is voluntary, and we are free not to participate. The need to come up with ways of enticing people to come to worship sometimes moves pastors in the direction of entertainment. Or else they proclaim the benefits that come from attending worship, prompting worshipers to judge the liturgy in terms of what they get out of it rather than by what they put into it.

To be sure, some liturgical rites have an obligatory character, particularly rites of passage like baptism, confirmation, marriage, and burial. But this applies only if one wants to be an active member of the Christian community. No one is forced to be baptized or to bring a child to baptism; no one is forced to be confirmed, married, or buried with the rites of the church. For the most part, worship—like free play—is a voluntary activity that one freely consents to and hopefully desires to participate in.

A second characteristic of free play involves stepping outside of ordinary or "real" life into a temporary sphere of activity with a character all its own. Every child knows that he or she is "only pretending." Play allows us to engage in fantasy. Victor Turner says that play is in the subjunctive mode because "subjunctivity is possibility. It refers to what may or might be."[16] Play can project a worldview, a condition that the child might wish for, just as the liturgy

16. Victor Turner, "Body, Brain, and Culture," *Zygon: Journal of Religion & Science* 18, no. 3 (September 1983): 235.

of the church also expresses what might be possible in God's kingdom. Therefore, the pretending character of play should not be opposed to seriousness. Play can be serious business. It is a way of working out serious issues in life, which is precisely why it requires stepping out of ordinary or real life. One gains a perspective on the issues of life by removing oneself temporarily from those issues.

The liturgy is performed by an assembly (*ekklesia*) that by its very definition is "called out" of the world. Like a legislative body, vested interests should be left behind when the legislature or congress convenes to do the public work of the body politic. Otherwise accusations of corruption arise, what we in America call "influence peddling." Politicians can get in serious trouble and sometimes even be sent to jail if they use their elected positions to enrich themselves or their friends. The liturgy should express a disinterested character as far as the world is concerned precisely so that it can see the world in a clearer light and be able to discern where prayer is needed and what should be done to fulfill the church's mission in the world. We need distance in order to gain perspective.

Play has this quality of disinterestedness. Not being a part of ordinary life, it stands outside of the immediate satisfaction of wants and desires. As an act of enjoyment that brings a certain satisfaction, play complements and enriches life. Liturgy, too, complements and enriches life, accompanying us in our daily work and struggles and giving us a way to rise above them with a vision of a larger goal or purpose. I will attend more to this aspect of liturgy when we study the role of festival in a later chapter.

The third quality of play is its limitedness in time and space. It begins at a certain moment, and it comes to an end at a certain moment. The child begins to play but is called home for dinner. Though playtime is at an end, it could begin again after dinner. Play possesses a repetitive character. It can be done again. Children often ask that a game or activity in which they find delight be repeated, and each time it is done it has a clear beginning and a clear ending. But eventually the child and parent must return to ordinary life. Perhaps it is bedtime.

Liturgy, too, has a moment in which it begins (sometimes announced by the ringing of the church bells) and a time when it ends (with a blessing and dismissal). In recent practice a tendency to prolong the time of gathering has taken shape, as well as the time of scattering after the dismissal. In terms of liturgical material, options are numerous at the beginning of the liturgy, including music (organ preludes, praise medleys) and prayers of gathering, confession of sins, rites of purification, and so forth. After the dismissal the lingering continues with a closing hymn, announcements, and so on. In the midst of all this people arrive and depart at will, making the boundaries of time more porous than they once were. However, it is not unusual for children to include other children who arrive after the playtime has begun. Perhaps we don't need to be so strict about when people arrive and when they leave. There is still a beginning and an ending. Since what happens in worship touches on eternity, the worshiping community continues to cross the boundary of time as it gathers and scatters.

More particular than the limitation of time is the limitation of space. All play moves and has its being within a geographic space that is marked off beforehand. This may be a playground or the backyard or the street in front of someone's house. Parents are often concerned that children be contained in their play so that they don't wander off into harm's way. When I was a youth, there was a stone quarry at the end of my street that was later paved over and turned into a shopping center. For the kids in the neighborhood, the quarry provided an expansive space for adventuresome play. We could sled down the hills in the winter and ride our bikes over paths through the brush or hide out behind large rocks and boulders playing war games. While the quarry seemed like a vast territory to us kids, it occupied only a few city blocks.

Liturgy, too, is performed in a given and limited space. Houses of worship have changed over the course of Christian history. House churches of the early Christians gave way to public basilicas in the later Roman and Byzantine Empires, and the great cathedrals of medieval

Europe provided a contrast to local, village churches. In mission situations today, congregations often worship in school auditoriums, gymnasiums, or shopping centers. Eventually the church reaches a point at which the congregation wants its own church home simply because, as in our personal lives, we begin to acquire furnishings that are both necessary and enriching. One could say that all Christian worship really needs is a table and some bread and wine. But then a covering over the table (and perhaps the people) is erected in case of inclement weather. Chairs or benches are acquired so that the people can sit, as well as a reading stand from which the word of God can be proclaimed. Of course there must be a place for baptisms, classrooms for instruction, a sacristy to keep vestments, and closets to store equipment. Perhaps the church has acquired artwork that it wants to display. Christian liturgy needs a place for the assembly to meet, and often the place is made sacred because of what happens in that space, even apart from the gathering for worship. Church buildings often possess an enchanting quality that casts a spell over those who enter.

A fourth characteristic of play is rules. Free play by an individual may be free of rules because the player can make them up as he or she goes along, but as soon as two or three are engaged in play, agreements must be made as to what is happening and what is allowed and not allowed. Changing the rules after the play begins is not allowed. Games, of course, always depend on rules because games involve competition, which means there will be a winner. Therefore everyone is concerned that the rules are applied fairly. That's why sporting events include disinterested umpires who are not partial to the players or teams.

The liturgy of the church also has rules. They are called rubrics (from the Latin word for red) because the directions for doing the liturgy were printed in red in liturgical books so that they would stand out from the spoken or sung text. Similar to the variety that exists among games, the rubrics or rules vary within the variety of churches. For example, the Catholic Church has very specific rules for how its liturgies are performed, while the free churches require far fewer directions. That being said, the free churches are certainly not without rules for the conduct of worship. Often these rules must be discovered in practice because they are not written down. Even written rules, however, vary in character. In our Lutheran liturgical traditions we used to have "shall" rubrics and "may" rubrics. The "shall" rubrics were things that had to be done and had to be done in a certain way: "Then the pastor shall face the congregation and say. . . ." The "may" rubrics were things that might be done but didn't have to be: "Then a closing hymn may be sung."

In play the player who breaks the rules or ignores them is a spoilsport, which is not the same as a cheat. The cheat agrees to follow the rules but tries to bend them to his or her own advantage. The cheat can be called out and advised to play fairly; he or she can continue to play. The spoilsport gets mad and says, "I won't play any more." The spoilsport is the kid who, as we used to say, "picks up his marbles and goes home." Indeed, by taking away some of the equipment that is needed for the game, the spoilsport effectively ends the game. He or she breaks the illusion or the fantasy that play creates by injecting a grinding note of realism into the situation. "I'm mad, and I won't play any longer." In effect, the play is over. A worldly situation has intruded on what should be an otherworldly experience. The spoilsport has broken the spell of enchantment and therefore must be ejected from future play. The players may decide that unless there is some kind of reconciliation, that person is not allowed to play again.

This kind of situation is not unknown in the life of the church. Those who break the rules by ending the enchantment that we are in the dimension of the kingdom of God in our liturgy must be expelled. They may have committed a moral scandal or taught false doctrine or disrupted the harmony of the congregation. These "this worldly" behaviors don't belong in the community, which is called to anticipate the life of the world to come in a liturgy that is "heaven on earth." Such people are ejected from the liturgical assembly, and their return is contingent upon amendment of life, reconciliation, and forgiveness.

This leads to another point concerning the nature of play. Playing together creates bonding and community. Children who are friends play together. It may be free play or, as they get older, organized play in sports or a school orchestra. Precisely because something special is shared in playing together the spirit of friendship is fostered, even to the point that children who play together form a club with its own secret rules, codes, gestures, and perhaps even a place to meet (a clubhouse). Certainly a sense of camaraderie develops among members of a sport team that is reinforced when the teammates go out together after games to review what has transpired over food and drinks.

Again, we can see how this applies to the liturgy of the church. The liturgy is performed by an assembly that is a congregation of people who get to know one another and "bear one another's burdens" (Gal. 6:2, NRSV) and "rejoice with those who rejoice" (Rom. 12:15, NRSV). In the liturgical life of the church this connection is evident as members of the congregation accompany one other in their life situations by including each other in public intercessory prayer and attending the rites and celebrations of their fellow members.

For all these reasons, liturgy has rightly been called "the playground of the kingdom of God." We look forward to and realize, in part, what is not yet but will be our reality in the fullness of God's kingdom.

5

Sacrifices and Meals

A. Sacrifices and Covenant Meals

Eating and drinking are essential human activities. Like other animals, humans need to eat and drink in order to replace the nutrients that the body uses for energy and to keep hydrated. The German philosopher Ludwig Feuerbach, in emphasizing the material basis of life, famously said, "We are what we eat." As Carl and LeVonne Braaten write, "Nothing more characterizes a person's connection with the earth than the food he eats."[1] The body is composed of the earth's elements and receives nutrients for life by consuming the food the earth produces. Those who live in the modern West are learning that we need to eat more nutritious food. Organically produced food is better than chemically altered and factory processed fare, and the less distance food travels from farm to table the better. Changing people's diets is not easy because the food people eat is fundamental to their understanding of themselves. Typically, ethnic groups in a pluralistic world identify themselves by their ethnic foods.

1. Carl E. and LaVonne Braaten, *The Living Temple: A Practical Theology of the Body and the Foods of the Earth* (New York: Harper & Row, 1976), 46.

It also works best for our bodies to eat regularly, which is not always possible in fast-paced modern society. Regularity is culturally as well as biologically conditioned. We eat breakfast after a night of fasting. If we eat a sufficient breakfast we can probably manage to get by with a snack or two until the late afternoon or evening meal. But we have developed culturally conditioned routines of eating three meals a day. *When* we eat often depends on our work schedules. Our modern tendency is to eat a light lunch in the middle of the work day and heavier fare in the evening, although eating heartily before we go to sleep might not be the best thing in terms of keeping weight down and getting a good rest.

Of more significance for our purpose, meals are eaten together with others, as far as that is possible. For humans, meals possess a social as well as a biological function. We bond with others by eating and drinking with them. Moreover, conversation usually takes place at meals. In this chapter we will see how rites of word and meal go together and also how meals acquired a sacred function.

The Sacred Character of Meals

The Orthodox theologian Alexander Schmemann writes:

> Centuries of secularism have failed to transform eating into something strictly utilitarian. Food is still treated with reverence. A meal is still a rite—the last "natural sacrament" of family and friendship, of life that is more than "eating" and "drinking." To eat is still something more than to maintain bodily functions. People may not understand what that "something more" is, but they nonetheless desire to celebrate it.[2]

In modern times we have all but lost the biblical perspective of sharing meals together. We've come to look at eating together merely in its social and physical context. That is, we see eating as a chance to fill our bellies, satisfy our taste buds, and enjoy a social gathering—joking, laughing, and talking about current events, business, or the weather. Many people think of meals only as an earthly activity with no spiritual

2. Alexander Schmemann, *For the Life of the World: Sacraments and Orthodoxy* (Crestwood, NY: St. Vladimir's Seminary Press, 1973), 16.

significance. But if we begin our meals by giving thanks we invoke God's presence with us as we eat, so meals are not void of spiritual significance.

Meals play a big role in the Bible. The biblical story begins and ends with a meal. It begins with Adam and Eve eating forbidden fruit against God's command and without God's presence. It ends with marriage supper of the Lamb in which the eternal relationship between Christ and his people is sealed in the heavenly banquet. There's a lot of eating and drinking in between those two meals, and in many cases God is sharing the meal with his people. Meals are a means of communion with God and with one another in the presence of God.

We see this in the visit of the three strangers to Abraham and Sarah (Genesis 18). Practicing typical Middle Eastern nomadic hospitality Abraham offers food and drink to the strangers, who then announce that Sarah, though ninety-nine years old, will finally bear Abraham's son of promise. The letter to the Hebrews comments that Abraham and Sarah entertained angels unawares (Heb. 13:2). As a proof text, it was used to shore up Christian practices of hospitality to strangers. But the Christian tradition has also taken these strangers to be a representation of the Holy Trinity, as we see in the famous Rublev icon. As such, Abraham's meal is understood to be a meal shared with God.

Covenant Meals

Covenant meals played an important part in ancient times, of which there are many examples. In Gen. 26:28-30, Isaac makes a water-rights covenant with the Philistine king Abimelech. The covenant brought union, fellowship, and peace between former enemies. Immediately following the making of the covenant, they "made a feast and they ate and drank" (Gen. 26:30, NRSV). The feast was a celebration of the covenant, symbolizing the newfound peace between them. We see the same thing in Gen. 31:44-54 between Laban and Jacob. After making a covenant together and offering a sacrifice to seal their covenant, Jacob "called his kinsmen to the meal," clearly to celebrate the covenant. Similar examples of covenant meals can be seen between Jethro and

Moses (Exod. 18:12, eaten "before God"), between Israel and Gibeon (Josh. 9:12-15), and between David and Abner (2 Sam. 3:20). This last example gives new meaning to David's words in Ps. 23:5 (NRSV): "You prepare a table for me in the presence of my enemies." The "table" represents peace, union, fellowship, and reconciliation.

The most significant example of a covenant meal, however, is in Exodus 24, at the climax of the sealing of the covenant between God and Israel. After Moses offers the sacrifice, sealing the covenant with the "blood of the covenant," he and the elders and Aaron and his sons enter into the presence of God on the mountain, where they "beheld God and they ate and drank" (Exod. 24:11, NRSV). If we aren't careful, we might miss the significance of the words "and they ate and drank." They ate and drank in God's presence. This was a very important part of the covenant process. It was a celebration of the new union between Israel and God, a union established by the blood of the covenant—that is, by sacrifice. The sacrifice effected reconciliation and included sharing a meal that celebrated communion between Israel and Yahweh. It was a *spiritual* feast, but it was a feast.

Sacrifice and Meals

Some consider sacrifices and meals as separate things, especially when it comes to understanding the Christian Eucharist. While Catholicism emphasizes the Eucharist as a sacrifice, the sacrifice of the Mass, Protestantism emphasizes the Eucharist as a meal, the Lord's Supper. But this is a false dichotomy. As Fr. Louis Bouyer explains, "What we call by the Latin word 'sacrifice' is nothing else than a sacred meal. More specifically, it is every meal that has retained its primitive sacredness, a sacredness that is attached to a meal perhaps more than any other human action."[3]

Bouyer draws upon the work of Royden Keith Yerkes, who examines the origin of sacrifice in the common meals of primitive hunting societies. As the killing of a large animal required more than one

3. Louis Bouyer, *Rite and Man: Natural Sacredness and Christian Liturgy*, trans. M. Joseph Costelloe (Notre Dame, IN: University of Notre Dame Press, 1963), 82.

hunter, so sharing the meat involved more than one family. The sharing of a large common meal established the bonds of community—whether of family, clan, or tribe—by which they entered into union "with the mysterious Power or powers which [they] felt within them and about them as life itself, and which they recognized in all their environments as both menacing and strengthening the life they loved and to which they longed to cling."[4]

We see this same connection between sacrifice and communion meal in the Levitical sacrifices outlined in the law of Moses. The entire burnt offering was given exclusively to God; hence it was completely burned. Various other sacrifices were to be eaten by the priests (Exod. 29:31–34; Lev. 6:16, 26; 7:6; 8:31; 10:12–14) or, in the case of the peace offerings, by the worshiper (Lev. 7:15–18) as a holy meal "before God." In fact, these "meals" were essential and not to be neglected (Lev. 10:16–20). They weren't designed to simply fill bellies but to celebrate the union between the community and God, a union made possible by sacrifice. Rather than being solemn and quiet, these communion sacrifices were joyous occasions, interactive and celebratory. They were meals eaten in the presence of God, sometimes even in the temple.

Communion Meals

While it is true that we have nearly lost the biblical understanding of communion meals in our modern society, there is one communion or fellowship meal that many of us have regularly participated in throughout most of our lives: the family dinner. Traditionally in America, the evening dinner hour is a time for the whole family to gather around the table together and share a meal (sadly, even this practice is going by the wayside). But this practice is more than a meal. It's not simply about the food; it's about sharing our lives together each day. The meal provides an opportunity for fellowship. After everyone scatters throughout the day, we come back together around the table to reconnect, to bond as a family. This practice touches on the concept

4. Royden K. Yerkes, *Sacrifice in Greek and Roman Religions and Early Judaism* (London: Adam and Charles Black, 1953), 25.

of a fellowship meal. It goes beyond food. It is a means by which we share our common spiritual relationship.

The communion or fellowship meal is quite common throughout the pages of the Bible. As mentioned above, most of the sacrifices ordained in the law of Moses were followed by a meal celebrating the union brought about by the sacrifice. The "peace offerings" (Lev. 7:15) and "votive offerings" (Lev. 7:16–17) especially emphasized the fellowship meal. The peace offering was partially burned; partially eaten by the priest, and the rest was consumed by the worshiper on either the day or the day after. It was a meal, with meat, bread, and drink (Lev. 7:11–14; Num. 6:17; 15:1–12). It is safe to assume that since the peace offering had to be eaten the same day and the votive offering had to be eaten by the second day that the sacrificial meat was shared with others. One does not eat a young bull alone. It was a communal act involving God, the priests, the worshiper, and the worshiper's family and friends. Nearly all other offerings (burnt offerings, sin offerings, etc.) had peace offerings associated with them, which included the communal fellowship meal. These meals held deep significance. They were not simply meant to satisfy hunger. Nor were they merely social in purpose. These meals celebrated union with God. They were eaten "before the Lord your God" (Deut. 12:7, 18; 14:23, 26; 15:20; 27:7).

One very special meal in the Old Testament combines the concepts of a covenant meal and a family fellowship meal—the Passover feast. This greatest of all Old Testament Jewish meals and feasts celebrated not only the great deliverance of the Jews out of Egypt but also their newfound relationship with God.

And the Lord said to Moses and Aaron, "This is the ordinance of the passover: no foreigner shall eat of it; but every slave that is bought for money may eat of it after you have circumcised him. No sojourner or hired servant may eat of it. In one house shall it be eaten; you shall not carry forth any of the flesh outside the house; and you shall not break a bone of it. All the congregation of Israel shall keep it. And when a stranger shall sojourn with you and would keep the passover to the Lord, let all his males be circumcised, then he may come near and keep it; he shall be as a native of the land. But no uncircumcised person shall eat of it. There shall be one law for the native and for the stranger who sojourns among you." (Exod. 12:43-49, NRSV)

The Passover Lamb was a sacrifice representing their deliverance from death. The family gathered together and the lamb was eaten in a fellowship meal with deep spiritual significance. The Exodus passage above states that the Passover meal could include foreigners or non-Israelites. But all who participated had to be circumcised. That is, they had to be brought into the covenant. (This practice is not observed in Jewish Passover seders today when Jews invite gentile friends and neighbors.)

In the Synoptic Gospels the Lord's Supper was instituted in a Passover *seder* (order). The Lord's Supper, as it continued to be observed in the church, was not a Christian Passover. The main item on the Passover menu—the roasted lamb—was not shared in the Lord's Supper (although the liturgy proclaims Christ as "the lamb of God"). The bread and wine shared in the Lord's Supper were common ingredients not only in Jewish meals but also in the meals of other peoples. The Lord's Supper is a shared meal before it is anything else. The philosopher Ludwig Feuerbach (whose famous slogan I quoted above) pointed this out in the early nineteenth century, but Christian theologians ignored much of what he said because of his purported atheism. About the Lord's Supper Feuerbach writes:

> Eating and drinking is the mystery of the Lord's Supper;—eating and drinking is, in fact, in itself a religious act; at least, ought to be so. Think, therefore, with every morsel of bread which relieves thee from the pain of hunger, with every draught of wine which cheers thy heart, of the God who confers these beneficent gifts upon thee,—think of man! But in thy gratitude towards man forget not gratitude towards holy Nature! Forget not that wine is the blood of plants, and flour the flesh of plants, which are sacrificed for thy well-being![5]

The Lord's Supper is first of all a meal. But it shares many of the characteristics of the Passover meal. Traditionally, it is shared only

---

5. Ludwig Feuerbach, *The Essence of Christianity*, trans. George Eliot (New York: Harper & Row, 1956), 133.

with those who have been brought into the new covenant of Christ by Holy Baptism, the Christian equivalent of circumcision. Meals are about hospitality, but they are never only about hospitality. Meals are about bonding—with God and with others. They are eaten in the presence of God. The Lord's Supper especially is eaten in the presence of God, and throughout the history of the Eucharist concern has been expressed about "fencing the table." Written at the end of the first century, the *Didache* clearly states that only the baptized, those who have been made holy, are to share in the Eucharist. In this regard it quotes Jesus' saying, "Do not give what is holy to the dogs"[6]. Before the distribution of the sacrament, the Eastern liturgies say, "Holy things for the holy people." Earlier in the service, before the greeting of peace, the deacon says, "Let all catechumens depart." Holiness is not so much a moral category as a religious one. It refers to that which belongs to God. The Lord's Supper is a holy meal because it is God's feast. The people who are invited to the Lord's Table are a holy people because they belong to God. God claims them in Holy Baptism. The gifts of God are for the people of God.

The Lord's Supper is not only a communion or fellowship meal (1 Cor. 10:16–17; 11:17–34) but also a covenant meal, not unlike the one mentioned in Exod. 24:11. In fact, when Jesus institutes the Lord's Supper, he uses the language of Exodus 24 with regard to the "blood of the covenant" (Matt. 26:28; Exod. 24:8). Jesus further connects the Lord's Supper to the ancient covenant meal tradition when he states that he will partake of it again with his disciples when it is fulfilled in the kingdom of God; just as the covenant meals were eaten in the presence of God, Christ himself—true God and true man—is present in the meal.

To emphasize the Lord's Supper as a meal does not mean, as we have seen, that it is inappropriate to speak of it as a sacrifice. All of the classical eucharistic prayers (anaphoras) make reference to the sacrifices of Abel, Abraham, and Melchizedek. The church fathers

6. Kurt Niederwimmer, *The Didache: A Commentary*, trans. Linda M. Maloney (Minneapolis: Fortress Press, 1998), 144.

understood these ancient sacrifices as "types" of the eucharistic sacrifice and the offerings of the patriarchs as figures of Christ. Abel offered a lamb, and Christ is "the lamb of God who takes away the sin of the world" (John 1:29, NRSV). In fact, the Orthodox Church uses those very words when the bread is offered on the altar for Holy Communion. Abraham offered his son, his only son Isaac, and "God so loved the world that he gave his only Son" (John 3:16, NRSV). The benefits of Christ's atoning sacrifice are conveyed in Holy Communion: forgiveness of sins, life, and salvation. Melchizedek, that mysterious priest-king of ancient Salem, offered bread and wine, just as we do.

Christ is present in the actions and elements of the Eucharist—the taking of bread and cup, giving thanks over them, and sharing them. The Lord's Supper as a covenant meal challenged the social setting in which it was celebrated in the Greco-Roman world. Acts tells us that while the early Christians in Jerusalem "spent much time together in the temple," they also "broke bread at home [or from house to house] and ate their food with glad and generous hearts." (Acts 2:46, NRSV). Emerging Christianity was essentially a fellowship meal. The social context of the celebration of the Lord's Supper was a gathering of the church either in the house of a member or in an inn rented for the occasion, similar to what other supper clubs did in the Greco-Roman world, to have a banquet. The form of the banquet was most likely a symposium.

The Symposium Meal

A symposium was a meal (that sometimes degenerated into a drinking party) in which the guests engaged in philosophic discussion. A number of literary symposia arose from ancient Greece and Rome, the most famous of which is probably Plato's *Symposium*. Blake Layerle[7] recognizes the form of the symposium in the Jewish Passover seder that was observed at the time of Jesus. Dennis E. Smith[8] sees the

7. Blake Leyerle, "Meal Customs in the Greco-Roman World," in *Passover and Easter: Origin and History to Modern Times*, vol. 5 of *Two Liturgical Traditions*, ed. Paul F. Bradshaw and Lawrence A. Hoffman (Notre Dame, IN: University of Notre Dame Press, 1999), 29–61.

cultural setting of the institution of the Lord's Supper as symposium. Symposia in the Greco-Roman world began with a meal (*deipnon*), after which thanksgiving was offered to the god of the feast, followed by the sharing of wine, which was accompanied by entertainment of various sorts in the form of a dance, a poem, a drama (the *symposion* proper). Philosophic discussion followed, accompanied by additional cups of wine (with copious drinking!). Women, who were sometimes the hosts of such gatherings, participated up to the point of the discussion, at which time they adjourned to their own place, leaving the men to talk and drink. This might be the background for Paul's statement that women should keep silent during the church gathering, asking their husbands about what was said when they got home (1 Cor. 14:34–35). But there is some discrepancy here because Paul indicated that the women could engage in prophesying, as long as their heads were covered (1 Cor. 11:5). The prophesying would likely have occurred during the symposium, not during the meal. At the Last Supper in the upper room, such drinking and discussion apparently took place, leaving the disciples drowsy and unable to watch with Jesus in the Garden of Gethsemane, while he prayed to the Father that the next cup would pass from him.

The symposium structure can best be seen in John 13-17. In the context of a meal, which is mentioned but not described, Jesus performs the dramatic action of washing his disciples' feet. Jesus' action serves as the basis for discussion of the new commandment Jesus gives his disciples (now called "friends")—that they love one another as he has loved them. Because this is a "last supper," there is also much discussion about Jesus' impending departure. The symposium ends with Jesus' high priestly prayer to his Father on behalf of his disciples.

The symposium structure can also be seen in the Jewish Passover seder. After the *berakoth* or blessings that mark the beginning of the meal, discussion ensues in connection with the strange food being

8. Dennis E. Smith, *From Symposium to Eucharist: The Banquet in the Early Christian World* (Minneapolis: Fortress Press, 2003).

eaten that night. Multiple cups of wine accompany the meal and discussion. The seder ends with a prayer of thanksgiving for the meal (*birkat ha-mazon*). A Christianized form of the Jewish meal prayers is seen in the *Didache*, in chapters 9 and 10.[9]

There is no reason to think that the Lord's Supper in the Corinthian church did not also follow the format of a meal (*deipnon*) with a symposium (*symposion*). The cup with its thanksgiving in Paul's text is "after supper." Is it possible that the words (cited by Paul) of Jesus over the cup—"Do this, as often as you drink it, in remembrance of me" (1 Cor. 11:25, NRSV)—refer to the multiple cups of the symposium and not to the frequency of the gatherings to share the meal, since a comparable specification, "as often as you *eat* this," does not accompany the command "do this" in connection with the bread? The typical drinking of wine throughout the meal and the symposium must have been observed in Corinth because Paul refers in 1 Cor. 11:21 to some people becoming drunk (as the guests were in Plato's *Symposium*). Hence, restraint is called for—not only in waiting for the slaves to arrive before the patrons and clients begin to eat but also in the amount of wine consumed. As there were obviously many problems with the celebration of the Lord's Supper at Corinth, we are advised against taking the early church as a model for our liturgical practices today.

Some have suggested that the social problems connected with the celebration of the Lord's Supper at Corinth—patrons, clients, plebs, and slaves not sharing the same meal and the same menu[10]—contributed to separating the sacramental meal from the context of an actual meal. The Eucharist was still being celebrated in the context of an actual meal in the *Didache* at the end of the first century. The more likely cause of the separation of the Lord's Supper from an actual meal was the imperial ban on supper clubs, which was imposed by Emperor Trajan early in the second century. The letter of Pliny the Younger,

---

9. See Frank C. Senn, *Christian Worship and its Cultural Setting* (Philadelphia: Fortress Press, 1983), 22–25.
10. Gerd Theissen, *The Social Setting of Pauline Christianity*, ed. and trans. by John H. Schütz (Philadelphia: Fortress Press, 1982), 145–74.

governor of Bithynia, to Emperor Trajan (ca. 112) reports that Pliny apprehended some Christians and interrogated them. In his interrogation he found that they were complying with the edict forbidding secret societies.[11] Christian gatherings for an evening meal, especially in public places, could easily have looked to the Roman authorities like other assembles of clubs and societies; so the Christians ceased having their suppers. From then on the Eucharist was more typically a morning rite involving readings and the sacramental meal of bread and wine, as we see in Justin Martyr's *Apology* 67. Even when supper gatherings were again allowed, Christians gathered for an *agape* feast in the evening but continued to celebrate the Eucharist in the morning, as we see in church orders such as *The Apostolic Tradition,* which has both a Eucharist and an Agape. In the Roman Rite only the evening Mass of the Lord's Supper on Maundy Thursday survived as an evening Eucharist.

Interest in recovering the celebration of the Lord's Supper in the context of an actual meal has recently resurfaced. This might account, in part, for the interest of Christians in experiencing Passover seders. But we cannot return to whatever it is that happened in the upper room on the night before Jesus' death. Furthermore, the Lord's Supper is more in accordance with the post-resurrection meals of Jesus. A new covenant has been inaugurated, and the Lord's Supper celebrates a new reality. Some of the old forms needed to be abandoned along the way. In the context of a purely sacramental meal the dynamics of the covenant meal were perhaps rescued, and the focus of the Eucharist could become the presence of Christ as food and drink without the distractions of other dynamics of the meal. But we cannot forget that the Lord's Supper *is* a meal. Liturgical renewal has not been amiss in trying to recover that character of the Eucharist.

---

11. Pliny to Emperor Trajan, *Documents of the Christian Church,* trans. Henry Bettenson (New York: Oxford University Press, 1947), 6–7.

Figure 9. The celebration of the Eucharist at Gereja Kebangunan Kalam Allah (Awakening the Word of God Church) in Banjarmasin, Kalimantan Selatan, Indonesia (Borneo). The church is in the Reformed tradition. The officiant is Pastor Ricky Rickstofer, who participated in the Embodied Liturgy course at Satya Wacana.

B. Word and Meal Joined

The Table of the Word

Our chief Christian liturgy is a service of word and meal.[12] Liturgical scholars have long pondered how a liturgy of the word that, like the public synagogue liturgy, includes the reading and study of Scripture was joined with a meal liturgy that, in Judaism, was a more private and domestic rite. The form of the symposium shows how a meal could have included readings and commentary, which was also the case with the Jewish Passover seder. Indeed, Paul indicates that members of the assembly in Corinth brought something to share at the meal: "When you come together, each one has a hymn, a lesson, a revelation, a

---

12. This section is based on a lecture given at the Pro Ecclesia Conference of the Center for Catholic and Evangelical Theology. See Frank C. Senn, "Do This: Eucharist and the Assembly's Liturgy," in *What Does It Mean to "Do This"?* (Eugene, OR: Cascade Books, 2014), 1–23.

tongue, or an interpretation" (1 Cor. 14:26, NRSV). Modern Protestants gather for a service of hymns and the word, to which they sometimes add Holy Communion, but early Christians gathered for a communion meal, to which they brought hymns and words.

This unity of word and meal is evident in the Sunday liturgy described by Justin Martyr in his *Apology*, chapter 67. He reports that "the memoirs of the apostles and the writings of the prophets are read as long as time permits. When the reader has finished, the president in a discourse urges and invites us to the imitation of these noble things."[13] However, we have few examples of homilies or sermons from the early church. One example might be the book of Hebrews in the New Testament, which reads like a midrash on Ps. 110:4. Hebrews was probably turned into a letter to give it more circulation and ascribed to Paul to give it more authoritative weight. The Second Letter of Clement from the early second century probably holds the distinction of being the oldest surviving sermon from ancient Christianity outside of the book of Acts. It is an exhortation to a congregation to act in justice and charity as befits the divine calling.

Commentaries on biblical books by the church fathers were written as homilies. They provide evidence that by the fourth century books of the Bible were read continuously. However, with the emergence of festival days (such as Easter, the Ascension, Pentecost, Christmas) and seasons of devotion (Lent and Advent), specific readings having to do with the events commemorated in the life of Christ or the purpose of devotion (such as the catechumenate or repentance) were chosen. These are pericopes, or "cut out" selections.

We see the development of a pericope system in Jerusalem in the fourth- and fifth-century pilgrimage rites. Christian pilgrims gathered at sites in the life of Christ in the gospels and read the appropriate account of what happened there from the Gospels. A pericope system attributed to Jerome, who spent his years in Bethlehem translating the Bible from Hebrew and Greek into the Latin we know as the

---

13. Justin Martyr, *First Apology*, ed. and trans. Edward Rochie Hardy, in *Early Christian Fathers*, ed. Cyril C. Richardson, vol. 1 of *The Library of Christian Classics* (Philadelphia: Westminster, 1953), 287.

Vulgate—called the *Comes Hieronymi* (Jerome = Jerusalem)—became the basis of the lectionary that emerged in the Western church. It was augmented by Alcuin of York, who worked on liturgical resources at the court of Charlemagne, to include additional days observed in the Frankish Church (including the season of Advent) that were not yet observed in the Roman Church. Alcuin also eliminated Old Testament readings and shortened many of the epistle and Gospel readings. This became the basis of the so-called historic one-year lectionary used in the Roman Catholic, Lutheran, and Anglican churches up until the late twentieth century.

At first, the leaders of the Reformation were drawn to the ancient practice of continuous reading (*lectio continua*) of biblical books, from which they also preached. This became a reality in the Reformed churches. But in the Lutheran churches as well as in the Church of England, there was a preference for the historic lectionary with its pericope system. After the Council of Trent, the Roman Rite also retained this historic lectionary, so that many similarities remained in the pericopes for the church-year lectionary in the Roman Catholic, Lutheran, and Anglican churches. Thus, an ecumenical lectionary existed among the Western churches before the three-year lectionary, which was developed first in the Roman Catholic Church, after the Second Vatican Council.

The bishops at the Second Vatican Council expressed the concern that the people should be exposed to a greater selection of Scripture, including the Old Testament. Certainly much of the Bible was read in the offices of the Liturgy of the Hours, but most people attended only masses or engaged in paraliturgical devotions. The Constitution on the Sacred Liturgy (*Sacrosanctum Concilium*) of the Second Vatican Council called for "more reading from holy Scripture in sacred celebrations, and it is to be more varied and suitable" (35.1) as well as preaching that "draws its content from scriptural and liturgical sources" (35.2).[14] In fulfillment of this desire, the Consilium for the Implementation of the

14.

Constitution developed and published *Ordo Lectionum Missae* with the reformed Mass in 1969.

The Roman Lectionary presented a new three-year series of readings for the Mass that supplanted the historic one-year lectionary in the Roman Catholic Church. It added an Old Testament reading with a responsorial psalm and even included a *lectio continua* principle in the epistle readings during ordinary time. In short order other churches adopted versions of the Roman three-year lectionary, including the *Lutheran Book of Worship* (1978) and the Episcopal *Book of Common Prayer* (1979). In adopting versions of this lectionary, Lutherans and Anglicans/Episcopalians in North America departed from their sister churches in Europe.

While a number of churches used versions of the Roman three-year lectionary, discrepancies remained in the choice of readings, especially in the readings for the season after Pentecost. The North American-based Consultation on Common Texts (CCT) worked with the international English Language Liturgical Consultation (ELLC) to put together a revision of the Roman Catholic three-year lectionary, which appeared in 1983 as the Common Lectionary.[15] This Common Lectionary found a way to incorporate some of the variations in the three-year lectionaries as options and added the further option of a quasi-*lectio continua* Old Testament track during the time after Pentecost to parallel the typological track that related the Old Testament reading to the Gospel. After a nine-year trial period, a Revised Common Lectionary was publicly released in 1992. It was immediately included in the worship books of the United Methodist and Presbyterian churches (1992 and 1993 respectively) and was subsequently adopted in whole or with emendation by eight other denominations in the United States, four denominations in Canada, and churches in the United Kingdom, Australia, New Zealand, and other places around the world. While work on the RCL began in English-speaking countries, the biblical citations can be read in any

---

15. See Horace T. Allen, Jr., "*Common Lectionary*: Origins, Assumptions, Issues," *Studia Liturgica* 21 (1991): 14–30.

language. As a result, non-English-speaking churches have also adopted the Revised Common Lectionary. A petition to the Vatican to adopt the Revised Common Lectionary as the Lectionary for the Roman Mass was turned down.

Fritz West points out that while Protestants and Roman Catholic use practically the same lectionary, they approach it with different hermeneutics (principles of interpretation).[16] The Protestant lectionaries are concerned not to skip verses and to provide the contextual lead-in verses in the periscopes because a primary concern in Protestant preaching is opening up the text in its context. The concern in the Roman Lectionary is to hear the living voice of Christ at the altar; hence the scriptural or historical context is not as important. The Roman Lectionary is a eucharistic lectionary, not a preaching lectionary, even though the late Methodist liturgist James F. White said that it is Catholicism's greatest gift to Protestant biblical preaching. We should also note that the Revised Common Lectionary (RCL) is not used primarily as a eucharistic lectionary in Protestant churches because the Eucharist is not celebrated in most Protestant congregations on most Sundays. Apart from this hermeneutical difference, the provision for an optional semi-continuous Old Testament track after Pentecost also makes the RCL less common than it might have been since churches that use the RCL are now divided on which Old Testament reading and responsorial psalm they use during the time after Pentecost. That being said, the RCL is common enough to give millions of Christians around the world the same readings on most Sundays, which provides a remarkable ecumenical sign of Christian unity in the Scriptures.

The Body Receiving the Word

We typically think of the word of God appealing to the mind, but it is received by the body. Even if it is read, the information is received through the eyes by sight (or, for the blind, by touch, using a braille

---

16. Fritz West, *Scripture and Memory: The Ecumenical Hermeneutic of the Three-Year Lectionary* (Collegeville, MN: Liturgical Press, 1997).

text). But "faith comes from what is heard," and Scripture was originally heard, not read, by worshipers. In today's liturgical assembly, it is common to have lay readers read the lessons. The Gospel has been traditionally read (or chanted) by the deacon. The readers need to practice reading the texts so that the delivery is loud enough and slow enough to be heard and absorbed by the worshipers. It is customary today for readers to announce the end of the reading by saying, "The Word of the Lord," to which the assembly responds, "Thanks be to God." It has also been customary for worshipers to stand when the Gospel is announced and read. The reading of the Gospel is framed by acclamations, such as "Glory to you, O Lord" (or Lord Christ) and "Praise to you, O Christ" (or Lord Christ). The Gospel may be carried in procession into the midst of the assembly and read from that location. This is a practice in both Eastern and Western churches. The Gospel book is carried by the reader, who is flanked by acolytes carrying torches. A thurifer (carrying the incense pot) may also carry incense in a thurible (the incense pot) ahead of the gospel procession. The reader holds the Gospel book so that the deacon can see it and read from it. The people, who are standing, face the spot from which the gospel is read. At the end of the reading the procession returns the Gospel book to the altar, ambo, or pulpit. Thus the body is standing and facing the direction of the reading. The procession from the altar to the midst of the assembly and the return procession are accompanied by the singing of the Alleluia by the choir and/or congregation. Sometimes the Alleluia includes a verse of Scripture related to the readings of that day in the liturgical calendar. In this way the body receiving the gospel text is engaged in singing as well as standing and turning and listening and watching. The word comes through several senses.

Bread and Wine

We turn next to what Augustine calls the "visible words" of the sacrament: the bread and the wine. To talk about the Eucharist without saying anything about its elements is like talking about marriage without mentioning sex. The bread and wine are, in fact, the *sacramenta*, the "sacred signs." Too many commentaries on the Eucharist ignore the *sacramenta* themselves. We take the bread and wine for granted, but they are rich symbols even apart from their use in the Christian Eucharist. The variety of breads in the world's cultures is astounding. At least in wheat-based cultures, it is a staple of life, rich in metaphor. Wine is associated with festivals, for it "gladdens the heart" (Ps. 104:15). As Gordon Lathrop writes, "The slight inebriation it causes can moderate our inhibitions, enable our communal speech, and encourage our shared joy."[17] Bread and wine were staples of meals in the ancient world.

As we have seen, the last supper of Jesus, according to the Synoptic Gospels, was a Passover seder that required unleavened bread. However, the Eucharist in the early church was not a continuation of the Passover seder. In fact, the Christian Eucharist owes a lot to the post-resurrection meals Jesus shared with his disciples. These were meals in which the purpose of Jesus' hospitality to his disciples (like the breakfast meal on the seashore in John 21) was forgiveness of and reconciliation with the failed disciples.

The Christian Eucharist was not a continuation of the Passover seder. Therefore the unleavened bread used at the Passover is not required for the Eucharist. However, the fact that the Western church increasingly used unleavened bread in the early Middle Ages became a source of contention between the Greek and Latin churches. In the ninth century the use of unleavened bread had become universal and obligatory in the West, while the Greeks, desiring to emphasize the distinction between the Jewish *Pesach* and the Christian Pasch, continued the exclusive offering of leavened bread. This issue became divisive when joined with other issues in contention between the Greek and Latin churches in the early Middle Ages and contributed to the Great Schism between Rome and Constantinople in 1054. Politics were obviously involved, but the theological touchstone became the use of unleavened wafers. In popular Greek opinion, the flour and

17. See Gordon W. Lathrop, *Holy Things: A Liturgical Theology* (Minneapolis: Fortress Press, 1994), 92–93.

water wafers of the "Franks" were not bread. Thus their sacrifices were invalid; they were acting like Jews, not Christians. Since their lifeless bread could only symbolize a soulless Christ, they had clearly fallen into the heresy of Apollinaris. In spite of the polemics at the time of the schism, this issue caused little or no discussion among the theologians at the Councils of Lyons and Florence. The Council of Florence reached an agreement between the Greek and Latin theologians that the consecration of the elements was equally valid with leavened and unleavened bread and that the priests should abide by the custom of their church.

Two seemingly contradictory developments dominated eucharistic faith and practice in the Western Middle Ages. On the one hand the eucharistic debates of the ninth and eleventh centuries over the real presence of the body and blood of Christ in the bread and wine led to the formulation and promulgation of the dogma of transubstantiation, which held that the bread and wine are changed into the body and blood of Christ at the words of Christ. Transubstantiation was promulgated as dogma by the Fourth Lateran Council in 1215. Yet in spite of the growing belief that the bread and wine are changed into body and blood, there remained an awareness that the Eucharist is essentially food intended for nourishment, and great concern was shown for the bread and wine as food and drink. The wheaten bread and the fine grape wine satisfy hunger and quench thirst, and concern was expressed for the quality of these elements.

Notwithstanding the eucharistic realism of the high scholastic period, the Augustianian distinction between the visible sign (*sacramentum*) and the sacramental reality behind it (*res*) continued to persist in pastoral teaching. And in spite of a formulary such as Hugh of St. Cher's—"When the bread becomes Christ's body, nothing at all remains of the bread, that is, nothing is shared in common"[18]—great care was taken in the production of the bread. Baking wafers became a ritualized procedure in religious houses, accompanied by the chanting

18. Cited in Miri Rubin, *Corpus Christi: The Eucharist in Late Medieval Culture* (Cambridge: Cambridge University Press, 1991), 37.

of psalms. Ministers in parish churches who baked wafers were to be vested in their surplices. The wafers were to be baked in a vessel coated with wax rather than fat or oil so that they were not burned. A twelfth-century tract answered the question concerning why only wheat was used: because Christ compared himself to a grain of wheat that falls into the ground and dies.[19]

In the liturgical renewal movement there has been a preference to use whole loaves of bread rather than individual wafers. More recently, however, churches have become more aware that some people have gluten allergies, and efforts have been made to provide the option of gluten-free bread for Holy Communion, which has resulted in the production of gluten-free wafers. Pastoral discretion suggests finding discreet ways of accommodating this need.

It has been noticed that celiac disease and gluten allergies have increased dramatically in recent years. Some reason that genetically modified wheat is to blame for the rise in celiac and gluten sensitivity, but that is not the case for the simple reason that GMO wheat simply isn't being grown commercially (yet). That doesn't mean wheat hasn't changed over the last half-dozen decades however. It *has* changed as the result of a process called hybridization. Some scientists (though not all) say that those changes could be one cause of an increased inability to tolerate gluten. In hybridization, scientists don't tinker directly with the plant's genome. Instead, they choose particular strains of a plant with desirable characteristics and breed them to reinforce those characteristics. When this is done repeatedly, successive generations of a particular plant can look very different from the plant's ancestors. Modern wheat is shorter, browner, and higher yielding than wheat crops of one hundred years ago. These wheat strains require less time and less fertilizer to produce a robust crop of wheat berries, which in turn produce more food for the world.

Dr. William Davis, author of the best-selling book *Wheat Belly*, raises questions about whether these changes in wheat have caused the spike in gluten-related health problems, including obesity and diabetes. He

19. Ibid., 38.

argues that modern wheat has been bred to contain more gluten and that small changes in wheat protein structure can produce a devastating immune response to wheat protein.[20] However, a study by Donald D. Kasarda, published in the *Journal of Agricultural and Food Chemistry* in 2013, casts doubt on part of Davis's hypothesis. Kasarda reports that the amount of gluten in modern wheat has not increased when compared with 1920s-era wheat.[21] So what is going on? The answer is not clear. Studies do show a significant increase in the incidence of celiac disease over the last several decades. Kasanda suggests that increased consumption of wheat in recent years—rather than increased gluten in the wheat consumed—might be partly to blame for increased incidence of celiac disease. He also says that the use of wheat gluten as an ingredient in processed foods might contribute to increased gluten intolerance. Gluten intolerance seems to be more prevalent in America than in other parts of the world. But since this impacts a main ingredient of the central Christian ritual, Christians need to give this issue attention.

Communion wine has drawn far less attention. The wine used in antiquity was strong and was cut with water for social drinking. Commingling of water and wine continued as a ceremony in the Roman Mass, like the fraction (breaking of the host). Nevertheless, transmission of the cup from one person to another was more liable to mishap than the transmission of wafers. By the twelfth century the cup was withheld from lay communicants out of fear that they might spill the blood of Christ. The communion cup was replaced in many places by a sip of unconsecrated wine for the sake of symbolic symmetry and to make it easier to swallow the host. Synodical legislation shows concern that the communion wine be fresh, that consecrating vinegar in the chalice be avoided, and that care be taken to ensure that more wine than water was in the chalice.

The Protestant reformers restored the cup to lay communicants.

20. William Davis, *Wheat Belly* (New York: Rodale Books, 2011).
21. Donald D. Kasarda, "Can an Increase in Celiac Disease Be Attributed to an Increase in the Gluten Content of Wheat as a Consequence of Wheat Breeding?," *Journal of Agriculture and Food Chemistry* 61, no. 6 (2013): 1155-59, http://www.ncbi.nlm.nih.gov/pmc/articles/PMC3573730/.

In fact, communion cups increased in size to accommodate a great amount of drinking from them. The Reformed churches also insisted that the plates and cups used in Holy Communion be simple wooden or pewter vessels rather than ornate goblets of gold or silver. As more people received Communion when it was offered (four times a year or once a month), large flagons were needed for the wine. Moreover, other means of receiving the communion elements emerged in the Reformed Churches. Rather than kneeling at the altar as the Lutherans and Anglicans continued to do, people came forward and stood or sat around the communion table; alternately, the elements were passed through the pews.

Communion practices changed drastically with the rise of the science of epidemiology and the tuberculosis epidemics of the late nineteenth and early twentieth centuries. Fear of contagion resulted in bans on the use of common drinking containers, including the communion cup. Individual glasses were first marketed in the 1890s, and their use became the rule in most Protestant congregations.

In 1869 Thomas Bramwell Welch, a strong supporter of the temperance movement in the United States, discovered a method of pasteurizing grape juice that halted the fermentation process. This enabled him to produce a nonalcoholic wine to be used for church services in his hometown of Vineland, New Jersey. Because of the social pressure of the temperance movement (and many Protestant churches were in its leadership), grape juice was substituted for wine in many Protestant congregations. Lost in this use is the idea that the wine is a symbol of festivity, of which grape juice cannot be.

The use of grape juice also increased the use of individual glasses because the beverage lacked alcoholic content to kill bacteria. (One might also question how adequately those individual glasses are cleaned after use. Considering that issue, some Protestants use disposable paper communion cups, which are tossed in a garbage bag after use. This practice shows a scandalous lack of respect for the holy sacrament.) Another practice involves fitting a cup with a pouring lip so that the wine can be poured into individually held glasses. It is evident that American Christians do not want to risk bodily interaction with their fellow believers.

In spite of a lack of scientific evidence that the common communion cup contributes to the spread of disease, people's fears of contagion are not easily overcome. Outbreaks of new viruses have caused further bans on the use of communion cups, so that the restoration of the cup has often been accomplished only through the practice of intinction. In this practice communicants dip the wafer or bread into the communion cup. While people's germ-ridden finger tips may touch the wine with intinction, the alcoholic content of the wine should kill any ordinary germs. However, the rim of the common cup should be wiped carefully after each use.

Common practice today typically involves the use of wafers along with the common cup. Consistency would suggest that the restoration of a common drinking cup should be matched by the restoration of a single loaf and that the Lord's Supper should look more like a meal. The idea of a common meal suggests one menu with only a discreet number of options for members of the assembly who truly have food issues, be it gluten allergy or alcoholism. Some communion practices make it look like we are once again providing different meals for different categories of people and therefore dividing the body of Christ. Pastoral sensitivity must be balanced with the purpose of the sacrament to effect, and not just symbolize, the unity of the church in sharing the one loaf and the one cup. As the apostle Paul writes to the Corinthians, "The cup of blessing that we bless, is it not a sharing in the blood of Christ? The bread that we break, is it not a sharing in the body of Christ? Because there is one bread, we who are many are one body, for we all partake of the one bread" (1 Cor. 10:16–17).

Delivering the Body to Our Bodies

It is unclear exactly how the body and blood of Christ were delivered to participants in the symposium meal that took place in a house church or rented inn. Most likely, the method was similar to other banquets. Participants reclined on couches arranged on three sides (triclinum) and food and drink was delivered to them by servants. Once the sacramental meal was separated from the actual meal and celebrated in the morning, communicants probably stood around the table to receive the bread and cup. In the basilicas of late antiquity communicants processed to communion stations where they received the bread and drank from a large cup or vat through a straw. The communion procession continued in smaller parish churches. By the high Middle Ages communicants knelt at chancel railings to receive the host. The cup at this time was not regularly administered to lay communicants. In the Lutheran Reformation and in Anglicanism communicants continued to kneel at the table to receive Communion, usually at chancel railings. In the Reformed churches several methods of administration of the sacrament were employed. In Strassburg communicants walked forward to receive the elements in front of the table, but they did not kneel. In other churches the bread and cup was taken to the communicants and passed by them through the pews. The Scottish Presbyterians came forward to the head of the central aisle of the nave and sat around a long table. In the liturgical renewal of the late twentieth century an ecumenical consensus in practice emerged: communicants walk to a communion station and receive the bread (either wafers or pieces broken from a loaf) from an ordained minister; then they proceed to a lay communion minister to receive the cup (either drinking from the cup or intincting the bread into the wine). This practice has become common in Roman Catholic, Anglican, Lutheran, Methodist, and Presbyterian churches. In Eastern Rite and Orthodox churches communicants come forward to the priest and receive the bread, which has been broken into the cup of wine, from a spoon.

Communion and Community

The connection between the sacramental body and the ecclesial body (the church) ensures that one cannot think about embodied liturgy without thinking about the corporate body. This eucharistic understanding of the church is the foundation for everything Paul addresses in chapters 11 and 12 of 1 Corinthians concerning divisions at the table and the competition that arises among those with different spiritual gifts. Such divisions and competitions fracture the body of Christ. Social divisions and vocational competition that might be practiced in worldly societies can have no place in the church as the body of Christ, in which every gift of the Holy Spirit is needed and welcomed. Because the unity and fellowship of the church is realized in the celebration of the Lord's Supper, we must give close attention to our communion practices. The liturgy forms the church just as it forms individual Christians.

As with the training of our physical bodies, whether for sports or music or yoga, formation does not happen in one or two training sessions. The training must be consistent over a long period of time, and it must be frequent rather than sporadic. Athletes know they need to exercise every day. Musicians know they must practice every day. The same can be said of those early Christians described in the second chapter of the book of Acts. Not only did they share all things in common and look after each other's needs, but they also frequently broke bread in their homes (that is, in the gatherings of the church)—not just once a week, but daily (Acts 2:46).

Offerings at the Eucharist in the early church included not only the bread and wine needed for the Lord's Supper but also the goods that were needed for the relief of the widows and orphans. Justin Martyr reports that at the Sunday Eucharist "those who prosper, and who so wish, contribute, each one as much as he chooses to. What is collected is deposited with the president, and he takes care of orphans and widows, and those who are in want on account of sickness or any other cause, and those who are in bonds, and the strangers who are sojourners among [us], and, briefly, he is the protector of all those in need."[22]

The church has always had its "poor box" (as well as ministries to the poor and needy). Quite literally, it is a box designated for donations (alms) to the poor. Also called a mite box or an alms box, the practice

---

22. Justin Martyr, *First Apology*, chap. 67, in *Early Christian Fathers*, 287.

and custom actually traces back to the temple of Jerusalem. Alms were placed in a basket at the back of the temple, and the poor were free to take as they needed from the donations made there. In more modern times, a box was used, and the funds were distributed to the poor. The practice of giving alms is widely referenced throughout the Bible and ties directly to Christian charity to those in need. Jesus assumed in the "Sermon on the Mount" that his disciples would continue the practice of almsgiving: "When you give alms, do not let your left hand know what your right hand is doing, so that your alms may be done in secret; and your Father who sees in secret will reward you" (Matt. 6:5, NRSV).

Martin Luther developed this ministry to the poor to an unprecedented extent and associated it with the Holy Communion. As Samuel Torvend points out in *Luther and the Hungry Poor,* Luther struck a nerve when he included in his attack on the sale of indulgences the implication that not everyone could afford to buy forgiveness in the afterlife for their dear departed relatives or themselves. Likewise, not everyone could afford to pay for votive masses for the relief of souls in purgatory. Many people in Germany at that time lived at a subsistence level. Luther raised the possibility that the poor were religiously disenfranchised because they could not contribute financially to their own spiritual destiny. In his *Ninety-Five Theses* he says, "Christians are to be taught that [the one] who gives to the poor or lends to the needy does a better deed that [the one] who buys indulgences."[23]

By 1523 reformed Evangelical churches were implementing Luther's ideas for the relief of the poor by establishing common chests in their churches. A chest into which communicants could place their alms was also placed in the church at Wittenberg. The town council administered the money collected in the common chest to those in need, and the recipients of alms could pay back the common chest if their situation improved.

One year during my pastoral ministry in Evanston, Illinois, Lent came early and I had forgotten to order Lenten coin boxes. Ash Wednesday was upon us so I was forced to improvise. I placed a large

---

23. Samuel Torvend, *Luther and the Hungry Poor* (Minneapolis: Fortress Press, 2008), 16–18.

bowl at the entrance to the chancel and invited people to empty their pockets of change when they came forward to receive Holy Communion. They would not know how much they contributed, and they would not receive any credit for it on their financial statements (see Matt. 6:5). The money collected was given to hunger ministries at Easter. It turned out to be one of the most popular practices I instituted in that congregation. Children even emptied their coin banks into the bowl. That impromptu alms bowl established a link between feeding our bodies and souls in the Eucharist and feeding the hungry poor in the world. Luther's post-communion prayer in his German Mass gives thanks for the gift of communion that "strengthens us in faith toward Thee and in fervent love toward one another." As we are fed in body and soul at the Lord's Supper, so we feed hungry bodies in the world as a grateful response to God's gift of grace to us.

Meditation on the Eucharist

The following exercise is *not* Holy Communion. It is a meditation on the communion elements using all five senses. In preparation for this meditation we will also do a few poses to stretch the body and open the heart space to receive the information that the senses bring.

Move into table pose on hands and knees. Alternately do the cat and dog poses by raising your chest and lowering your abdomen and then lowering your chest and raising your back. As you exhale move into child's pose. As you inhale slide forward onto your belly. Exhale. Bring your hands alongside your ribs and on inhale lift your chest and head into cobra pose. Lower to the floor on exhale. If you are able, bring your hands under your shoulders; and on inhale lift your chest and head into high cobra with your arms straight. On exhale go into downward dog. Then take a sitting position.

Make available a freshly baked loaf of bread and a cup or bowl of wine. Sit in a circle in lotus position. Turn on a recording of a repetitive communion hymn that refers to the bread and cup, such as the Taizé mantra "Eat this bread, drink this cup." Listen to the words as the bread and cup of wine are passed around the circle. As the bread and cup of wine are passed around the circle the first time, look at each element as you receive it. As the bread and cup of wine are passed around the circle the second time, smell each element as you receive it. As the bread and cup of wine are passed around the circle the third time, touch each element as you receive it. As the bread and cup of wine are passed around the circle the fourth time, taste each element as you receive it.

What did you learn about the bread and wine from each of the five senses (hearing, seeing, smelling, touching, tasting)?

As Lorin Roche writes, in Tantra practice "we are invited to enter the heart through the door of the senses."[24] As we follow any or all of the senses, we find ourselves entering the heart space or heart chakra (*hrdaya*). The heart chakra is the center of love and devotion. The Tantra tradition in yoga is allied with the devotional (*bhakti*) movement in Hinduism. As Tantra turns away from renunciation of the world to embrace the body, everyday life, and the sensual world, so the bhakti movement turns away from Brahman mysticism to practice devotional rituals that show love to one's gods.

Is it possible that by opening our hearts to the information about the bread and wine, which is received through the senses, we can develop a love for these elements and for the sacrament in which they are used? Can we develop a passionate love for the Christ who comes to us in the bread and wine? See the classic communion hymn, "Deck Thyself, My Soul, in Gladness" (*Schmücke dich*).

Bhakti is devotion and love, especially of the deity. Yoga provides techniques that can be used by the body to aid any bhakti, also a Christian eucharistic devotion.

24. Lorin Roche, *The Radiance Sutras: 112 Gateways to the Yoga of Wonder and Delight* (Boulder, CO: True Sounds, 2014), 195.

6

Penitential Bodies, Celebrating Bodies

A. Fasting and Feasting

We've been discussing meals, particularly the Lord's Supper or the Eucharist, and we've established that the Lord's Supper was originally celebrated in the context of a banquet, probably a symposium meal. Yet even when it is separated from an actual meal, it is still a feast.

We know the custom of fasting before a feast. One eats less to whet his or her appetite for the good foods at the feast. You don't want to approach a great dinner on a full stomach, so it is not surprising that this basic principle was applied to the Eucharist. We will see in this lesson the development in Christianity of fasting before receiving Holy Communion. But first the general concept of fasting should be considered.

Fasting Customs

Fasting is a natural occurrence; we do it every night while sleeping. We call the morning meal "break[the]fast." It comes from the old English word *fasten*, which means "to fix" or "make firm." Under no circumstances is fasting starvation. Fasting is practiced in all the great religions of the world—Hinduism, Buddhism, Judaism, Christianity, Islam—and the rules of fasting are always relaxed in the case of children, the elderly, and the sick. Fasting is a natural form of detoxification. Taking in food introduces bacteria into the body, especially when eating meat. It is more important for those who regularly eat meat to fast in order to detoxify the body. Fasting almost always involves refraining from eating meat, just as feasting is almost always centered on roasted meat.

It is noteworthy that in the northern hemisphere, where Christian traditions of fasting began, the coming of winter is a time of feasting (e.g., Christmas) because the animal herds have been culled in preparation for winter. Grains that are used to feed the herds must be sufficient through winter when the animals can't graze. After Carnival time (*carnival* means "farewell to meat") Lent begins, which is a time of fasting. This is also a time when the weather begins to get warmer. Fasting should not be done during a cold season because the body needs food to convert into energy to deal with the cold. By the end of Lent animals have given birth, providing fresh meat to eat (e.g., roast lamb).

Fasting has been promoted by the great religions because it can help people to be more introspective. By paying attention to what is going on in our bodies we can learn things about ourselves and the importance of food in our lives. When the fast begins, there is usually an initial desire to eat because the body is being deprived of substances it has come to rely on and crave. This experience introduces the theme of temptation. Those who fast discover that after the first several days the body becomes used to the different intake of food. Fasting actually promotes vigor because breathing is freer, the tired feeling caused by overeating is removed, and the blood pressure is lowered. Thus, health benefits are linked to fasting.

Fasting was observed among the Jews, and the practice was assumed in early Christianity. In the Sermon on the Mount Jesus reviews the pious Jewish practices of almsgiving, prayer, and fasting, telling his disciples: "And whenever you fast, do not look dismal, like the hypocrites, for they disfigure their faces so as to show others that they are fasting. But when you fast, put oil on your head and wash your face, so that your fasting may be seen not by others but by your Father who sees in secret; and your Father who sees in secret will reward you" (Matt. 6:16–18, NRSV). Fasting that makes one "look dismal" was associated with mourning and penitence. People in those situations did not bathe. Mourners looked disheveled, and penitents sat in sackcloth and ashes. Such persons gained sympathy from others, and the hypocrites purposely looked as dismal as they could to win approval from others for their piety. Jesus tells his disciples to wash and look joyous as they fast because they are fasting out of devotion to him. That being said, Jesus' assumption is that his disciples will continue the practice of fasting.

When we look at the Old Testament, only one commanded fast is found—in Leviticus 16, for the Day of Atonement (Yom Kippur). All other fasts were voluntary. Since this command to fast was directed to the nation of Israel and since the Day of Atonement was fulfilled in Christ, it is no longer a fast that applies to Christians.

Nevertheless there were instances of both voluntary individual fasting and national fasts called for in response to emergency situations. As an example of an individual fast as a sign of repentance see 2 Sam. 12:16–18, where David is fasting and weeping for his dying child, the love child of his illicit affair with Bathsheba. For examples of national fasts see Es. 4:3, 16, where the Jews in Persia fast when threatened with extermination at the hands of Haman; Jon. 3:6–10, where Nineveh fasts after Jonah pronounces judgment on them; and Joel 2:12–13 (NASB), where the people fast in the face of a national threat:

> "Yet even now," declares the Lord,
> "Return to Me with all your heart,
> And with fasting, weeping and mourning;
> And rend your heart and not your garments."
> Now return to the Lord your God,
> For He is gracious and compassionate,

Slow to anger, abounding in lovingkindness
And relenting of evil.

Both Moses and Elijah fasted for forty days on Mount Sinai in relation to their mission. This was a prototype of Jesus' forty-day fast in the wilderness after his baptism.

While these fasts are not related to feasting, fasting related to feasting goes back all the way to the beginning of the biblical story. "Then the Lord God commanded the man, 'You may freely eat fruit from every tree of the orchard, but you must not eat from the tree of the knowledge of good and evil, for when you eat from it you will surely die'" (Gen. 2:16–17, NRSV).

Temptation, Fall, and Fasting

The first sin in the Bible was a violation of a dietary restriction. Even in the Garden of Eden, a restriction on dietary behavior was imposed. As the Jewish scholar Nahum Sarna comments, "Unrestricted freedom does not exist. Man is called upon by God to exercise restraint and self-discipline in the gratification of his appetite. This prohibition is the paradigm for the future Torah legislation relating to the dietary laws."[1]

Interestingly, after the prohibition on eating from the tree of the knowledge of good and evil, the Genesis story relates the story of the creation of Eve, saying that it was "not good for the man to be alone" (Gen. 2:18, NRSV). Immediately after the creation of the woman the food prohibition is again referred to in Gen 3:1, creating a structure that alternates the individual creation narratives with references to the food prohibition.

In Gen. 3:1 the serpent questions the validity of the command to the woman. In fact, the serpent contradicts the stated penalty of certain death, suggesting instead that they would become like God (*Elohim*), "knowing good and evil" (Gen. 3:5, NRSV). The reasoning process of the woman includes three elements, "that the tree was good for food, and

---

1. Nahum M. Sarna, *Genesis*, JPS Torah Commentary (Philadelphia: Jewish Publication Society, 1989), 21.

that it was a delight to the eyes, and that the tree was to be desired to make one wise" (Gen. 3:6, NRSV). This led her to take it, eat it, and give it to her husband who also ate (Gen. 3:7).

After the disobedient act, the couple knew they were naked, and so they covered themselves and hid. When YHWH Elohim called to them, he immediately asked Adam if he had eaten from the tree (Gen. 3:11). The man responded that the woman whom God had given him gave him fruit from the tree and he ate; the woman likewise defers to the deception of the serpent when she is interrogated. Next comes a series of curses (Gen. 3:14-19) in which God begins by pronouncing judgment on the serpent. Along with the penalty of going on his belly comes the statement that he will eat dust all the days of his life (Gen. 3:14). As Sarna suggests, "The transgression involved eating, and so does the punishment. As the serpent slithers on its way, its flickering tongue appears to lick the dust."[2] Enmity would arise between the serpent and the woman and her offspring, who would bruise the serpent's head and in turn be bruised in the heel. The woman is assigned great pain in childbearing and a potentially dysfunctional relationship with her husband. Because the man listened to his wife and ate what he was commanded not to eat, the ground is cursed, resulting in great toil to produce the food they would eat in the future (Gen. 3:17-19). "Once again, the punishment is related to the offense. The sin of eating forbidden food results in complicating the production of goods."[3] Then the judgment of death is pronounced, with the foreboding words, "for you are dust, / and to dust you will return" (Gen. 3:19, NRSV).

Of what significance is this account to fasting? At least three ideas present themselves and are picked up by the New Testament, referred to often in the church fathers, and prove foundational to a Christocentric, biblical theology of fasting: (1) the notion that the created world, including food, may be regulated by God for his purposes, requiring disciplined obedience on the part of humanity; (2) the messianic idea that the offspring of the woman will reverse the

2. Ibid., 27.
3. Ibid.

effects of the fall, a theme that will later be symbolized by fasting passages; and (3) the unsettling reality that the body is somehow disconnected from the sustaining force of life.

In the context of Genesis 2–3 we find that food is used as a tool of discipline by God both before and after the fall. As Thomas Brodie notes, "Among human needs and activities, eating is fundamental, thus making it a suitable representative for human conduct in general."[4] Before the fall, all manner of food was allowable, with one exception. Was this directive a test by God to examine the loyalty of the man and woman? It appears so, since a direct command was given, and a penalty was prescribed for disobedience. Without speculating too much about the purposes of God in giving this prohibition, one may surmise a couple of relevant points. First, the creation should be viewed as fundamentally good, but second, even in the Garden of Eden potentially subversive elements lurked. The crafty serpent was ready to deceive, and the food that led to separation from God was readily available. Amidst the goodness of creation, God called the woman and man to a disciplined obedience—abstinence from something that might appear desirable.

It is interesting to note that later Christian fathers, particularly in the Byzantine tradition, interpret the fall of humanity in terms of a failure to maintain a decreed fast. According to St. Basil the Great, in his *First Homily on Fasting*, Adam, the first-created man, loved God of his own free will and dwelt in the heavenly blessedness of communion with God in the angelic state of prayer and fasting. The cause of this first man's fall was his free will: by an act of disobedience he violated the vow of abstinence and broke the living union of love with God. That is, he held in scorn the heavenly obligations of prayer and fasting by eating of the Tree of Knowledge of Good and Evil. Lack of abstinence, then, was the cause of the Fall. Because of this original greed, the soul becomes dimmed and is deprived of the illumination of the Holy Spirit.

Additionally, the apocryphal intertestamental book of *The Life of*

---

4. Thomas L. Brodie, *Genesis as Dialogue: A Literary, Historical, and Theological Commentary* (Oxford: Oxford University Press, 2001), 151.

Adam and Eve (6:1) says that Adam engaged in a forty-day fast in penitence for his fall (the Slavonic adds that Eve fasted forty-four days).[5] This is an interesting correlation with the forty-day fasts of Moses, Elijah, and Jesus, as well as the Christian idea of a forty-day Lenten fast in imitation of Jesus fasting in the wilderness.

While Jesus' forty-day fast in the wilderness involved the temptation of food, it was really about distracting Jesus from his mission by getting him to look after his own needs. The tempter says, "If you are the Son of God, command these stones to become loaves of bread," but Jesus counters the devil with the word of God from Deuteronomy: "One does not live by bread alone, but by every word that comes from the mouth of God" (Matt. 4:3–4, NRSV). Jesus proves his true messiahship by keeping the fast to the end.

The condition of life in which food is procured with great difficulty in the fallen creation is overturned in the new creation in which God provides a feast for his people on his holy mountain and death itself is swallowed up forever.

> On this mountain, the Lord of hosts will make for all peoples
> a feast of rich food, a feast of well-aged wines,
> of rich food filled with marrow, of well-aged wines strained clear.
> And he will destroy on this mountain
> the shroud that is cast over all peoples,
> the sheet that is spread over all nations;
> he will swallow up death forever. (Isa. 25:6–8a, NRSV)

Christians are born again as new creatures in Christ. But because we live in the tension between the old creation and the new, the regulation of food continues to play a part in the Christian tradition.

Jesus and Fasting

At the time of Jesus the codification of Jewish dietary laws was in a state

---

5. The two versions may be compared in *A Synopsis of the Books of Adam and Eve*, ed. Gary A. Anderson and Michael E. Stone, 2nd rev. ed., SBL Early Judaism and Its Literature 17 (Atlanta: Scholars Press, 1999).

of flux, with various parties developing different practices. Fasting was a hot topic, and it is not surprising that Jesus was asked about it.

In Matthew the disciples of John the Baptist ask Jesus about fasting. Since the Baptist was noted for his severity regarding food (Matt. 11:18; Mark 1:6; Luke 7:33), it is not surprising that his disciples also fasted. They wanted to know why Jesus' disciples didn't fast. Luke depicts the Pharisees asking the questions (Luke 5:30, 33), and Mark writes that the questions came from both the Pharisees and John's disciples (Mark 2:18). In all three accounts the clear assumption is that Jesus' disciples were not observing proper fasting practices, at least not ones that conformed to the customs of emerging Pharisaic Judaism. So where did Jesus stand on the debates about fasting within emerging Judaism?

Jesus clearly taught that his disciples were in a new situation because of his presence among them, which is evident in the two analogies he offers: placing a new patch on old cloth and putting new wine in old wineskins (Matt. 9:16–17; Mark 2:21–22; Luke 5:36–38). These examples convey that Jesus' teaching could not be blended with rabbinic traditions. In response to the questions about fasting he says, "The attendants of the bridegroom cannot mourn as long as the bridegroom is with them, can they?" Then he adds, "But the days will come when the bridegroom is taken away from them, and then they will fast" (Matt. 9:15, NRSV). Jesus viewed fasting as a sign of mourning, which is inconsistent with the joy of the bridegroom's presence. In standard Christian interpretation, the bridegroom allegorically represents the Messiah. As long as Jesus was with his disciples, they didn't fast. When Jesus departed from his disciples, they would fast (though Jesus would still be present in the Eucharist).

In addition to the basic fact that one can't feast and fast at the same time, the tradition also developed in Christianity that the Lord's Day, on which the Eucharist is celebrated, is never a day of fasting—not even in penitential seasons like Lent (Sundays are "in" Lent but never "of" Lent). Conversely, the Eucharist is not celebrated on a fast day. This practice has been maintained in the Eastern churches but not in the Western ones. While Holy Communion can be served from the

Presanctified Gifts (or reserved elements)—that is, leftovers from Sunday's Eucharist—on a fast day, the Eucharist itself (a fresh consecration, made so by the eucharistic prayer) is not celebrated on those days.[6]

Christian Fasting

The first statement about Christian fasting practices can be found in the church manual from the end of the first century known as the *Didache*. It gives the following instruction to its largely Jewish Christian community: "Let your fasts not [take place] with [those of] the wicked [i.e., hypocrites]. They fast on Monday and Thursday; you, though, should fast on Wednesday and Friday."[7]

Again, as in the Sermon on the Mount, there is the assumption that Christians will continue the custom of fasting. However, these Semitic Christians in northern Palestine or Syria (where the *Didache* may have been compiled) are to distinguish their fast days from those of the Jews by fasting on Wednesdays and Fridays. As such, these days became fixed in Christian tradition as weekly fast days. By the time of Tertullian of Carthage (ca. 200) the Friday fast was regarded as a weekly commemoration of the passion of Christ. Thus there developed early in Christian history a weekly commemoration of the death and resurrection of Christ in the Friday fast and the Sunday Eucharist.

It is noteworthy that the verses about fasting in the *Didache* follow the instructions about preparation for baptism. "Before the baptism, let the person baptizing and the person being baptized—and others who are able—fast; tell the one being baptized to fast one or two days before" (7:4).[8]

The fact that the faithful accompany those preparing for baptism in their fasting is also mentioned in Justin Martyr's *Apology*. Justin tells the Roman Senate, "Those who are persuaded and believe that

---

6. See Robert Taft, *Beyond East and West: Problems in Liturgical Understanding* (Washington, DC: Pastoral Press, 1984), 66–68.
7. Kurt Niederwimmer, *The Didache: A Commentary*, trans. Linda M. Maloney, ed. Harold W. Attridge (Minneapolis: Fortress Press, 1998), 131.
8. Ibid., 125.

the things we teach and say are true, and promise that they can live accordingly, are instructed to pray and beseech God with fasting for the remission of their past sins, while we pray and fast along with them."[9]

The practice of fasting along with the candidates for baptism continued. When a forty-day period of preparation of the elect for baptism at Easter developed in the fourth century, a forty-day period of fasting also developed in which the faithful fasted along with the candidates—hence the origin of the season of Lent. In time, Lent became a whole season of fasting, which was followed by a whole season of feasting. During the paschal (Easter) season, there is no fasting, even on Wednesdays and Fridays.

During the rest of the year, fasting was done on Wednesdays and especially Fridays. Must of us are aware that Roman Catholics have more or less observed the Friday fast of not eating meat, although fish has been allowed. However, the Orthodox fast is more rigorous. Unless a fast-free period has been declared, Orthodox Christians are to keep a strict fast every Wednesday and Friday. The following foods are avoided:

• Meat, including poultry, and any meat products such as lard and meat broth.

• Fish (meaning fish with backbones; shellfish are permitted).

• Eggs and dairy products (milk, butter, cheese, etc.).

• Olive oil. A literal interpretation of the rule forbids only olive oil. Especially where olive oil is not a major part of the diet, the rule is sometimes taken to include all vegetable oils, as well as oil products such as margarine.

• Wine and other alcoholic drink. In the Slavic tradition, beer is often permitted on fast days.

9. Justin Martyr, *First Apology*, chap. 61, ed. and trans. Edward Rochie Hardy, in *Early Christian Fathers*, ed. Cyril C. Richardson, vol. 1 of *The Library of Christian Classics* (Philadelphia: The Westminster Press, 1953), 282.

In terms of the communion fast, the Orthodox abstain from all food and drink from the time that they retire the night before (or midnight, whichever comes first). Married couples should also abstain from sexual relations the night before communion. When communion is in the evening, such as the Presanctified Liturgy during Lent, this fast should be extended throughout the day until after communion. For those who cannot keep this discipline, a total fast beginning at noon is sometimes prescribed.

The Lenten fast for the Orthodox is also observed on Sundays, except that wine and oil are permitted; otherwise the strict fasting rule is kept. For Western Christians, whatever is observed as the Lenten fast—whatever is "given up for Lent," as people say—need not be applied to Sunday.

Unfortunately, these fasts are often observed in the breach. Fasting has been much relaxed in Catholic practice since the Second Vatican Council. Protestants who choose voluntarily to abstain from something in particular during Lent may be more disciplined in carrying out their intention because they see it as promoting some good for them and for others, such as a contribution to aid world hunger.

In spite of errors and abuses, fasting acquired a central place in the Christian life throughout Christian history. At its best, fasting was a clue to all Christian living, a perspective on the whole of discipleship. To be a Christian meant to participate in a great feast, the Eucharist. It meant also to observe a great fast, which is true in several respects. Fasting shows that discipleship is always cruciform. It reminds us that we can't follow Jesus unless we say no to ourselves and take up the cross. Fasting reveals that Jesus requires us to combat—and enables us to conquer—the sinful desires and habits that continue to plague us. Fasting reveals that the Christian life is a life of charity. But we need to remember that fasting went along with prayer and almsgiving. Time not spent preparing meals can be devoted to prayer. Money not spent on buying food can be given to the poor or to hunger ministries.

I should be clear that Christians do not fast because they think the material creation is evil. Early Christianity struggled mightily with

Gnosticism, and the gnostic religion was eventually rejected. God didn't impose a fast on Adam because creation is bad—even the knowledge of good and evil is not bad in itself. Understood more precisely, Adam was not ready to handle that knowledge. When he took the forbidden fruit, it blew up in his face.

Fasting is not a renunciation of creation; rather, it celebrates and honors the goodness of creation by saying that we can appreciate it more if we abstain from it for a while. This is probably most evident in the pious custom of abstaining from marital relations on fast days. Christians don't practice abstinence out of a prudish hatred of sex but out of admiration for its mysterious potency. Sex is so pleasurable that our senses must be trained before we can handle it well. Abstinence is the fast that prepares us for the feast of marriage. Even for those who are married, Saturday night or even a six-week Lenten sexual abstinence honors creation by insisting we take time to appreciate the great gifts God has given us so that we can receive them back with thanksgiving.

The Feast

This brings us to the day of the feast. The great feasts of the liturgical year have been occasions for real feasting as well, especially at Christmas and Easter. Here the cultures of the world take over with ethnic food for the holidays. It is helpful that in Europe the Christian fasts of Advent and Lent occurred during the times of harvest and culling of the herds before winter and the births of new livestock in early spring. This provided meats for the Christmas and Easter celebrations. Roast lamb has been a paschal meat for Christians as well as for Jews. Throughout many countries in Europe, especially in Eastern Europe, dyeing Easter eggs became an art. Easter baskets of dyed eggs (in addition to all sorts of feasting foods) may be blessed by the priest on Holy Saturday in Polish, Ukrainian, Russian churches.

In America the custom of the parish Easter breakfast is observed in all churches. In my former congregation we had a "Break-the-Lenten-fast" party after the Easter Vigil Liturgy, which was held in the parish hall. Everyone brought party food and beverages, including wine, to share. We also had an Easter breakfast prepared by the youth on Easter morning. In the Orthodox churches, the Vigil may go on all night, so the parish breakfast usually occurs at breakfast time. People bring their ethnic foods, and it is usually a feast to die for. Afterwards, people go home to bed and return for Vespers on Easter evening.

Pentecost doesn't seem to have particular foods associated with it, but in late medieval England it was the occasion of the parish ale festival (perhaps relating to the taunts of those who said that the disciples, filled with the Holy Spirit, were drunk). The Feast of Corpus Christi became an occasion for a town fair, as did many of the saints' days in medieval Europe. In addition to the food and drink, a feast usually included some form of entertainment. Singing, music, juggling, acrobatics, and plays could all be seen at medieval fairs. All the liturgical festivals of medieval Europe were celebrated with fairs and communal feasting. In a later chapter we will see that the feast of Corpus Christi in particular helped give birth to Western theater; several cycles of mystery plays were associated with this feast, as was one of the greatest annual processions in the Christian repertoire of processions. At the center of it all was the veneration of the food that was received and worshiped as the body of Christ.

A Yoga Sequence: Tonifying and Detoxing the Body

It's time for another yoga sequence. Not surprisingly, the old yogis who gave much attention to bodily functions also gave a great deal of attention to food and diet and developed practices related to both intact and outtake, digestion and elimination. Worried about how Indonesian food might affect my digestive processes, I had a private lesson with my yoga teacher to develop a simple sequence—*Agni,* or fire tonifying and soothing—that I could take with me and do in my room. I usually did the sequence first thing in the morning; it is comprised largely of abdominal poses and twists that create heat (*tapas*) in the belly. In the Vedic literature *tapas* refers to heat in the sense of generating energy. But it also refers to austerity, penance, and pious activity. Taken in its literal sense, "to burn," it can refer to overcoming the challenges in life as demonstrated in the challenges of the yoga poses. My little sequence served the simple purpose of helping with the challenges of digestion. Thanks to Nick Beem for the sequence.

Lay on your back. Bring your knees to your chest. Take hold of them with your hands; bring them in and extend them out five times. Inhale as you bring your knees toward your face; exhale as you push them away.

Put your hands behind your thighs. Raise your legs straight up and lower your knees to your chest five times. Inhale as you raise your legs; exhale as you lower them.

With your legs straight up, circle them like a windmill five times in one direction and five times in the reverse direction.

Place your feet on the floor behind your buttocks, body-width apart. Stretch out your arms in a T. Lower your knees to the right and then to the left (like windshield wipers) five times. Turn your face to the left when your knees are to the right, and vice versa. Then do the same thing with your feet off the floor, bringing your knees toward your armpits.

Roll over onto your belly. Place your hands alongside your ribs and raise your chest to a low cobra. Inhale as you lift and lengthen, exhale as you lower—five times. Then hold cobra while you breathe in and out of your belly.

Lift one leg and your chest and lower back down—five times for each leg.

Raise both arms and legs off the floor (locust pose) and hold for five breaths. Breathe in and out of your belly.

Turn over to table pose (hands and knees on the floor). Inhale and lift your chest. Then exhale to child pose with uddiyana bandha. A bandha is a lock—in this case an abdominal lock. It is created by exhaling completely, chin down to lock out more breath. Without inhaling, suck the abdominal muscles in and up, pulling the navel toward the spine. Pull the abdomen and diaphragm up into the cavity of the rib cage. Do this as you move into child pose and hold the lock as long as it is comfortable.

Inhale and move back to table pose. Do this a few times, slowly. Then relax, inhale to the belly, exhale, and resume normal breathing while observing a brief savasana.

Figure 10. *Penitensya*. A flagellant procession in the Philippines during Holy Week.

B. Penance and Festival

People instinctively want to respond in some bodily way when they desire to show sorrow for sin and repentance. When I was a boy, I had a good friend with whom I often got into impromptu wrestling matches. He was just slightly bigger than me, and one day, when we were about eleven or twelve, I got thrown down to the ground and had the wind knocked out of me when I landed. He told me he was sorry for being so rough. He picked up a stick and told me to hit him with it. I declined, but we immediately reconciled and reaffirmed that we were friends.

But I remember to this day the fact that he would have been willing to suffer bodily pain as his penance for hurting me.

In the Old Testament bodily practices of penitence included fasting, sitting in ashes, and tearing one's clothes. Such practices—and more—continued in the Christian tradition.

Repentance and Forgiveness

Repentance and the forgiveness of sins are at the very heart of Jesus' preaching. In Mark's Gospel, he begins his messianic work with the appeal, "Repent and believe the Gospel" (Mark 1:15, NRSV). In Luke, he takes leave of his disciples with the charge that "repentance and the remission of sins should be preached in my name to all nations" (Luke 24:47, NRSV). As we see in the parables of the lost sheep, the lost coin, and the lost son in Luke 15, the divine willingness to forgive the repentant sinner knows no bounds. "There is joy is the presence of the angels of God over one sinner who repents" (Luke 15:10, NRSV).

Sin separates us from God and from others. Cut off from God we are cut off from the source of life, and we perish eternally; but "one who believes and is baptized will be saved" (Mark 16:16, NRSV). Baptism is the full and final forgiveness of sins. When those pilgrims who were gathered in Jerusalem on the day of Pentecost heard Peter's sermon and asked what they should do, he said, "Repent and be baptized, every one of you in the name of Jesus Christ so that your sins may be forgiven; and you will receive the gift of the Holy Spirit" (Acts 2:38, NRSV). The Spirit is the giver of life and salvation.

Certainly forgiveness is available at any time. Jesus included in his model prayer the petition, "Forgive us our sins, as we forgive those who sin against us" (Matt. 6:12, ICEL/ICET). In the case of serious sins, however, especially those with social consequences, forgiveness is not just a matter between God and the sinner. It comes through the mediation of the church, of which the Christian is a member by baptism. When a Christian sins, he or she dishonors and defiles the church.

Our interest here is in ritual processes of forgiveness and

reconciliation. Jesus expressly grants to the church disciplinary authority over believers who commit sin. In Matt. 18:15-17, the process is laid out: first, the brother who committed the sin is to be admonished privately by an individual. If he does not listen, then two others are to be brought along as witnesses. If he refuses to listen to them then he is to be denounced to the church. If the highest tribunal cannot bring about his repentance, then he is to be treated "as a gentile and a publican." This means, in accordance with Jewish practice, that he is to be excommunicated. In the Lutheran Church, this process is called the Office of the Keys in the truest sense, hearkening back to Matt. 16:19, where Jesus gives the keys for binding and loosing to Peter (which may refer to more matters than sins). In Matthew 18 Jesus gives to the community of disciples the authority he gave to Peter in Matthew 16: "Whatever you bind on earth shall be bound in heaven; and whatever you loose on earth shall be loosed in heaven" (Matt. 18:18, NRSV). *Binding* and *loosing* are rabbinical expressions; they mean "to forbid" and "to permit." Their secondary meanings are "to impose a ban" and "to lift the ban." When the sinner is "bound" on earth he is not only banned from the earthly fellowship but also from the kingdom of heaven. A similar authority over sin is found in John 20, in which the risen Christ gives to his apostles authority to "forgive" or "retain" sins. This is the same as the binding and loosing in Matthew 18.

The apostle Paul deals with a concrete case of sin in 1 Corinthians 5, for which the ban or excommunication must be imposed. Faced with this appalling crime of incest, the community should have broken off all relationships with the evil doer in obedience to an earlier instruction of the apostle. They neglected to do so, and Paul does it himself on their behalf. Conscious of his union with them in the Spirit he pronounces judgment in the name of Jesus "to deliver up such a one to Satan for the destruction of the flesh, that his spirit may be saved in the day of the Lord" (1 Cor. 5:5, NRSV). This "delivering up to Satan" is nothing less than excommunication. What the apostle expects in terms of "the destruction of the flesh" is not clear; it could be understood literally in terms of the man's physical body, or it could be understood figuratively in terms of the purging of evil desires. However, Paul still hopes for the man's salvation, "that his spirit may be saved in the day of the Lord" (1 Cor. 5:5, NRSV), but no mechanism is provided for reconciliation. Paul clearly expects that the man will be banned from the meal fellowship, the Lord's Supper. "I wrote to you in my letter not to associate with sexually immoral persons—not at all meaning the immoral of this world, or the greedy and robbers and idolaters, since you would then need to go out of the world. But now I am writing to you not to associate with anyone who bears the name of brother or sister who is sexually immoral or greedy, or is an idolater, reviler, drunkard, or robber. Do not even eat with such a one" (1 Cor. 5:9–12, NRSV).

Confession of Sins and Reconciliation in the Early Church

In both 1 John and in the letter of James we find references to confessing one's sins. In 1 John we read, "If we say we have no sin, we deceive ourselves, and the truth is not in us. If we confess our sins, he who is faithful and just will forgive us our sins and cleanse us from all unrighteousness" (1 John 1:9, NRSV). In James, the confession of sins to another person, perhaps to the elders of the church, occurs in the context of the ministry to the sick—and "the prayer of the righteous is powerful and effective" (James 5:16, NRSV). Confession is connected with healing because it was commonly assumed that sickness was in some way a punishment for sins. Therefore healing was physical, spiritual, and moral—in modern terms, holistic. Orders for the visitation of the sick in the church always included individual confession of sins as well as anointing of the body and Holy Communion.

The confession of sins is regarded as a way to prepare for participation in the Eucharist in the *Didache* (14:1): " Assembling on every Sunday of the Lord, break bread and give thanks, confessing your faults beforehand, so that your sacrifice may be pure."[10] It is possible

10. Niederwimmer, *The Didache*, 194.

that this confession refers to setting things right with a fellow believer with whom one shares the meal since the reference to the purity of one's offering is mentioned in connection with the confession. The *Didache* depends heavily on the Gospel of Matthew, and in the Sermon on the Mount Jesus teaches that we should be reconciled with our brother, particularly if he has something against us, before we offer our gift at the altar (Matt. 5:23–24) The ancient church orders, such as the *Apostolic Constitutions*, devote considerable attention to this ministry of reconciliation. The bishops are instructed to hold court on Monday in order to settle disputes. This allows the greatest amount of time to work out reconciliation between Christians before the Sunday Eucharist.

Forgiveness and reconciliation after baptism is possible. Because of human weakness, a relapse can always occur, but forgiveness is excluded only when the sinner hardens his heart against God, thus committing the "sin against the Holy Spirit" (Matt. 12:31). This sin is unpardonable because the sinner is intent on rejecting grace, and therefore his heart is set against repentance. In the letter to the Hebrews this unpardonable sin is called apostasy, a deliberate renunciation of Christ (Heb. 6:4–6). Apostasy was a big problem in the early church because of intermittent persecution. One of the major controversies of third-century Christianity concerned whether those who lapsed from the faith under persecution could be restored to the communion of the church.

Perhaps this is the issue behind one of the most interesting documents concerning penance in the early church, *The Shepherd*, by Hermas, written in the middle of the second century. Hermas was the brother of Pius I, who was bishop of Rome from 140 to 150. During this time, the church was concerned about the increasing laxity with regard to sin, a concern that gave rise to the Montanist movement. In this imaginative piece of Christian literature the angel of penance says to Hermas that the Lord knew of human weakness and established a means of repentance after baptism, though not all may use it. The implication is that repentance might not be real in many of the baptized, especially if they denied Christ in the Roman court, with plans to seek forgiveness afterwards. Such repentance would not be sincere; it was preplanned and there was no real change of heart. However, after a long and hard penance, a change of heart might be possible. Also, the angel speaks of only one means, which could imply that penance could be used only once in a lifetime.[11]

Public Penance

In spite of the deliberate obscurity this document, it might herald the emergence of the public penance practiced in the church from the second through the sixth centuries.[12] The earliest witness to this public penance is Tertullian of Carthage. In his treatise *On Penitence* (*De Paenitentia*), ca. 200, Tertullian uses the image of a closed door being left slightly ajar. Those who sin after baptism can come into the vestibule for a second penance, but only once. In Tertullian's description the sacrament of penance can be used not only for the big three sins—apostasy, murder, and adultery—but also for all graver sins of flesh or spirit and even for sins committed in the heart. The balancing act involves making penance an unattractive process, but not so unattractive that those who need the cure avoid the remedy. "But if a man is obliged to a second penitence, his spirit must not be cast down. Of course, he should be reluctant to sin again, but to repent again he should not be reluctant. He should be ashamed to place himself again in danger, but to be saved again no one should be ashamed" (7:13).[13]

Tertullian gives us the actual ritual process of penance, which he calls by the Greek word *exomologesis*, "to make a confession." It includes confession, prostration, lying in sackcloth and ashes "to cover his body with filthy rags,"[14] fasting, weeping, bowing before the feet of the

---

11. See Bernhard Poschmann, *Penance and the Anointing of the Sick*, trans. Francis Courtney (New York: Herder & Herder, 1964), 26–35.
12. Ibid., 35–80.
13. Tertullian, *Treatises on Penitence*, trans. and annotated by W. P. LeSaint, Ancient Christian Writers 28 (Westminster, MD: Newman, 1959), 29.
14. Ibid., 31–32.

presbyters, and kneeling before one's fellow believers, asking for their prayers. He writes in *On Penitence 9*:

> Exomologesis does all this in order to render penitence acceptable and in order to honor God through fear of punishment, so that in passing sentence upon the sinner it may itself be a substitute for the wrath of God and, by temporal punishment, I will ot say prevent eternal tormengs but rather cancel them. Therefore, in humbling a man it exalts him. When it defiles him, he is cleansed. In accusing, it excuses. In condemning, it absolves. In proportion as you have had no mercy on yourself, believe me, in just this same measure God will have mercy upon you.[15]

Tertullian acknowledges that public penance is a difficult thing to undertake but nonetheless salutary. He sees a value in bodily mortification, living unwashing, wearing rough sackcloth and ashes, one's face wasted with ashes. "Well, is it fitting that we beg for pardon in scarlet and purple?"[16]

These practices described by Tertullian are replicated in the ancient church orders and carried into the medieval pontificals (books of rituals for bishops). Public penance includes sitting in the vestibule in sackcloth and ashes, hanging one's head in shame, fasting, weeping, bowing to the feet of the presbyters, and kneeling to the congregation as they enter the assembly hall beseeching their prayers.

Debates over public penance were intense during the third and fourth centuries. Some, like the Montanists, held that the church had no authority to forgive sins committed after baptism. Tertullian himself became a Montanist and argued this point in his later treatise *On Purity*. Some advocated a more lenient approach to post-baptismal sin than the one-time public penance. A practice developed one allowing private penance for private sins and requiring public penance for public sins. Both private and public penance extailed temporary excommunication. Ambrose of Milan argued in his *De paenitentia* that someone who has done private penance still needs to be restored to communion through public reconciliation. In Ambrose's discussion it is apparent that there is an examination of the penitent to judge if his

15. Ibid., 32.
16. Ibid., 34.

penitence has been sincere, and the same kind of practices described by Tertullian are in effect—such as weeping, assuming a pitiable condition, and prostrating oneself at the feet of the church's ministers.

St. Jerome (d. 420) makes some incidental comments to Oceanus about the public reconciliation of the Roman lady Fabiola. She had divorced her first husband and married again. After her second husband died she became a penitent by putting on sackcloth and making a public confession of her error before the "whole city of Rome," taking her place in the order of penitents (*ordo paenitentium*). According to Jerome, as a sign of sincere repentance she disheveled her hair, took on a ghastly appearance, and prostrated herself before the bishop, the presbyters, and all the people to ask for their prayers. After she had gone through all this she received reconciliation in the sight of the whole church on "the day before the Pasch" (which could mean Maundy Thursday).[17]

Pope Innocent I (d. 417) is the first explicit witness to the rite of reconciliation being celebrated on Holy Thursday. In his letter to Decentium he writes:

> But on the matter of penitents, whether they are doing penance for more weighty or lighter offences, the custom of the Roman Church makes it clear that they are to be reconciled (*remittendum*) on Holy Thursday unless an illness intervenes. It is the business of the bishop (*sacerdos*) to judge the seriousness of the sins that he may mark the penitent's confession, his weeping and tears, and then order reconciliation (*dimitti*) when he sees there has been a fitting satisfaction.[18]

I should note here that all penitents were reconciled on Holy Thursday so they would be able to receive Holy Communion at the day of its institution.

The old Gelasian Sacramentary provides the basic elements of the rite of reconciliation of the penitents on Holy Thursday as we move into the Western Middle Ages:

---

17. Jerome, *Epistula 77 ad Oceanum* 4, cited in Ephrem Carr and Duane Etienne, "The Rite for Public Reconciliation of Penitents in the Roman Pontifical," *Resonance* 2 (1966), 22.
18. Innocent I, *Epistula 25 ad Decentium* 7, 10; trans. in Ephrem Carr and Duane Etienne, ibid. 23.

- The penitent is led from the church porch or narthex to the "bosom" (*gremio*) of the church.

- He prostrates on the ground.

- He is led and presented to the bishop by the deacon. The text of the deacon's speech is provided.

- The bishop exhorts him and prays over him for reconciliation. Several prayers for reconciliation are provided.

- The greeting of peace is extended and the forgiven sinner takes his place in the ranks of the faithful to receive Communion.

- The Mass of Reconciliation of the Penitents with proper prayers follows.[19]

As this rite was passed on in Carolingian Gaul, litanies and the penitential psalms were added to the beginning of the liturgy in the atrium of the church, as we see in Ordo Romanus L (the Roman Pontifical ca. 950).[20]

In summary, we can conclude the following about the development and practice of canonical public penance: It is seen as a way of extending the forgiveness of sins in baptism one more time. It is observed in close analogue to Christian initiation. It is a celebration of *metanoia*, or reinitiation, into the converting community. It always requires excommunication and aims at reunion with the one who alone has power to forgive sins in his body the church. Thus baptism and penance are closely connected. Incorporation into the body of Christ in Holy Communion is the culmination of the rites of both Christian initiation and penance.

It was inevitable that in the pastoral life of the church the order of catechumens and the order of penitents would be coordinated. Each required enrollment into the order, instruction, and dismissal after

---

19. *Liber Sacramentorum Romanae Aeclesiae Ordinis Anni Circuli (Sacramentarium Gelasianum)*, ed. Leo Cunibert Mohlberg, OSB (Roma: Casa Editrice Herder, 1968), 56–60.

20. Michel Andrieu, *Les Ordines Romani du Haut Moyen Age*, 5 (Louvaion: Spicilegium Sacrum Lovaniense Administration, 1961), XXV, 24–58.

the liturgy of the word by means of prayer, the imposition of hands, fasting, and almsgiving. Intense preparation for baptism and reconciliation occurred during the forty days of Lent, with baptism at the Easter Vigil and reconciliation on Holy Thursday. The focus on preparation of catechumens for baptism and reconciliation of penitents during Lent gave this season both its catechetical and its penitential character. At one time, Ash Wednesday was the day on which ashes were imposed on the sackcloth-wearing penitents. By the tenth century all had become penitents; all received the ashes.

Flagellant Movements

If life in the church was becoming increasingly lax, the religious orders made up for this lack by adopting penitential disciplines, including self-flagellation. There have always been lay people who themselves are not in a position to enter a monastery or join a mendicant order of friars (brothers) who nevertheless identify with them and support them with their prayers and gifts and sometimes adopt their practices as best as they can (as oblates). Wearing hair shirts and self-flogging were voluntary penitential practices taken up also by lay people. One of the most famous of such persons was Sir Thomas More, chancellor of England under King Henry VIII.

During the times of great plagues in the Middle Ages we see the emergence of penitential processions, led by friars and joined by lay people, who asked for God's mercy. This accounts for the emergence of the Flagellant movement in the thirteenth century. In response to plague, political instability, and prophecies of the end of the world great processions were organized in northern Italy in 1260.[21] All ages and classes of society joined them. Clergy and laity, men and women, even young children, scourged themselves in reparation for the sins of the whole world, which had brought about the plagues. Great processions, amounting sometimes to ten thousand people, passed through the cities beating themselves and calling the faithful to

---

21. See R. W. Southern, *Western Society and the Church in the Middle Ages* (New York: Penguin Books, 1970), 275ff.

repentance. With crosses and banners borne before them by the clergy, they marched slowly through the towns. Stripped to the waist and with covered faces, they scourged themselves with leathern thongs until the blood flowed (there are contemporary drawings of the processions), chanting hymns and canticles of the passion of Christ, entering the churches, and prostrating themselves before the altars. This penance continued for thirty-three days in honor of the years of Christ's life on earth. The processions continued in Italy throughout 1260 and by the end of that year had spread to countries beyond the Alps. The ecclesiastical and civil authorities expressed concern about this unsettling display of piety, but gave mixed messages of discouragement and encouragement. While the processions abated for a while, they flared up again in 1347 in the wake of the Black Death that swept across Europe and devastated the continent. Earthquakes in Italy and the scandal of the divided papacy intensified the feeling in the popular mind that the end of the world was at hand and these feelings gave rise to new penitential processions.

The diffusion of the penitential spirit produced popular *laudi*, folk songs of the passion of Christ and the Sorrows of Our Lady. The most famous was *Stabat mater dolorosa* ("The Sorrowful Mother Stood"). One of the most powerful and immediate of medieval poems, it meditates on the suffering of Mary, Jesus Christ's mother, during his crucifixion, and it came to be sung by groups doing the popular devotion known as the Stations of the Cross, which we will discuss in a later chapter.

In the wake of the Flagellant movement many brotherhoods (confraternities) sprang up that were devoted to penance and the corporal works of mercy. The *Battuti* of Siena, Bologna, and Gubbio founded *Case di Dio*, which were centers for devotional and penitential exercises as well as hospices for the sick and the destitute. The confraternities created permanent ecclesiastical organizations, and some have continued, at least as charitable associations, until the present day.

Flagellant movements continued to spring up in various European countries up through the end of the fifteenth century. As the number grew, charismatic leaders emerged within the movement, casting doubts on the necessity or even desirability of the sacraments administered by priests, practicing absolution, casting out evil spirits, and claiming to work miracles. They asserted that the ordinary ecclesiastical jurisdiction was suspended and that their pilgrimages would be continued for thirty-three-and-a-half years. Doubtless some of them hoped to establish a lasting rival to the Catholic Church, but very soon the authorities took action and endeavored to suppress the entire movement. Even so, the message conveyed by the ecclesiastical authorities was unclear; they alternately condemned and supported these movements by the pious, and the Flagellant tendency was by no means eradicated.

The generating cause of these movements was always an obscure mixture of horror concerning the corruption in the church, a desire to imitate the heroic expiations of the great penitents, and apocalyptic vision. In simplest terms, the Flagellant movement was really a revival movement and, like all revival movements, it produced charismatic leaders, accomplished some genuine repentance and good works, but then died down—only to have its fires rekindled again. The Flagellant movement was but one of the manias that afflicted the end of the Middle Ages. Others included the dancing-mania, the Jew-baiting rages, which the Flagellant processions encouraged, the child-crusades, and the like.

Against this background perhaps we can gain a better sense of the rapid spread of the Protestant Reformation. Remember that Luther's Reformation began because of a debate over a penitential issue: whether the pope had the authority to remit eternal as well as temporal punishments for sins by releasing souls from purgatory through letters of indulgences. While the reformers eschewed bodily punishments, they did revive forms of public church discipline that involved excommunication and reconciliation. This was especially modeled in Calvin's Geneva.[22]

22. See Robert Kingdon, "Worship in Geneva Before and After the Reformation," in Karin Maag and John D. Witvliet, eds., *Worship in Medieval and Early Modern Europe: Change and CXontinuity in Religious Practice* (Notre Dame, IN: University of Notre Dame Press, 2004), 41–60.

The Flagellants continued even after the beginning of the Reformation. In France, during the sixteenth century, we find Black, White, and Blue Brotherhoods. At Avignon, in 1574, Catherine de' Medici herself led a procession of Black Penitents. In Paris, in 1583, King Henry III became patron of the White Brotherhood of the Annunciation. On Holy Thursday of that year he organized a great procession from the Augustinians to Notre Dame, in which all the great dignitaries of the realm were obliged to take part. The laughter of the Parisians, however, who treated the whole thing as a jest, obliged the king to withdraw his patronage. There was no laughter in Spain, however, as Blue Penitents wearing hoods to disguise their identities from friends and neighbors paraded their bloodied bodies through the streets, whipping themselves as they went.[23]

A unique penitential exercise in Spain was the *auto de fe*, a theater of penance in which those guilty of certain crimes were paraded through the streets, wearing emblems of their crimes, to the public square where they were given an opportunity to publicly confess their sins and repent before punishment was meted out. If they did repent, they received absolution and ordinary penances rather than severe punishment. Lamentably, heretics and witches were burned at the stake. Repentant heretics received the mercy of being strangled first.[24]

Throughout the seventeenth and eighteenth centuries flagellant processions and self-flagellation were encouraged by the Jesuits in Spain and Austria, as well as in the countries they evangelized. The penitential piety and the flagellant processions took root in Catholic countries, especially in the Philippines, Mexico, and the provinces in South America. The spirit of reparation in Catholic piety in the seventeenth century may even have been a response to the Protestant Reformation. Groups of Catholics took on themselves punishment for the sins of the whole church. This is the reason the flagellants wore hoods: they were not doing penance just for their own sins but for the

23. See Edward Muir, *Ritual in Early Modern Europe* (New York: Cambridge University Press, 1997), 65.
24. Ibid., 205–7.

sins of the whole church. In a sense they were participating, like the apostle Paul, in "the afflictions of Christ" (Col. 1:24).

These processions continue even to the present day in Spain, Central and South America, and the Philippines as part of Holy Week observances. Particularly in the Philippines, the *penitensya* are noteworthy for their bloody realism. While the Catholic hierarchy now tries to discourage these displays of piety, the practice seems to be expanding rather than diminishing. However, it is a spiritual practice in which the participants make their confession and share a fellowship meal together to further the bonds between them before the day of the procession. Like in modern marathon races, first aid stations are available along the penitential routes.[25]

Festival and Carnival

We move now from bodily excesses in penance to bodily excesses in festivals. If penance entails stripping down and punishing the body, a festival is an occasion to dress up and indulge the body. Festivals are known for their costumes, as well as eating and drinking—usually to excess. Indeed, excess is a basic characteristic of festival. In fact, we intentionally overdo it.

Festivals are celebrations. In his important little book, *In Tune with the World*, the German philosopher Josef Pieper calls attention to the elements of rejoicing and affirmation in festival.[26] For Pieper, a festival is a time when we affirm *all* of life by saying yes to part of it. Festival is an affirmation of something good that has happened, and that something is the occasion for the festival. However, we celebrate the good for its own sake, not to accomplish something. We celebrate the liturgical festival because "today Christ is born," because "Christ is risen. Alleluia," because "the Spirit of the Lord fills the whole earth."[27]

Among all liturgically inspired festivals, Carnival is the archetypal

---

25. See http://ireport.cnn.com/docs/DOC-948133.
26. Josef Pieper, *In Tune with the World: A Theory of Festivity*, trans. Richard and Clara Winston (Chicago: Franciscan Herald, 1965).
27. Standard liturgical proclamations for the three major festivals of Christmas, Easter, and Pentecost.

form against which all other festivals must be measured. Carnival occurs just before Ash Wednesday. It is one final splurge of excess before the coming of the time of fasting.

A Carnival season could last from the Epiphany until Ash Wednesday. The word means "farewell to the meat," and refers to eating up the meat before the Lenten fast begins. The last day of Carnival is called *Mardi Gras* in French, which means "fat Tuesday." The great *Mardi Gras* celebration in New Orleans in the United States has lost its liturgical connection with Ash Wednesday. Many churches do hold Fat Tuesday celebrations with traditional meals of pancakes and sausage. The idea was to use up the far, such as butter and milk before Lent. The famous *Mardi Gras* celebration in New Orleans, which includes a parade and parties, is highly secularized.

Throughout history, the very tension between Carnival and Lent suggested a season in which the pieties and social order of Christian life could be mocked and inverted.[28] It was fair game to make fun of bishops and kings in the masquerades, pantomimes, and plays that characterized Carnival in the cities. Carnival was a time when the subordinate groups—servants, the poor, children, and so on—were given license to speak. Role reversal was common, such as men dressing as women and women dressing like men. In Carnival or carnivalesque festivals like Midsummer Night, there was also a great deal of sexual energy.

Carnivalesque-type festivities from the Middle Ages continued in the Reformation, where entertainments were used to mock Catholicism. For example, in Wittenberg during *Fastnacht* (the night before Lent began, called *Fastenzeit* in German), the university students marched through the streets with a sham pope, who was pelted with dung in the marketplace, and chased those portraying the cardinals through the streets of the city. This example illustrates, as Harvey Cox says, that "festivity is not superficiality."[29] It recognizes tragedy. The students and good burghers of Wittenberg must have recognized the tragedy of

28. Muir, *Ritual in Early Modern Europe*, 86–104.
29. Harvey Cox, *The Feast of Fools: A Theological Essay on Festivity and Fantasy* (New York: Harper & Row, 1969), 24–26.

the growing schism in Christendom even as they had fun mocking the pope and the Roman Curia, which they did because of the tremendous grievances they had against the Roman Holy See. Also, says Cox, "Festivity is not frivolity." The students' actions were not frivolous. Flaunting the highest authorities in Europe, whose power still reached into Saxony in spite of the protection of the Elector, was risky. Their frivolity was not disguising a serious situation. But the students sensed the potential for evangelical freedom in their professor's call for reform, and that was something worth celebrating, in spite of the danger their street theater presented to themselves. True festivity requires freedom. Like play, it cannot be coerced. Unlike play, it can be real.

Figure 11. Young Ibans of the Sea Dayak people in Borneo dressing for a festival.

7

Young Bodies, Healthy Bodies

A. Baptism and Confirmation

Societies practice many rites of passage as part of their cultural life. Among them are childbirth, puberty, initiation into adulthood, vocation, marriage, sickness and death. The French comparative sociologist Arnold van Gennep (1873-1957) provides an important interpretation of rites of passage in *Les rites de passage* (published in English in 1960 as *The Rites of Passage*).[1] In the book he offers a structure for transformative ritual practices he considers universal and common to all cultures. Although they vary greatly in intensity, specific form, and social meaning, rites of passage are ceremonies used by societies to mark the passage or transition of an individual or a group from one social status or situation to another. Rites of passage resolve *life crises*; they provide a mechanism for dealing with the tensions experienced by both individuals and social groups during transitional occasions including—but not limited to—birth, puberty, marriage, and death. In chapter 4 I mentioned that Van Gennep compares rites of passage to

---

1. Arnold van Gennep, *The Rites of Passage*, trans. Monika B. Vizedom and Gabrielle L. Caffee (Chicago: University of Chicago Press, 1960).

taking a journey: there is a leave-taking, a transition (called the liminal stage), and an arrival (incorporation into a new status).

These rites of passage are sometimes called "occasional services" or "pastoral offices" in worship books. In this chapter we will focus first on rites for children and youth and then on rites related to health and healing. In chapter 8, we will focus on marriage and burial.

Although this section focuses on rites for children and youth, I want to point out that Christianity has no specifically child or youth rites of passage. In some societies childhood rites are highly developed. For example, the Balinese culture observes a twelve-day ceremony, a forty-two-day ceremony, a three-month ceremony, a touching-the-ground ceremony, a 210-day ceremony, a puberty ceremony, and a tooth-filing ceremony.[2] In Western societies parents mark significant milestones in a child's development, but usually only birthdays merit a festive celebration.

Christianity does not typically provide such rites. While most churches practice infant baptism, baptism itself is not a child rite. Although it is often practiced as a rite celebrated soon after birth in which relatives gather and welcomed a baby into the family, it is actually regarded by the church as a rite of new birth and initiation into the body of Christ. However, because it is so commonly celebrated with newborn infants I will comment on baptism as a youth rite.

In churches that practice only believer's baptism, a special effort is often made to baptize adolescents who are within the orbit of the congregation (for example, whose parents and families are members). Baptism in these churches can also become a sort of puberty rite of initiation (although, again, baptism is not a rite limited to youth). Such churches do, however, offer a rite of welcome and dedication of children born into their families. In the oldest manuscript of the Byzantine liturgy, the *Barberini Euchologion* (ca. 800), there are prayers for infants to be used on the eighth day after birth at the naming of the

---

2. See Gusti Nyoman Darta, Jean Couteau, Georges Breguet, *Time, Rites, and Festivals in Bali* (Indonesia: BAB Books, 2013), 126ff.

child, and on the fortieth day, which are to be used before the child is enrolled as a catechumen.

Churches that practice infant baptism usually have a rite of confirmation or affirmation of baptism. Confirmation need not be only a teenage rite, although the fact that a congregation's confirmation ministry usually includes early adolescents has allowed some characteristics of a puberty rite of passage to accrue to it. In the Jewish tradition there is a puberty rite of passage when a boy becomes *bar mitzvah* (son of the commandments) at age thirteen and a girl becomes *bat mitzvah* (daughter of the commandments) at age twelve. Thereafter they undertake adult responsibilities in the synagogue and in Jewish life. Confirmation in Christian practice has come to be viewed in a similar way, although the age of youth confirmation is arbitrary, ranging from middle school through high school and even college. In churches that confirm baptized youth, an unbaptized youth who attends confirmation class will be baptized first before being confirmed.

Baptism of Infants and Young Children

The church has been willing to baptize infants and young children born into Christian families, perhaps even from the beginning. The Scriptures do not specifically enjoin the baptism of infants, but neither is such baptism forbidden. Rather, the church is commanded to baptize all peoples (Matt. 28:19), and there are examples of whole households being baptized (e.g., Cornelius in Acts 10). The suggestion that the households in Acts might have included children is, admittedly, an argument from silence. In the first two centuries, no direct testimony to the practice of infant baptism can be found, but by the beginning of the third century Tertullian indirectly testifies to the fact. Tertullian was opposed to the practice, which means that it was being done. In *On Baptism* he cites Matt. 19:14, "Forbid them not to come to me," and writes: "So let them come when they are growing up, when they are learning, when they are being taught what they are coming to: let them be made Christians when they have become competent to know

181

Christ. Why should innocent infancy come with haste to the remission of sins?"[3]

According to *The Apostolic Tradition*, Hippolytus of Rome testifies to children being baptized with the women after the baptisms of the men at the beginning of the third century.[4] If the children could not answer for themselves, someone else answered for them. While the time and author of this church order have been questioned, there is no doubt that children were being baptized in the third century. Origen and Cyprian are also witnesses to the practice. Without developing a doctrine of original sin, as Augustine later did, Origen appealed to Old Testament examples of ritual defilements in need of purification and extended baptismal forgiveness to ritual impurity associated with childbirth. In his *Homilies on Leviticus*, Origen states, "While the church's baptism is given for the remission of sin, it is the custom of the church that baptism be administered even to infants. Certainly, if there is nothing in infants that required remission and called for lenient treatment, the grace of baptism would seem unnecessary."[5] As Jean LaPorte points out, it is not the stain of original sin that Origen is referring to here but the defilement of blood (this is a homily on Leviticus!).[6] Origen thus sees baptism as a ritual purification, and the Eastern fathers continued to appeal to Old Testament models such as circumcision.

John Chrysostom, bishop of Constantinople (397–404), argues that infants should be baptized even though they are sinless so that they might be given "further gifts of sanctification":

> You have seen how numerous are the gifts of baptism. Although many men think that the only gift it confers is the remission of sins, we have counted its honors to the number of ten. It is on this account that we baptize even infants, although they are sinless, that they may be given the

3. Tertullian, *De baptismo* 18, in E. C. Whitaker, *Documents of the Baptismal Liturgy*, 2nd ed. (London: SPCK, 1970), 8–9.
4. Bradshaw, Johnson, Phillips, *The Apostolic Tradition*, 112.
5. Origen, *Homilies on Leviticus* 8.3, cited by Johannes Quasten, *Patrology: The Ante-Nicene Literature after Irenaeus* (Westminster, MD: Newman, 1964), 83.
6. Jean LaPorte, "Models from Philo in Origen's Teaching on Original Sin," in *Living Water, Sealing Spirit: Readings on Christian Initiation*, ed. Maxwell E. Johnson (Collegeville, MN: Liturgical Press, 1995), 112–13.

further gifts of sanctification, justice, filial adoption, and inheritance, that they may be brothers and members of Christ, and become dwelling places for the Spirit.[7]

In the Christian East, a tradition arose in which the baptismal theology for infants was adapted from the baptismal theology for adults, with the exception that infant baptism was not understood as a remission of sins, which, in the case of children, was considered unnecessary. But numerous benefits of baptism were stressed for the infant candidates, just as with the adults. Baptism was interpreted in covenantal terms as a union with Christ and all of the graces that flow from him.

As for Augustine of Hippo, it is important to note that the great North African church father did not defend infant baptism on the basis of original sin but taught a doctrine of original sin on the basis of the fact that children were baptized. This was a typical patristic appeal to the *lex orandi* (the rule of prayer) as the basis of the *lex credendi* (the rule of belief). In the context of the Pelagian controversy, Augustine repeated his emphasis that baptism is regeneration, which was made in reference to the Donatist controversy. His argument goes something like this: new life is possible only if sins are forgiven. Since infants are baptized, forgiveness of sin must also apply to them. Since infants are not capable of sinning, the sin forgiven must refer to the sin inherited from their parents and so on, back to Adam and Eve. Later on it was argued that infants should be baptized because they are born in original sin, but Augustine did not make that argument.[8]

Therefore it is clear that the ancient church baptized infants, even though adult baptism was clearly the norm. Everett Ferguson makes a persuasive case on the basis of dates on tombstones that young children were baptized if they were in danger of dying.[9] The bishops assuaged the anxieties of parents about the eternal fate of their children by baptizing them, perhaps when the child was on his or her

---

7. John Chrysostom, *Baptismal Instructions*, trans. Paul Harkins, Ancient Christian Writers 31 (Mahwah, NJ: Paulist, 1963), 56–65.

8. Everett Ferguson, *Baptism in the Early Church: History, Theology, and Liturgy in the First Five Centuries* (Grand Rapids: Eerdmans, 2009), 808–16.

9. Ibid., 372–77.

deathbed (adult deathbed baptisms were also common). After the fifth century the infant mortality rate, which was exacerbated by declining social conditions in the West, prompted parents to rush their children to the font as quickly as possible. At that point in history, the doctrine of original sin provided a justification for the growing normalcy of the practice of infant baptism. However, the doctrine of original sin does not account for the growing normalcy of the practice of infant baptism in the East, though we have seen, the Eastern Church appealed to other "honors" conferred at baptism.

Nevertheless, except for solitary voices like Tertullian's, the church in antiquity never found a reason *not* to baptize infants and young children. Ferguson's argument about the concern of parents to have their children baptized in emergency situations in which the child was likely to die is demonstrated in the life of Augustine himself. Augustine's mother Monica arranged for her son to be baptized when he was seriously ill as a youth but then cancelled the rite when Augustine recovered. Once the practice of infant baptism became more common, church fathers like Augustine were able to further develop views about the efficacy of the sacrament, even with regard to the faith of the infant. Augustine wrote to Bishop Boniface in Numidia with regard to the pastoral issue of Christian parents desiring to have their child baptized:

> Even if that faith that is found in the will of believers does not make a little one a believer, the sacrament of the faith itself, nonetheless, now does so. For, just as the response is given that the little one believes [the response of the parents at the child's baptism], he is also in that sense called a believer, not because he assents to the reality with his mind [the infant cannot assent] but because he receives the sacrament of that reality.[10]

This discussion of the relationship between baptism and the doctrine of original sin emerged in the heat of the Pelagian controversy, which was thought to undermine the absolute necessity of God's grace. But I would like to step back and look at baptism in the light of Augustine's less polemical writings, especially his *Confessions*. In this spiritual

10. Augustine, *Letter* 98.10, p. 432; cited in Ferguson, *Baptism in the Early Church*, 807.

autobiography Augustine records that he was enrolled as a catechumen on his eighth day. His mother Monica was a baptized Christian; his father Patricius was a Christian catechumen. This was a usual arrangement at the time. Women were more likely to receive the water-bath than men because they did not have public responsibilities that might compromise the values of the gospel. Having not received the water-bath as a youth, Augustine delayed his own baptism until the age of thirty, when he was under the influence of Ambrose of Milan. Yet, between his enrollment as a catechumen and his baptism and first communion at the age of thirty, Augustine still regarded himself as a Christian. He had received the sign of the cross at his enrollment, which he counted among the many *sacramenta* that were included in Christian initiation. "As a catechumen, I was blessed regularly from birth with the sign of the Cross and was seasoned with salt, for, O Lord, my mother placed great hope in you."[11]

The norm of Christian initiation entailed a whole ritual process that led from enrollment into the catechumenate, the catechumenate itself, election as a candidate for baptism, the water-bath, the Spirit-related ceremonies of anointing and the laying on of hands, the kiss of peace and welcome into the assembly, and first communion. The catechumenate was a process that could last three years or even a lifetime. If infants were baptized, they could not experience the learning and ministry activities of the catechumenate. The catechumenal acts were truncated to the recitation of the Apostles' Creed and Lord's Prayer by the godparents. However, the exorcisms that also accompanied the catechumenal process remained, and since all of the exorcisms were retained in the preliminary rite, the role of exorcism was magnified in the medieval order of baptism (exorcism is discussed in the second part of this chapter). The essential elements of the water rite remained in the medieval order: the blessing of the water; a three-fold renunciation of Satan and a three-fold profession of faith in creedal form; an anointing of the child between the shoulders; a triple immersion in the name of the Father, Son, and Holy Spirit; an

11. Saint Augustine, *Confessions* 1.11, trans. R. S. Pine-Coffin (Baltimore: Penguin Books, 1961), 31.

anointing with chrism on the back of the head; being clothed in a white baptismal dress; and the presentation of a lighted candle.

At this point in history, some dislocations took place in regard to the rite. Baptisms could still be celebrated at Easter or Pentecost if the child was born within eight days of either feast. If the bishop was present, the post-baptismal ceremonies (what became the rite of confirmation) were completed, and the child was communed. But increasingly the rite was performed in the parish church as soon after birth as possible. In this case the local presbyter (priest) presided. However, the bishop retained his prerogative to be the minister of initiation. His role was primarily associated with the post-baptismal anointing and laying on of hands. As a result, this part of the order was lopped off and became a separate sacrament of confirmation.

Children could still receive Communion at their baptism. While an infant could not swallow the bread, the priest could dip his finger in the cup of wine, and the infant could suck the wine off the priest's finger. The doctrine of concomitance (which held that the entire Christ is received under either species) made it possible to commune infants in one kind only—the wine. However, growing scrupulosity over spilling the precious blood of Christ in the transmission of the cup led to the removal of the cup from lay communicants. The East solved the problem by communing the faithful using intinction (dipping the bread in the cup of wine), which was done by breaking the communion bread into pieces in the cup and then communing the faithful from a spoon. In the West the cup was simply removed from lay communicants. At that point in time, infants received neither the bread nor the cup. When the Fourth Lateran Council in 1215 prescribed that all of the faithful who had attained the age of discretion (seven years) were under obligation to make a confession to the priest before receiving Communion and forbade the administration of first communion before confirmation (a practice that would be continued in the Protestant churches), this effectively stopped the practice of infant communion (except in places like Bohemia, which continued to commune infants). Thus we come to the end of the Middle Ages in the West with the ancient church's unitary rites of Christian initiation broken up into separate sacraments that were theologically interpreted as separate means of grace: baptism, confirmation, and communion.[12] The infant norm was assumed in both Catholic and emerging Protestant orders of baptism.

In 1523 Luther translated the medieval order of baptism from the 1493 Magdeburg Agenda into German. He revised it in 1526, drastically simplifying the order by using the Gospel text from Mark 10:13–16 ("And they brought little children to him . . . "). Other Reformation orders followed. While Lutheran orders retained a brief exorcism, the sign of the cross, Luther's "flood prayer" as a kind of blessing of the font, vesting of the child in the baptismal dress, and presenting the lighted candle, the Reformed order eliminated all "ceremonies" except the use of water itself. The Anglican Prayer Book order was closer to the Lutheran order but added a thanksgiving for the regeneration of the child and an admonition to the godparents.

Sixteenth-century practice assumed the continued immersion of the naked baby. This practice continued in the Eastern Orthodox churches. But by the seventeenth century the mode of baptism in both Protestant and Catholic practice became affusion (pouring) on the head rather than immersion. As less water was needed the fonts became smaller, and the child was not undressed.

The naming of the child is associated with the pouring of the water ([Name], I baptize you in the name of the Father, and of the Son, and of the Holy Spirit). At the beginning of the Catholic order the priest asks the parents, "What name have you given your child?" The act of naming someone or something has come to be called a christening (from the name of Christ), and this aspect of child baptism has become so important that sometimes the whole order is referred to as a christening rather than baptism. The public naming of the child became so important that churches that do not practice infant or child baptism nevertheless provide a rite for the naming and dedication of a child born into a Christian family.

---

12. See J. D. C. Fisher, *Christian Initiation: Baptism in the Medieval West* (London: SPCK, 1965).

When missions to non-Christian lands began producing adult converts, distinct orders for the baptism of adults and the baptism of children were developed rather than one order of baptism for all candidates no matter what the age. The 1662 *Book of Common Prayer* includes an order of baptism for use with those who are able to answer for themselves, which basically amounts to changing the Scripture reading, admonition, and questions.

Recent liturgies of Holy Baptism have tried to recover the creedal confession of "one baptism for the forgiveness of sins." I hold up as one example the order for Holy Baptism in the *Lutheran Book of Worship* (1978), which is intended for use with both children and adults. It restores the post-baptismal ceremonies of the laying on of hands, anointing with oil (the seal of the Spirit), and the presentation of the lighted candle. *Evangelical Lutheran Worship* (2006) added a provision for vesting the newly baptized after the water-bath. In chapter 3, I raised the possibility of returning to the practice of baptizing babies naked, as the Orthodox continue to do. This requires fonts with enough depth and width to get a baby immersed or even submersed in the water. By so doing, it makes sense to dress the baby in the white baptismal garment after the baptism.

Here I have only indicated the changes that occurred in orders of baptism when infant baptism became a more common and even normative practice. But I want to stress again that baptism is not an infant rite; it is a rite that is applied to infants who are included in the "all people" to whom Jesus refers when he commissions his apostles to go, teaching, baptizing, and making disciples (Matt. 28:16–20).

Many churches continue to practice infant baptism, and it has received additional support from feminist theology. In her book, *Fragments of Real Presence: Liturgical Traditions in the Hands of Women*, Teresa Berger writes about the disconnect between the birthing waters of the womb and the birthing waters of baptism. The closeness of these two "bodies" of water is apparent, and the dissonance between them in liturgical settings, she suggests, is yet another consequence of the erasure of women from liturgical history and theology. The lived experiences of women are not taken into consideration in traditional liturgical theology. But Berger notes that while images of death and resurrection are prominent in understanding baptism, some traditions, especially in Syria, emphasize birthing and adoption.[13]

In a way typical of feminist theological methodology, Berger looks to her own experience of nurturing and birthing her son to construct a theology of baptism that brings the waters of the womb and the font into intimate contact. She begins by suggesting that focusing on natality—the simple fact that every human being is birthed of a woman's womb—can help to bridge this dissonance. Second, she suggests that pregnancy can be viewed as a type of catechumenate, an intimate time of spiritual preparation during which a child is prepared for birthing into the physical world. Here, Berger recounts how her pregnancy was a deeply spiritual time, during which she prayed with her son, sang songs of praise with him, and read the Scriptures out loud to him. She touched the place where she felt his face at the time of the kiss of peace during Mass. She even allowed a woman pastor-friend to pray for her child with the laying on of hands, just prior to his birth. It was a deeply spiritual time for her and her son, together. This prenatal period has long been a field of interest to medical professionals, who have determined that a child is able to recognize the voice of her parents very early in the pregnancy and that, during later months, the child becomes fully responsive. Berger asserts that this prenatal period should be left to medical professionals to define and that theologians should move their conversations away from abortion and toward the ways in which the womb is a site for a child's first spiritual formation, particularly in the lives of the unborn children of Christians.

Berger suggests three ways that we can take concrete, liturgical steps towards reclaiming baptism as an act of birthing (see John 3:5). First, we can look at pregnancy as a sacramental time, which divulges a unique insight into the heart of God towards creation. Second, we can acknowledge the unborn in concrete ways, such as writing their

---

13. Teresa Berger, *Fragments of Real Presence: Liturgical Traditions in the Hands of Women* (New York: Crossroads, 2005).

names in the book of life, thereby seeking the prayers of the people as the child is developing in the waters of the womb. She notes that this practice would be especially helpful in the event of a miscarriage or stillbirth since mothers often have anxiety over the fate of their unborn children. Finally, we can create liturgical resources that draw on this image and explicitly name God as a maternal figure who gives birth through baptism. The Holy Spirit is the creative energy of God, and the East Syrian tradition refers to the Spirit in the feminine gender as "she." Liturgical resources developed for this purpose could make specific references to this usage. In addition, the actual celebration of the baptism of the newborn infant could replicate the experience of infant care, complete with immersion of the child in the bath water, anointing of the child with baby oil (which often occurs after a bath), and wrapping the child in a warm white blanket after the water-bath takes place.

Baptism as a Puberty Rite

The practice of infant baptism was categorically rejected in the sixteenth century by the Anabaptists, who insisted on baptizing only those who could make a conscious confession of faith. The name "Anabaptist" originates from their practice of rebaptizing persons who had already been baptized. Anabaptist communities like the Mennonites thereafter only practiced the baptism of believers.

The English Baptists were offshoots of the Puritan Separatists and were influenced by the example of the Mennonites in the Netherlands. The Anabaptists and the Baptists who followed them were primarily concerned to create a church of true believers; infant baptism, at least within the context of the society of Christendom, made the church indistinguishable from the rest of society. The Anabaptists therefore "re-baptized" those who made a profession of faith and did not count the original baptism as valid. The Baptists, as a matter of principle, only practiced a "believer's baptism" and made no provision for the baptism of infants or young children. The problem of what to do with the children of Christian families was solved with a child dedication rite, which could suggest the possibility of enrollment as a catechumen as in the ancient church. At first the Baptists followed the practice of the Puritans and Separatists and used the mode pouring or sprinkling water over the heads of the candidates. They later opted for the more ancient example of immersion and usually insisted on total submersion.

Since Baptist meetinghouses did not have baptismal facilities indoors, a river, stream, or pond frequently sufficed. The event was typically public and drew attention of townspeople and differing faiths. Inclement weather was not a deterrent for early North American Baptists who wished to baptize outdoors. New England and Canadian Baptist records are replete with episodes of winter baptisms for which ministers broke the ice on ponds or rivers and candidates were baptized in ice-cold water. Some Baptist congregations, however, held off on baptisms until Easter.

In the 1800s, especially in the northern regions, new church buildings featured indoor baptisteries that were usually located under the floor of the pulpit area. An exceptional example of American Baptist baptismal architecture was created at the Sansom Street Baptist meetinghouse in Philadelphia. Designed by Pastor William Staughton (1770–1829), a baptistery in the center of a circular auditorium emphasized baptism as a central feature of the church. A tank or baptismal pool became a fixed feature of the architectural designs of Baptist churches and the churches of other denominations that performed only believer's baptisms.

We must keep in mind that churches practicing infant baptism also practice the baptism of older youth and adults. In many parts of the world today adult baptism in these churches is as common as infant baptism. Consequently, liturgical renewal in the late twentieth century addressed the need for more robust adult rites of initiation. Accordingly, liturgical revision tried to recover some of the more ancient practices that had fallen away during the Middle Ages in the Rite of Christian Initiation of Adults (RCIA), which was promulgated in the Roman Catholic Church in 1972. This ritual process replicates the sequence of catechumenate, election, water-baptism, Spirit-conferral, first communion, and mystagogy that is found in the ancient church orders. Versions of the RCIA have been implemented in other denominations (e.g., Anglican, Lutheran, Methodist, and Reformed). The RCIA restores many of the ancient ceremonies that impact the body.

One of the noteworthy features of church architecture in the late twentieth century has been the provision of larger fonts with flowing water and baptismal pools in Greek Orthodox, Roman Catholic, and mainline Protestant churches, since these churches baptize older youths and adults as well as infants. Advocates of liturgical renewal have shown an interest in larger fonts and the use of more water for baptism, just as they have shown a preference for real loaves of bread and shared chalices of wine for Holy Communion. Some of the new baptismal pools in Roman Catholic churches are very impressive. One of the most impressive I have seen is the circular pool at St. Benedict the African Roman Catholic Church in Chicago, which is partly surrounded by a curved, sloping walkway that leads from the church entrance down to the level of the main worship space. The entire space of St. Benedict the African suggests an African hut, which reflects the African American heritage of the parish church and the surrounding community. I saw some baptismal pools in Roman Catholic, Anglican, Lutheran, Methodist, and Presbyterian churches in Singapore, including outdoor pools at both Covenant Presbyterian Church and Yishun Christian Church in Singapore (which houses both Anglican and Lutheran congregations). Especially impressive is the combined font and pool at St. Mary of the Angels Roman Catholic Church, Bukit Batok, Singapore. This modern building has a massive tomb-shaped pool cut from a single piece of Chinese black granite; a smaller font higher up allows water to flow down into the pool. The font/pool is located in the center of the worship space, suggesting the centrality of baptism for the life of the church. The black font contrasts with the white granite altar, which suggests the concept of yin-yang in the Asian cultural context.

Figure 12a. The baptismal font and pool in St. Mary of the Angels Catholic Church in Singapore.

The appearance of immersion pools in churches that also practice paedobaptism (infant baptism) and the use of more water will prompt more ministers and candidates to go into the water, raising the issue of

193

what to wear in the water. I have already commented on the Orthodox practice of baptizing babies naked. While the Orthodox are not particularly adverse to baptizing naked youth and adults, for the sake of modesty and as an accommodation to Western cultural sensitivities priests usually allow older candidates to wear white underwear or bathing suits and sometimes even shorts and a white t-shirt. Some Baptists provide their candidates with a white gown to wear over one's underwear or bathing suit or clothes. In most instances ministers and candidates go into pools, lakes, and streams wearing their clothes. But this carries modesty to an extreme; one does not wear clothes to take a bath.

Western people and Western Christians in particular feel a sense of shame about their bodies that can have unfortunate psychological consequences. Adolescents especially are self-consciousness about being even partially undressed in certain public settings. The changes to the body that occur in puberty often make adolescents feel self-conscious and awkward about their bodies. Adolescent girls appear to be particularly vulnerable to developing a negative body image, which is exacerbated by commercial portrayals of "ideal" bodies. The exposure of bodies virtually and in the flesh for sexually exploitative commercial purposes is ubiquitous in Western or Westernized cultures. A Christian counteroffensive might be a willingness to practice baptisms that look more like a bath and to encourage by example the acceptance of our bodies as gifts of God, especially in the baptismal situation of utter holiness. Tied in with the teaching that baptism makes them a child of God, precious in God's sight, catechesis of youth should help them develop a better self-image. Since the body is acted upon in the initiatory sacraments, it seems fitting that some attention should be given to bodily care and self-esteem.

What is done with bodies in baptism? Catholics practice immersion, in which the candidate stands in the pool and water is poured over the candidate's head. Baptists practice submersion, in which the minister places one hand over the candidate's face and the other hand around the candidate's back for support while the candidate holds his or her nose and the minister bends the candidate backwards into the water. This is done three times—in the name of the Father, Son, and Holy Spirit (although some Baptists baptize only in the name of Jesus). There's no doubt that this can be a scary experience, particularly for young adolescents who might be afraid of the water. In any event, the newly baptized emerge from the water, dripping wet; thankfully, churches that practice immersion or submersion provide changing facilities. In this way, it is still possible to put on new white baptismal clothes even if one is bathed in clothing.

As we consider baptism as a rite that is also applied to youth, it is interesting to point out that Baptists hold different beliefs concerning the timing of baptism for children who profess faith in Christ. Some argue for "immediate participation," meaning that children should be baptized as soon as they can confess faith in Christ at their own level of comprehension. This can mean that very young children are baptized (which moves Baptists closer to paedobaptists in their actual practice). But most Baptist congregations wait to baptize children until there is evidence of regeneration and the ability to reason independently in spiritual matters, which is around age eleven or twelve (which brings Baptist youth close in age to confirmation youth in other churches). Just as larger Protestant congregations send a letter of invitation to parents advising them of the beginning of an age- or grade-appropriate confirmation class, some large Baptist congregations send letters to parents of prospective baptismal candidates, inviting them to speak with their youth about baptism. Some congregations provide mentors for their youth candidates (which is not unlike godparents in paedobaptist churches). Instruction classes are arranged for mentors and candidates in which candidates share their testimonies with the group and learn about the meaning of baptism, the distinctive Baptist heritage, and the responsibilities of church membership. The candidates are then scheduled for a future baptismal service. Some congregations even plan a special youth baptismal service that includes candidate testimonies, a pastoral message to the candidates, and the baptisms. Parents are able to help the young person into and out of the water, and the rite concludes with a time for family and friends to gather around the young candidate, lay hands on him or her and pray, which is not unlike the post-baptismal elements of rite that became the separate rite of confirmation. To offer a rite of church membership at a later time begs the question of the relationship between baptism and church membership.

Confirmation as a Rite of Passage

The rite of confirmation has a murky origin and an even more muddled theology. The most cogent explanation for its origins is that bishops retained their prerogative to be the minister of initiation even when baptisms were increasingly celebrated in parish churches. The portion of the rite they retained for themselves was the laying on of hands to petition the gifts of the Holy Spirit, the anointing of the forehead as the seal of the Spirit, and the greeting of peace. Hence the baptized were either brought to the bishop, or the bishop visited the parishes to do the confirmations.[14] This rite applied to any person who had been baptized, no matter the age. But with the prevalence of infant baptism, the candidates for confirmation tended to be older children and youth.

The delay of confirmation by the bishop altered the sequence of Christian initiation. The elements of rite associated with confirmation (laying on of hands, chrismation, and the greeting of peace) should have been the hinge between the baptism and first communion. Since it was possible to commune infants, the hinge was dislocated. The Fourth Lateran Council rectified this situation by decreeing that Communion should be given after confirmation, which was to be administered only on reaching the age of reason. However, by the time of Lateran IV (1215), infant communion was no longer practiced in most of the Western church. First communion was to be administered only when the child reached an age of discretion as a result of the requirement that one make a confession to a priest before receiving

---

14. There was some confusion over which particular rite—the laying on of hands or the anointing—was unique to the bishop's ministry. See Maxwell E. Johnson, *The Rites of Christian Initiation: Their Evolution and Interpretation* (Collegeville, MN: Liturgical Press, 1999), 204–7.

communion, which was also set at the age of discretion. Thus, both penance and confirmation were to occur before first communion. Sometime after the thirteenth century, the age of confirmation and first communion began to be delayed further—from seven, to twelve, and even to fifteen years of age after the Reformation.

While recommending that confirmation be delayed until seven years of age, the 1917 Code of Canon Law in the Roman Catholic Church still allowed it to be given at an earlier age.[15] In 1932 the Sacred Congregation for the Sacraments allowed, as necessary, confirmation to be administered *after* first communion. This novelty, originally seen as exceptional, became more and more the accepted practice as the age of first communion remained at seven or eight but confirmation became an adolescent rite that was regarded as an occasion for professing personal commitment to the faith on the part of someone approaching adulthood. In other words, confirmation became a rite of passage from childhood faith to a more "mature faith," which has precipitated a pastoral discussion over how "mature" a youth should be in order to undergo a rite in which a mature faith is professed.

What does the rite of confirmation mean when it is separated temporally and spatially from baptism? A homily attributed to Faustus of Riez, a fifth-century south Gallican bishop, provides an example of what became the classic Western theology of confirmation:

> What the imposition of hands bestows in confirming individual neophytes, the descent of the Holy Spirit gave people then in the world of believers . . . The Holy Spirit, who descends upon the waters of baptism by a salvific falling, bestows on the font a fullness toward innocence, and presents in confirmation an increase for grace. And because in this world we who will be prevailing must walk in every age between invisible enemies and dangers, we are reborn in baptism for life, and we are confirmed after baptism for strife. In baptism we are washed; after baptism we are strengthened. And although the benefits of rebirth suffice immediately for those about to die, nevertheless the helps of confirmation are necessary for those who will prevail. Rebirth in itself immediately saves those needing to be received in the peace of the blessed age.

---

15. See Gerard Austin, *The Rite of Confirmation: Anointing with the Spirit* (New York: Pueblo, 1985), 29.

Confirmation arms and supplies those needing to be preserved for the struggles and battles of this world.[16]

The discussion of the possibility of dying after baptism might still reflect the kind of emergency health situations that prompted parents to bring their children to the font. If the child lives, maintains Faustus, confirmation is needed to equip the young Christian to do spiritual combat against spiritual enemies. The grace of confirmation strengthens one to be a soldier of Christ in the church militant. In this connection, the gesture used while saying *Pax tecum* (Peace be with you) to the person he had just confirmed was interpreted in the Roman Pontifical as a slap, a reminder to be brave in spreading and defending the faith: *Deinde leviter eum in maxilla caedit, dicens: Pax tecum* (Then he strikes him lightly on the cheek, saying: Peace be with you.). The gesture actually was more of a caress on the cheek. It was omitted in the revised rite of confirmation in 1971, but some episcopal conferences allow the gesture to be continued. Just as some adolescent Baptist youths might be apprehensive about being submerged in the water at their baptism, so some Roman Catholic youths have fretted over the bishop's slap in the face.

Confirmation was administered haphazardly during the Middle Ages. Sometimes an episcopal visit consisted of little more than the bishop riding through a village on horseback, laying hands on youth who were lined up along the way as he went. Not surprisingly, parents also neglected to get their youth to the bishop's church for this extra rite. Martin Luther called confirmation "monkey business" (*apfenspiel*) and emphasized catechetical instruction instead, for which he provided a *Large Catechism* and a *Small Catechism* that Lutherans use to this day. In some church orders the gesture of the laying on of hands by the pastor continued. In Strassburg, Martin Bucer prepared an evangelical rite of confirmation with laying on of hands in blessing to be used at the completion of a period of catechetical instruction. The rite was construed as a renewal of baptismal vows and was a response

16. *Corpus Christianorum, Series Latina* 101, 37f., in *Sources of Confirmation: From the Fathers through the Reformers,* trans. Paul Turner (Collegeville, MN: Liturgical Press, 1993), 35–36.

to Anabaptist accusations that the magisterial Reformation allowed "moral laxity" by practicing infant baptism.

By the end of the seventeenth century Lutheran and Reformed pietists seized on the idea of confirmation as a renewal of baptismal promises and made it an opportunity for adolescents who were baptized in infancy to make a personal profession of faith. In Prussia confirmation became a maturity rite that made young men eligible for higher education or apprenticeship and young women eligible for "finishing school" or to "come out" in society, meaning they were eligible for marriage. Confirmation was only administered to those who had finished elementary school, and it was required in order to become a communicant member of the church and to be married in the church. Rationalists explained that while baptism made one a Christian, confirmation made one a member of the church. If the pietists looked for confirmation to be a conversion experience, the rationalists turned it into a festival of youth. Like baptism, it became a great family celebration. These pietistic and rationalist strains were also brought into the Scandinavian state and folk churches, and confirmation instruction was tied in with the public education system. Confirmation and graduation from elementary school occurred in close proximity. For all of these reasons, confirmation was clearly construed as a rite of passage from childhood to adulthood.[17]

Lutheran immigrants brought these traditions to America and other parts of the world. Confirmation classes were organized and taught by the pastor. The content centered on the Bible and the catechism. Students between the ages of twelve to fifteen went through two or three years of instruction that in more recent times has included confirmation camps, retreats, and hands-on experiences such as mission projects. Engagement in acts of ministry, such as serving soup kitchens or helping in a homeless shelter, allows confirmation students to experience faith in practical ways that employ the body as well as the mind. At the end of their period of study the candidates are publicly examined, which historically took place before the whole

17. See Arthur C. Repp, *Confirmation in the Lutheran Church* (St. Louis: Concordia, 1964), 61–84.

congregation, with the pastor asking questions and the youth giving rote answers. In more recent times it has become more of a guided conversation with leaders of the congregation. The rite of confirmation tends to be celebrated on or about the day of Pentecost and is construed as an affirmation of baptism.

What difference does confirmation make? What does one "get" for being confirmed? In increasing measure, first communion has been separated from confirmation. Some suggest that one is given the opportunity to exercise adult responsibilities in the life of the church after being confirmed, such as serving on committees or the church council. In this way, the idea of confirmation as a kind of youth rite of passage similar to bar/bat mitzvah lingers on.

A Youth Rite of Passage: *Quinceañera*

Other youth rites of passage that are associated with particular ethnic traditions are held at about the same age as confirmation, such as *Quinceañera* (the feminine form of "fifteen years old" in Spanish), also called *fiesta de quince años, fiesta de quinceañera, quince años,* or simply *quince.* This is the celebration of a girl's fifteenth birthday in parts of Latin America and among Mexican-Americans. This birthday clearly marks the transition from childhood to young womanhood. It is celebrated as a kind of "coming out" party or cotillion, which once upon a time publicly signified that the girl was prepared to be married. In the years prior to their fifteenth birthdays, girls were taught to cook and weave as well as bear and rear children by the elder women in their communities in preparation for their lives as married women. Although it is agreed that the traditions of *quinceañeras* originated in ancient Aztec culture, the celebrations today have a pronounced religious overtone.

On her fifteenth birthday a Mexican or Mexican-American girl will go through a rite of dedication to the Blessed Virgin Mary and a renewal of baptismal vows in a church ceremony, which is attended by several other young ladies and young men. The event might be preceded by classes that cover such topics as marriage, sex and family, and the meaning of the sacraments of initiation (especially our baptismal calling, the role of Mary, and prayer in general), as well as dating, friendship, and relationships. While most commonly celebrated in Catholic parishes, Protestant congregations in Latin America also observe this rite of passage and provide appropriate religious instruction (but not the dedication of the girl to the Blessed Virgin Mary). The religious service is usually followed by a formal party or dance, or a less formal event.

A Youth Rite: Diving for the Cross

The Orthodox churches do not have a rite of confirmation such as the Western churches have, but this does not mean that the educational component of "youth ministry" falls out of the picture in Orthodox church life. Along these lines, the Greek Orthodox Church has its own way of enabling young men to renew their baptism: diving for the cross on the feast of Epiphany (January 6). A custom observed in Greece, Bulgaria, and other southeastern European countries, this ritual for young men was brought by immigrants to their new homes in other countries.

The tradition is carried on in Tarpon Springs, Florida, a town on the Gulf of Mexico known for its sponge diving and Greek heritage. Greek Orthodox boys, ages sixteen to eighteen, participate in the event. The day begins with an 8:00 a.m. Divine Liturgy at St. Nicholas Greek Orthodox Cathedral. Barefoot and wearing bathing trunks and white t-shirts imprinted with "Epiphany Day" and an image of the cross, the divers march through the streets to Spring Bayou. They are blessed by the archbishop, board rowboats, and circle a designated area. Following the release of a dove (a symbol of baptism), the bishop tosses a handmade white cross into the waters of the bayou, and the boys dive into the chilly waters, each frantically trying to be the one to retrieve the cross, as thousands of spectators watch their every move. The dive is understood as a ritual that recalls Jesus' baptism by John the Baptist in the River Jordan. It is also the culmination of an intentional effort on the part of the Greek Orthodox Church to steep the young men in the tradition of the church and form them as faithful Christians. A local newspaper article reports, "As his parents stood nearby holding his towel, Michael Vlamakis, 17, of Palm Harbor, tried to imagine what the dive would be like. 'I feel like it would be almost like experiencing the baptism of Christ again,' he said. 'It's like a leap of faith.'"[18] Local tradition plays a big role in this practice because the boys' fathers and grandfathers, uncles and cousins, and perhaps older brothers have participated in the dive. It is considered to be both a spiritual and a cultural event—an affirmation of baptism.

Figure 12b. Boys diving for the cross on Epiphany Day in Tarpon Springs, Florida. This annual tradition in the Greek Orthodox Church is considered to be an affirmation of baptism.

B. Ministries of Healing and Exorcism

Christianity received from the Hebrew Scriptures the view that the created world is inherently good (Genesis 1). Like Judaism, Christianity holds that the creation and the human body are good and should be

---

18. Stephanie Wang and Keyonna Summers, "First-Timer Grabs the Epiphany Cross in Tarpon Springs," *Tampa Bay Times*, January 6, 2013, http://www.tampabay.com/news/humaninterest/first-timer-grabs-the-epiphany-cross-in-tarpon-springs/1269275.

cared for. The hope of the resurrection and the promise of eternal life do not mean that we should ignore human need in this world. The ministry of Jesus included healing the sick and casting out demons as signs of the wholeness of life brought about by the coming of the kingdom of God; Jesus' healing ministry set a model for the early church.

The sociologist Rodney Stark argues that Christianity's attention to health and wellness facilitated its rise in the Greco-Roman. During the early centuries of Christian growth, a series of natural disasters (including earthquakes and epidemics) disrupted the Roman Empire. Stark believes that "Christianity offered a much more satisfactory account of why these terrible times had fallen upon humanity, and it projected a hopeful, even enthusiastic, portrait of the future."[19] Stark also points out that the chaos associated with urban living during this period of history—with its disease, misery, and fear—provided Christians with the opportunity not only to imagine a better world in the distant future but also solutions for present-day problems. The church community provided a social net in which the needs of widows and orphans were met and the sick were nursed, their infections and sores ministered to. The poor were clothed and fed, and regular housecleaning made for a cleaner living environment. Each of these practices attended to the needs of the body and helped to keep bodies healthy.

Ministries to the sick and dying continued throughout the history of the church. The medieval monasteries took care of the sick and became hospices for the dying. When the monasteries were dissolved during the Reformation, the former cloisters often became hospitals, and former monks and nuns continued their former work of caring for the sick. Spurred on by the Reformers, common chests were set up in the cities to care for the needs of the destitute. In the name of Christ and the common good, congregations, cities, and private citizens took it upon themselves to create health-care institutions that cared for all

---

19. Rodney Stark, *The Rise of Christianity: How the Obscure, Marginal Jesus Movement Became the Dominant Religious Force in the Western World in a Few Centuries* (Princeton: Princeton University Press, 1996), 74.

people. Pietistic centers of activity, such as Halle, Germany, developed orphanages, homes for the elderly, hospitals, sanitariums, clinics, and even the occupation of family physician. In the eighteenth and nineteenth centuries, Methodists in Great Britain worked for greater justice in society, such as abolition of the slave trade, better working conditions for laborers, and a healthier society. By working to reform orphanages and workhouses, they helped to put an end to child labor, torturous punishments, and filthy conditions. In Germany, pietistic inner-mission societies engaged in the same work. By the twentieth century, secular versions of their ideas helped to create the social-safety net for the poor, which can still be found in most developed nations, especially in northern and western Europe. In the United States, a different vision of public health reform depended less on government action. Christians of all sorts, such as Lutheran pastor William Passavant (1821–1894), built health institutions across the nation. Their vision stretched from the founding of hospitals and nursing homes to the founding of hospices and neighborhood clinics. Christians in the United States today lobby for government policies that help feed poor people and reduce poverty not only in the United States but also throughout the world.

A positive Christian view of the body lies in the background of the development of modern physical fitness. One of the important influences on modern physical education was the "Swedish System" founded by Pehr-Henrik Ling (1776–1839), the son of a Lutheran pastor who studied theology at Lund University and finished his degree at Uppsala. As a result of his own experiences with exercise (he was also a fencing master at Lund University), he studied anatomy, physiology, and medicine. Aware of the contemporary work of Friedrich Jahn in Germany, who is considered "the father of gymnastics," Ling developed a medical or therapeutic form of "light gymnastics" that, in comparison with the German "heavy gymnastics," employed little if any equipment apparatus and focused on calisthenics, breathing, and stretching exercises, as well as massage. In 1813, Ling promoted these practices through the Royal Gymnastic Training Institute in

Stockholm, which he founded with government cooperation, serving as its principal. (Contrary to what some have claimed, he was not the father of "Swedish massage." But the true pioneer of this massage modality, the Dutch physician Georg Johann Mezger, named it "Swedish" in honor of Ling.)

Ling's theories and practices became influential not only in the physical education philosophy of school systems in Europe and North America but also in the physical training of military recruits through the use of calisthenics. Ideas of physical fitness were promoted by the Young Men's Christian Association (YMCA), which was founded in London by George Williams in 1844 as an explicitly Christian organization. As it spread across the British Empire and arrived in the United States, the YMCA quickly became an international organization that aimed to put Christian principles into practice by developing a healthy "body, mind, and spirit." The work of the YMCA in India was significant, including its influence on the development of Hatha postural yoga.[20] From its beginnings as a Bible study group for young men it became a major youth organization dedicated to physical fitness. In 1869 the first YMCA building with gymnasiums opened, and swimming pools soon followed. Boston YMCA staffer Robert J. Roberts is credited with coining the term "bodybuilding" in 1881. He developed exercise classes that anticipated today's fitness workouts. The YMCA is also credited with inventing basketball for use in its urban gyms and volleyball for use in its summer camps. As an organization associated with the nineteenth century physical culture movement, the YMCA promoted fit bodies and healthy living, and boys and men exercised and swam naked until the 1970s when the YMCA opened its membership to women and girls. We also need to note that the male camaraderie of the YMCA (many of its "secretaries" [directors] were lifelong bachelors) fostered intimate male relationships and a culture of "cruising" by single men that flourished in YMCA gyms and hotels. This homoerotic presence in the Ys diminished in the 1970s with the

20. See Mark Singleton, *Yoga Body: The Origins of Modern Posture Practice* (Oxford and New York: Oxford University Press, 2010), 91–94.

advent of the gay liberation movement and the emergence of other venues for gay meetups.[21] Today the YMCA is a family-oriented institution still known for its gyms, pools, and educational programs.

The Young Women's Christian Association (YWCA) was founded in London in 1855 through the convergence of the social activist Lady Mary Jane Kinnaird and the evangelical Christian Emma Robarts. Mary Jane Kinnaird was a philanthropist concerned about the safety and well-being of young women who moved to London city, often alone, to work or serve in the Crimean War. She raised funds and in 1855 set up housing for young single women in London. Equipped with a library, Bible classes, and an employment bureau, the housing provided a "warm Christian atmosphere."[22] Kinnaird and her associates aimed to help young women cope with the pressures of work and believed it was important to care for their souls as well as their physical and mental health. Like the YMCA, the YWCA followed the path of the British Empire around the world, was brought to the United States, and became a worldwide organization by 1998. In the twentieth century it promoted women's rights and healthy race relations, especially in the United States.[23] Like the YMCA, it also provides youth activities and athletics.

Throughout the history of Christian missionary work, medical missions have gone hand in hand with evangelization. Although missionaries from Europe and America went to other countries to save souls, they also recognized the need to improve the quality of life among the people with whom they worked. Possibly the first medical missionary was Dr. Kaspar Gottlieb Schlegemilch, who traveled to India in 1730 under German and Danish sponsorship. Unfortunately, he died of dysentery after only about a month in India. Other Danish and German doctors followed, but they too remained only a short time or

21. John Donald Gustav-Wrathall, *Take the Strangers by the Hand: Same-Sex Relations and the YMCA*, (Chicago Series on Sexuality, History and Society) (Chicago and London: The University of Chicago Press, 1998).
22. See Anna Rice, *A History of the World's Young Women's Christian Association* (New York: Woman's Press, 1947).
23. See the essays by Adrienne Lash Jones, Margaret Spratt, and Michelle Busby in Nina Mjagkij and Margaret Spratt, eds., *Men and Women Adrift: The YMCA and the YWCA in the City* (New York and London: New York University Press, 1997).

died of tropical diseases. In 1793 Dr. John Thomas was sent to India by the Baptist Missionary Society in England. Accompanied by the evangelist William Carey, they established the first Protestant mission in India. The first American medical missionary was Dr. John Scudder, who went to Ceylon in 1819 and later moved to India. Seven of his sons later worked in India as well, several of them as physicians. Another member of this family, Dr. Ida Scudder, established the Christian Medical College in Vellore, India, becoming somewhat of a legend among early medical missionaries. The American Dr. Peter Parker was sponsored by the American Board of Commissioners for Foreign Missions. In 1834 he traveled to China to begin a medical mission. As a surgeon, he performed many of the first surgical procedures in China and trained many young Chinese students in medicine.[24] Probably the most famous medical missionary was Alsatian-born Dr. Albert Schweitzer, who set up a hospital at Lambarene in Gabon Province of French Equatorial Africa. In India, Albanian-born Mother Teresa is famous for her work among the poor and sick of Calcutta. Both she and Schweitzer received the Nobel Prize for Peace for their humanitarian work, in 1979 and 1952 respectively.

The point of this brief review is to provide a general context for the rituals related to the Christian ministries of health and healing. Christianity has, from the beginning, been concerned with healthy bodies as well as sound minds and good spirits. In the following sections, we will look specifically at rites for the churching of women, visitation of the sick, and exorcism.

The Churching of Women

Christianity inevitably put its stamp on rites concerned with the resocialization of women after childbirth because in traditional societies pregnant women were viewed as dangerous, capable of polluting men as well as sacred objects and places. In fact, as Mary Douglas notes, all social activities had to be protected from female

---

24. See Stephen Neill, *A History of Christian Missions* (Harmondsworth, UK: Penguin Books, 1964), 255.

pollution.[25] Commenting on birthing rites, Arnold van Gennep cites W. H. R. Rivers's 1906 ethnography of the Todas of India at length.[26] Among these people a series of pregnancy rites are performed, the first of which separates the pregnant woman from her village. After an extended liminal period, a ceremony is held in which the woman drinks sacred milk to purify herself, her husband, and their child. Subsequently, the family is reintegrated into their social group. No longer a polluting women, she is reestablished in her village with the status of mother.

The church's rite of the churching of women is less a rite of purification than a thanksgiving for the woman's survival of childbirth. It was performed even when the child was stillborn or died unbaptized. Although the ritual contains no elements of purification, it was related in theological interpretation to the Jewish practice in Lev. 12:2–8, which prescribes the purification of women after giving birth. In basic terms, women were relieved of normal responsibilities after childbirth—forty days for boys, eighty days for girls. A burnt offering of a sheep and a sin offering of two pigeons or turtledoves were to be made at the end of this period of seclusion. Mary Douglas points out that the purity code in Leviticus is not related to bodily health concerns in the modern sense.[27] It has to do with being a holy people who belong to God. The loss of life-giving body fluids such as vaginal blood and semen required atonement even if the life-giving purpose of procreation was served; this recognizes that God is the author and giver of life. In terms of this practice, it's pointless to second-guess God, from whose mouth issued the instructions in the Torah. Leviticus is about practice, not theory.

However, in light of the New Testament, the Christian ritual drew on the imagery and symbolism of the purification in Luke 2:22–40 of the Virgin Mary, who was in fact carrying out the prescriptions of Leviticus. Although some Christian traditions believe she gave birth

---

25. See Mary Douglas, *Purity and Danger: An Analysis of the Concepts of Pollution and Taboo* (London: Routledge and Kegan Paul, 1966), 152ff.

26. Van Gennep, *Rites of Passage*, 42ff.

27. Mary Douglas, *Leviticus as Literature* (Oxford: Oxford University Press, 1999).

to the Christ without incurring impurity, Mary went to the temple in Jerusalem to fulfill the requirements of the Law of Moses and thus accepted her own humanity. In the liturgical calendar, this event is observed February 2, along with the presentation of Jesus in the temple, which involved an offering of two turtledoves to "redeem" him from priestly service.

No Christian rites concerning pregnancy and childbirth have been found in documents from the early centuries. It is possible that Christians followed local or ethnic customs. Even after the fourth century, when the more public church had to provide rites of passage for the sanctification of life situations, we find no rites for the churching of women in the church orders or the sacramentaries. The first rites show up in the late Middle Ages. In the Sarum (Salisbury) Manual the rite consists of Psalms 121 and 128, the Lord's Prayer, some versicles and responses, and a prayer—all said on the church porch. The woman was then sprinkled with water (the *asperges*) and led into the church while more psalms and/or the Magnificat or Nunc Dimittis were chanted. Luke's account of the presentation of Christ in the temple was sometimes read.[28]

An order for the churching of women is not found in the Lutheran or Reformed books. The churching rite in the 1549 Book of Common Prayer was essentially the Sarum rite, but it was moved into the church, and the *asperges* was dropped. In 1552 the title was changed to "The Thanksgiving of Women after Childbirth." In the 1662 Book of Common Prayer, Ps. 116:1-12 or Psalm 127 was substituted for Psalm 121. The rite continued in abbreviated form in the American Book of Common Prayer (1790). In the 1928 revision a prayer was added for the child, thereby continuing the trend of making this rite a thanksgiving for childbirth and less concerned with the reincorporation of women into church and society. In the 1979 Book of Common Prayer the order is entitled "A Thanksgiving for the Birth or Adoption of a Child." It may take place during the communion service and includes the Magnificat,

---

28. See Marion J. Hatchett, *Sanctifying Life, Time, and Space: An Introduction to Liturgical Study* (New York: Seabury, 1977), 88.

Psalm 116, or Psalm 23 and a series of prayers, from which an appropriate one is chosen.

Post-Natal Yoga Practice

The order for the churching of women and the idea behind it may be a ritual worth reviving in Western societies, especially as we compare the postpartum care of women in the United States with maternity leave benefits in other Western countries and the communal care given to new mothers in traditional societies. The rite assumes that a new mother needs a time of rest before resuming her social responsibilities. As I know from personal experience many young families today are separated by geographic distance from their families of origin. Paid (or unpaid) leave from employers is not adequate, especially for new fathers, and community support for postpartum mothers tends to be minimal. Mothers don't get the rest and re-creation they need.

The yoga studio in which I practice offers prenatal and postnatal yoga classes for expectant and new mothers respectively. Most of the classes are offered by the co-owner of Grateful Yoga Evanston, Lela Beem, who herself went through childbirth two years ago and who trains yoga teachers to specialize in prenatal and postnatal yoga teaching. I asked her to tell me about her practice, especially for postpartum mothers. She wrote several paragraphs, and I include them here for the information and wisdom they impart.

> Postpartum care is quite minimal in the United States. One six-week appointment with a midwife or OB/GYN and that's it. A woman might get twelve weeks of maternity leave if she is lucky. There is a growing movement to honor the forty- to eighty-day rest period once again, but unfortunately since men don't have paid paternity leave yet, most women don't get this luxury.

> Postpartum yoga is one of the ways that we serve this population of women during what would otherwise be a very isolating, exhausting, and anxiety-provoking time.

> Prior to six-weeks postpartum, women are encouraged to do only minimal exercise, such as kegals and pelvic tilts. These first six weeks are some

of the most challenging, and an emerging field of postpartum doula care has started to gain in popularity. A woman hires another woman who is a trained professional with some proficiency in newborn care and lactation education to come to her home and help her take care of herself and her household. Sometimes all a postpartum doula does is let the mother take a nap and a shower. She might even cook a meal for the woman's family.

Once a woman has gotten permission to resume exercise from her care provider, she can attend group or private postnatal yoga classes. Some classes include the baby; others are just for the mothers.

A yoga class is a special time in a woman's week to connect with other mothers and be open about the challenges of the postpartum time. Perhaps due to some of the historical shaming of public discussion of women's physiological processes, women nowadays are very eager to connect with other women and educate themselves about how to care for their bodies post-birth. Many women struggle with feeling guilty for leaving their newborns and husbands for the hour or for having to return to work.

In a postnatal yoga class, women are encouraged to begin to reengage and tone the muscles of the pelvic floor and transverse abdominal muscles. Regardless of having had a cesarean or vaginal birth, each woman needs a significant amount of time to recover not only from labor and birth but from pregnancy itself.

The asymmetries and lack of stability in a postpartum body is remarkable. This is partially due to the level of the relaxin in a woman's system during pregnancy and lactation, which keeps the ligaments softer and stretchier. Women often find themselves with severe back and hip pain, neck and wrist problems from breastfeeding, and a general sense of uncenteredness that comes from having your whole life and body turned upside down.

Learning how to reactivate the core muscles (pelvic floor, transverse abdominus, gluteal muscles, adductors, quadriceps, multifidi) help mothers move with more confidence into their new roles. Immediately post-birth, women are required to lift and carry and clean, especially if they have other children at home. Without learning how to reengage the core musculature, they are extremely vulnerable to muscular strain, pelvic organ prolapse and long-term diastasis recti (separation of the rectus abdominal muscles).

Yoga helps a woman reconnect with herself post-birth, remember how to relax during a stressful time, and replenish her vital essence that is so depleted during this sleepless and complex time of life.

Another thing I would like to mention on this topic is that in Ayurveda [an Indian medical system that is in close alliance with yoga], the 40 days post-birth is considered an exceedingly delicate time in which Vata (wind element) is extraordinarily off-balance. Women are discouraged from going outdoors, recommended to eat warm, wet foods that are high in healthy fats, and [told] to bind the abdomen. Ayurvedic wisdom says that women should bind their bellies after childbirth to decrease Vata because of the vacuous state of the abdomen after the baby is born. As well, the loss of blood and fluid puts the woman at a risk for deep energetic and physical depletion, so she must take at least forty days to replenish herself and receive support.

In my opinion, it is a great loss to women and families that there is such a rush to "get on with it" after having a baby. Traditional cultures give women more time to heal, more space to bond with their babies, and more encouragement to ask for help. Perhaps we have lost some of this also because of the rapid secularization. Certainly, church communities had this support system built in for families. Now we have less access to this and have to seek out other mothers in support groups, yoga classes, and family drop-in centers.[29]

Liturgical Ministry to the Sick

When people are seriously sick they are separated from normal life and responsibilities, and the community brings them appropriate rites that provide comfort and healing. Rites dealing with the sick are properly rites of passage because they deal with the transition from health through the period of sickness back to health—or, in some cases, to death.

Prayer and anointing of the sick was practiced in the Jewish community. In Leviticus 13–14 the purity laws were applied to lepers. The leprosy described in Leviticus does not correspond to actual leprosy (Hansen's disease) or to any known dermatological ailment. The concern is with the disintegration of the skin to the extent that the innards of the body are exposed, which is a sign of corruption—death overtaking life. Healing requires a seven-day isolation period, the burning of contaminated clothing, and the shaving of the head. On the eighth day the right earlobe, thumb, and big toe are anointed,

29. Lela Beem (Co-owner of Grateful Yoga in Evanston, Illinois), email to the author, January 16, 2015.

paralleling the anointing of the priests—a reminder that the healing of the sick is a call to service. As with the purification rite after childbirth, a sin offering is to be made.

In the Gospels Jesus heals many people of their diseases, including leprosy. In Luke 17:11–18 Jesus encounters ten lepers who keep their distance but cry out to Jesus for mercy. He does not directly heal them but tells them to go and show themselves to the priests. They are cleansed as they go on their way and one, a Samaritan, who would have shown himself to the priest on Mt. Gerizim rather than in Jerusalem, returns to give thanks to Jesus, prostrating himself before him.

James 5:13–16 presumes a continuation of rites for the sick that were practiced in the Jewish community, which included prayer by the elders of the church, anointing with oil, and confession of sins. It was commonly assumed that there was a connection between sin and sickness: "Therefore confess your sins to one another, and pray for one another, so that you may be healed" (James 5:16, NRSV).

These elements of rite continued as the church's ministry to the sick developed. The ancient church orders prescribe that the sickness of a member should be reported to the bishop. If some of the laity have been given the gift of healing they may also visit the sick, pray for them with the laying on of hands, and anoint them. The bishops blessed the oils used in the ministry to the sick, so presumably this oil was available to be taken by lay people and applied to the sick, extending the bishop's ministry to his flock. Justin Martyr reports in his *First Apology* (67) that consecrated Eucharistic elements are taken to the sick by the deacons after the Sunday liturgy. Later on the sacrament was reserved after the Eucharistic celebration precisely for this purpose.

In the Carolingian reforms of the ninth century, the rites for the visitation of the sick became more elaborate. Because illness often was a prelude to death, the seven penitential psalms were used as well as the litany of the saints. The confession of sin became more prominent than prayers for healing. Because of the need for absolution the visitation of the sick became a priestly duty. Anointing became "extreme unction" (or the last rite), both because it was done toward the end of the visitation and because it was often the last rite performed before death.

The reformers objected to the designation of the New Testament's ministry to the sick as a "last rite." Luther wondered, "Why do they make an extreme and a special kind of unction out of that which the apostles wished to be general?"[30] He pointed out that the Apostle James intended it for healing, but also noted that "the prayer of faith will save the sick man" (Jas 5:15) and wondered if we have that faith today.

In their reforms, the reformers made visitation of the sick a more regular part of pastoral duty. The German Church Orders typically provided an exhortation, individual confession and absolution, psalmody and readings, a homily, and celebration of Holy Communion. Anointing was dropped except in the *Manual of Olavus Petri* (1529) in Sweden. The Mark Brandenburg Church Order (1540) and the first Book of Common Prayer (1549) provided for the communion of the sick from the reserved sacrament on the day on which Holy Communion was celebrated (an extended distribution). This practice was dropped in the 1552 edition. An order for the Celebration of Holy Communion in the house of the sick was provided with special propers (prayers and readings). All later editions of the Book of Common Prayer provided propers for a celebration of Holy Communion in the presence of the sick person, usually surrounded by family members. Some of the Reformed churches objected to private celebrations of Holy Communion and sometimes also to private confession and anointing. But it usually included prayer and the laying on of hands in blessing.

A significant recovery of the ministry to the sick in the Catholic Church was made after the Second Vatican Council. In particular, a concerted effort was made to play down the aspect of the anointing of the sick as a last rite and to make the ministry of healing, as it was now termed, a more regular part of Christian life. Special communion ministers were designated to take the reserved sacrament to the sick.[31]

30. Martin Luther, "The Babylonian Captivity of the Church," *Luther's Works* ed. Abdel Ross Wentz (Philadelphia: Fortress Press, 1959), 118.
31. See the articles pertaining to the ministry of the sick in Peter E. Fink, *The New Dictionary of Sacramental Liturgy* (Collegeville, MN: Liturgical Press, 1990), 1161–89.

In Lutheran and Episcopal churches, a similar development includes the use of oil for anointing and communion of the sick from the elements used in the congregation's celebration of Holy Communion. The anointing of the sick has become a practice also in Pentecostal churches. The charismatic renewal of the 1960s and 1970s brought anointing of the sick with the laying on of hands into mainline Protestant churches. Sometimes special public healing services are offered in the mainline churches, or anointing and prayer for the sick is made available in conjunction with the celebration of Holy Communion. Persons desiring prayer and anointing go to a designated station after receiving the communion elements. Laypersons are trained to perform this ministry, just as communion ministers are trained to take Holy Communion to the sick and homebound.

Many existential questions surround the ministry to the sick in the modern world, that is, the world of sophisticated medical science and technology. Can we maintain a connection between sin and sickness in the modern world? Is prayer and anointing effective in healing the sick? Is healing the same as curing illness? Does God set aside natural processes to bring about a supernatural healing? Ronald Grimes raises the question of "ritual failure" more generally.[32] Do rites of healing, like all rites, sometimes fail to accomplish their purpose?

These are not questions with easy answers, and I will not attempt to answer them here. I will only point out that from the earliest times, prayer and the anointing of the sick was cherished among Christians—not only for those in immediate danger of death but also for those experiencing only the beginning signs of danger from illness. To this was added confession and absolution, the consolation of the gospel, and Holy Communion. In liturgical renewal this sacramental ministry of healing has been restored and is very popular when it is made available. One possibility involves providing an opportunity for anointing and laying on of hands in the public liturgy for any who desire to receive this ministry, perhaps during and after Holy

32. See Ronald Grimes, *Ritual Criticism: Case Studies in Its Practice, Essays on Its Theory* (Columbia: University of South Carolina Press, 1990).

Communion, thus bringing together two elements in the church's rites of healing. Some people have even received anointing and laying on of hands on behalf of others who cannot be present. But that practice raises questions. If someone can't be baptized on behalf of someone else, can one be anointed on behalf of someone else? I think it is a practice that should not be encouraged.

The Christian rite of anointing the sick in the early Middle Ages, before the ancient Christian ministry of healing had become the sacrament of extreme unction, called for anointing the five sense organs, the neck, the throat, the region between the shoulders, the breast, and parts of the body which were painful—as many as fifteen different places. In other words, much of the body was anointed. Today the anointing is restricted to the forehead and maybe one or two other places. As contemporary sacramental practice has preferred more water in bigger fonts for Holy Baptism, whole loaves of bread and larger chalices of wine for Holy Communion, perhaps we also need to consider more use of oil in the Anointing of the Sick. These sacramental rites are signs of the coming Kingdom of God. They need to witness to fullness of life under God's reign, not to paucity.

Exorcism

Not all afflictions of the body and mind are instigated by natural causes or even unhealthy lifestyle choices. Many people throughout human history and around the world today believe in a spirit world in which evil spirits take hold of a body and inhabit it. The apostle Paul writes in Eph. 5:12 (NRSV) that "our struggle is not against enemies of flesh and blood, but against the rulers, against the authorities, against the cosmic powers of this present darkness, against the spiritual forces of evil in the heavenly places."

In the Synoptic Gospels Jesus performs as many exorcisms as healings. In fact, healing and exorcism go together. Especially in the fast-paced Gospel of Mark, Jesus' advancing of the kingdom of God is accomplished by assaulting demons and evil spirits. It is as if the physical territory itself needs to be cleansed of evil spirits because

Jesus performs exorcisms on the gentile side of the Sea of Galilee as well as on the Jewish side. The most dramatic exorcism involves the Gerasene demoniac in Mark 5:1–20. The demons, who call themselves "Legion, for we are many" (5:9), are expelled from the man and transferred into pigs who run to the edge of a cliff and fall off into the water and drown. Spirits need a body, and apparently even an animal body will do.

The ancient Christians took exorcism seriously, and it became a regular feature of catechetical rites leading to baptism. The baptismal profession of faith is preceded by a renunciation of Satan and all his works and pomps (honors). With the prevalence of infant baptism after the period of antiquity, the catechumenal rites primarily became acts of exorcism. While Luther eliminated these exorcistic prayers from the 1526 revision of his Order of Holy Baptism, the order still begins with the stark words: "Depart thou unclean spirit and make room for the Holy Spirit," followed by "Receive the sign of the holy cross on both thy forehead and thy breast."[33] The sign of the cross was often an apotropaic act used to ward off evil. Lutheran church orders retained this act of exorcism, but the Reformed regarded it as a "papal relic"—a source of superstition that had to go. Exorcism in baptism became as much of a controversy between Lutherans and Reformed in the Reformation and post-Reformation periods as disagreement over the presence of Christ in the Eucharist.[34] After the Enlightenment, however, Lutherans also dropped the exorcism from their baptismal orders.

Yet in the global church today we are aware of the prevalence of demon possession and the use of exorcism, especially in Africa, Asia, and Latin America. What are we modern Western Christians to make of this? Should missionaries be extending psychiatric care as part of medical missions?

In the West we have been reconsidering the category of the demonic. Psychiatrist M. Scott Peck's *People of the Lie*[35] offers case

---

33. *Luther's Works*, trans. Ulrich S. Leupold (Philadelphia: Fortress Press, 1965), 53:107.
34. Bodo Nischan, *Prince, People, and Confession: The Second Reformation in Brandenburg* (Philadelphia: University of Pennsylvania Press, 1994), 199, 133, 243.

studies of people whose behavior is not only a sin against others but an act perpetrated with evil intent for the sake of sheer meanness. But does demon possession entail more than this? Is it possible to see bodies so possessed by evil spirits that they act in unhuman ways, as Hollywood filmmakers have portrayed?

On the streets of Yogyakarta, Indonesia, I saw for myself a man whose body was possessed by an evil spirit. He was down on all fours on the sidewalk, writhing with contorted facial expressions and empty-looking eyes and making animal-type sounds. As a former urban pastor I've seen and dealt with street people who suffer from schizophrenia. I never saw anything like this. A crowd had gathered but was keeping its distance, and a policeman stood nearby, not intervening. On the chance that he might have been a street performer I asked my Indonesian companion, a woman with a master's degree from Trinity Theological College in Singapore, what was happening. Without a second's thought she said, "Oh, he's possessed," as if this was something she was used to seeing. Later I asked my friend Emil Salim, who earned his PhD in philosophy from the University of Arizona, if exorcism is taught in the Presbyterian seminary in Jakarta where he taught. "Not formally in class," he said, "but it is understood that pastors need to know about performing exorcisms. I suppose they pick it up in fieldwork education."

I've heard firsthand accounts of exorcisms in Lutheran churches in Madagascar and Tanzania. The Canadian Lutheran pastor Philip E. Gagnon has encountered people possessed of evil spirits in Western Canada and has prepared a manual of exorcism.[36] The Roman Catholic Church appoints exorcists who perform exorcisms under carefully controlled circumstances and with a complete manual of exorcism. Pentecostals practice exorcism and use as ministers those who have the gift.

Demon possession afflicts the body. We see this in the episode of Jesus casting the demon out of the Geresene man in Mark 5. The man

---

35. M. Scott Peck, *People of the Lie* (New York: Touchstone, 1983). See also Peck's book *Glimpses of the Devil* (New York: Free Press, 2005).

36. Philip E. Gagnon, *Deliver Us from Evil: A Manual of Exorcism* (Edmonton, AB: Philip Gagnon, 2014).

possessed unusual physical strength, breaking the shackles that held him (5:3). He went into frenzies of rage (5:5). He may have had a split personality (5:6–10). There was evidence of clairvoyance—the demon knew Jesus' name (5:7)—as well as a transference of symptoms; "Legion" asked to be sent into the swine (5:12). The demons manifested themselves as they came out of the afflicted man.

I am not going to review any of the rites of exorcism here because I have not performed them or even experienced an exorcism. I don't believe that exorcisms should be performed by those who aren't trained or who lack the gift. From what I've read and heard, exorcism can be physically and spiritually dangerous. It is often performed by a team, with assistants who help the minister of exorcism. If there is any possibility of violence, the afflicted person is sometimes tied down, and prayers invoking God's protection on the afflicted, bystanders, and the exorcism team are offered, which suggests the possibility of physical and spiritual danger from expelled evil spirits. The name of the demon needs to be ascertained in order to call it out, and the person from whom an evil spirit has been expelled will undoubtedly need special care.[37]

I've often pondered why demon possession is more common in some geographic places than in others. I think Athanasius's *On the Incarnation* provides an answer. As he surveys the world in the first quarter of the fourth century, only a decade or so after the legalization of Christianity by the Roman state, the church father asks: "When did the deceitfulness and madness of daemons fall under contempt, save when the Word, the Power of God, the master of all these as well, condescended on account of the weakness of mankind and appeared on earth?"[38]

In the view of Athanasius, the advent of the divine Word in human life and history pushed back the idols, the oracles, the demons, and the magicians. His view suggests that evil spirits are less plentiful where the worship of Christ has been established. But Jesus tells a parable

---

37. These and other issues are discussed in Gagnon's *Deliver Us from Evil: A Manual of Exorcism.*
38. Athanasius, *On the Incarnation* 46, trans. Penelope Lawson (Crestwood, NY: St. Vladimir's Seminary Press, 1953), 83.

that suggests the enemy can reclaim lost territory. "When the unclean spirit has gone out of a person, it wanders through waterless regions looking for a resting place, but not finding any, it says, 'I will return to my house from which I came.' When it comes, it finds it swept and put in order. Then it goes and brings seven other spirits more evil than itself, and they enter and live there; and the last state of that person is worse than the first" (Luke 11:24–26, NRSV). We saw the horrible evil inflicted on the world from the former European home of Christianity in the guise of godless Soviet Communism and neo-pagan Nazism in the mid-twentieth century. Today, young people from Europe and North America are seduced into taking up the cause of radical Islamic jihad, launching brutal terrorist attacks on innocent people. With secularization and the diminishing of Christian worship, is it possible that evil spirits are becoming more rampant in places where we assumed they were long gone?

The desire for exorcism seems to be increasing in North America. It is a ministry that needs to be taken seriously since possession is a terrible affliction of body and soul that works against God's kingdom. But it is a ministry that requires great care and oversight. Special training and skill are needed to distinguish between psychological and spiritual afflictions. I understand that sometimes the more sensational aspects of demon possession appear only after the rite is underway. As in most endeavors, the exorcist learns from experience. I cannot see exorcism being properly carried out except within the support structure of a community of faith—which is the context for all ministries of healing. If we are learning anything about what makes for healthy bodies today, it is that healing must be holistic, addressing both body and mind and connecting the individual with a supporting community.

Figure 13. A painting by the Spanish artist Francisco Goya (1746-1828) showing an exorcism being performed by a Catholic priest.

8

Sexual Bodies, Dead Bodies

A. Marriage Rites

Marriage and burial are two of the most important rites of passage because they deal with the immense realities of sex and death respectively. Before I discuss Christian marriage and burial rites in this lesson, I want to treat sex and death together because from biological, psychological, and sociological perspectives they are more related than we may think.

The Biology of Sex and Death

Human beings are created with an instinct to procreate, and the sentence of death hangs over all of us. Beginning with Sigmund Freud, psychoanalysis has explored the connection between sexuality and death as two instincts that counter but complement each other. If a society ceases to reproduce itself, there are profound social consequences, including social death.

While we might think of sex and death as diametrically opposite phenomena, they are connected at a deep level. Biologically, sex is related to procreation, which we consider to be an enlivening endeavor. We typically think of death as occurring only at the end of life. But from a biological perspective sex and death are related. In the animal kingdom lessons abound concerning the connection between reproduction and death. Pacific salmon, for instance, return after three or four years in the ocean to swim hundreds of miles upstream—against gill nets, predators, and dams—to the tributaries where their lives began. Once there, they spawn and die. The female praying mantis bites off the head of her partner while mating. In several marsupial mice species, the immune systems of the mice collapse after their first mating, which leads to death shortly thereafter.

Scientists have observed that death is the price multicellular creatures must pay in order to reproduce. The biologist William Clark observes, "Obligatory death—as a result of senescence (natural aging)—may not have come into existence for more than a billion years after life first appeared. This form of programmed cell death seems to have arisen at about the same time cells began experimenting with sex in connection with reproduction."[1] Perhaps one legacy of this original immortality is the telomerase, the so-called immortality enzyme, which is found within the cells of testes and ovaries. Absent from normal cells that age and die, telomerase allows cancerous cells to reproduce without limits.

In a fascinating book that reveals counterintuitive insights, Tyler Volk and Dorion Sagan show that death is a creative biological process at work within us and that we should be happy our sex lives aren't perfect.[2] In this two-books-in-one Volk writes about death and Sagan writes about sex.

Volk gives numerous examples of death as part of growth and development. For example, in our embryonic bodies, death is the sculptor that shapes our hands and feet. In the womb a developing

---

1. William Clark, *Sex and the Origins of Death* (New York: Oxford University Press, 1996), xi.
2. Tyler Volk and Dorion Sagan, *Death and Sex* (White River Junction, VT: Chelsea Green, 2009). The book was published so that the reader can read about death or sex and then turn the book over and upside down to read about sex or death.

fetus first grows finlike hands, and the digits are carved out by the death of web cells between the digits. Programmed cell death triggers many other metabolic processes responsible for cell differentiation, the mechanism of development and complexity. To wish to be free of programmed cell death would be to wish for cancer: undifferentiated, unrestrained, practically immortal cell growth. Death doesn't come from forces outside of our bodies, bringing ill health; death comes from healthy cells at work in the body. Death cells ensure that we will not be immortal—but also that we will become who we are created to be.[3] The ancients understood this. As St. Athanasius reminds the pagans, "You must know . . . that the corruption which had set in was not external to the body but established within it."[4] As the medieval antiphon says, "In the midst of life we are in death."

Sagan begins his portion of the book by equating immortality with eternal sameness. An amoeba that reproduces asexually by dividing into perfect copies of itself is immortal in this sense. But, as Sagan notes, "eternally-the-same" is not an existence we should wish for. We do not reproduce or clone ourselves perfectly. Human beings are not identical copies of one another that roll off the assembly line "in a cookie-cutter mold off an evolutionary assembly line." ". . . It's the little things," he writes, "from freckles to the shape of a lip, from a way of speaking to the curve of a hip, or the uniqueness of his words or her thoughts, that mark the loved one as our loved one, as opposed to some random drone."[5] Through sexual reproduction we don't simply reproduce (which is what asexual reproduction allows simple organisms to do). Rather, we reproduce imperfectly. These imperfections not only enable us to cherish our mates, but they also spice up the evolutionary process.

Humanity is not immune from this law of death as the cost of sex, which we find in other species. Death is built into our healthy bodies, and sex is risky business, fraught with peril. Before the modern age it was not uncommon for women to die in childbirth. Death rates

3. Volk, *Death*, ibid., 32–39.
4. Athanasius, *On the Incarnation* 44 (Crestwood, NY: St. Vladimir's Seminary Press, 1953), 80.
5. Sagan, *Sex*, x.

for women giving birth or seeking abortions are still high in underdeveloped countries. The sex act itself can prove lethal for heart patients, although an active sex life has been a healthy cardiovascular activity for many other people. In modern times, the AIDS epidemic adds to the relationship between sex and death. Unprotected sex with multiple partners can be deadly. Thus sex and death are connected in many and various ways.

Of course, sex and death maintain a number of connections besides being biological processes and taboo topics in polite company. Few people question the premise that life's greatest drives are to reproduce (even though we do it imperfectly) and to avoid death (even though it is unavoidable). The Austrian psychoanalyst Sigmund Freud and the French social theorist Michel Foucault argue that the two are fused together—that the death instinct pervades sexual activity—a connection easily seen by the language Foucault uses, framing orgasms as *petit mort*, or "mini-deaths." Indeed, there are some who say that "spilling the seed" diminishes one's life force. Some yogis practice retention of both breath and semen, thus holding on to life forces and increasing their internal energy. One tantric text holds that "while the sperm remains in the body, there is no fear of Death."[6] Therefore, the object of tantric practice is to keep the sperm in the body. This is why true Tantra promotes the idea of separating orgasm from ejaculation. Jain ascetics and other celibates practice semen retention to devote their energy to good works, reasoning that one loses energy as soon as ejaculation occurs—energy that can be used for other purposes. Ejaculation should be saved for procreation since procreation expands the life force by creating a new human being, even though it may leave the married couple feeling depleted.

Without procreation, of course, a social group may cease to exist. Take, for example, celibate religious orders or communities (e.g., the Shakers) that fail to attract new members. It has been suggested that a primary reason for the decline of mainline Protestant denominations

---

6. Cited in Mircea Eliade, *Yoga: Immortality and Freedom*, trans. Willard R. Trask (Princeton: Princeton University Press, 1958), 248.

in the United States is the low birthrate among the members. The whole of Europe is currently experiencing the social changes resulting from the failure of a society to reproduce itself.

As fascinating as the connections between sex and death may be, from this point on I will treat sex and death as separate ritual processes related to marriage and burial. The rites of marriage and burial are ways by which a society manages the powerful biological realities of sex and death that concern all individuals and human societies.

The Institution of Marriage

In the second creation story in Genesis 2–3 (NRSV) the Lord God creates man and then woman from man. The woman is to man "bone of my bones and flesh of my flesh" (2:23). "Therefore a man leaves his father and mother and clings to his wife, and they become one flesh" (2:24).

As the first creation story leads to the institution of the Sabbath, so the second creation story leads to the institution of marriage. The Torah is concerned with both law and custom.

The two creation stories are not unrelated. In the sexual union of the man and the woman—so intimate that they become "one flesh"—there is the potential of receiving the blessing of fruitfulness, that is, the procreation about which the first account speaks (1:28). Male-female sexuality is thus ordered to an end. At the same time, "both were naked, but they were not ashamed" (2:25), which adds to the basic meaning of the marriage as intended by God: the man and the women are free from the constraints of their own bodies and their own sex. Their nakedness expresses their freedom to interact with each other; sex will be a matter of mutual pleasuring as well as procreation. Pope John Paul II expresses this thought in his theology of the body:

> The human body, with its sex—its masculinity and femininity—seen in the very mystery of creation, is not only a source of fruitfulness and of procreation, as in the whole natural order, but contains "from the beginning" the "spousal attribute," that is, *the power to express love: precisely that love in which the human person becomes a gift* and—through this gift—fulfills the very meaning of his being and existence.[7]

227

The idea of basing marriage on love would seem to be inherent in the institution of marriage "from the beginning." But in the biblical narrative the fall is yet to come, and marriage too is a fallen institution. Throughout most of human history, as Stephanie Coontz relates, "marriage was not primarily about individual needs and the desires of a man and a woman and the children they produced. Marriage had as much to do with getting good in-laws and increasing one's family labor force as it did with finding a lifetime companion and raising a beloved child."[8]

Hence marriage became a social institution that concerned families more than individuals. In some cultures like India, even young children could be betrothed to each other for a future marriage when they came of age. And while the institution text in Genesis might imply a monogamous marriage, with monogamy becoming the accepted norm in Judaism and Christianity, polygamy, particularly in the form of polygyny (one man, multiple wives), has been common throughout human and biblical history. What has remained constant is not that marriage is based on love, although people have fallen in love throughout history, but the ontological condition of marriage: that a man and a woman copulate with the possibility of producing offspring—a conjugal union. Even that assumptions up for grabs in the modern world since birth control technology has made it possible to have sexual relations without consideration of children, and Western societies are now legally recognizing marital partnerships of the same sex. These partnerships, cannot, within their same-sex union, procreate.

The sexual revolution of the 1960s has taken its toll on an institution that was already "fallen" from the beginning. All these changes must fit within the legal strictures of the modern state, which defines what marriage is and grants couples the license to marry, taking over the role that families and religion once played in making these decisions.

7. John Paul II, *Man and Woman He Created Them: A Theology of the Body*, trans. Michael Waldstein (Boston: Pauline Books and Media, 2006), 186 (italics in the original).
8. Stephanie Coontz, *Marriage, A History: From Obedience to Intimacy or How Love Conquered Marriage* (London: Viking Penguin, 2005), 6.

In the United States and many other Western nations, marriage is legally a civil institution in which family and religion play a subordinate role. Historically, the French Revolution was the catalyst for the total separation of the civil and religious aspects of marriage, with the civil aspect being determinative. While clergy in the United States may receive a license to function as a civil magistrate for a particular wedding and the wedding may be held in a church building, the legal aspect determines the social recognition of the marriage.

Marriage Rites

Next we will examine the Christian rites for "solemnizing" a marriage. The role of the church in solemnizing a marriage is different from the role of the state. As much as the interests of church and state colluded in the society of Christendom, a distinction was still made in the marriage rites themselves. In the Middle Ages the legal, contractual aspects of marriage were solemnized on the church porch or in the vestibule. The sacramental aspect of marriage was celebrated at the altar and actualized in coitus on the marriage bed (which was sometimes blessed by a priest). The state is interested in regulating the legal arrangements of marriage as a social good for this world. The church is interested in proclaiming what marriage is by divine institution and intention. And because marriage is, like everything else in this world, a fallen reality, the Orthodox theologian Alexander Schmemann writes that marriage does not need "to be blessed and 'solemnized'—after a rehearsal and with the help of the photographer—but *restored*." He goes on to say that "this restoration, furthermore, is *in Christ* and this means in His life, death, resurrection and ascension to heaven, in the Pentecostal inauguration of the 'new eon,' in the Church as the sacrament of all this. Needless to say, this restoration infinitely transcends the idea of the 'Christian family,' and gives marriage cosmic and universal dimensions.[9]

Schmemann is saying that marriage must be related, as the apostle

---

9. Alexander Schmemann, *For the Life of the World: Sacraments and Orthodoxy* (Crestwood, NY: St. Vladimir's Seminary Press, 1973), 82 (italics in the original).

Paul says, to the mystery (sacrament) of Christ and the church (Ephesians 5). The restoration of marriage is not about in-laws or civil laws; it is not about economics and sexual politics. It is about the kingdom of God. It is not only about what God intended "in the beginning" but also what will be brought to fulfillment in Christ—not paradise restored but a new creation finally celebrated at the marriage supper of the Lamb (Revelation 19). The purpose of the Christian liturgy of marriage is to ritualize this new creation—to make it, if not a *reality*, then a *vision* of what is possible. For this reason what makes Christian marriage different from other marriages in the cultures of this world is the celebration of the Eucharist, the meal of the kingdom of God.

For the first millennium of its existence the church had no marriage rites of its own. As a meal fellowship, it had only the Eucharist. Since Christians were drawn from every race and nation, Christians followed the cultural practices of their own ethnic groups. But the Eucharist always made the difference, transforming the new household into a cell of the coming kingdom of God.

Marital rites in human societies involve a process in which the bride and groom are separated from their parents and from the ranks of the single men and women in the community. The joining together of the couple as husband and wife is usually celebrated publicly. Further rites integrate the newly married couple into the community according to their new status as a couple. The public character of the marriage rite conveys the legal and social difference between a couple that is simply cohabiting and a couple that is married.

The Roman world into which Christianity moved proved influential on later Christian marriage rituals; Christianity in turn passed many Roman practices into Western culture. The Roman groom was usually older than the bride by about ten years, having already served in the military and practiced arguing a law case before a court. He was in a position to leave his father's house and set up his own household. Even so, marriage was arranged by the *paterfamilias*. The role of families in selecting mates for their children is common in many cultures. It is largely a modern Western phenomenon that two persons meet, fall in love, and choose to marry each other.

Marion Hatchett provides a succinct description of the ancient Roman marriage rites, from which I note the following stages in the ritual process of matrimony.[10]

1. Betrothal. The betrothal took place at the home of the parents of the bride. A contract was signed, the groom presented the bride with a betrothal gift and placed a ring on the fourth finger of her left hand. A banquet followed.

2. Wedding Day preparations. On her wedding day the bride dedicated her playthings to the gods and was dressed in her wedding garments, which included a girdle (symbol of virginity), a flame-colored veil, and a floral crown.

3. Marriage vows and banquet. The bride and groom came together and made a solemn vow before witnesses, after which the wedding official (*pronuba*) joined their hands. A sacrifice was offered to Juno, the goddess of marriage and a banquet followed. Gifts were given to the wedding guests.

4. Bridal procession to her new house. At nightfall the bride was led to her new home. The groom had left earlier in order to be home to receive her. She was carried over the threshold by her friends, not by her husband. Together the bride and groom lit a fire in the hearth with a torch fire that had been brought from the home of the bride's family.

5. Preparation of the marriage bed. The pronuba oversaw the preparation of the marriage bed. The bride went through the ritual of loosening her girdle. Prayers were offered to the gods of marriage. The company departed.

6. The new husband and wife welcome their relatives to their home. On the next day the groom celebrated a feast, and the bride received her new relatives and offered a sacrifice to the gods of the hearth.[11]

10. Marion J. Hatchett, *Sanctifying Life, Time, and Space: An Introduction to Liturgical Study* (New York: The Seabury Press, 1976), 39–40.

Roman Christians continued to observe these rites, with a few substitutions. The bishop or a presbyter attended the wedding, offered a blessing in place of the pagan prayer, celebrated the Eucharist in place of the sacrifice to the gods, and blessed the marriage bed. Many of these customs were absorbed into Western culture, and the Christian components were filled out with prayers for a nuptial Mass and nuptial blessings in the sacramentaries.[12]

During the Middle Ages not all marriages were solemnized by the presence of clergy. Nor were all marriages celebrated with a nuptial Mass. Furthermore, only weddings that celebrated a nuptial Mass could be held in the church building. The church understood the *form* of the marriage rite to be vows of faithfulness recited in the presence of witnesses and the *matter* of marriage to be the act of coitus. The celebrants of marriage were the bride and groom. According to the church, it was considered sufficient if the marriage vows were exchanged in the presence of witnesses. As in Roman times, marriages were often arranged by the fathers of the couple who were often glad to keep "mettlesome priests" out of the arrangements.[13] Nevertheless, in the society of Christendom marriage was regarded as a sacrament, and it was regulated in canon law.

The Protestant reformers played into the interests of family and state (that is, royal marriages) by desacralizing marriage. Paradoxically, while Martin Luther emphasized the married state as divinely instituted so as to downplay the medieval elevation of the celibate state, he also denied that sacramental status of marriage. The Reformation church orders reformed many of the marriage regulations in canon law.

The Protestant reformers also abolished the nuptial Mass, in addition to other votive masses (masses offered for special intention).

11. Full details of marriage laws and customs with all their variations are given in Susan Treggiari, *Roman Marriage: Iusti Coniuges from the Time of Cicero to the Time of Ulpian* (New York: Oxford University Press, 1991; Oxford: Clarendon Press paperback, 1993).

12. Concerning the innumerable variations in medieval marriage rites see Kenneth W. Stevenson, *To Join Together: The Rite of Marriage* (New York: Pueblo Publishing Company, 1987), 30–36.

13. See Edward Muir, *Ritual in Early Modern Europe* (Cambridge: Cambridge University Press, 1997), 31ff.

However, the Protestants took the lead in performing weddings in the church building (a public place), hoping to curb the increase of Romeo-and-Juliet-type elopements that were upsetting the parents. The Council of Trent came under similar pressure to rein in clandestine marriages, and decreed in 1563 that marriages should be entered into parish registers by the priest.[14]

Luther was socially conservative enough to retain some of the civil aspects of the marriage rites, including the announcement of the banns (publicizing the proposed marriage) three times in three weeks before the wedding took place in case there were any legal objections to the marriage. He retained the exchange of promises and rings on the church porch (the legal requirements), followed by "What God hath joined together, let not man put asunder." Next came a procession into the church building and up to the altar as Psalms 127 and 128 were sung. At the altar, Scripture was read (Gen. 2:18, 21–24), a homily given, and a prayer of blessing offered. But the Eucharist was not celebrated.[15]

Reformed rites of marriage were typically celebrated on Sundays (a day off from work) and could be celebrated at the congregation's main worship service. Martin Bucer at Strasbourg encouraged couples to receive communion at that service. The Book of Common Prayer (1549, 1552, 1559) enjoined "the newe married persones (the same daye of their marriage)" to "receive the holy communion." The 1662 edition admonished the couple to receive Holy Communion as soon as possible after the marriage service, which was a concession to the Puritans who objected to having weddings, with their accompanying festivities, on a Sunday or at the Eucharist.

Thus the marriage rite was separated from the Lord's Day and eventually also from the Eucharist. Furthermore, the Protestant rites make no provision for the blessing of the marriage bed by the priest, the purpose of which was fertility. In Protestant eyes much superstition surrounded this practice, and "the gift and heritage of

14. See John Bossy, *Christianity in the West, 1400–1700* (Oxford: Oxford University Press, 1985), 19ff.
15. Martin Luther, "The Order of Marriage for Common Pastors" (1529), *Luther's Works*, trans. Ulrich S. Leupold (Philadelphia: Fortress Press, 1965), 110ff.

children" petitioned in the intercessions[16] was understood as a matter of God's will.

While the Roman Catholic Church recognized marriage as a natural institution, after the Council of Trent it reemphasized marriage as a supernatural institution and one of the seven sacraments of the church, elevated to this status by Christ's participation in the wedding at Cana (John 2:1–11). More Christian couples had a nuptial Mass celebrated than before the Tridentine reforms, and the Catholic Church continued to teach that marriage between any two baptized Christians, as long as it was entered into with the intention to contract a true marriage, was a sacrament. But the Catholic Church made it mandatory for a marriage to be performed by a priest in the presence of two or three witnesses and entered into the parish register. In particular, they wanted to prevent any marriages between spiritual kinships, such as godparents marrying godchildren, which could happen if the bride was a ward of the godfather.

The French reacted to this ecclesiastical control of marriage, making civil marriage mandatory in 1791 as a result of the French Revolution. In France and in other European countries the civil marriage was legalized in the civic building, but couples could have a nuptial Mass or a Protestant service celebrated afterward. The United States was faced with the unusual situation of a secular state with a religiously pluralistic people. It solved this dilemma by issuing licenses to clergy to serve as civil magistrates for individual weddings.

In more recent reforms of marriage rites, receiving the Eucharist is again an option in Protestant marriage rites, and the Catholic Church likewise encourages Catholic couples to receive communion. However, this situation presents certain hospitality issues when many of the guests who attend a wedding are not members of that church body or may not be Christians. Since the Eucharist is the liturgy of the church, those who are eligible communicants should not be excluded from receiving communion. In other words, communion should not

---

16. The Book of Common Prayer According to the Use of the Episcopal Church (New York: The Church Hymnal Corporation and The Seabury Press, 1977), 429.

be offered only to the bride and groom or only to the wedding party (which may also be denominationally or even religiously mixed). A clear statement indicating who may receive communion solves this problem, and most guests to the church respect prevailing practices of eucharistic hospitality.

In the Orthodox Church, the marriage service is the church's recognition of a union that God has already begun to work in the lives of two Christians. As long as the union remains within the reality of this world, it will be subject to sin, pain, and death. However, through the sacred mystery of the Eucharist, the union enters at the same time into a new reality: God's Kingdom. In Christ, marriage is restored to its initial perfection, and in the sacrament, this union is made open to the possibility of what God intended marriage to be from the beginning—an eternal life of joy in union with him.

Thus, the marriage service, which includes the legal aspects observed in the vestibule, goes beyond a legal contract. There is no exchange of vows at the altar in the Orthodox rites. The couple have freely and coequally made a commitment to one another and consented to God's presence in their union. There is no phrase "'till death do us part" because if marriage is brought into the Kingdom of God, death, as a separation, is powerless over it. Christ has destroyed death by His Cross and Resurrection; therefore, the union of man and woman in Christ is eternal. The eschatological nature of the mystery of marriage is symbolized by the crowns worn by the bride and groom as they are led to and around the altar.[17]

Marriage and the Theology of the Body

Marriage is not practiced only by Christians, of course. Pope John Paul II stresses in his theology of the body that marriage is a "primordial sacrament."[18] Even so, it serves ontologically as a sign in this world of the life of the Holy Trinity. If we are created in the image of God ("Let us

17. John Meyendorff, *Marriage: An Orthodox Perspective* (Crestwood, NY: St. Vladimir's Seminary Press, 1989).
18. John Paul II, *Man and Woman He Created Them*, 503.

make humankind in *our* image," Gen. 1:26, NRSV—*Elohim* is and speaks in the plural) and if the God who creates us—male and female—is a community of persons, then we are created to be a community of persons who share our life and love with each other and with the world. This is what marital spirituality is all about: participating in God's life and love and sharing it with the world. While marriage is certainly a sublime calling, it is not ethereal but tangible. God's love is meant to be lived and felt in daily life as a married couple lives according to the full truth of the body. In the words of Pope John Paul II:

> In fact, on the road of this vocation, how indispensable is a deepened knowledge of the meaning of the body in its masculinity and femininity! How necessary is an accurate consciousness of the spousal meaning of the body, of its generative meaning, given that all that forms the content of the life of spouses must always find its full and personal dimension in shared life, in behavior, in feelings! And this is all the more so against a background of a civilization that remains under the pressure of a materialistic and utilitarian way of thinking and evaluating.[19]

The theology of the body also shows how the call to celibacy affirms both the goodness of sexuality and the vocation of marriage and family. It doesn't diminish sexuality as the world-renouncing asceticism of ancient and medieval spirituality did. The celibate doesn't reject sexuality but rather uses it to make a gift of self to Christ and his church. Love is what drives us to give of ourselves, whether it be in marriage or in celibacy. Celibacy actually affirms the goodness of the sexual act by sacrificing it for the sake of the kingdom. The vocation of the voluntary celibate is to point to the eschatological reality in which there is neither marriage nor giving in marriage. The pope deftly holds up the witness of both marriage and celibacy.

These are high doctrines of marriage in the Orthodox and Catholic traditions. Protestants, too, consider marriage to be a way of living out one's baptismal calling. In fact, Protestants view marriage as a more

19. Ibid., 222.

honorable Christian calling (vocation) than celibacy. As Luther puts it, there is no higher calling than to be a bishop to one's own children.

The Pastoral Practice of Marriage

In spite of this high view of marriage, some (mostly Protestant) clergy in America have wondered aloud whether the church should even be in the marriage business. Indeed, marriage *has* become a business, with couples looking for church buildings to rent and clergy to hire for the occasion, since oftentimes they are not members of a church. While this can be a lucrative source of income for congregations and clergy, weddings are very time consuming. For the conscientious pastor weddings require premarital counseling, liturgical planning, rehearsals, and the need to open the church building early to let people in and to lock up after all have left. Saturday weddings often bump up against the parish's liturgical schedule if the church has Saturday evening services. Sunday church weddings are often impossible unless they are included within the Sunday liturgy. In earlier days pastors tended to preside only at the weddings of their church members, but in culturally pluralistic countries like the United States interdenominational and even interfaith weddings are commonplace. Yet in spite of the difficulties and aggravations, many pastors are reluctant to give up an opportunity to work through issues of marriage and faith with couples, even if they are not church members, and to witness to what the Bible and the church teach about marriage as a divine institution.

The issue of solemnizing same-sex marriages, now that they are legal in some Western countries (including Canada and the United States) , presents a new challenge to pastors and congregations. While same-sex marriages are not new in human history, they are new to recent history and to Christian practice. Same-sex marriages were legal in ancient Rome, even if not viewed favorably by conservative Roman moralists. Many Romans, for example, could not countenance a man taking the submissive role in the sex act. Christians did not engage in same-sex marriage, and it was the Christian-influenced revision of the legal code under Emperor Theodosius that brought an end to homosexual marriage in the Roman Empire.

Obviously, the purpose of marriage for procreation cannot be met in homosexual marriage, and churches have resisted the move toward same-sex marriage on this basis. But governments legalize marriage according to their own notions of the common good. Marriage has always been seen as an institution that places a restraint on unbridled sexuality, so it makes sense that the state would apply this social good to homosexuals as well as heterosexuals. Ironically, it is an attitude of social conservatism. In the United States, this issue has been decided by the Supreme Court on the basis of equal rights under the law.

If Christian churches solemnize same-sex marriage, they need to recognize that there is no biblical command or promise concerning same-sex marriages. Scripture readings used in Christian marriage rites that apply to the divine institution of marriage (e.g., Gen. 1:26–28; 2:18–24; Eph. 5:21–33; 1 Pet. 3:1–9) are obviously not applicable to a same-sex marriage. However, readings about God's covenant faithfulness, the fulfillment of hope (such as the eschatological feast and marriage supper of the lamb), and sacrificial love are fitting for the covenant commitment the partners are making.

Marriage in Human Culture

Marriage has meant different things in different cultures. As Luther expresses at the top of his order of marriage, "Many lands, many customs." In traditional societies, the ritual process surrounding marriage is more precisely demarcated than in modern Western or Westernized societies where the couple may be post-adolescent adults who freely choose their partners. Nevertheless, the ritual process still includes the following elements of rite: betrothal (proposing and accepting marriage); meeting each other's families and receiving their affirmation; going through the liminal period of the engagement, during which the couple learns how to work together in planning a wedding; breaking ties with singleness (bachelor parties); a formal statement of marital vows in front of witnesses; a public reception and wedding banquet (often also a rehearsal dinner the night before the wedding); the withdrawal of the married couple to the marriage bed (the honeymoon); and the welcoming of relatives and friends to the couples' new home.

These rituals are also imbued with cultural customs, and in non-Western societies they can be quite protracted and elaborate. I was privileged to attend a wedding reception at Satya Wacana Christian University in Indonesia that clearly surpassed any wedding reception that I have experienced in America; practically the entire community was invited, and I understand that this is not unusual. In Indonesia the betrothal period is often quite lengthy because the families take time to get to know one another. Gifts are given on many occasions. The students in my class enacted the ritual of the new couple visiting the parents of the groom after the wedding to receive wedding gifts from them.

Partner Yoga Sequence

In these chapters I have provided some yoga sequences that "act out" aspects of the lessons. For marriage rites it seems appropriate to provide a sequence for couples. Partner yoga has become a popular and fun way to practice yoga in recent decades. Any historical roots of partner yoga are probably found in tantric practices.

The word *tantra* stems from the Sanskrit root *tan*, which literally translates as "to weave." It aims to weave various life experiences together into a non-dualistic experience of reality. As it is currently interpreted and popularly practiced, Tantra is associated with the concept of sacred sexuality. Figures showing the yab yum (father mother) embrace and sculptures on medieval temples showing various positions of sexual interaction testify to the couple character of historic Tantra. This is not all that Tantra is about, and the Neo-Tantra that is practiced today is sometimes considered a defilement of the essence of tantric bliss, which was really about union with the divine.[20]

20. Georg Feuerstein, *Tantra: The Path of Ecstasy* (Boston: Shambhala, 1998), 271.

Nevertheless, partner yoga probably gained popularity through tantric couples' workshops which work on intimacy between partners.

Partner yoga can be practiced with a life-mate, a friend, or another participant in a yoga class. Some yoga classes assign partners at the end of the class and do some partner yoga *asanas*. I first experienced partner yoga in a general YMCA yoga class, but I believe that partner yoga can be especially helpful to couples who are proposing to become life partners or married couples. Partner yoga allows two people to transform traditional *asanas* into postures for more than one participant that are mutually beneficial for both partners. It requires developing trust in and working cooperatively with the partner. The practice of partner yoga involves breathing, touching, *asanas*, trust, humor, and playfulness. Thanks to Per Erez for his suggestions.

Pranayama. Begin by feeling your partner's breath and begin to breath together. This can be done in a couple of different ways. Partners may sit back to back and engage in deep breathing at a steady rate of inhale and exhale so that they can feel each other's breath and breathe in sync in close proximity to the lungs. If you link your arms, this will bring your backs closer together.

Alternately, partners may sit facing each other with one palm on your partner's chest and the other palm on top of the partner's palm that is on your chest so that you are feeling each other's heartbeat. Partners should look into each other's eyes. Look first into each other's left eye. Then turn your heads to clear the vision and look into each other's right eye. Again turn your heads to clear the vision.

Seated twist. If you are seated back to back, rest your hand on your opposite knee and reach your other hand back to rest it on your partner's opposite knee. This will require each of you to twist your spines and abdomens. Do this in both directions. If you are seated facing each other, take hold of opposite arms around your backs (for example, extending your right arm to your partner's left arm, which is behind his or her back) and gently pull each other into a twist. Do this also on the other side.

Double downward dog. One partner does downward dog in the regular way. The other partner does downward dog but places his or her feet on the partner's back. Change places.

Double tree pose. Hold hands for support and move your opposite legs up the standing leg to an equal height that you can agree on, to the thighs if possible. Change sides.

Double boat pose. Sit on the floor and extend your feet to touch each other's feet and hold hands. Lean back (keep spines straight) and raise your feet together so that your bodies each form a V (or together a W). Hold this and other poses as long as you like.

Forward and backward bends. One partner is in child pose or seated forward fold while the other partner lays his or her back on the partner's back, allowing his or her spine to follow the curve of the partner's spine. Partners should change positions.

Final savasana. Partner savasana could be simply lying side by side holding hands.

Figure 14a. The crowning of the bride and groom in the marriage liturgy of the Syro-Malabar Church in Kerala, India.

B. Burial Rites

The man and woman God placed in the garden of the world were tempted to be "like God" and had to be reminded of their finitude. The Lord God does not wipe out the "fallen" creation; it continues laboriously. In pain the woman gives birth to children and the man provides for their sustenance by the sweat of his brow. The race survives and may even thrive, but the individuals return to the ground from which they were created, for "you are dust, and to dust you shall return" (Gen. 3:19, NRSV). Each of us is born. We strive, and we may thrive; but we die.

The Biology of Death

We came to life when the breath of life was breathed into us; we begin to die when we've lost the ability to breathe on our own. Each breath provides the oxygen necessary to the rest of the body for survival. Very simply, dying starts to happen when the body doesn't get the oxygen it needs to survive. Today ventilators can prolong life by infusing oxygen into the body, though not indefinitely, especially if other complicating factors are in play.

Different cells die at different speeds, so the length of the dying process depends on which cells are deprived of oxygen. The brain requires a tremendous amount of oxygen but keeps very little in reserve, so any cutoff of oxygen to the brain will result in cell death within three to seven minutes. When blood is cut off from the heart, a heart attack occurs and can take a life fairly swiftly without immediate intervention. Since our bodies aren't designed to last forever, sometimes the body's systems simply wear out with age. Certain outward signs appear when these systems begin slowing down. The person begins sleeping more to conserve the little energy that's left. When that energy is gone, the individual may lose the desire to eat and then to drink. Swallowing becomes difficult, and the mouth gets very dry; forcing the person to eat or drink can cause choking. The dying person loses bladder and bowel control, but accidents occur less frequently as the gastrointestinal functions shut down and the dying person consumes less.

The stage just before a person dies is called the agonal phase. The dying person is often disoriented, and it seems like he or she can't get comfortable. It also seems that the person can't catch his or her breath. There may be agonizing pauses between loud, labored breaths. If fluid is built up in the lungs, then the congestion may cause a sound known as the "death rattle." As the cells inside a person lose their connections, the person may start convulsing or having muscle spasms.[21]

When the heartbeat and breath stop, the person is clinically dead. Circulation stops, and no new reserves of oxygen are reaching cells. However, clinical death also denotes that the process is reversible by means of CPR, a transfusion, or a ventilator. The point of no return is biological death, which begins about four to six minutes after clinical death. After the heartbeat stops, it only takes those few minutes for brain cells to begin dying from lack of oxygen. Resuscitation is impossible at this point.

Because the body begins to decompose quickly and emit odors, there's not a lot of time for sitting around and staring at the corpse. The body cools to room temperature, and rigor mortis sets in between two and six hours after death. The living organisms that live in the intestines begin to break down their host by moving to other organs and feeding on the body. The skin changes color, bloating occurs, and gas is emitted, causing odors. The rate of decomposition depends on atmospheric conditions and the steps that are taken to preserve the corpse (e.g., embalming or refrigeration).

Burial Rites

The ancients learned the biology of death by observation and experience. Some burial customs were dictated by the practical necessity of disposing of the body as quickly and reverently as possible. In warm countries this meant almost immediately, although Egyptian

---

21. Sherwin B. Nuland, *How We Die: Reflections on Life's Final Chapter* (New York: Knopf, 1994).

embalming and wrapping practices made it possible to delay burial for an extended period of time while arrangements were carefully made. The embalming practice included removal of the internal organs, which are a swamp of organisms (although the ancient Egyptians didn't know that), and stuffing the cavity with cotton. This prevented rapid decomposition. Hindus burned the body in order to release the soul and encourage it to move on to its next reincarnation.[22]

Because of the need to dispose of the body in short order, most rites of death focus on the period of mourning. In Judaism this rite became quite elaborate. The dead body was considered unclean; without embalming, it was washed, clothed, and prepared for almost immediate burial. But the period of mourning was divided into three sections of three days, seven days, and thirty days, plus an observance of the anniversary of the death. The activities prohibited to the mourner were extensive.

While Christians made little contribution to marriage rites, they transformed the rites of death that were practiced in the pagan world because of the Christian belief in the resurrection of the body. Christians inherited from Judaism a preference for burial of the dead rather than cremation, which was preferred in the mid- to late Roman Republic and the early Roman Empire into the first and second centuries CE. Changes in preference from cremation to burial (inhumation) in the late Roman Empire probably reflect Christian influence.

Some Roman practices either fell away or were transformed in Christian practice, but the basic ritual process remained unchanged. The body of the deceased was prepared for burial at his or her house and transported in a procession to the place of disposal (cremation, inhumation) with a stop at a public place (forum, church building) along the way. For both pagans and Christians memorial services were held in commemoration of the deceased at prescribed intervals after death. Let us first look at the Roman rituals of death before we discuss

22. Cedric Mims, *When We Die: The Science, Culture, and Rituals of Death* (New York: St. Martin's, 1998).

the changes in funeral practices made by Christianity that were passed on to Western culture.[23]

At the time of death the eyes of the deceased were closed by a senior member of the family, and a coin for Charon the ferryman to transport the soul of the deceased across the River Styx was placed in the mouth of the deceased. The body was cleansed and dressed by the family and then transported on a bier in a procession to a cemetery outside the city walls as dirges were sung, accompanied by brass instruments (tuba and cornu). At the cemetery a *laudatio funebris* or eulogy (a formal oration or panegyric) was given in praise of the dead. For a public figure, the procession stopped at the forum, and the eulogy was delivered there. At the grave a sacrifice was performed in the presence of the corpse. The sacrificial victim was then allotted for consumption among the participants. The portion for the deceased was put on a spit and cremated with the body, if the body was cremated. The family ate the portion that was due the living. Roman funerals typically occurred at night, so this sacrificial feast was actually a supper. After the funeral the family members went through rites of purification because of the defilement of being in contact with the corpse. On the ninth day after the person died, the funeral feast and rites—called the *novendialis* (nine days)—were held. A libation to the *Manes* (deified souls of the ancestors) was poured onto the grave. This concluded the period of full mourning.

In February—the last month of the original Roman calendar when March 1 was New Year's Day—the dead were honored at a nine-day festival called the *Parentalia*, which was followed by the *Feralia* on February 21, the day on which the potentially malign spirits of the dead were propitiated. During the *Parentalia*, families gathered at cemeteries to offer meals to the ancestors (*refrigeria*) and then shared wine and cakes among themselves. Tombs for wealthy, prominent families were constructed as "houses," with a decorated room for these banqueting festivities.

---

23. See J. M. C. Toynbee, *Death and Burial in the Roman World* (Baltimore: Johns Hopkins University Press, 1971), 43–72.

At the death of a Christian the eyes were closed, and the body was cleansed, anointed, and dressed; but there was no coin for Charon. This anointing is not to be associated with what became extreme unction (see previous chapter) but rather with baptism; a kind of perfume was used to mask the odor of decay (just as the myrrh-bearing women intended to do on Jesus' body on the morning of the third day). The practice of anointing the body for burial continued in later centuries, although it was done as part of the funeral service. Christians, like Jews, practiced burial rather than cremation, both in respect of the body and as a symbol of the resurrection of the body. The funeral procession was accompanied by psalms and alleluias, not dirges. In the procession, white garments were worn rather than dark ones. This may simply reflect the fact that no one rolled on the ground as a sign of mourning. The sacrifice at the cemetery and future meals on the tops of tombs (*mensae*) was the Eucharist. Especially in the age of persecution, Christians gathered at the tombs of martyrs to celebrate the Eucharist. To the pagan Romans this would look like a *refrigerium* because of the bread and wine. During the age of persecution, Christians could generally gather in the cemeteries at night for the Eucharistic meal without being disturbed because the Romans respected burial customs. Gatherings in the cemeteries at night also gave Christian women an opportunity to be out after dark without the usual restrictions. The danger, as far as the Christian bishops were concerned, was that Christian gatherings in the cemeteries could be as riotous as pagan gatherings, and they issued admonitions for restraint. In Milan, Ambrose abolished Christian *refrigeria* altogether.[24] Gifts brought to the graves or unclaimed remains of the deceased were to be distributed to the poor.

A striking example of an ancient Christian burial prayer is from the prayer book (*Euchologion*) of Bishop Sarapion of Thmuis in Lower Egypt in the first half of the fourth century.

> O God, you have authority of life and death, God of the spirits and master of all flesh; you kill and make alive, you bring down to the gates of Hades

24. See Geoffrey Rowell, *The Liturgy of Christian Burial* (London: SPCK, 1977), 11.

246

and bring up; you create the spirit of mortals within them and take to yourself the souls of the saints and give rest; you alter and change and transform your creatures, as is right and expedient, being yourself alone incorruptible, unalterable and eternal.

We pray to you for the repose and rest of this your servant; give rest to his soul, his spirit, in green places, in chambers of rest with Abraham and Isaac and Jacob and all your saints; and raise up his body in the day when you have ordained, according to your promises which cannot lie, that you may render to it also the heritage of which it is worthy in your holy pastures. Remember not his transgressions and sins and cause his going forth to be peaceable and blessed. Heal the grief of his relatives who survive him with the spirit of consolation, and grant to us all a good end, through your only-begotten Son, Jesus Christ, through whom to you is the glory and the strength in the Holy Spirit, forever and ever.[25]

This prayer is an example of the combination of beliefs about the afterlife that Christianity inherited from Greek mythology (the soul is transported to the Elysian Fields—although "green places" could also be a reference to Psalm 23) and the resurrection of the dead in Jewish thought. The same blending of Greek and Hebrew ideas about soul and body is found in contemporary Jewish ideas of the afterlife.[26] The idea of God giving rest to the soul need not imply that the soul has an active existence apart from the body and is therefore, in some sense, immortal; the idea of "rest" implies quite the opposite. The commitment to biblical views are evident in the symbolic decorations on the tombs of Christians; the biblical motifs include baptism, loaves and fishes pointing to the Eucharist, the Good Shepherd, Daniel among the lions, the three young men in the fiery furnace, Job delivered from his miseries, and Christ raising Lazarus. Many of these symbols are images of deliverance.

Christians commemorated the dead with special services on specific days after the death. The most common days of commemoration were the third, seventh, and fortieth. The third day is clearly associated with the resurrection of Christ on the third day. The seventh day is symbolic

25. Lucien Deiss, *The Springtime of the Liturgy* (Collegeville, MN: Liturgical Press, 1979), 207–8.
26. See Jeffrey Burton Russell, *A History of Heaven: The Singing Silence* (Princeton: Princeton University Press, 1997), 18ff., 40ff.

of the Sabbath rest in Genesis. The symbolic meaning of the fortieth day remains unclear, although there are plenty of biblical references to draw upon for an interpretation.

Attitudes toward Dead Bodies

In spite of parallels in ritual processes, there was bound to be a collision between Christian and pagan (and Jewish) attitudes toward dead bodies. Christians consider the bodies of the saints to be sources of holiness rather than defilement. The location of a deceased saint actually served to make the space holy. One church father in the fourth century said that the River Tiber in Rome was sanctified because the graves of Peter and Paul were on either side of it. Cemeteries were regarded as sacred places, and when Christians could erect basilicas for use in public gatherings they often erected them over the graves of martyrs. The most famous church to be built in a cemetery (a necropolis, or city of the dead) was St. Peter's Basilica on the Vatican Hill outside the city of Rome. Relics of the martyrs and saints were also transported to various places to be enshrined in the altars of churches even inside the city walls, which caused disgust among the pagans. A riot broke out in Gaza City in 496 when pagans thought Christians were bringing a dead body into the city.

Christians wanted to be surrounded by the bodies of the saints. They gloried in the faithful departed in a way that Peter Brown says "would have been profoundly disturbing to pagan and Jewish feeling."[27] Altars increasingly looked like tombs. In fact, they *were* tombs, with pieces of dead saints actually entombed in them. The *mensa* became the tabletop for the celebration of the Eucharist. A city like Rouen, which lacked its own local saints, could boast in 496, "Our habitation is now among the legion of Saints and the renowned powers of the Heavens."[28] Within the span of a century, from the beginning of the fourth century to the beginning of the fifth, a complete revolution happened in the world

27. Peter Brown, *The Cult of the Saints: Its Rise and Function in Latin Christianity* (Chicago: University of Chicago Press, 1981), 7.
28. Ibid., 38.

of late antiquity with regard to attitudes about the dead. As Béatrice Caseau states, "That which had defiled the space in the eyes of the pagans sacralized it in the eyes of Christians."[29]

As we move into late antiquity and the Middle Ages we find cemeteries planted around church buildings and the faithful departed being interred within the church building itself. The Orthodox churches in the eastern Mediterranean continued the Jewish practice of gathering the bones of the deceased into ossuaries. This involved disinterring the remains after one to three years, washing the remains with wine and perfume, and placing them in an ossuary box in an ossuary room in or near the church building. The remains of Orthodox monks were disinterred after one to three years, cleaned, and the bones were desposited in the monastery's charnel house, usually in categories of skeletal remains (e.g. skulls with skulls, femurs with femurs, etc.). The remains of a Christian were treated with reverence, in conformity with the biblical teaching that the body of a believer is a "temple of the Holy Spirit" (1 Cor. 3:16–17), having been sanctified by baptism, Holy Communion, and participation in the mystical life of the church Christians in both the East and the West have been happy to be surrounded with the remains of the faithful departed, whether in a church cemetery or interred within the church building, ossuaries, or (in modern urban practice) columbaria in or near the church building, containing the ashes of the deceased.

Christian Funeral and Burial Practices

Profound changes occurred in the Christian funeral practices in the medieval West. The ancient Christian singing of alleluias and psalms of praise in processions was replaced with penitential psalms and dirges. Black or violet replaced white as the color of the liturgical vestments, and the Mass for the dead came to be called the "Requiem Mass" because of the opening words of the Introit antiphon: "aeternam dona

29. Béatrice Caseau, "Sacred Landscapes," in G. W. Bowersock, Peter Brown, and Oleg Grabar, *Late Antiquity: A Guide to the Postclassical World* (Cambridge, MA: Belknap Press of Harvard University Press, 1999), 37.

ei (eis), Domine, et lux perpetua luceat ei (eis). Requiescat (-ant) in pace. Amen" (Eternal rest grant unto him/her/them, O Lord, and let perpetual light shine upon him/her/them. May he/she/they rest in peace). There is no Gloria in excelsis Deo and no recitation of the Creed, which may reflect the fact that Requiem Masses were usually celebrated on weekdays when these items were omitted in the Roman Mass; the alleluia chant before the Gospel is replaced by a tract (a sentence between the Epistle and Gospel readings), as in Lent (no Alleluia); the kiss of peace is omitted (perhaps because communion was not administered to the congregation); and the Agnus Dei is altered in its last phrase—"give us peace" is changed to "give them eternal rest forever"; *Ite missa est* is replaced with *Requiescant in pace* (May they rest in peace); the *Deo gratias* (Thanks be to God) response is replaced with "Amen." Other omissions include the use of incense at the introit and the Gospel, lit candles held by acolytes when a deacon chants the Gospel, and a benediction (since the service continued at the grave). The sequence hymn, *Dies Irae*, sung between the tract and the Gospel, became an obligatory part of the Requiem Mass. As its opening words—*Dies irae* (day of wrath)—indicate, this poetic composition speaks of the day of judgment in fearsome terms; it then appeals to Jesus for mercy. The Requiem Mass also emphasizes the resurrection of the body and the last judgment, which is a counterbalance to the focus on the purification of souls in purgatory that dominated thinking about death and pious practices on behalf of the dead in the medieval West.

The Requiem Mass was actually the termination of a series of prayer offices known as the Office of the Dead. Originating in the seventh or eighth century, this office differs in important points from the other offices of the Roman liturgy. It lacks the Little (Interval) Hours, the Second Vespers, and Compline. In this respect it resembles the ancient vigils, which began at eventide (First Vespers), continued during the night (Matins), and ended at the dawn (Lauds); Mass followed and terminated the vigil. The absence of the introduction "O Lord, make haste to help me," the Gloria Patri in the psalms, and the hymns may also recall more ancient times when these additions had not yet been made. The psalms are chosen not in their serial order, as in the usual Roman Sunday and weekday offices, but because certain verses, which serve as antiphons, seem to allude to the state of the dead. The lessons from Job, so suitable for the Office of the Dead, were also read in earlier centuries at funeral services. This all-night vigil is the origin of the "wake."

This round of offices originated in the monasteries as a way of keeping vigil for deceased brothers or benefactors, as did All Souls' Day on November 2, which originated in the Cluniac monasteries circa 1000. All Souls' Day was joined with All Saints' Day on November 1 as a way of remembering all the faithful departed at the beginning of November. In western Europe this coincided with the change of seasons before the onset of winter. The two commemorations were days of extraordinary busyness for clergy and laity. They involved gathering the relics of the saints for display on All Saints' Day and cleaning the cemeteries for All Souls' Day. The full round of the offices of the dead were observed.[30]

The combination of mass death from plagues and increasing prosperity in the late Middle Ages contributed to increasing provisions in wills and through burial societies (confraternities) for offices and masses for the repose of souls in purgatory. The demand was so great that priests were ordained who did no pastoral work other than offering votive masses for the dead. The social historian John Bossy refers to the social piety of providing for the relief of the souls of family and friends in purgatory as "charity for the dead."[31] Since purgatory was a form of penance extended into the afterlife the attitude of the dying person at the time of death was considered of vital importance for his or her fate in the hereafter, making ministry at the time of death also of great importance. We will see in the next lesson that the ministry of healing became "the last rites" with confession and absolution, last anointing (extreme unction), and communion for the

---

30. See Frank C. Senn, *The People's Work* (Minneapolis: Fortress Press, 2006), 199–213.
31. Bossy, *Christianity in the West*, 26ff.

journey (viaticum). Orders for the Commendation of the Dying were also developed.[32]

The Reformation rejected votive masses and purgatory and therefore abolished the Requiem Mass. However, psalms and readings from the Office of the Dead provided material for the new Protestant burial services. Some medieval practices continued, especially in Lutheranism. A simple procession was made from the house of the deceased into the church and then from the church to the cemetery for burial. The funeral sermon took the place of the Requiem Mass and elements from the Office of the Dead (psalms with antiphons, lessons with responsories, hymns, sermon, Gospel canticle and prayers) provided an order and content for a funeral liturgy. The procession to the cemetery included the hymn *In media vita* in Luther's German version, *De profundis* (Psalm 130), as well as other hymns. Some church orders included the committal of the body into the grave retained the medieval form.[33] The form of the prayer office provided a model for orders for the Burial of the Dead in American Lutheran service books (e.g., *Church Book* 1891, *Common Service Book* 1917, *Service Book and Hymnal* 1958).

In the Reformed tradition burial took place "without any ceremony" and was followed by a service of readings, psalms, sermon, and prayers in the church.[34] The Book of Common Prayer (1549) provided propers for a Eucharist to be held in the church before or after burial, but this was abolished in the 1552 and subsequent prayer books of the Church of England (1559, 1604, 1662). The Book of Common Prayer provided sentences to be said during the procession from the house of the deceased to the church. The procession was met at the church stile by the priest and continued into the cemetery for the service of committal. The 1662 prayer book provided Psalms 39 and 90 and the lesson from 1 Corinthians 15 after the Order for the Burial of the Dead,

32. See Philip H. Pfatteicher, *Commentary on the Occasional Services* (Minneapolis: Fortress Press, 1983), 142–56.
33. See Craig Kostlofsky, *The Reformation of the Dead: Death and Ritual in Early Modern Germany, 1450–1700* (Basingstoke, UK: Macmillan, 2000).
34. William D. Maxwell, *The Liturgical Portions of the Genevan Service Book* (Edinburgh: Oliver and Boyd, 1931), 58–59, 160–64.

apparently as propers for an order of Morning or Evening Prayer in the church before or after the cemetery service—a use that continued into the nineteenth century.

A feature of all Protestant funeral liturgies was a reluctance to deal with the corpse or directly address the dead. Changes in the Book of Common Prayer rite exemplify this. While in the 1549 edition the dead were addressed directly in the committal, "I commend thy soule to God the father almighty, and thy body to the grounde, earth to earth, asshes to asshes, dust to dust," in the 1552 and subsequent editions the priest turned away from the corpse and faced the living when he said, "Forasmuche as it hath pleased almightie God of his great mercy to take unto himselfe the soule of our dere brother here departed: we therefore commit his body to the ground, earth to earth, asshes to asshes, dust to dust."[35] The dead person is spoken about but not spoken to; the dead were no longer part of the living. The final prayer in the 1552 burial service reworked from a prayer in the 1549 edition the phrase "both thys our brother, and we, may be found acceptable in the sight" to say "may we be found acceptable in thy syghte." The boundaries of human community were thereby redrawn to exclude the dead. As such, Protestantism severed the unity of the communion of saints in the church militant and the church triumphant.

A revolution in both Catholic and Protestant funeral rites occurred in the late twentieth century as a result of liturgical renewal. After the Second Vatican Council the title "Requiem Mass" was often replaced by the term "Mass of the Resurrection" or "Mass of Christian Burial," although "Requiem" was never official terminology. In line with this shift, the use of black vestments was made optional (and had mostly disappeared by the late twentieth century, at least in the United States); many priests preferred white, the color of joy associated with Easter, or purple, a muted version of mourning. The texts used for the service were similarly changed, with the overall theme of the service being a proclamation of the promise of eternal life made by Jesus. In

35. *The First and Second Prayer Books of King Edward VI*, Everyman's Library 448 (London: J. M. Dent, 1910), 269–70, 424–25.

253

the spirit of Vatican II, the people participated more in the singing of hymns. Dirges were abandoned in favor of alleluias and songs of joy.

Liturgical renewal also had an impact on Protestant practice, especially in American Lutheran, Episcopal, Methodist, and Presbyterian traditions. The order of service became the liturgy of the word, with the possibility of celebrating the Eucharist, indicating a new appreciation of the role of the sacrament in Christian life. Today's prayers take notice of the faithful Christian who has died, mentioning the deceased by name, and a commendation of the faithful departed concludes the service in the church. There is a recovered sense that death cannot break the communion of saints. Hence, the paschal spirit is introduced into the funeral liturgies, and the custom of lighting the paschal candle and placing it next to the coffin has emerged, especially in those churches that use the paschal candle at the Easter Vigil and for baptisms. White is the preferred liturgical color, although Lutherans continue to use the color of the day or season. Churches also provide palls (preferably white) to place over the coffin during the service. This equalizes the worth of the coffins and serves as another symbol of baptism.[36]

The ancient ritual structure of death and burial has been challenged by the exigencies of modern urban life. People more often die in hospitals or nursing homes than in their own homes, and families are no longer involved in the preparation of the body for burial. This task has been taken over by professional funeral directors. Funeral homes developed as an institution in the nineteenth century to provide places where the body could be displayed so that the family could gather for a wake or vigil and receive friends. Sometimes, as a matter of convenience, the funeral service was also held in the funeral home. This encouraged the use of soft sentimental music, excessive flowers, exorbitant expenditures on coffins and vaults, and even the postponement of the actual lowering of the body into the grave and

---

36. See Philip H. Pfatteicher, *Commentary on Lutheran Book of Worship* (Minneapolis: Augsburg Fortress, 1990), 474–507.

burial. Taken together, these practices became part of "the American way of death."[37]

Cremation has become more popular even among Christians as an alternative to inhumation because it is less expensive and it seems more ecologically friendly. However, it should be noted that it is not ecologically unfriendly to bury bodies in wooden boxes that will eventually decompose. It is the use of concrete vaults and metal coffins that is ecologically unfriendly. Inhumation is a better symbol of the hope of the resurrection of the body than cremation. If cremation is practiced, the disposal of the ashes needs to respect the remains of the body as much as inhumation (burial).

Cremation has also led to a reduction in the number of funeral services. Memorial services can be arranged at a time convenient to far-flung family members, relatives, and friends. Unfortunately, memorial services tend to become remembrances of the deceased (which much eulogizing) rather than a proclamation of the hope of the resurrection. That proclamation is more likely to be made with the body of the deceased front and center in the church building. There is no reason why cremation cannot follow a funeral service.

Some churches have installed columbaria as a form of a modern urban church cemetery to contain the ashes of the faithful departed. These may be located within a church building or in an outside garden. The positive implication of columbaria is that Christians are still surrounded by the physical remains of their saints, and the ashes, as remains of the body, are treated with honor and respect.

.

37. See Jessica Mitford, *The American Way of Death* (New York: Simon & Schuster, 1963).

Figure 14b. Traditional song and dance at a funeral of the Toraja people indigenous to a mountainous region of South Sulawesi, Indonesia, who are known for their elaborate funeral rites.

9

Cultural Bodies, Artistic Bodies

A. Liturgical Inculturation

We have already seen how deeply ritual practices are embodied in the cultures of peoples. As we look at the expressions of art, music, and dance in Christian liturgy we will see how the relationship between worship and culture is a constant and complicated issue for the church. Issues of liturgical inculturation have become increasingly urgent as Christianity has spread around the world and is growing quickly in places where it has not been long established, especially in Africa and Asia. But immigration and population mobility has also raised the issue of cultural pluralism for established churches in Europe and the Americas.

It is not easy to come up with a universally agreed upon definition of culture because culture is composed of many aspects. However, I think it is possible to agree generally on what those aspects of culture are.[1]

---

1. See Anscar J. Chupunco, "Liturgy and the Components of Culture," in *Worship and Culture in Dialogue*, ed. S. Anita Stauffer (Geneva: Lutheran World Federation, 1994), 153–66.

Components of Culture

The components of culture include the practical aspects of life: the provision of food through planting and hunting or herding, cooking and eating habits, the building of shelters, and provisions for social organization and ways of doing business. To a great extent food, styles of clothing, and types of shelter are determined by geographic and climate conditions. And yet the food people put into their bodies for nourishment, how they dress, and the kind of buildings they erect are also culturally conditioned. That's why we see people bringing their foods, clothing, and architecture with them when they move to another location, even in a different climate. Hence Chicago can hold its annual "Taste of Chicago" event, which features many different ethnic foods from the various ethnic cultures in this very multicultural city. These ethnic groups also continue to have their own festivals, with parades and ethnic food and drink. On the streets of cities like Chicago, you can see people wearing distinctive ethnic dress. And immigrant groups erect churches and temples that reflect their cultural heritage.

In these ways specific aspects of culture are passed on from one generation to another, including the stories that provide people with their identity and also their values. Values include how particular cultures celebrate family life, extend hospitality to nonfamily members, and select and honor leadership. Social groups also have their languages and rituals by which they celebrate their stories and enact their rituals. Children need to be taught these things if the cultural way of life is to continue.

So cultures provide some kind of educational system to pass on their myths and rituals. This is to say that culture has structures, some of which are educational. Educational structures may be as simple as learning from parents in the home, or they may be as highly developed as schools of various levels. Cultural structure can be maintained through institutions. Political organization and religious systems are also a part of the cultural structures.

Finally, cultures are expressed through arts and crafts, stories, music, and dance. Some of these forms may be folk expressions, and others may be artistic expressions. The artistic expressions (e.g., painting and sculpture, poetry and novels, learned music and ballet) are generally called "high culture." While rooted in local cultures, they are capable of transcending local cultures because they are expressed in more universal ways.

As we can see, the many and varied aspects of culture make it difficult to come up with a comprehensive definition of culture.

One additional aspect of culture in the modern world is that cultures are decidedly pluralistic. There are few local cultures in the world today that have not been influenced by other cultures as a result of trade and commerce, migrations of people, and the worldwide web.

Culturally, Indonesia is a very complex nation. It includes on its many islands a number of indigenous cultures, but it has been influenced by Western culture through commercial dealings and global technological sharing. While Indonesia is predominantly a Muslim country, remnants remain of the more ancient Hindu religion. At the Borobudur Temple near Yogyakarta an annual world gathering of Buddhists is held on the temple grounds. What's more, Christianity has a toehold going back to the colonial period of the Dutch East Indies.

The Church as a Culture

Our concern in this chapter is to discuss liturgical inculturation, which is a complicated topic because, first of all, the liturgy itself is a cultural expression. Put more specifically, it is the cultural expression of a social group called the church. Liturgy is not a cultural void waiting to be filled with the expressions of other cultures. It is already quite full of its own cultural expressions, some of which can be traced back to the origins of Christianity.

The first Christians were Jews who lived in two cultural worlds: the world of the Jewish people and the world of the Greco-Roman commercial and political state, which first-century Jews also inhabited, whether in Palestine or in the diaspora. We should not ignore the fact that many Jews in the diaspora lived east of the Roman Empire in East Syria, Persia (modern day Iraq and Iran), and even India. So, from its beginning, gentile Christianity was Hellenistic in the west and Semitic in the east. Consequently, liturgical texts emerged in both Greek and Syriac. But as the gospel was spread beyond the earliest centers of Christianity, particularly Antioch and Alexandria, the issues involving inculturation naturally arose.

Dynamic Equivalence

Issues of inculturation came up first in the need to translate the Christian Scriptures into other languages, including Latin. Jews had already translated the Hebrew Scriptures into Greek before the time of Christ (the Septuagint); quotations of the Old Testament in the New Testament are from the Greek translation, not the Hebrew. This gave early Christians permission, as it were, to translate their Scriptures in the interests of the mission of the gospel. The Eastern Church was quicker to do this than the Western Church. We have early versions of the Bible in Coptic, Ethiopic, and Arabic. One of the great accomplishments of translation came about when the Greek brothers from Constantinople, Cyril and Methodius, invented the Slavic alphabet in order to translate the Bible and the liturgy into the Slavic languages. When Russia was ready to embrace the Orthodox faith around 900, a Slavonic version of the Bible and the Divine Liturgy already existed.

Translation brings up the issue of what linguists call "dynamic equivalence." Sometimes a word in one language doesn't translate literally into a word in another language, and some equivalent must be found in the new language. In more recent times, the issue of dynamic equivalence has been raised in the effort to use language that conveys what the original expression intends rather than a literal equivalent. For example, how should one translate the Latin "et cum spiritu tuo" into English? Literally it could be translated "and with your spirit." But what does "spirit" suggest to modern people? It was argued that the Latin original was itself a translation of a Hebrew/Aramaic form of greeting, so it could also be translated "and also with you." This was the translation chosen in 1970 and accepted in ecumenical use. But in 2011 the Roman Catholic authorities stated that translations must be more faithful to the original Latin. Hence, English-speaking Catholics now say, "and with your spirit," just as they say in the Nicene Creed that the Son is "consubstantial with the Father" rather than "of one being with the Father." This form of translation, which is literally faithful to the original text, is called "formal correspondence."

Creative Assimilation

The liturgy has also been inculturated through what the Philippine Catholic liturgist, Anscar Chupungco, OSB, calls "creative assimilation."[2] In short, this is the issue of dynamic equivalence applied to symbolic actions rather than texts. Creative assimilation means using the cultural forms of the local culture to do something in the liturgy that was instituted in a different form. For example, liturgical renewal in the mid-twentieth century was interested in reviving an expression of the enacted greeting of peace in the eucharistic liturgy. We saw in chapter 3 that in the ancient church it was an actual kiss of peace on the lips.[3] This practice remained a liturgical action for centuries, expressing the fact that the Lord's Supper was celebrated in a state of communal reconciliation. But by the Middle Ages it was thought inappropriate for clergy and laity to kiss one another. So the clergy only greeted the other clergy, and the laity was left to their own devices; the kiss of peace died out among them. When those establishing liturgical renewal sought to restore it, kissing one another on the lips wasn't deemed acceptable in some cultures. French and Russian men might kiss one another; American men do not. Thus the handshake has become the way in which the greeting of peace is enacted in America—or in some cases a hug. But in other cultures people don't shake hands; they bow to one another. In the African

2. Anscar J. Chupungco, "Two Methods of Liturgical Inculturation," in *Christian Worship: Unity in Cultural Diversity*, ed. S. Anita Stauffer (Geneva: Lutheran World Federation, 1996), 77–94.
3. See Michael Philip Penn, *Kissing Christians: Ritual and Community in the Late Ancient Church* (Philadelphia: University of Pennsylvania Press, 2005).

Catholic rite of Zaire, the equivalent of a kiss as a gesture of reconciliation became washing hands with one another in the same bowl, so as to say by this symbolic action, "Whatever I have against you, I wash away."

Another example of creative assimilation involves how the practice of foot washing is done on Maundy (or Holy) Thursday. Revived in liturgical renewal circles as a symbol of servanthood, this symbolic action admittedly hadn't had much of a career in the history of liturgy. The church of Milan under Ambrose practiced it and so do the Mennonites. We Americans have resisted the restoration of the practice, arguing that washing someone's feet after they've traveled by foot over dusty roads isn't in our cultural context. Some have suggested handwashing as an equivalent practice, but this doesn't seem like a servant action in the same way that washing feet does; we don't usually wash one another's hands. However, nurses' aids in hospitals and nursing homes wash patients' feet. I have also heard of a large Lutheran congregation located in the center of a large American city that holds a Thursday night meal to which the street people are invited and foot washing is practiced. This must be a welcome gesture for people who walk for much of the day in less-than-adequate footwear. Washing hands is not a good equivalent. Moreover, washing hands in a liturgy during Holy Week might even suggest to some astute Bible readers Pontius Pilate's gesture at Jesus' trial.

Another example of creative assimilation is the substitution of communion elements in places that don't produce wheat bread and grape wine. In this age of global commerce wheat bread and wine are probably available in most countries, but there may be situations in which it is necessary to find some equivalent. In Japan, rice cakes and saki are sometimes used. The bread assimilation should be a basic foodstuff, and the wine assimilation should be something alcoholic that would be served at festive banquets.

Organic Development

A third form of inculturation is called organic development, which is the development of new texts and new ritual actions in new situations for which there are no models to follow from the past. Examples might include interfaith worship in situations that allow for this or in situations in which national or local disaster might call for it. In America, community interfaith services on the National Day of Thanksgiving have been held that allow for particular religious expressions within one liturgical structure. In such a service in my local community breads from different cultures are blessed and distributed.

Another example might be the development of rites for blessing same-sex unions in countries that recognize same-sex marriage and in which gay church members desire this form of pastoral care. Obviously the church's traditional marriage rites—which include reading the institution texts from Genesis and their citations in the words of Jesus and Paul, the blessing of the conjugal union, and the petition for the gift and heritage of children—cannot be used. But the Bible's analogy between Yahweh's covenant fidelity to Israel and marriage can be evoked in a service in which two people pledge lifelong care and support of each other.

Sometimes rites of passage or recognition of ancestors in indigenous cultures need to find a Christian expression, particularly when people from those cultures become Christians. Not everything from one's native cultures needs to be left behind. These are all cutting-edge issues, but that is the nature of organic development.

Cultural Accumulation in the Liturgy

The liturgies we have inherited are full of cultural expressions that have accumulated over the centuries. We can note instances of Jewish, Greek, and Roman cultures, as well as whatever other cultures the liturgy passed through on its way to our use. Heading north and west of the Alps, these may be German, French, English, or Dutch. Heading north of the Danube they may be Slavic, and heading east of Palestine they might be Syriac or Arabic. Heading south into Africa they may be Coptic and Ethiopic. Cultures change as social conditions change and as history moves on. So there may also be medieval, Reformation, or post-Reformation cultural influences in our received liturgies. As missionaries introduced the liturgy into new lands where it hadn't previously been, it was evitable that sooner or later the cultural expressions of the lands would find some kind of expression in the liturgy. What is remarkable is how long it took. New cultural contributions will be added to cultural expressions that have already accumulated in the liturgy. Seldom are the cultural inheritances of the past completely discarded. Remnants of cultures from other times and places persist because we have made them our own.

There are also subcultures within Christianity—that is, the denominations. In Indonesia, I have seen Catholic, Reformed, Baptist, and Pentecostal churches. What's more, there are Lutherans in the Batak Christian Protestant Church. Here are quite distinct Christian traditions, whose forms and practices are influenced by the theological issues, historical origins, and further developments of denominational traditions. However, the Christian liturgy will retain certain core practices no matter what time or place it is celebrated in. There will be readings from Scripture. The sacraments of Holy Baptism and Holy Communion will be celebrated, even if they are celebrated differently in different churches. Prayers of thanksgiving, supplication, praise, and intercession will be offered.

These core elements in the liturgy remain in every one of its cultural settings and in most of the denominational expressions of Christianity. The Bible and the sacraments provide Christianity with a worldview and a value system that is expressed in the liturgy and shared among all Christian denominations, no matter what their theological differences and ethnic particularities may be. This basic Christian worldview and value system bumps up against the cultures of the world as the church proclaims the word of God in different times and places. In the interaction between church and society, between liturgy and culture, some of these cultural expressions will be appropriated into the liturgy; other cultural expressions will be resisted. In order to understand these and other dynamics in the relationship between worship and culture, let us consider the "Nairobi Statement on Worship and Culture."

The Nairobi Statement on Worship and Culture

The Lutheran World Federation sponsored a global study of worship and culture. They came up with a statement, adopted in Nairobi, Kenya, in January 1996.[4] This statement has been highly regarded by other Christian traditions as a way of sorting out the complex relationships between worship and culture. The statement holds that there are four ways in which worship and culture are related and that all four should be evident to some extent in every liturgy.

1. Worship is transcultural. Certain core elements of the liturgy transcend all cultures.
2. Worship is contextual. Liturgy is rooted in the lives of the people of local churches. Dynamic equivalence is held up as one way to make that happen.
3. Worship is countercultural. Liturgy embodies the values of the kingdom of God and may stand over against values embedded in the world's cultures.
4. Worship is cross-cultural. Liturgy should give expression to the cultural contributions of all the people gathered in the assembly, especially in multicultural contexts.

As an exercise, think about the liturgies in which you have participated, particularly in your own local congregation, and analyze them according to this model. List all of the elements in the liturgies that you have experienced that are transcultural, contextual, countercultural, and cross-cultural. By means of this exercise you might discern ways to do your liturgies that are more sensitive to the diverse cultures in your own congregation and more dynamically related to the cultures of the world in which we also live and move and have our being.

---

4. See Stauffer, ed., *Christian Worship*, 23–28.

It is possible to see all of these elements embedded in liturgy, although in different ways. For example, a church may use an order of service rooted in the historical tradition. The congregation meets in a building, the architectural design of which reflects the local structures rooted in the culture of that community. The liturgy includes women and children in a way that is not typical of the place of women and children in that society. It uses musical selections that derive from a wide range of times and places.

Music in worship especially has the ability to reflect a wide range of cultural expressions. Within one liturgy the music might include medieval church chant, Reformation chorales or psalmody, Victorian-era British hymns, and Christian folk or contemporary Christian rock music. Such a range of musical selections reminds us of the length and breadth of Christian culture. What kind of cross-cultural music was used in your church's worship last Sunday? Even if your hymns were selected from a standard worship book or hymnal, what times and places were represented in the selection?

The Slow Process of Inculturation

Many leaders and members who desire their church to be more adept at reaching out to the culture in which the congregation lives and moves and has its being wonder why inculturation does not happen faster. When we speak of inculturation we often limit ourselves to adaptation, which entails making the gospel and the liturgy at home in a new cultural setting. But what Michael Amaladoss, SJ, author of *The Asian Jesus*,[5] calls "the gospel-culture encounter" may call for more than mere adaptation. It may call for rooting the gospel and the liturgy in the indigenous culture. For example, Amaladoss, an Indian-Asian Jesuit theologian, drew upon Indian and Asian images to proclaim Christ in his cultural context. But to call Christ a sage or an avatar is not to compare Christ to Confucius or to Krishna. It is simply to use images that are familiar to Asians or Indians. Christ may even be contrasted

5. See Michael Amaladoss, *The Asian Jesus* (New York: Orbis Books, 2006).

with Confucius or Krishna. When the gospel encounters a culture, it involves a call to conversion: a turning to God, as revealed in Christ, and a turning away from cultural pride.

Culture is a social product. As such, it shares in the limitations of humans and of human society. Culture expresses both the good and the bad in human society. For example, family may be a venerated institution in a culture, and for this very reason may become an object of idolatry. Sometimes following Christ requires us to leave our families of origin. This is no less the case in predominantly Christian societies than in predominantly non-Christian societies.

Cultural components include not only language, literature, and art but also economic and sociopolitical structures. These various structures mutually influence each other, so the gospel needs to enter into dialogue with all of these cultural structures. Here the values of the gospel and the values of a culture may be at variance, which is true even of predominantly Christian countries like the United States. Sometimes Christians have to stand against the culture in which we live. The commercial exploitation of Christmas, which begins as early as two months before December 25, is an annual example. Churches are slowly discovering the countercultural power of the Advent season to stand athwart the onslaught of commercialism.

The process becomes more complex with changing cultural perspectives. The gospel entered history embodied in Jewish culture, and the New Testament contains four gospels that embody the circumstances, needs, and perspectives of four different communities of Christians. The good news found further embodiment in Greek and Roman cultures, as well as other dominant cultures, throughout the course of history. We need to recognize that all cultures are ambiguous, including the cultures through which Christianity has passed. From the perspective of the gospel, each culture is comprised of good and bad elements. For example, many cultures in which Christianity has become embedded have been hierarchical and oppressive of women. The gospel and the liturgy, therefore, carry a great deal of baggage as a result of these cultural elements. These issues need to be addressed in the world today, which tends to be more democratic and concerned about the equality of the sexes. Liturgical celebrations have become more inclusive of the talents of people in the congregation and have provided for the role of women as liturgical ministers, even in the Roman Catholic Church, which steadfastly preserves a male priesthood.

The gospel-culture encounter is also an intercultural encounter. The process of cultural interaction depends on whether the cultures are strong or weak, developed or non-developed, dominant or subaltern. I should mention, in this connection, that ideology (or theology) sometimes privileges certain cultures over others. For example, some insist that the Judaic and Greco-Roman cultures are normative for Christianity. But if the kingdom of God is not of this world, that assumption cannot be correct. Using items like vestments, which derive from ancient Roman culture, is for the sake of continuity with Christian history, not because Roman culture is superior to the other cultures through which Christianity has passed.

Another reason for the slow process of inculturation is that culture is not religiously neutral. The cultures that the gospel encounters are not found in a pure, nonreligious state. Every culture is animated by a religious component that seeks to answer ultimate questions of meaning. The religion may be popular or developed, folk or elite, which means that when the gospel encounters a culture it may also be encountering religious beliefs and values embedded in that culture. Pagan practices and sensibilities still linger deep under the surface of the so-called culture of Christendom in Europe. The American civil religion was as much formed by the philosophy of the Enlightenment as by the Christian gospel. Therefore the church must keep its antennae raised in order to discern cultural views that may be at variance with the gospel of Christ.

Inculturation can also be an interreligious process. The gospel sometimes aims at completely replacing other religions, as Christianity tried to do with paganism when the church became the official cultus of the Roman state. Sometimes, where Christianity has not been dominant, it has simply lived peacefully alongside other religions and hoped for the best, as it did for centuries in the Middle East under various Muslim rulers. But we ought to be aware that religious sensibilities are found in every culture. One reason that younger churches are often reluctant to practice inculturation is because they must first gain some distance from the culture out of which their Christian converts come before they can enter into dialogue with that culture.

The complexity of this intercultural and interreligious process increases when we realize that the Spirit of God is present and active in all of the cultures and religions of the world, as Pope John Paul II says in his encyclical, *The Mission of the Redeemer*. Any gospel-culture encounter needs to take this pluralism seriously and should not easily dismiss creative initiatives as syncretistic, as happened in the infamous Chinese Rites controversy in the seventeenth and eighteenth centuries. The dispute arose among Roman Catholic missionaries in religious orders over whether Chinese ritual practices of honoring family ancestors and other formal Confucian and imperial rites qualified as religious rites, making them incompatible with Roman Catholic belief. The Jesuits argued that these Chinese rites were secular and thus could be tolerated as practices in which Christian converts could engage. The Dominicans and Franciscan argued otherwise and reported the issue to Rome for adjudication. At first the Vatican Congregation for the Propagation of the Faith in 1645 condemned the use of Chinese rites. In 1656 the Congregation reversed itself and lifted the ban. Several universities, the Chinese emperor, and several popes weighed in on the discussion, with many Dominicans and Franciscans changing their positions. However, in 1704 Pope Clement XI banned the rites, and in 1742 Pope Benedict XIV reaffirmed the ban. Not until 1939 did Pope Pius XII issue a decree allowing Christians to participate in the observance of ancestral rites and Confucian honoring ceremonies. The Second Vatican Council developed a generally positive principle of admitting indigenous ceremonies into the liturgy of the Catholic Church.[6]

Sometimes inculturation has been seen as the translation and adaptation of a preexistent, "pure" gospel that has already found privileged and normative expression in Judaic and Greco-Roman cultures. But inculturation is not the adaptation of a preexisting practice into a new cultural situation.[7] Inculturation (or indigenization, as it is sometimes called) is a faithful living and celebration of the gospel in one's own cultural context.

In actuality, inculturation is a natural process. People who hear the gospel respond to it spontaneously in their commitment, reflection, prayer, celebration, and action. As new converts join the church they do not leave behind their cultural mindset and practices. Inevitably, the collective forces of a congregation or denomination bring their cultural components with them, influencing the life of the church. I think of how the hierarchical state-supported churches in Europe became democratically organized voluntary associations (denominations) in America. And in time, churches in America began to be run like corporations, even using business models to plan the mission. In America and in other places around the world today, we see the entertainment culture influencing how we worship and do evangelism. Evangelicals especially have embraced the entertainment culture in how they worship. The real issue is not whether inculturation will take place but when the brakes should be applied. Maybe not every cultural expression is appropriate in the liturgy.

An enormous challenge to liturgy today comes from the global consumerist culture. Many congregations used to rely on denominational products to provide resources for worship. For some congregations this may have consisted only of the denominational hymnal. On the Internet anyone can get a license and download whatever material is needed for worship, whether it's denominational or not. While there is nothing wrong with using worship material from other denominations or ecumenical organizations, the temptation

6. See George Minimike, *The Chinese Rites Controversy: From Its Beginning to Modern Times* (Chicago: Loyola University Press, 1985).
7. See G. A. Arbuckle, "Inculturation, Not Adaptation: Time to Change Terminology," *Worship* 60 (1986): 511–20.

becomes relying on these resources instead of preparing our own. I have found, in visiting other churches, that intercessions have been downloaded that promote ideological concerns while lacking specificity when it comes to praying for particular church leaders, national and local political leaders, and international and local disaster victims. The local pastor sometimes does not take the trouble to make the intercessions as specific as possible to the assembly that is actually praying them.

A wider pastoral issue is that consumers (which includes all of us) construct and reconstruct their own self-identities on the basis of the goods that they purchase. The coherence of a religious tradition is challenged when individuals construct meaning on their own and even shop for churches that match their self-identified meanings. In the processing of "shopping" for a church that satisfies their perceived needs or views, they end up judging traditions rather than receiving meaning from them. As a result, liturgy is often in tension with the assumptions and attitudes of modern life.

Individualism versus Community

Modern life is characterized by individualism, competition, and the demand for protection of individual rights, especially in the West but increasingly also in other parts of the world. In religion, the personal relationship with God is often prized above the communal nature of the church. Consequently, prayer and piety become individualistic and emotional. Many forms of mystical prayer encourage the perspective of "alone with the Alone."

On the other hand, liturgy, especially sacramental liturgy, expresses the symbolic actions of the community. In baptism, the community welcomes new members. The Eucharist is a celebration of community, which is symbolized by the sharing of food. Through the sacraments the church becomes the body of Christ, but this communal dimension is present in other rites of the church as well. In the early church, reconciliation was an occasion when the community accepted back notorious public sinners through the processes of public penance. At the anointing of the sick the community prays for and with a sick member. Ordination is the designation by the community of persons who are authorized to speak and act in its name. In marriage a new unit of the community is founded by a man and a woman who make their vow of faithfulness to each other before witnesses. Unfortunately, in many of these rites today only the needs of the individual or the relationship between the couple and God are stressed. The communal celebration of the liturgy and its embodiment in daily life are a vital counter to the pervasive individualism of modern societies. .

Postmodern Pluralism

While modernity was fond of bringing things together and building big unities, postmodernity recognizes the fragmentation and pluralism that exists in modern societies. Modernism drives towards globalization while postmodernity respects diversity and particular identities. But the struggle for a sense of identity in a pluralistic culture may lead to fundamentalism, a phenomenon that can be seen in all religions and that has become a major academic study. *The Fundamentalism Project*, sponsored by the American Academy of Arts and Sciences under the direction of Martin E. Marty and R. Scott Appleby, is an international scholarly investigation of conservative religious movements throughout the world.[8] The study comes to various conclusions, some of which have been criticized. One basic feature that emerges is an aversion to pluralism. Even non-fundamentalists find pluralism difficult to affirm. But increasingly, cultural pluralism is affirmed as a gift of God and the manifestation of human creativity. Simultaneously, there is much talk of the global village. Taking both centrifugal and centripetal factors into consideration it is possible to understand unity not as uniformity but as the dynamic convergence of diversity.

Pluralism is not new in the world. What *is* new is the realization that unity does not mean the suppression of pluralism.[9] Pluralism is

---

8. See especially Gabriel A. Almond, *Strong Religion: The Rise of Fundamentalisms around the World* (Chicago: University of Chicago Press, 2003).

not negative; it can have a positive significance. We can recognize and accept differences as manifestations of the diverse gifts of the Holy Spirit without the need to abandon our particular confessional gift. While respecting the identities of others we can maintain our own sense of identity. This is the tolerance that liberal societies try to cultivate, and with human nature being what it is, tolerance cannot be taken for granted.

We also need to recognize the cultural pluralism in each local congregation. People do not leave their cultures behind when they join the church, and yet they are joining a community that already has a culture. In this way there is a gospel-culture encounter for each individual Christian. Within each congregation dialogue must take place between worship and culture because the congregation lives simultaneously in the culture of the church and the culture of the world. The discussions need to occur not only between us and others but among ourselves in our own communities. How shall our liturgical life, which has a culture of its own, relate to the cultures of the world, from which our members come, bringing the world with them? Each congregation must face this complex question. Just as each local congregation relates to the larger Christian culture of its denomination, it also possesses its own local culture as a social group and must relate to the various cultures in the world in order to live out the gospel. The conversation inevitably continues on every issue that arises. That's what it means to be "in mission."

From Entertainment to Enchantment

Finally, I note that there has been a movement from entertaining passive seekers (as in the 1980s) to engaging participants actively in worship. This is sometimes done in so-called contemporary worship by appealing to the senses and bodily postures in the style of rock concerts with their strobe lights and stage smoke and hand clapping and arm waving and sometimes even encouraging the audience to

9. See Michael Amaladoss, *Making All Things New: Dialogue, Pluralism, and Evangelization in Asia* (New York: Orbis Books, 1990).

join in singing with the band. It is a change of direction in Protestant worship not unlike the reorientation of Catholic worship from attending mass to participating in the liturgy after the Second Vatican Council.

Fantasy is "in," as we see in the video-game craze and the enormous success of the *Harry Potter* and *The Lord of the Rings* books and films. The emerging church phenomenon taps into the appeal of enchantment, devoting a lot of attention to the ambience of the worship space and the order and content of the service. These communities recognize that worship is more than words. But I would like to note that the multisensory catholic liturgical tradition, as manifested in several denominational traditions, is also capable of producing enchantment. The chanting, vestments, icons, candles, and incense are quite capable of drawing worshipers into a different world, a reality that is different from "this world," which they experience in their everyday lives. It is not surprising that many young people find the liturgical experience attractive. It is sensual—it appealing to the senses. It is worship drawn into the body and liturgy enacted by the body.

B. Artistic Bodies

The human body needs shelter from the natural elements—the heat of the sun, rain and snow, wind and cold. We live and work and also worship in buildings that affect the movement of the body and interactions among bodies. These buildings are usually expressions of the cultures in which people live. Artists also present the body in various forms in paintings and sculptures. These works of art are housed in our homes and places of work and also in our places of worship.

Figure 15. A contemporary Byzantine icon.

Church Architecture

The community of faith, like any social group, needs a place to gather in order to be together. Our gathering places are determined by our bodily needs. As we continue to meet in these places, the places also shape our bodily participation in the liturgy.

The word *church* in Greek, *ekklesia*, means those who are "called out" of the world to engage in a "public work" (*leigtourgia*). Christians originally met to share a meal together—the Lord's Supper—study the Scriptures, and pray. They did not need a temple, such as the pagans or even the Jews had in Jerusalem. In fact, the early Jewish Christians continued to worship in the temple alongside other Jews as long as the temple existed. But they were also meeting in one another's houses for their meal fellowship. The need for bodies to gather around a table shaped the development of church architecture, and the domestic setting of the house church provided the first basic model.

In time Christian congregations also acquired houses from members that they could redesign by knocking out some walls to create an assembly area for word and sacrament, as well as a baptistery, a sacristy, and a schoolroom. An example of such a house church (ca. 230) was excavated in Dura-Europos in eastern Syria.

With the triumph of Emperor Constantine and the legalization of Christianity, royal audience halls called basilicas were turned over to the church, or comparable structures were built. The basilica served various purposes, from law courts to indoor shopping malls. The chair or cathedra for the magistrate, governor, or emperor when he came to visit became the seat of the bishop. The benches that formerly served as seats for councilors became seats for the presbyters, who surrounded their bishop. With it longitudinal axis the basilica could accommodate large crowds and splendid processions, particularly when the faith came under imperial patronage. The people gathered in the long, narrow, rectangular body of the building, called the nave. Until pews were invented in the fourteenth century, worshipers simply moved about to follow the action of the service: Scripture readings, prayers, processionals, the sermon, and (increasingly in the West) the celebration of masses on various side altars throughout the church. Platforms for singers extended out of the apse and into the nave. One end of these featured a pulpit, and a prominent altar table occupied the middle. The pulpit was not originally used for preaching. Scripture readers and other worship leaders used the pulpit, but the bishop preached from his seat (*ex cathedra*).

This longitudinal or rectangular structure remained a characteristic of Western church buildings. The Romanesque (Roman-like) churches of the early Middle Ages and the Gothic churches of the high Middle Ages continued the longitudinal design and grew even longer in abbey and cathedral churches where provisions were made for stalls in which monks or canons (cathedral clergy) could face each other to sing the prayer offices antiphonally (two choirs singing back and forth to each other).

Byzantine basilicas became less rectangular as a dome was placed over the central gathering area. A bema or platform in the center of the space was used by cantors and choirs, and the bishop and presbyters sat there for the liturgy of the word, with the people gathered around. For the liturgy of the meal the clergy processed along a pathway called the *solea* to the apse or sanctuary where the altar-table was located. The communal character of liturgy continued to be emphasized in the East, whereas a more hierarchical character defined liturgy in the West as church buildings became longer and narrower. In both East and West, the altar area on the east end of the building (in the apse) was closed off from the people by screens or rails.

The average late antique and medieval church provided the worshiper with ample visual imagery and sensory stimulation. Glittering mosaics covered the walls and ceilings of Byzantine churches, which can still be seen in the churches of Ravenna, Italy. Walking into a medieval church was like entering a tunnel of sacred imagery. A carved or painted reredos as the backdrop behind the main altar; statues, paintings, and tapestries along the walls and in side chapels; stained-glass windows; mosaics, paintings, and even tombstones on the floors all suggested that one was entering a different world. The Byzantine iconography, capped with the image of Christ the All-Ruler (Pantocrator), suggested heaven on earth. In medieval Gothic churches the great crucifix or rood scene (Jesus on the cross, with his mother and the beloved disciple at the base) over the rood screen, loomed above all. Many of these images were donated and cared for by guilds and members of the parish, who also bore the not inconsiderable expense of providing candles and lamps to illuminate all of that visual richness! Well-off landowners and merchants commonly willed items to the church or left endowments to fund replaceable items like candles for years to come. Often their wills provided very specific instructions about how and when these items should be displayed.[10]

The Reformation inherited these buildings and worked around their limitations. Eventually form followed function. The proclamation of the word received a new emphasis in both Protestant and Catholic liturgy, requiring that people gather around the pulpit in order to hear the preacher. Pews or benches were added so that people could sit during long sermons. In time the pews were boxed to keep out the draft, and worshipers brought coal-burning foot warmers in the winter. The nave, which was full of pews, precluded much ritual movement during the liturgy.

As new buildings were erected for Protestant liturgy, more experimentation took place in terms of liturgical arrangements. Medieval pulpits had traditionally been placed along the north wall, and Reformed churches continued this arrangement because the congregation could be gathered closer to the pulpit. Lutheran conservatism dictated retaining a semblance of the older architectural arrangement, but altars and pulpits moved closer together.

The Renaissance neoclassical style of architecture opened up assembly halls in all churches with a single nave and the elimination of nooks and crannies. The opera houses of the Baroque era, with their galleries and center front stage, also influenced church buildings in the various confessions. Choirs and organs in Roman Catholic and Lutheran churches were moved from the chancels (the area behind the cancelli or railings) to the rear or side galleries. This enabled musical

---

10. See Eamon Duffy, *The Stripping of the Altars: Traditional Religion in England, 1400-1580* (New Haven: Yale University Press, 1992), 355ff., 504ff.

forces to work together above and out of sight of the congregation. In Roman Catholic churches the liturgy became a spectacle not unlike the popular operas of the period. Likewise, church buildings were decorated in the manner of the theaters, with chubby naked angels flying around. What Lutheran Baroque churches lacked in visual art (they did have some) they made up for in the sonorous amplitude of the music. Reformed worship space tended to be bare of decoration and sound—other than the congregational singing of psalms in unison.

The Romantic movement of the nineteenth century, with its idealization of the Middle Ages, made a return to gothic architecture in churches and other public buildings. As a rule, Gothic churches tended to scatter the people into different compartments. In Anglican and other Protestant churches amateur choirs filled the divided chancels, with an organ console buried in their midst. If the organist also directed the choir, he accomplished this feat with an intricate arrangement of mirrors. Protestant churches influenced by revivalism and the experience of the camp meetings favored an auditorium plan in which the pews slanted toward the platform in the front or in the corner so that everyone could see the preacher. Choir and organ occupied a slightly raised gallery above and behind the preacher, creating a theatrical sense of performance with the congregation as the audience.

These architectural plans and their effects on worshipers may have accentuated the concern of the modern liturgical movement in the twentieth century to promote both the gathering of the people around the altar table and also their overt participation in the liturgy. Altars were arranged free standing along the long wall so that the presiding minister could face the people (*versus populum*). Alternatively, churches were built "in the round," around the table. In a return to the early church the meal was the focus of the assembly. Even pulpits could be dispensed with as preachers simply stood in the congregation and talked to the congregation rather than orating from on high. A simple ambo or reading stand served as the "throne of the Word." Choirs were no longer front and center, but perhaps to the side, but nevertheless still understood as part of the assembly and not separate from it. Chairs for presiding ministers were cut down so that they no longer looked like thrones and were placed basican-style behind the table or in the front row of the assembly's seating. The liturgical ministers stood out from the assembly by wearing vestments rather than placing themselves in a position to "hold court."[11]

Church architecture in the past has reflected the cultures of Roman and Byzantine public buildings, of Gothic design with its pointed arches and vaulted ceiling, of Baroque theaters, of Georgian-era neoclassical styles, and of modern Bauhaus—all of which follow a European trajectory. As church buildings were erected in the rest of the world, they continued to reflect European Gothic or Renaissance styles. Very rarely does one see Christian church buildings that borrow from indigenous Asian culture, such as a Japanese pagoda or an Indian temple. It might be argued that this kind of architecture confuses Christian churches with the shrines and temples of other religions. But ancient Roman basilicas also possessed a sacred dimension, with the image of the divine emperor often placed in the apse. Those Roman basilicas, however, were also public buildings designed to shelter large numbers of people, which the temples to the deities did not. This is a main requirement of church architecture and it must be a place of assembly. Modern architectural designs can work just as well to serve that purpose, even if they look like shopping malls. Actually, the Roman basilicas were also shopping malls on market days.[12]

The Visual Arts

The visual arts in church buildings are more amenable to local cultural expression, and there are various uses for the visual arts in worship. The worship space requires at least an altar table, a reading desk or ambo, and a baptismal font. But there may also be altar and pulpit hangings, banners, crosses, candlesticks, eucharistic vessels, icons and

11. For a succinct article on this history see Mary M. Schaefer, "Architecture, Liturgical," in *The New Dictionary of Sacramental Worship*, ed. Peter E. Fink (Collegeville, MN: Liturgical Press, 1990), 59–66.
12. See R. Kevin Seasoltz, *A Sense of the Sacred: Theological Foundations of Christian Architecture and Art* (New York: Continuum, 2006).

pictures, statuary, and stained glass windows[13]—and the designs of these items can reflect particular cultural expressions. It is interesting that the stone baptismal pool and altar in St. Mary of the Angels Catholic Church in Singapore are black and white, respectively. Does this suggest yin and yang? If so, what does that saying about the understanding of baptism and the Eucharist? That one receives grace in baptism and responds to grace in the Eucharist?

Because this is a book about embodied liturgy, I want to focus on the portrayal of the body in liturgical art. Not all Christians agree that visual representations should be part of Christian worship, as art goes against the commandment that prohibits graven images. The Iconoclastic controversy of the eighth and ninth centuries tore apart the Byzantine Christian Empire. It was settled by the Seventh Ecumenical Council in 787 (Second Council of Nicea), which affirmed that while God cannot be portrayed in a picture Christ can be portrayed according to his human nature. The council allowed images of Christ and the saints to be placed on walls, ceilings, vessels, clothing in both public and private places, and to be carried in outdoor processions.[14] The council made a distinction between veneration (*proskynesis*, or prostration) and adoration (*latreia*). Adoration is pure worship as an expression of total submission that can be given to God alone. Icons can be venerated but not worshiped—not even the icons of Christ. As gestures of respect, incense and candles may be burned in front of icons. This decision of the Second Council of Nicea is celebrated every year in the Eastern Orthodox churches as the Triumph of Orthodoxy Sunday. The Orthodox Church regards icons as a Christological issue as much as an artistic one. In fact, they don't speak of "drawing" or "painting" icons but of "writing" them. Icons are a unique genre of liturgical art because they don't have a vanishing point within the image; the vanishing point is in the beholder. We are drawn into union

---

13. See Marchita B. Mauck, "Art, Liturgical," *New Dictionary of Sacramental Worship*, 66–71.
14. For a detailed analysis of the theological controversy over icons and its conciliar outcome see Jaroslav Pelikan, *The Christian Tradition, 2: The Spirit of Eastern Christendom (600-1700)* (Chicago and London: University of Chicago Press, 1974), 93–133.

with Christ and the saints by venerating the icons. In other words, the viewer is invited to transcend the image and venerate the prototype.

Eastern icons are objective in a way that Western art is not. Since the ancient Greeks were quite capable of portraying the human body in an ideal form, especially in sculpture, it is not as if Greek icon writers were incapable of producing more realistic art. The icons produced for liturgical use are not realistic; they are representational. But Western art, like Western sacramental theology, was moving in a realistic direction. By the high Middle Ages the sculptures on church facades had become very realistic. In fact, the artists sometimes portrayed their friends and neighbors in the sculptures.

By the time of the Renaissance, artwork was becoming not only more realistic but also more subjective, even more psychological. Feelings are expressed in Renaissance art, as we see in Leonardo da Vinci's *Last Supper* (1498). *The Last Supper* is an example of the way in which Renaissance artists wanted to draw the viewer into the painting by depicting a vibrant scene filled with real psychology and emotion. Each of the apostles is portrayed with different reactions to Christ, revealing that one will betray him.

From the standpoint of scientific anatomy, there was a new interest in the human body during the Renaissance. *The Creation of Adam*, by Michelangelo (1511), which is arguably the most famous section of the Sistine Chapel, expresses the idea of man being a cocreator with God. But it also shows the Renaissance interest in anatomy; God is resting on the outline of the human brain. Who has not marveled at the multitude of naked men and women in the Sistine chapel paintings? Michelangelo, like Leonardo, performed numerous dissections of human corpses in order to gain an in-depth and realistic look at the parts and structure of the human body.

Michelangelo's *David* (1504) is the first freestanding nude statue since antiquity. Michelangelo believed that sculpture was the highest form of art because it echoes the process of divine creation. His *David* is the perfect example of the Renaissance's celebration of the ideal human form; it conveys rich realism in form, motion, and feeling.

Michelangelo also sculptured the completely naked *Resurrected Christ* (1519-20), holding a cross. It is displayed in the church of Santa Maria sopra Minerva in Rome. On the orders of a seventeenth-century pope, Christ's genitals were covered with a bronze cloth. Realism and emotion are also evident in Michelangelo's *Pietà* (1498-1500). Who has not marveled at the perfect proportions of Christ's dead body and the stately body of his grieving mother in St. Peter's Basilica? While Mary's face appears peaceful, her left hand, turned upward in helpless resignation, betrays the true intensity of her grief. In the face of the Savior, *Pietà* reveals only slight traces of the suffering Christ endured. The expression is peaceful, relaxed, not yet rigid, and without lingering agony. The body of Christ is highly polished to absolute anatomical perfection.

These sculptures were not created as liturgical art. *David* stood in the public square of Florence, and the *Resurrected Christ* was commissioned by a Roman patrician. *Pietà* was created as a monument for a cardinal's grave, though in the eighteenth century it was moved into St. Peter's Basilica. While nudity was acceptable in church art of the Renaissance, it became less so in the following centuries. While nudity continued to be prominent in Baroque paintings, the pelvic area was usually covered with a loin cloth or something else that obscured a full vision of the genitals.

Paintings of the passion and crucifixion of Christ took on dark tones, especially in Spanish mysticism. The famous painting of the crucifixion of Christ by the Spanish painter Francisco Zurbarán (1598-1664) is noted for its dark tones reminiscent of the passionate poetry of St. John of the Cross. The figure appears suspended above the earth, as though from another world. The serenity of the face of Christ contrasts with the bloody realism of his wounds.

If we jump ahead four centuries to a modern Spanish painter, Salvador Dali, his famous *Christ of Saint John of the Cross* (1951), based on a drawing by St. John of the Cross, depicts Christ on the cross in a darkened sky floating over a body of water, complete with a boat and fishermen. Although it is a depiction of the crucifixion, it is devoid of nails, blood, and a crown of thorns because, according to Dali, he was convinced by a dream that these features would mar his depiction of Christ. Similarly, the importance of depicting Christ at an extreme angle in the painting was also revealed to him in a dream.[15] The geometric features of the triangle and circle are evident in the painting although not drawn—the triangle formed by Christ's extended arms and shadow of the right arm on the crossbeam and the circle formed by enclosing the entire cross in a circle with Christ's head as the center of the circumference.

Dali's other famous portrayal of the crucifixion, also called *Corpus Hypercubus* (1954), depicts Christ on the polyhedron net of a hypercube (a geometric, multidimensional form) and adds elements of surrealism. It fuses Dali's interests in Catholicism, mathematics, and science to create a new interpretation of a much-depicted subject. Levitating before a hypercube, Christ's physique is almost athletic and bears no signs of torture. The artist's wife, Gala, poses as a devotional figure, witnessing Christ's spiritual triumph over bodily harm.

In both of these depictions of the crucifixion, the reality of a torturous death is absent. Does this represent an aversion to the horrors of the recent conflagrations of World War II and the Spanish Civil War? Is it of a piece with the tendency of liturgical art of the post-World War II period to depict Christ suspended over the cross but not on it, his naked body clothed with his high priestly robes? It seems to be an effort to replace the man of sorrows with the risen and ascended Lord. A sense of Christ's ascension can also be felt in Dali's *Corpus Hypercubus*.

Returning to the sixteenth century, an iconoclastic streak surfaced in the radical Reformation. Andreas Bodenstein von Karlstadt launched an iconoclastic campaign in Wittenberg in 1522 while Martin Luther was sequestered in the Wartburg for safekeeping. Images and statues were vandalized and removed from church buildings, and stained-glass windows were smashed; paintings of the saints were whitewashed. Luther returned and put a stop to this revolution. Artists like Lucas

15. See Alyse Gaultier, *The Little Book of Dali* (Paris: Flammarion, 2004).

Cranach the Elder and Lucas Cranach the Younger became the reformer's collaborators and painted altarpieces in Lutheran churches. Interestingly, the Lutheran altar paintings tended to be representations of the word and the sacraments rather than the saints. One famous altar painting by Cranach the Younger shows the reformers preaching, baptizing, and celebrating the Lord's Supper. In his famous painting of the Last Supper of Christ the reformers are portrayed as the apostles. However, further iconoclasm occurred in the Protestant Reformation, beginning in Zurich under Ulrich Zwingli in 1525, in the Netherlands,[16] and in England during the Puritan Commonwealth.

How should the artist portray Christ? No one knows what Jesus looked like. The tendency has been to portray Jesus as a man whose features are culturally familiar. This is why we have pictures of Jesus with blue eyes and long blond hair in American churches and homes. In my class presentations at Satya Wacana I showed images of Christ from Native American, African, and Asian cultures.

As an example of a Native American Christ, I showed an Epiphany scene: the visit of the chiefs to the infant Jesus as envisioned in Crow art by Fr. John Giulian. In a second example, the artist shows a world-weariness born of an unremitting suppression of culture, which Christ also shares.

The Asian Christ is similar to a guru who is seated and giving two mudras (hand gestures). His right hand shows the mudra of *Abhaya*—symbolizing protection, peace, benevolence, and dispelling of fear—while his left hand displays the *Varada* mudra, which symbolizes "open-handed" generosity, such as charity or the granting of wishes. An oil painting by M. P. Manoj is based on the original drawing by Joy Elamkunnapuzha. It was also executed in mosaics by V. Balan on the facade of the Chapel at Dharmaram College in Bangalore, India.

The African portrayal is the scene of the Last Supper from *The Life of Jesus Christ: An African Interpretation*, by the Mafa People in Cameroon.

---

16. See Henry Luttikhuizen, "The Art of Devotion before and after the Introduction of Calvinism," in *Worship in Medieval and Early Modern Europe: Change and Continuity in Religious Practice*, ed. Karin Maag and John D. Witvliet (Notre Dame, IN: University of Notre Dame Press, 2004), 281–99.

The Mafa people portray the Gospel stories in an African village setting as they imagine them to be from the perspective of their culture in terms of dress, architecture, environment, and customs.

Finally, representing Indonesian art, I showed several biblical scenes painted by Ketut Lasia. Lasia is a Balinese artist who is known for his depictions of Biblical narratives in the traditional Balinese style and context. He was born of a Hindu family in Tabesji, a village in Bali known for its painters. He was converted by Dutch missionaries and thereafter devoted his life painting biblical scenes in the Balinese style.

What kind of images best serve the needs of public worship? In my opinion, icons. They have a sacramental quality. In fact, they reflect the grace of the primary sacrament, who is Christ, the Word made flesh, the image of the invisible God. The depictions of biblical stories remind us of salvation history. The images of the saints remind us of the Holy Spirit's sanctifying work in his people in all times and places. Images serve their purpose if they lead us to the worship of God, the Holy Trinity, and draw us into the family of God, the communion of saints.

Figure 15a. Crow Native American Epiphany scene by Fr. John Giulian.

Figure 15b. Crow Native American Christ of the passion by Fr. John Giulian.

Figure 15c. Indian mosaic of Christ the Guru by V. Balin.

Figure 15d. Cameroon Last Supper scene.

Figure 15e. Sculpture of Christ the King in a Hindu-Javanese version in the Temple Ganjuran, Bantul, Yogyakarta (left). Painting of the Last Supper of Jesus and his disciples by Balinese artist Ketut Lasia (right).

10

Breathing Bodies, Singing Bodies

A. The Spirit and the Breath

Christian liturgy is a celebration of good news, and good news is celebrated with a festival. One cannot have festivity without music, and one cannot make music without breath or wind. Proper breathing is necessary for singing. Wind is needed to produce sounds through tubes, such as woodwind and brass instruments and the pipe organ. Bowing or plucking strings and hitting wires (piano) and taut surfaces (drums) create vibrating air columns. Breath and wind is needed to make music. But let us focus here on the voice that utters words of praise in honor of God.

Yogic Breathing

I didn't understand or make good use of breathing until I began to practice yoga. The yoga traditions have developed very sophisticated teachings about the breath (*prana*) and what it can do to energize the body. Through their exploration of the body and breath, the ancient yogis discovered that *prana* (life force/energy) can be further subdivided into energetic components they called *vayus* (winds). The five *vayus* of *prana* have very subtle yet distinct energetic qualities, including specific functions and directions of flow. The yogis were able to control and cultivate these *vayus* by simply bringing their focus and awareness to them.

The most important *vayu* is *prana vayu*. *Prana vayu* is situated in the head and centered in the "third eye" in the middle of the forehead. It nourishes the brain and the eyes and governs reception of all things: food, air, senses, and thoughts. This *vayu* is the fundamental energy in the body; it directs and feeds into the four other *vayus*.

Vyana vayu is situated in the heart and lungs and flows throughout the entire body. The flow of *vyana vayu* moves from the center of the body to the periphery. It governs circulation of all substances throughout the body and assists the other *vayus* with their functions.

Udana vayu is situated in the throat and flows in a circle around the neck and head. It functions to "hold us up" and governs speech, self-expression, and growth. The mouth emits breath as we speak.

Samana vayu is situated in the abdomen, and its energy is centered in the navel. The flow of *samana vayu* moves from the periphery of the body to the center. It governs the digestion and assimilation of all substances: food, air, experiences, emotions, and thoughts.

Apana vayu is situated in the pelvic floor, and its energy pervades the lower abdomen. The flow of *apana vayu* moves downward and out; its energy nourishes the organs of digestion, reproduction, and elimination. *Apana vayu* governs the elimination of all substances from the body: carbon monoxide, urine, stool, and so forth. A great deal of what we take into our bodies—and into our minds—is not needed and should be eliminated.

If you want to use yoga *asanas* with these *vayus*, the following is a suggested sequence that I received from my teacher, Nick Beem.

Preparation: Move back and forth from table to child pose, four breaths on inhale, four breaths on exhale. Maintain this ratio of breaths in and out as you move into and out of every pose.

Prana vayu: From child pose slide into cobra pose. From cobra move into downward dog. From downward dog step forward and move into warrior 1. These asanas open the chest and take in prana/energy.

Vyana vayu: Step forward into mountain pose. Raise your arms overhead, then sweep them back as you move into chair pose. Do this movement several times. Then step into warrior 2. These asanas serve to circulate energy.

Udana vayu: Step into mountain pose and do a standing back bend. Then lay down on your back and do extended bridge pose, raising and lowering your arms overhead as you lift and lower your pelvis. These asanas serve to move energy upward.

Samana vayu: Lay on your back and extend your legs upward, lowering and raising each one several times. Remember to breathe! Then bring your knees to your chest, extend your arms outward, and bring your legs to each armpit while turning your head in the opposite direction (an abdominal twist). These asanas serve to balance energy.

Apana vayu (butterfly pose): Lie on your back and bring your feet together. Bring your knees up on inhale while contracting the pelvic muscles (mula bandha, or pelvic lock). Hold the lock and then exhale. Do this movement several times. This asana serves to eliminate energy.

The Spirit, the Breath of God

I began to see that the yogic emphasis on the breath has correlations with the biblical view of the breath/wind/spirit (*ruach, pneuma, spiritus*). The biblical Christian recalls that "By the word of the Lord the heavens were made, and all their host by the breath of his mouth" (Ps. 33:6, NRSV; see also Gen. 1:1). And "the Lord God formed man from the dust of the ground, and breathed into his nostrils the breath of life; and the man became a living being" (Gen. 2:7, NRSV).

In Ezekiel 37 the prophet has a vision of the resurrection as he is bidden to prophesy to the dry bones of God's people Israel. He prophesies and brings the bones together, with sinews on the bones and flesh over the sinews. Finally, the Lord says, "Prophesy to the breath, prophesy, mortal, and say to the breath: Thus says the Lord God: 'Come from the four winds, O breath, and breathe upon these slain, that they may live.' I prophesied as he commanded me, and the breath came into them, and they lived, and stood on their feet, a vast multitude" (Ezek. 37:9–10, NRSV).

According to Acts 2 a violent wind filled the house where the disciples of Jesus were gathered on the day of Pentecost, energizing them to go out into the world to proclaim the resurrection of Jesus. In the Nicene Creed we confess that the Holy Spirit is "the Lord and giver of life"—the breath-giver.

The resurrection of the dead is connected with the work of the Holy Spirit in the third article of the Creed. The Holy Spirit is the energy by which God creates the world, gathers the people of God (the church), and raises our mortal bodies from the dead.

"Do you not know that your body is a temple of the Holy Spirit within you, which you have from God, and that you are not your own? For you were bought with a price; therefore glorify God in your body" (1 Cor. 6:19–20, NRSV). St. Paul applies this to moral behavior, but the principle of the indwelling Spirit also applies to worship through the breath.

Pranayama

In yoga practice, the postures (asanas) are supported by the energy of the breath (prana). Prana encompasses more than the air we breathe. As the yoga teacher Richard Freeman says, "It is an intelligence that organizes sensations throughout the body into patterns, and then presents those patterns of feeling and sensation to our awareness."[1] Yoga practice incorporates disciplines of breathing (pranayama) to attune the yogin to his or her body by focusing on the breath. The yogin will pay attention to the duration of the inhales and exhales and to the transitions between them, as well as to internal patterns of breath throughout the body. By controlling the breath the yogin controls what the body is doing. The yogin uses the breath to empower and stabilize the posture. Stable posture was the goal of the ancient

---

1. Richard Freeman, *The Mirror of Yoga: Awakening the Intelligence of Body and Mind* (Boston: Shambhala, 2012), 24.

yogins because stability supported meditation, which is aided by chanting. Singing teachers know that breath and posture are important to the production of sound. You can't cramp the lungs and diaphragm and expect controlled sound to come out of the mouth via the vocal cords.

Physical postures and gestures have widely different cultural meanings, but biologically we are all the same. Inside every physical movement we make we are breathing at a particular rate and depth, taking in oxygen, which the blood pumps through our bodies. Breath and pulse are present in every sound, every movement, and every pregnant silence. Whether our hands are lifted high in ecstatic praise or our open palms are resting on our knees in meditation, we can do nothing without breath and pulse. As emergency responders know, breath and pulse are the most basic signs of life. Just as there is no life without them, there is no movement without them either. Whether we are walking outside in the middle of the day or sleeping in our beds in the middle of the night, breath and pulse are happening in us until our bodies die. Even when we appear to be still this movement of heart and lungs continues; our breath and pulse energizes our bodies to stretch and walk, to embrace and caress, to strike or cower. Whether we are standing in praise or kneeling in confession, our breath and movement is by the design of our Creator.

As a way to pay better attention to the power of breath and pulse, do the following exercise, which I have borrowed from from Dr. Amy Schifrin:

To speak of the use of the body in worship, the place to start is with your breath. So lie down on the floor and put a heavy book across your abdomen, and breathe. Your shoulders do not need to move, but watch your belly rise and fall. The air fills your lungs, your diaphragm moves. Once you see the movement of your breath as the book rises and falls, take it off your belly and put your hands there so you can feel the change as you inhale (expand) and exhale (contract). Now stand up and breathe and see what happens. (If you start moving your shoulders up and down with every breath, lie down and try it again.)

Amy comments:

> Without such diaphragmatic breathing, your tone of voice will be diminished; your ability to speak or sing a complete phrase will be interrupted. Without being able to have a measure of control of your breathing, your ability to read texts in the assembly will be interpretively diminished, for when you have to stop to take a breath before St. Paul finishes his thought, his intent as well as yours may not come to fruition for the hearer. Without a fullness of breath, your heart will also be beating faster, and your rate of speech easily conveying your body's physical anxiety.[2]

Whether for speaking or singing we also need to learn how to parcel out the air to give us the support we need to get through a phrase. Try this exercise:

Sit up straight, place your hands on your knees. Breathe in four counts, then breathe out four counts. Now breathe in four counts but breathe out five counts. Next breathe in four counts and breathe out six counts, and so on. This is pranayama—control of the breath.

This is *pranayama*—breath control. Speaking and singing requires breath control—parceling out the breath in a controlled exhale to complete verbal thoughts and musical lines.

Chanting

There is a venerable tradition of Mantra yoga. Mantra meditation involves chanting a word or phrase until it is internalized, the mind and emotions are transcended, and the higher consciousness is clearly revealed and experienced. Many of the yoga traditions practice the chanting of sutra texts at the beginning and end of yoga practice to implant the texts in one's mind. This practice has been adopted in certain Christian contexts, such as the mantra-like chants associated with the Taizé monastic community in France. Mantras bring us into

2. Amy C. Schifrin, "A Primer for Presiders: Your Body in Worship," January 28, 2015, in *Let's Talk: Honoring the Body* 18, no. 2 (Easter 2013): http://mcsletstalk.org/honoring-the-body/primer-presiders-body-worship/.

a heightened awareness and focus on the texts, whether for Hindus chanting the yoga sutras or for Christians chanting psalm verses. In fact, in the Benedictine monastic practice of chanting psalms a long pause is taken between the two parts of each verse to allow for breathing; with the breathing comes space for meditation. Usually the psalms are sung antiphonally—that is, two choirs singing to each other. The breath comes between the verse and the response, and the pause often feels quite long (longer than we are used to), offering space for the breath and for the Spirit.

One of the skills choirs are taught is to listen to one another. In yoga practice it is common to chant *om* together, which should be sounded *a-u-m*: a (the sound *awe*), u (the sound *oo*), mmmm. Practitioners need to listen to one another when transitioning from the *a-u* to the *mmmm*. Because the word may have religious connotations—it derives from Omkara, a Hindu deity—let us instead chant *Amen*. We can still achieve an open sound on the *A* and a buzzing sound on the *n*.

Sit up straight. Place your hands on your knees. Close your eyes. Take a deep breath and listen to one another as we move from Aaa to mennn with one voice. Do this several times.

Historically, the function of music in worship is traced to a use we hardly think about today: the chanting of sacred texts. Scripture was not "read" in the assembly but "recited," which means chanted. Scriptures continue to be chanted in the Eastern Orthodox liturgies. There have been different methods of chanting Scripture readings. The medieval Gregorian system was one method. Martin Luther provided ways of chanting psalms, collects, the Epistles, and the Gospels in his German Mass and provided samples that pastors could use for practice. The point is that the reader's voice becomes the voice of the psalmist, the prophet, the evangelist, the apostle, and Christ himself. The recitation of tones establishes who is speaking and minimizes human interpretation of the texts, which is always a problem when readers want to be dramatic and impose their interpretation on the text. It is the reader's job to proclaim the text, not to impose his or her self on it. The tone serves the word. Luther actually made a theological statement about the words of institution in the German Mass by having them chanted using the same tones as used for chanting the gospel. These words were a form of gospel proclamation.

Something similar may be said about liturgical texts such as prayers and responses. Chanting prayers, like chanting Scripture readings, certainly helped to project sound before the days of electronic amplification, the historic prayers of the church possess an objective quality. They should be presented in a matter-of-fact way. The traditional reciting tones soften the human petitions, becoming more ecstatic when the concluding ascriptions of praise and glory to God are sung. The traditional reciting tones for the congregation's responses help the people to sing in unison, minimizing the tendency of some people to push themselves forward by being more dramatic than their neighbors when speaking a text.

Thus the elementary function of music in worship consists in its ordering and regulating force. When the word is vested in musical tone, it exercises a stronger regulative power than the spoken word. It helps to weld a miscellaneous group of people into one body. Liturgy needs to be sung—even sung throughout. In the Orthodox liturgy nothing is spoken except the homily.

Music Serves the Word

Music in worship has a diaconal function: it serves the word. This is why the church has been concerned when musicians, who may have their own agenda to promote their musical craft and to express themselves as artists, have gone beyond what the word requires and call attention to themselves. This has happened over and over again in the history of the liturgy, in every historical period in which we have knowledge of how the music was used in worship. Music is an art form, and the artist may have a different vision to convey than the liturgy. And, of course there is a human tendency to promote ourselves, so all liturgical ministers, not least the leaders of the people's song, are tempted to impose themselves on the people's work, the liturgy, rather than assisting the people in their worship (the diaconal function).

The difficulty in joining music with text is evident in the selection of hymn tunes. There are often multiple tunes that could fit a hymn text; finding the right match is often a matter of trial and error. That's why we find different tunes in different hymnals for the same text.

Music Glorifies God

While we don't want the music to obscure the word, we must also recognize that music serves the glory of God. We can be "lost in wonder, joy, and praise" as we sing to the glory of God. Music helps to join the worship of the earthly church with that of the angels, the archangels, all the company of heaven. Worship as eschatological mystery—as the hidden beginning of the last things, as the place where the joyful feast of the kingdom of God becomes present—is experienced already here on earth in the worship of the believing and hoping congregation. If the last things have already appeared on earth in the resurrection of Jesus Christ and the outpouring of his Spirit, if men and women really speak prophetically in the assembled congregation, then the music that serves the word and glorifies God is surely not the least of the signs of the eschatological and spiritual character of the church. The very fact that the audible form of the music merges the intelligibility of the word (1 Corinthians 14) with its spiritual exuberance—a union in which neither of the two essential elements is destroyed—is a good reason for singing the liturgy in all its parts.

Music Serves the People

There is really no part of the liturgy that cannot be sung, including psalms, hymns, and spiritual songs, but also prayers, readings, and blessings. In some Pentecostal churches, especially African-American ones, even the sermon is chanted. This flies in the face of the way music is approached today in many of our societies. People no longer come together to sing; they listen to music through earphones, privately. Not only have they lost the ability to sing, but they have also lost the sense of community that is created when people sing together. The church may need to become the music teacher to the world and teach people to sing all over again. It won't be the first time that the church has preserved a culture the world has lost.

Group singing can create a feeling of connectedness. Even people who have no particular religious persuasion gush with enthusiasm as they leave a great rock concert, ebullient with a feeling of joy and connectedness. Singing together with lots of people speaks to us on an emotional level.

Where does this feeling come from and why do we have it when we sing together? An entire branch of the neuroscience community studies the effects of music on the brain, trying to answer questions like this one. One theory involves oxytocin. Oxytocin (not to be confused with OxyContin, the pain-killing drug) is a hormone produced by the human brain that contributes to feelings of trust for the people around us. It is most known for its role in sexual behavior; oxytocin levels are high after orgasm, which leads people to feel tremendously bonded with their partner. The former studio musician and neuroscientist Daniel Levitin says it's a bit like neurochemical soul glue.[3]

If this claim is true, it means that when people sing together their brains make oxytocin, which makes them feel trust, solidarity, and connectedness with the people around them. Another fascinating discovery is that oxytocin is released in the brain when two people have an orgasm together, but not when they have orgasms by themselves!

In the psalms, we are told frequently to sing together. God has designed us in such a way that corporate singing draws us out of our self-centered worlds and lets us know that *we are not alone*. We are not alone in our walk with the Lord. We are, to borrow the language of the *Book of Common Prayer*, "very members incorporate in the mystical body

---

3. Daniel Levitin, *This Is Your Brain on Music* (London: Plume, 2006).

of thy son, the blessed company of all faithful people, and also heirs, through hope, of thy everlasting kingdom."[4]

Music is a gift God has given to all people, and to the church in particular, to help declare this fundamental truth, which seems to be grounded in our biochemistry that we are not meant to be alone. We often feel alone and disconnected. It is a consequence of the fall of humankind into sin, which has been defined as that which separates us from God, from one another, and from the creation itself. But the gift of music has survived the fall and is one of the primary gifts God has given to help us know and feel that we are not alone. That certainty can be reinforced if we sing together.

In another book, Levitin claims that there are six functions of song (music) in human culture, which he backs up with scientific data and from his own experience as a musician and record producer (in his pre-research scientist days).[5] He seeks to answer the questions, "Why is there music?" and "Are we musical because our brains made us that way, or are our brains adapted to music because we are musical?" Levitin explores the social advantages to being a musical being through the six categories of song: friendship, joy, comfort, knowledge, religion, and love.

Songs of friendship are songs of camaraderie and togetherness; creating a functional large group. Songs sung in group experiences, such as at a campfire or in a sports stadium ("Take Me Out to the Ball Game"), may come to mind. Levitin notes, "Music has historically been one of the strongest forces binding together the disenfranchised, the alienated."[6]

Songs of joy, in particular, release oxytocin in the brain. This obviously would help in creating a group of people who can work together to create a larger society. Levitin quotes new research that suggests music, especially joyful music, affects our health in

---

4. *The Book of Common Prayer* (The Church Hymnal Corporation and The Seabury Press, 1977), 339.
5. Daniel Levitin, *The World in Six Songs: How the Musical Brain Created Human Nature* (New York: Dutton, 2008).
6. Ibid., 61.

fundamental ways. Music modulates levels of dopamine (the "feel-good" hormone) in the brain.

Songs of comfort are fundamental to growing up. Mothers the world over sing lullabies to their children. Many children learn to self-comfort by singing to themselves songs that their mothers sang as lullabies. Singing can sooth and comfort infants in ways that other actions cannot. Lullabies even share similar musical structures.

Songs of knowledge are ubiquitous in all societies. How do children learn their alphabet (the alphabet song)? How do children learn songs of physical knowledge about their world ("The Wheels on the Bus," "Twinkle, Twinkle Little Star")? How do children learn to work together ("Clean Up, Clean Up, Everybody, Everywhere")? How do children learn to count? Memory songs involve learning sequences ("There Was an Old Lady Who Swallowed a Fly"). Most of these songs are learned through oral tradition—children at young ages do not yet read.

Songs of religion are found throughout world religions and have been used to communicate beliefs. Levitin writes:

> Ceremonies with music reaffirm the propositions, and the music sticks in our heads, reminding us of what we believe and what we have agreed to. Music during ritual is designed, in most cases, to evoke a "religious experience," a peak experience, intensely emotional, the effects of which can last the rest of a person's life. Trance states can occur during these experiences, resulting in feelings of ecstasy and connectedness.[7]

Songs of love help to communicate emotion. When someone hears "their song," it brings to mind a specific time, place, and emotion. Even when a particular song is heard many years later, people are able to travel back in time through memory. Worshipers remember hymns and songs they learned in church in their younger years or that were associated with important events in their lives, such as a wedding or funeral.

Levitin concludes, "Although the important functions of music can be described in these six categories, the specific ways that people from

---

7. Ibid., 222.

different musical cultures have found to make music are very diverse."[8] Levitin's list may not be exhaustive, but it demonstrates the point that different kinds of songs affect us in different ways. Christian liturgy employs a variety of psalms, hymns, and spiritual songs that tap into these various qualities and emotions. One of the spiritual advantages of praying through the Psalter as in the daily prayer offices of the Church, is that the psalms cover every attitude in worship from praise to lament and every condition of the soul from gratitude to repentance and every kind of prayer from thanksgiving to supplication. If the attitude and condition of a particular psalm is not your attitude or condition at the moment, it may be someone else's in the assembly.

We gather to support one another on the journey into God's kingdom. We uphold one another with the breath, which is the life source and the energy of the Holy Spirit. Whether the congregation is reading texts or singing songs, worship in the assembly is an exercise in shared breathing.

Group Meditation

Sit in lotus pose in a circle. Inhale as you extend your arms upward. On exhale chant "Veni" (Come). Inhale as you extend your arms outward. On exhale chant "Sancte" (Holy). Inhale as your bring your hands to prayer position over your heart. On exhale chant "Spiritus" (Spirit). Inhale as you fold your torso forward. On exhale chant "Amen" (So be it).

8. Ibid., 281.

Figure 16a. Alfanda.

Javanese instruments, including gamelans, gongs, drums, and wooden flute are used to accompany Javanese tunes based on a pentatonic scale in this Christian Church across the street from Satya Wacana Christian University in Salatiga, Central Java, Indonesia. Lfanda Abhor Ardana, a student in the author's course in Embodied Liturgy, put together this indigenous Javanese worship service as a graduation project for his degree from the Faculty of Performing Arts. The photo was taken by Priska Lydia S. Pulungan, a lecturer in English at Satya Wacana Christian University who served as a translator in the author's classroom.

Figure 16b. Priska Lydia S. Pulungan and Alfanda Abhor Ardana model Javanese formal churchgoing attire, including sarongs made of batik, a cloth indigenous to Java.

B. "Psalms and Hymns and Spiritual Songs"

St. Paul refers in Col. 3:16 and Eph. 5:19 to singing "psalms and hymns and spiritual songs." The material in both letters in these chapters is similar, even verbatim. It is possible that Ephesians was copied from Colossians, or both were copied from some other document. The material in both letters concerns Christian life, particularly relationships in the household. The "psalms and hymns and spiritual songs" may refer to "household devotions" rather than public worship. However, hymns were among the spiritual gifts contributed to the assembly (1 Cor. 14:26).

Is there a distinction between psalms, hymns, and spiritual songs? Whatever the author intended by this phrase, distinctions can be made. In the Christian context, *psalms* refers to the biblical psalms. In the context of ancient cults, *hymns* refers to songs addressed to a deity. *Songs* are what people sing to one another for encouragement or to express certain doctrines or sentiments. These distinctions are seldom made today. Much psalm singing is metrical, which makes the psalms seem like strophic hymns and songs. Many musical items are called hymns, even if they are not addressed to God, because they are "traditional." And many songs, judged on the basis of their lyrics, are really hymns but are called songs because they are contemporary.

Psalms

There are no specific references to the singing of psalms in Christian public worship before the fourth century. Jesus and his disciples sang a psalm after the last supper (in the Passover context this was probably one of the Hallel Psalms, 13–18) before they went out into the night (Matt. 26:30; Mark 14:26; Luke 22:31). The Psalter was the hymnbook of the second temple, though we don't know what role psalmody played in synagogue prayer in the first century. However, it is likely that Christians sang psalms in their homes and from there the psalmody found a natural inclusion in the prayer offices when these were offered publicly.

Psalms were sung in the public liturgies of the basilicas during the processions of the entrance, the offertory, and communion, as well as in processions through the streets from one station to another. Much of Christian worship in late antiquity was processional in character.

Canticles, which are another type of biblical song with psalm-like character, attained use in Christian liturgy.[9] Biblical canticles not from the Psalter are sung in the prayer offices. The Roman Breviary uses seven Old Testament canticles at Lauds (morning prayer) in place of a fourth psalm and adds two more on Friday and Saturday. The Greek Orthodox Church has the same nine canticles at Matins. From the New Testament canticles the Liturgy of the Hours includes the Canticle of Zechariah (Luke 1:68–79), commonly referred to as the *Benedictus* (from its first word), at Lauds; the Canticle of Mary (Luke 1:46–55), commonly known as the *Magnificat* (from its first word in the Latin text), at Vespers; and the Canticle of Simeon (Luke 2:29–32), commonly referred to as the *Nunc dimittis* (from the opening words) at Compline. When you consider the amount of singing in the prayer offices—psalms and canticles, plus versicles and responses that are psalm verses—to pray the daily offices is nothing else than to pray the Bible.

Early Christians also developed *psalmi idiotici* (private psalms), that is, compositions that imitated the biblical psalms. One of the best known is the Gloria in Excelsis Deo, "Glory to God in the highest." This prose hymn begins with the words that the angels sang when the birth of Christ was announced to shepherds in Luke 2:14. Other verses were added early on, forming a doxology, which in the fourth century became part of morning prayer and is still recited in the Byzantine Rite Orthros (morning) service. The Latin translation is attributed to Hilary of Poitiers, which became the standard Sunday and festival canticle of praise in the Roman Mass. It begins with praise to God the heavenly king and almighty Father: "We worship you, we give you thanks, we praise you for your glory." Then it becomes a supplication of mercy from the Son: "Lord Jesus Christ, only Son of the Father, Lord God, Lamb of God, you take away the sin of the world, have mercy on us."

9. See Frank C. Senn, *Introduction to Christian Liturgy*, 178.

It ends with an ascription of praise to the Holy Trinity: "For you alone are the holy One, you alone are the Lord, you alone are the Most High, Jesus Christ, with the Holy Spirit, are most high in the glory of God the Father."

Another important nonbiblical canticle is the Te Deum Laudamus. Traditionally ascribed jointly to Ambrose and Augustine, it more likely originated in southern Gaul in the fifth century. Like the Gloria in Excelsis it begins by addressing God: "We praise you, O God; we acknowledge you to be the Lord." Next it addresses Christ: "You, Christ, are the king of glory." With its references to the prophets, apostles, and martyrs, it may have been sung in procession to the baptismal font and was also used as a song of thanksgiving for deliverance. The Te Deum is sung at the end of Matins on all days when the Gloria is sung at Mass, which includes all Sundays outside of Advent and Lent, as well as all feasts and all weekdays during Eastertide. Concluding psalm verses were added later and came to be regarded as part of the canticle. The Te Deum Laudamus is almost creedal in both its praise of the Holy Trinity and its Christology.

We don't know how the psalms were chanted in the ancient church, but eight Gregorian plainchant tones (one for each musical mode), to which any of the psalm texts could be recited, developed in the early Middle Ages. These tones were devised so that the antiphon that is sung between verses or at the beginning and ending of the psalm or canticle transitions smoothly into the psalm tone.

Anglican chant was developed at the time of the English Reformation and appears to be an adaptation of the plainchant method for singing the psalm texts in English. It was sung in four-part harmony by cathedral and collegiate choirs. A system of chanting psalms, not unlike the method of Anglican chant, was devised in the Protestant monastery at Taizé, France, after 1955 by Jacques Berthier (1923–94). The *Lutheran Book of Worship* (p. 291) and *Evangelical Lutheran Worship* (pp. 337–38) also provide a collection of tones for chanting the psalms and canticles.

A notable contribution of the Reformed tradition was the Geneva

Psalter. As encouraged by Calvin, psalms were set to French verse by Marot, with tunes by Louis Bourgeois. Psalms 42, 100, and 124 are tunes sometimes still used in hymnals. This type of psalm singing continued in the Reformed tradition in other places, such as the Scottish Psalter. Interestingly, the first book published in the British colonies in America was the Massachusetts Bay Psalter (1636).

A responsorial psalmody has emerged in the Roman Catholic Church in which a cantor sings a refrain that is repeated by the congregation. Then the cantor or a choir sings the verses of the psalm and the congregation repeats the refrain after each verse or several verses. There has also been a global effort to recover the use of psalmody in the Reformed churches, which once sang only psalmody. Responsorial psalmody has been composed in various languages for use in Reformed/Presbyterian churches, although the use of indigenous music idioms has been slow to develop.[10]

Hymns

Form critics have detected in the New Testament the citation of early Christian hymns, specifically in John 1, Phil. 2:5–11, and Revelation 4–5. The earliest known Christian book of hymns, psalms, or odes is the *Odes of Solomon* (ca. 100—no relationship to the ancient Israelite king). Pliny the Younger, in his letter to the Emperor Trajan (ca. 112), reports that Christians gathered before dawn "to recite a hymn [*carmen*] antiphonally to Christ, as to a god."[11] Pliny interpreted this to suggest Christians regarded Christ as a god because in the ancient world hymns were addressed to deities.

The earliest Christian hymn still in use is "Shepherd of Tender Youth." Attributed to Clement of Alexandria (ca. 170–ca. 220), best-known English translation is by Henry M. Dexter (1821–90).[12] Another

10. See *Psalms for All Seasons: A Complete Psalter for Worship*, ed. Martin Tel, John Witvliet, and Joyce Borger (Grand Rapids: Faith Alive Christian Resources, 2012).
11. *Documents of the Christian Church*, trans. Henry Bettenson (New York: Oxford University Press, 1947), 6–7.
12. See *Hymns for Worship* (Grand Rapids: Faith Alive Christian Resources, 2010), hymn 18.

third-century Greek hymn is the *Phos hilaron*, "Joyous Light of Glory" sung in Vespers.

Strophic hymns and spiritual songs became popular in Syria in the fourth century, especially those composed by Ephrem the Syrian (ca. 306–373). Over four hundred hymns attributed to Ephrem are extant; there were undoubtedly others that are lost. Ephrem wrote hymns because Bardaisan and Mani composed hymns. His hymns were meant to teach the faith and strike against heresy. Stanzas with a repeating melody made the song easy to learn.

Another great Eastern hymn writer was John of Damascus (ca. 676–749), a Syrian Christian monk and priest who was born and raised in Damascus and died at his monastery, Mar Saba, near Jerusalem. Some of his Easter hymns, such as "Come, You Faithful, Raise the Strain" and "The Day of Resurrection," are sung in Western churches in the translations of John Mason Neale.

Hilary of Poitiers (d. 367) is mentioned by Isidore of Seville as the first to compose Latin hymns. Ambrose of Milan (ca. 340–397) is considered the father of Latin hymnody. Clothing Christian ideas in classical phraseology, Ambrose appealed to popular tastes. Several of his hymns are still sung, such as "O Splendor of God's Glory Bright" and "Savior of the Nations, Come."

Other great Latin hymn lyricists include the Spanish Christian poet Aurelius Clemens Prudentius (348–ca. 413), who left us "Of the Father's Love Begotten" (Christmas) and "Earth Has Many a Noble City" (Epiphany). Verantius Honorius Fortunatus (530–609) penned "Welcome, Happy Morning" (Easter) and "Hail, Thee, Festival Day" (stanzas for Easter, Ascension, and Pentecost).

While strophic hymns found a welcome place in Eastern liturgies, in the West they were primarily confined to the prayer offices. Strophic songs came into the Mass during the Middle Ages as sequences to the Gradual and Alleluia. In the Latin Mass of the Middle Ages, it became customary to prolong the last syllable of the Alleluia while the deacon was ascending from the altar to the ambo to chant the Gospel. This prolonged melisma was called the *jubilus* because of its jubilant tone. It was also called *sequentia*, "sequence," because it followed (*sequere*) the Alleluia. Notker Balbulus (ca. 840–912) developed sequence hymns by setting words to this melisma in rhythmic prose for chanting as a trope (so that these hymns were also called proses). The name *sequence* came to be applied to these rhythmic prose and rhymed texts.

Sequences continued to be composed throughout the Middle Ages and were sung on major festivals. One of the reforms of the Roman Missal of Pius V (1570) reduced the number of sequences for the entire Roman Rite to four: *Victimae paschali laudes* (eleventh century) for Easter; *Veni Sancte Spiritus* (twelfth century) for Pentecost; *Lauda Sion Salvatorem* (ca. 1264) for the Feast of Corpus Christi; and *Dies Irae* (thirteenth century) for All Souls and in Masses for the dead. In 1727, the thirteenth-century *Stabat Mater* for Our Lady of Sorrows was added to this list. In 1970, the *Dies Irae* was removed from the Requiem Mass of the revised Roman Missal and was transferred to the liturgy of the hours to be sung *ad libitum* (at will) in the week before the beginning of Advent.

Hymns continued to be composed during and after the Reformation. Some of the early Reformation hymns were versifications of canticles in the Mass, such as "Kyrie, God Father in Heaven Above" (Kyrie) by Martin Luther, "All Glory Be to God on High" (Gloria in Excelsis) by Nicholas Decius, and "Lamb of God, Pure and Sinless" (Agnus Dei) also by Nicholas Decius. But the Reformation and post-Reformation periods are better known for their spiritual songs, and many songs were composed to teach doctrine. The Jesuit Robert Bellarmine famously charged that more souls were lost from singing Luther's songs than from reading his theology.

Spiritual Songs

The background of German Reformation song is the *genre* of vernacular carols that were added for the congregation to sing in connection with the Latin sequences. For example, to the sequence for Easter, *Victimae paschali laudes* (Christians to the paschal victim offer praises)—usually attributed to the eleventh-century Wipo of Burgundy—was added the vernacular carol *Christ ist erstanden* (Christ is arisen). This became the basis of Martin Luther's *Christ lag in Todesbanden* (Christ lay in death's strong bands).[13]

The sequences, both Latin and vernacular, became one of the first sources of Lutheran Reformation spiritual songs. It is simply not true that Luther made use of tunes from the beer hall. Most of his tunes were based on Gregorian chant; others drew upon the *Meistersinger* tradition of German art song. Luther wrote thirty-six German hymns and spiritual songs and encouraged others to write hymns as well. Lutheran hymnody and spiritual songs flourished in the post-Reformation period.

The Reformed tradition confined congregational song to versifications of biblical psalms and canticles. Isaac Watts (1674–1748), who is credited with seven hundred and fifty hymns, was the first to move beyond this restriction. Charles Wesley (1707–1788) penned about six thousand hymns and songs. After the Wesleys, hymn and song singing became a standard part of Protestant worship. Spurred on by Watts and Wesley, many nonconformist churches produced lively popular songs that expressed one's personal relationship with God. Later songs came to be used in the revivals that occurred between 1800 and 1920. Songs such as "Washed in the Blood of the Lamb" came from the hymnbook of Dwight Lyman Moody (1837–99) and Ira David Sankey (1840–1908).

The Negro spiritual is an indigenous contribution by African-American slaves to the revival tradition. Often referencing symbolic aspects of biblical images such as Moses and Israel's exodus from Egypt in songs like "Michael Row the Boat Ashore," the lyrics of these spirituals express the slaves' aspirations for freedom.

Gospel music has a complex religious and musical history. Developed in the revivals, especially in the cities, gospel songs drew on both European and African roots. In recent times, gospel song has become a style associated with African-American worship, which may be attributed to the legacy of Thomas A. Dorsey in Chicago in the 1930s.

---

13. See *Lutheran Book of Worship* (Minneapolis: Augsburg, 1978), hymns 37, 36, 34.

Best known as the author of the song "Precious Lord, Take My Hand," who had spent the 1920s writing secular music, turned fulltime to gospel music, established a publishing house, and invented the black gospel style of piano music.

In the 1960s both Roman Catholics and evangelical Protestants turned to popular genres of music to provide songs for Christian worship. Roman Catholic songs tended to follow the folk idiom, using acoustic instruments such as guitar and flute, whereas evangelical Protestants turned to rock music, using electronic instruments. The Contemporary Christian Music industry in Nashville developed from Christian popular music.

The use of Christian popular music was promoted by the church growth movement to reach the unchurched and has become ubiquitous, not only in North America but also throughout Asia.[14] While music in the church has drawn upon the musical styles of the various cultures through which Christian liturgy has passed, there has not been previously the intentional effort to use popular styles such as we see in evangelistic circles today. Indeed, "popular" music forms a new genre that is neither art music nor folk music, and it is closely associated with the commercialism of the mass media.[15]

In contemporary worship services the liturgy has actually become one part song and one part spoken message. This follows the revival form of worship in which "preliminaries" included songs and testimonies, led to the sermon, which was followed by some kind of response in the form of an act of commitment. Contemporary Christian Music has become ubiquitous in evangelical worship, in which the songs are led by an instrumental combo with a soloist or a small group of vocalists. In Pentecostal praise and worship services there is greater participation by the worshipers in the singing. This music with a base in America has been imported in evangelical and Pentecostal worship throughout the world and competes with efforts to create a truly indigenous worship music.

14. See Jeffrey A. Truscott, *Worship: A Practical Guide* (Singapore: Genesis Books, 2011), 84–88.
15. See Steve Miller, *The Contemporary Christian Music Debate: Worldly Compromise or Agent of Renewal?* (Waynesboro, GA: OM Literature, 1993).

Nevertheless, new hymns and songs that utilize indigenous musical styles have been composed in east Africa, southern Africa, Asia, the Caribbean, and Latin America. Some of these have found places in Western hymnals and become popular. Examples include "Christ Has Arisen, Alleluia" (east African), "We Are Marching in the Light of God" (South African), and "Cantad al senior un cantico nuevo" (Brazilian). These songs from the global church have become well known in America. In fact, with the use of recorded music all music is more or less portable, and can therefore be removed from its original setting.[16]

Choral Music

Choral music in worship means music sung by the choir but not by the rest of the congregation. The choral usurpation of the congregation's song developed slowly, over a long period of time. However, the Introits, Kyries, Glorias, Graduals, Credos, Offertory psalms, Sanctus settings, Agnus Dei settings, and communion psalms which came to be sung exclusively by choirs in the Catholic Church could be sung by the people, and under liturgical renewal they have been. In a similar way, all the music sung by choirs in the Orthodox church can be sung by the people, and increasingly it is.

Martin Luther not only promoted the restoration of congregational song, but he also promoted the work of noted contemporary composers such as Josquin des Prez (1450/1455–1521). Music for choirs (chorale settings, motets, cantatas) continued to be composed for Lutheran worship, reaching a high point in the church music of Johann Sebastian Bach (1685–1750) in the baroque period. Bach's cantatas were based on the Gospel reading or hymn of the day, and were located in the liturgy around the sermon. The high point of concerted church music was Bach's settings of the St. John and St. Matthew Passions, sung in the Good Friday services in Leipzig. These cantatas and passions are considered liturgical music since they were composed for use in worship.

16. See Mark Katz, *Capturing Sound: How Technology Has Changed Music* (Berkeley: University of California Press, 2004).

Handel's oratorios are examples of sacred music, but not liturgical music, although choirs do sing choruses from various oratorios in worship. They were composed as unstaged operas on biblical themes when the opera houses and theaters were closed during Lent.

In Roman Catholicism there was a reaction to polyphonic liturgical music after the Council of Trent and Giovanni Pierluigi da Palestrina (ca. 1525–94) developed a chaste polyphony in which the text was not obscured, influencing later composers of Catholic mass settings. Catholic composers produced innumerable settings of the Mass, culminating in the works of the Viennese composers Haydn, Mozart, and Schubert, which were actually used to celebrate mass.

In Anglicanism, cathedral and college choirs sang settings of the psalms and canticles in Morning and Evening Prayer. In the Restoration period choirs also sang anthems at the end of Evensong that, in keeping with the Reformed tradition, were settings of biblical texts. However, they originated in the Marian antiphons that were sung in English cathedrals after Vespers.[17]

Today in Protestant churches around the world choirs sing special music called "anthems" as part of the order of worship. The anthems are usually sung during the offering to cover the action of gathering the people's gifts. Sometimes, the choir music overshadows that simple ritual action. In Africa several parish choirs might singe and compete with one another.

Instruments

I called this lesson "singing voices." But human beings extended their singing with the use of musical instruments that produce sound through vibrations. Instrumental music, often associated with pagan cults, was forbidden by early church fathers, which has remained the rule in Eastern Orthodox worship. Pipe organs first appeared in church buildings in the fourteenth century. At first, they were used for

17. Robin A. Leaver, "Liturgical Music as Homily and Hermeneutic," in *Liturgy and Music: Lifetime Learning*, ed. Robin A. Leaver and Joyce Ann Zimmerman (Collegeville, MN: Liturgical Press, 1998), 340–59.

ceremonial occasions and not to accompany congregational singing. Lutherans retained organs and expanded their use to introduce and later to accompany congregational hymns and chants. The Reformed tradition, beginning with Ulrich Zwingli, removed organs from churches. Puritans in England also removed organs from Anglican churches, but they were brought back during the Restoration period. Choral and instrumental music, including organs, returned to the Reformed tradition in force during the revivals because of music's capacity to stir the emotions. Contemporary services tend to prefer the use of electronic instruments, which have their limitations. Unlike acoustic instruments, they do not help with congregational singing because they do not produce vibrating air waves. While the pipe organ has limitations in some genres of contemporary and global church music, it is still the most effective instrument for leading a large group of people in communal singing.

Psalm 150 ends with the words, "Let everything that has breath praise the Lord" (150:6). While this verse refers to the human voice first of all, wind instruments also require human breath to be played, and trumpets and trombones have also found a place in Western church music. The pipe organ remains the largest wind instruments, and though its sounds are not produced by human breath, a lot of *prana* (energy) is forced through its pipes by mechanical means. The pipe organ is superior to electronic organs in leading congregational song because its vibrating wind columns attract the vibrating wind columns produced by the human vocal chords.

However, pipe organs are expensive, and the heat and humidity in some parts of the world are not conducive to maintaining them. The same atmospheric conditions affect pianos. The choice does not need to be between pipe organ and pianos on the one hand and electronic instruments on the other. The Western church has employed other acoustic instruments in the string, woodwind, and brass families in worship. Mark Bangert has surveyed acoustical instruments in other parts of the world that are waiting to be employed in Christian worship.[18] While we may associate African music and its rhythmic vitality with drums, shakers, and other percussion instruments, there are also African string and wind instruments. Bangert notes the Zimbabwean xylophone and the mbiras (a thumb piano). Latin American/Caribbean music features guitars, bass, flute, trumpet, and percussion instruments such as the guiro, tambourine, conga, and maraca. Asia is so vast and diverse that it defies categorization. The music of north India is different from the music of south India. The ancient culture of India boasts an assortment of strings, winds, and drums. The sitar, which looks like a very large guitar, has been associated with the Brahman caste and would raise issues with the poorer castes if used in Christian worship. China, South Korea, and Japan seem to favor Western classical and popular music and have therefore been slow to develop and export indigenous music, so it is not surprising to find little interest in the musical inculturation of Christian worship. Southeast Asia constitutes another diverse region. Among Thai instruments are the *ching chap* (a small hand cymbal), drums, *ranat ek* (xylophone), and *khaen* (a mouth organ made of bamboo pipes). Certainly Indonesia is famous for its gamelan orchestras, which are supplemented with drums and large gongs. I understand that churches in Bali have tapped into this kind of instrumentation.

Selection of Music

It remains to be said that psalms and hymns and songs should be selected for use in orders of service according to their function within the liturgy, their relation to the church year's festivals and seasons, and the biblical readings in the liturgy—a task that requires team planning by the pastor and the musicians.

There are some principles of music selection that apply to all worship situations. First and foremost, all music chosen for the assembly or choir should be within the capabilities of the group that is singing. Pastors and musicians have to know their people.

18. See Mark Bangert, "Liturgical Music, Culturally Attuned," in *Liturgy and Music*, 360–83.

Second, whether the music is traditional or contemporary, classical or popular, there are some things that just should not be put before the assembly because some music doesn't lend itself to group singing. Some songs have been written with a soloist in mind. Some hymns and songs have easily learned refrains but irregular stanzas. The stanzas can be sung by cantors or choirs while the people sing the refrain.

Third, responsorial singing is especially useful in congregational processions. We will see in chapter 11 that processions are an important, time-honored way of engaging people bodily in worship. People can process without the need to read words, joining in with the singing of antiphons or refrains as they move. I noted that responsorial singing is often used today in Roman Catholic liturgy as a means of singing psalms and canticles. The call-and-response songs from Africa have a similar character that requires listening more than looking—hearing the words rather than reading them in a book or on a screen. "Faith comes from what is heard," said St. Paul (Rom. 10:17, NRSV). Hearing the words and repeating them should be joined to those moments in the liturgy when the congregation is in motion, or activities are going on, such as the entrance, the offertory, the communion, and dismissal.

One further word about processions: when done inside the church building the choir does not process—the people process. The choir should be in place to lead the people in singing, preferably in a location where they can be the unseen engine empowering the voice of the people. Choir processions are a different matter.

Finally, it is always helpful for congregations to make musical notation available. While not everyone can read music, some people can, and they become the leaders of congregational singing whether they are in the choir or not. Notes projected on screens can be advantageous because people sing better when looking up rather than down. Projection screens are becoming common in all kind of churches around the world, not only in evangelical megachurches. This type of technology, in particular, has some advantages over books, especially for visitors.

In processions, however, neither books in the hand nor projections on a screen are helpful. What is helpful is for the ears to hear and the eyes to watch where one is going. In these situations, books and folders are at least portable and can be carried in procession; screens require one to look in a particular direction. This topic leads us to the next lesson: liturgy in motion. Historically, Christian liturgy East and West has maintained a processional character. The whole body can be more engaged in worship if people are moving. But processions call for music that people can sing as they walk, watching where they are going—that is, music of a call and response or responsorial character.

11

Bodies in Motion

A. Dance and Processions

Worship involves motion: God's movement toward humans and the human movement toward God in response. This gets acted out in liturgy, which necessarily means that liturgy is always in motion.

The African theologian Elochukwu E. Uzukwu notes, "Animals display particular motions at play or during mating, in asserting territoriality, sensing danger, or expressing aggression." Among humans, he writes, "the gesture retains the characteristic of motion. It is a movement of the body; a measured movement."[1]

In this chapter we will consider specific ways in which the body is actively in motion in liturgy—through dance, processions, and dramatic reenactments. These three activities actually go together. In the first section, our topic will consider dance and processions, and in the second we will look at liturgical drama and plays.

---

1. Elochukwu E. Uzukwu, *Worship as Body Language, Introduction to Christian Worship: An African Orientation* (Collegeville, MN: Liturgical Press, 1997), 1.

Dance

Dances are known in all human cultures throughout the world. Archeology has unearthed examples of prehistoric dancing as it has dug up artifacts and old buildings. Pictures of women dancing adorn both Egyptian tombs and Greek urns. Dancing was used in religious rituals and as a way to reenact myths. Dances accompanied seasonal rites, initiation rites, weddings, funerals, coronations, and other festivals. They involved costumes, body painting, masks, and handheld weapons or bouquets, as we see in the elaborately staged Ramayana Ballet Purawisata outside Yogyakarta. Undoubtedly, dancing was a form of entertainment and pleasure in ancient times, just as it is today, and was very much a part of public lives as well. Barbara Ehrenreich wrote a book asking what happened to this sense of collective joy in modern Western societies.[2]

There is no doubt that dancing is found throughout Hebrew and Jewish traditions. Psalm 150:4 (NRSV) says, "Praise God with timbrel and dance." After the crossing of the Red Sea, Exodus tells us that "the prophet Miriam, Aaron's sister, took a tambourine in her hand; and all the women went out after her with tambourines and with dancing. And Miriam sang to them: 'Sing to the Lord, for he has triumphed gloriously; / horse and rider he has thrown into the sea" (Exod. 15:20–21, NRSV). Not to be outdone by the women, King David danced before the ark when he brought it up to Jerusalem. His wife, Saul's daughter Michal, objected to her husband's public nakedness (he was probably wearing an apron that flapped around in his energetic movements, exposing his private parts). But David responds, "It was before the Lord [whose presence was with the ark], who chose me before your father, and above all his house, to appoint me as prince over Israel, the people of the Lord—and I will make merry before the Lord" (2 Sam. 6:21, NRSV).

Perhaps the example of David dancing before the ark inspired the

2. Barbara Ehrenreich, *Dancing in the Streets: A History of Collective Joy* (New York: Metropolitan Books, 2006).

custom of the celebration of *Simchak Torah* in the synagogue. This festival marks the conclusion of the annual lectionary reading of the Torah and the beginning of a new annual cycle of readings. The main celebration takes place in evening and morning services. In both Orthodox and Conservative congregations, this is the only time of year the Torah scrolls are taken out of the ark and read at *night*. Both at night and in the morning, the last portion (*parashah*) of Deuteronomy and the first *parashah* of Genesis are read. On each occasion, when the ark is opened, the worshipers leave their seats to dance and sing and process with all the Torah scrolls in a joyous celebration that often lasts for several hours.

Dancing is an important part of Jewish life. It was practiced among Ashkenazi Jews of Eastern Europe, where dancing to klezmer music was an integral part of weddings in the shtetl. To this day, dancing is an integral part of Jewish weddings. Especially popular is a circle dance called the *hora*, which originated in the Balkans. In Hasidic Judaism, dance is a means for expressing joy and is believed to have a therapeutic effect: it purifies the soul, promotes spiritual elation, and unifies the community. A Hasidic melody became the basis of the song *Hava Nagila* that, from its obscure roots, came to be a song of celebration of the state of Israel. The song is often combined with dancing the *hora* at Jewish celebrations in America.

Dancing in Church

As far as I can tell, dance was not part of worship in the early church. Dancing only appears in the New Testament in two contexts: Herod's banquet (Mark 6:21–22, with disastrous results for John the Baptist) and the celebration of the prodigal son's return (Luke 15:22–27).

By contrast, dance played a prominent role in many pagan cults, such as the orgiastic cult of Dionysius. Because early Christians did not want to be associated in any way with such rites, they most likely avoided dancing in house-church meetings. However, I would not categorically state that the charismatic worship at Corinth in the context of a symposium meal excluded dance as a contribution to the assembly (see Cor. 14:26). Elizabeth Fiorenza wonders if the women of Corinth were becoming too exuberant for Paul's taste and if the apostle's admonition to the women to keep their hair covered was meant to prevent them from letting it flow freely in ecstatic dancing, which was common in the ecstatic worship of oriental dieties.[3]

Certainly Christians were admonished to avoid dancing, which was usually associated with drinking and sexual immorality in Roman culture. The church fathers on the whole took a dim view of social dancing and even reinterpreted references to sacred dance in the psalms. Clement of Alexandria, writing around 195, interpreted Old Testament Scriptures in such a way as to erase any reference to literal dancing. Thus "Praise with the timbrel and the dance" (Ps. 150:4) is interpreted as the church meditating on the resurrection of the dead "in the resounding skin." However, Clement does instruct Christians to "dance in a ring, together with the angels, around Him who is without beginning or end," which Louis Backman suggests might be a ring dance around the altar table.[4] More typically, Commodius (writing around 240) associates dancing with worldliness: "You are rejecting the law when you wish to please the world. You dance in your houses. Instead of psalms, you sing love songs." Writing about a decade later, Cyprian makes a distinction between godly and ungodly dance: "The fact that David led the dances in the presence of God is no sanction for faithful Christians to occupy seats in the public theater. For David did not twist his limbs about in obscene movements. He did not depict in his dancing the story of Grecian lust."[5]

References from the church fathers in the fourth century indicate that Christians, especially the women, did dance, perhaps even in the church buildings during festivals and in the cemeteries at the graves of the martyrs in the fourth century. Basileios, bishop of Caesarea, lashed out at women who "shamelessly attract the attention of every man.

3. Ibid., 66.
4. E. Louis Backman, *Religious Dances in the Christian Church and in Popular Medicine*, trans. E. Classen (London: Allen and Unwin, 1952), 21–22.
5. Quotes from the church fathers taken from "Dancing," in *A Dictionary of Early Christian Beliefs*, ed. David W. Bercot (Peabody, MA: Hendrickson, 1998), 187.

With unkempt hair, clothed in bodices and hopping about, they dance with lustful eyes and loud laughter; as if seized by a kind of frenzy they excite the lust of youths. They execute ring-dances in the churches of the Martyrs and at their graves."[6] Of course, we cannot say whether the women's dancing was lewd or only seemed that way to the bishop.

Toward the end of the century Gregory of Nazianzus, bishop of Constantinople (379–81), seemingly gave in and suggested a more somber approach to singing and dancing. "Let us sing hymns instead of striking drums, have psalms instead of frivolous music and song . . . modesty instead of laughter, wise contemplation instead of intoxication, seriousness instead of delirium. But even if you wish to dance in devotion to this happy ceremony and festival, then dance, but not the shameless dance of the daughter of Herod."[7] John Chrysostom, bishop of Constantinople after Gregory, extolled dancing on the feasts of the martyrs. "You have reveled in the holy martyrs in these recent days; you have taken your fill of the spiritual feast . . . You have danced a beautiful dance throughout the whole city, led by your noble general."[8] The bishop may be referencing a dance-like procession through the streets in which the relics of a martyr—their "noble general"—were being carried ahead of the procession.

Perhaps the most positive affirmation of dance in the church comes from Ambrose, bishop of Milan.

> The dance should be conducted as did David when he danced before the ark of the Lord, for everything is right which springs from the fear of God. Let us not be ashamed of show of reverence which will enrich the cult and deepen the adoration of Christ. For this reason the dance must in no wise be regarded as a mark of reverence for vanity and luxury, but as something which uplifts every living body instead of allowing them to rest motionless upon the ground or the slow feet to become numb.... This dance is an ally of faith and an honoring of grace. The Lord bids us dance.[9]

6. Quoted in Backman, *Religious Dances*, 25.
7. Ibid., 31–32.
8. John Chrysostom, *Homilies on the Statues* 19.1; cited in Andrew B. McGowan, *Ancient Christian Worship: Early Church Practices in Social, Historical, and Theological Perspective* (Grand Rapids: Baker Academic, 2014), 132.
9. Marilyn Daniels, *The History of Dance in Christianity* (New York: Paulist, 1980), 18–19.

The evidence suggests an ambiguous attitude on the part of the church fathers toward dance, particularly in connection with liturgy. It was apparently happening and the bishops were constrained to keep it under control but allowed it. We should note that the basilicas of late antiquity (fourth through sixth centuries) and the medieval churches were large open spaces unencumbered by pews. Many functions went on in church buildings beside worship. One of the reasons for erecting screens between the nave and sanctuary in the churches of the East and West was to allow clergy to go about their liturgical functions without being disturbed by other activities that were taking place in the building. Markets could be held in the churches as well as Christmas and Easter dinners. Dancing in church was a possibility, and perhaps it accompanied these festive meals in the nave. But liturgy was also done in the streets in late antiquity in the form of processions that could have also included dancing.

During the early Middle Ages in western Europe carols were sung at Christmas and Easter and danced in stanza-chorus form. "To carol" actually means to dance. As Marilyn Daniels informs us, during the stanza, which means "to stand or halt," the people stood with their attention generally directed to the center of the circle for what was being celebrated. If it was a line dance carol the focus would be on the destination of the dancers. During the repeated choruses the people danced, using a three-step or *tripudia*. The tripudium was danced at both a slow and medium speed, usually in an attitude of joy or jubilation (*jubilate* is another translation for *tripudia*). The step (which can be traced to ancient Rome) involved three steps forward and one step backward and was used in ring dances, line dances, and processionals. This movement came to signify man's humility—"I go forward, yet I falter"—and was an act of reverence that is the basis for genuflection used in Christian worship.

In the early medieval period (from the sixth to tenth centuries) the priests and bishops joined in with the dancing of the people. In the high Middle Ages (from the eleventh to thirteenth centuries) the clergy had their own dances separate from the people. By the late Middle Ages (fourteenth to fifteenth centuries) synods and councils made efforts to suppress dancing entirely.

Yet some dances were encouraged. In response to the Black Death in the fourteenth century (1347–73), the dance of death (*danse macabre*) was performed like a morality play. Many late medieval depictions of this dance portray people in dancing skeleton costumes. Peasants believed that if they could catch the devil, they could drive him off. The dance of death symbolized this hope.

A dance before the Holy Sacrament was instituted in Spain by Cardinal Ximenes (1436–1517) in 1499 when he restored the old Hispanic (Mozarabic) rite. Called *Los Seises*, meaning "the sixes," this dance was performed by two divisions of six choirboys in colorful costumes as an act of devotion before the reserved sacrament. Because of its popularity it spread beyond Toledo and Seville and was performed on Corpus Christi and is still performed day.[10]

In America a religious group known as the Shakers (an offshoot of the Quakers) included dancing in their worship. The Shakers lived in male and female communities, known for their simple wooden furniture as well as their dancing. Their dancing appears to have been a form of line dancing, with men and women on separate sides of the dance hall. Because they were celibates and no new members have joined them in recent years, the group has mostly died out.

A church that has integrated dancing into the liturgy and continues to thrive is St. Gregory of Nyssa Episcopal Church in San Francisco. The architectural space is arranged into two separate spaces: one for the word and the other for the eucharistic meal. During the liturgy of the word the worshipers sit on two sides facing each other (like in cathedral or monastic stalls) with an ambo in the middle. For the liturgy of the meal the worshipers dance a *tripudium* into the adjoining room and stand around the table. A carol dance concludes the service, and portrayals of dancing saints adorn the walls.

In the second half of the twentieth century in Europe and North

---

10. See J. G. Davies, *Liturgical Dance: An Historical, Theological, and Practical Handbook* (London: SCM, 1984), 54–55.

America there were efforts to revive liturgical dance.[11] This usually meant a solo dancer or a troupe of dancers acting out parts of the liturgy or the readings. On the whole, the practice has not been successful because it has usually been performed by professional dancers, whose movements are not easily emulated by ordinary worshipers. In more successful efforts, lay participants were taught some simple movements.

Incorporating dance into worship has been more successful in places where dancing is a more common form of expression. Uzukwu notes "the dance, which involves an expansive, rhythmic, nonverbal movement of the body, is one key way of interaction in Africa."[12] In the Ethiopian Orthodox Church there is a sixteen hundred-year-old torch dance observed as part of the annual Meskel celebration. The Meskel celebration includes the burning of a large bonfire, or *Demera*, a practice that is based on the belief that the Empress Helena, mother of the Emperor Constantine, had a revelation in a dream in which she was told to make a bonfire and that the smoke would show her where the true cross of Christ was buried. The veneration of the cross is especially popular in Ethiopia, and dances are a part of many celebrations in African churches.

Entrance Processions

In chapter 1 we discussed postures in worship (for example, kneeling, raised arms, folded hands, bowed heads, even prostration). Doing these poses involves movement of one's own body. Processions are a form of solemn dance that can involve the whole liturgical assembly. Christian worship has been processional since the fourth century.

I don't know what the liturgical practices were in the Christian house churches with their symposia in which the word and discussion were added to eating and drinking the Lord's Supper, I suspect some amount of reclining at table was practiced. But as soon as Christianity

11. See Robert E. Webber, ed., *Music and the Arts in Christian Worship*, vol. 4, bk. 2, *The Complete Library of Christian Worship*. (Nashville: Star Song, 1994), 719–68.
12. Uzukwu, *Worship as Body Language*, 6.

became a legal cult in the Roman Empire by the Edict of Milan in 313, and began moving into large public halls known as basilicas for their liturgical assemblies, liturgy was set in motion.

The Emperor Constantine handed over the Lateran Palace as a residence for the bishop of Rome (the pope). The great basilica of St. John Lateran was built as the cathedral of the diocese of Rome (which it still is). But the eucharistic ecclesiology of the ancient church, expressed as far back as in the letters of Ignatius of Antioch (ca. 110), holds that in each local church there is one bishop and one Eucharist. This means that the whole diocese of Rome had to gather around its bishop for the eucharistic celebration. How was this going to be accomplished with a growing Christian population in so vast a city? Christian basilicas couldn't even be built in the city center because it was already occupied by the Forum, the Senate, the Colosseum, and pagan temples. The only place for new construction was in the suburbs. So Christian basilicas were built in a circle around the city, and the pope had to get from one to another to celebrate the Eucharist on Sundays and festivals. This was called stational liturgy—moving from one station to another. The solution was to organize processions from the Lateran Palace to whatever station the pope was celebrating the Eucharist. Since the shortest distance between two points is a straight line, the processions traveled through the (pagan) center of the city singing psalms and litanies and attracting participants as it went. This is liturgical evangelization.

Psalms and litanies were also sung by Christian pilgrims to the Holy Land during the fourth century. A detailed description of pilgrimage rites in the *Diary of a Pilgrimage* of the Spanish religious woman Egeria as she recorded what she experienced in her pilgrimage to the Holy Land in 381-84. This practice was to process from a gathering place, such as the Church of the Holy Sepulcher in Jerusalem (also known as the Martyrium), to a site associated with an event in the life of Christ, singing psalms and litanies on their way. In the procession the people responded with a refrain or antiphon as a cantor or a choir of monks or nuns sang the stanzas. The psalms were followed by litanies, which were prayers sung while walking, to which the worshipers responded with the petition *Kyrie eleison* (Lord have mercy). When the pilgrims reached their destination, a reading appropriate to that place (usually from a Gospel) was read. These pilgrim processions were quite a walk—such as from the Martyrium in Jerusalem up the Mount of Olives on Palm Sunday and the Ascension and then back again; or from Jerusalem to Bethlehem and back again on the Epiphany.

The entrance procession into the Roman basilicas included an Introit psalm, a Kyrie litany, and an opening hymn, followed by the prayer and the liturgy of the word (the readings). Notice the structural similarity with the pilgrimage rite: psalms, litany, hymn, readings.

Other moments of movement in the Roman Eucharist or Mass included the throngs of people in the basilica when they brought forward their gifts, especially bread and wine (which were gathered by acolytes) and when they went to a communion station to receive the consecrated bread and wine. Psalms were sung during these moments as the people moved throughout the basilicas (unencumbered by pews, benches, or chairs).

Upon coming into power, the Emperor Constantine decided to vacate the old capital of Rome and build a new capital city named after himself on the site of ancient Byzantium on the Bosporus, the city of Constantinople (modern Istanbul). Constantine did this for a number of reasons: it removed him from the influence of the old senatorial families in Rome; it placed him more strategically in the center of the Roman world (straddling Europe and Asia); and it provided him with an opportunity to build a city in which Christian institutions rather than the Roman pagan institutions were in the heart of the city. The new Rome was built as a processional city, with grand boulevards connecting the imperial palace, the government buildings, the Hippodrome, and the Great Church (under the Emperor Justinian in the sixth century this became the Hagia Sophia, the greatest church building in Christendom). In this new capital church and society were unified by liturgical processions that occurred along the boulevard from one station to another, drawing on the full forces of church and state and thousands of bystanders. Processions were organized for a variety of occasions: national thanksgiving, such as a coronation of an emperor, a military victory, the transfer of the relics of a saint, or deliverance from plagues or earthquakes; national lament in the face of disaster, whether military or natural; or to ward off disaster, such as a plague or a siege, in which case the processions had a penitential character. Again, the processions were accompanied by psalms and hymns and litanies. The entrance rite of the Byzantine Divine Liturgy, can be seen as a continuation of the material that was sung outside of the church building, inside the building. The Trisagion (Thrice-Holy hymn) was the song of entrance into the church.

The entrance rite of the Byzantine liturgy may be compared with that of the Roman liturgy once both were celebrated almost exclusively inside the church building (this is a little lesson in comparative liturgics). The psalmody and litanies became truncated. What survives in the Byzantine liturgy today are three psalm antiphons with brief litanies before the Trisagion hymn. In the Roman Mass before 1969 the Introit and the Kyrie responses (repeated nine, six, or three times) before the Gloria in Excelsis survived. The Introit consisted of an antiphon, a psalm verse (not a whole psalm), the Gloria Patri, and the antiphon repeated.

Stational Processions

Stational liturgy and processions were carried into the rest of Europe, East and West, by missionaries from Constantinople and Rome. Stational processions moved a crowd of people from one site to another. Throughout the Middle Ages, stational liturgy served the same purposes established in antiquity: processions to pilgrimage sites, episcopal stational liturgy, aversion to plagues and natural disasters, transfer of relics, and so forth. These processions were occasional, but four annual stational processions connected with days in the church year have more or less survived into our time: Candlemas, Palm Sunday, Rogationtide, and Corpus Christi. I'll look at these processions, along with those of Holy Week.[13]

Candlemas

The Feast of the Presentation of Jesus in the Temple and the Purification of Mary on the fortieth day after the Nativity, according to the Gospel of Luke, spread from Jerusalem over the entire church and was later kept on February 2 in the Western calendar (forty days after December 25). The popular name "Candlemas" comes from the blessing of the church's supply of candles for the year and the candlelight procession. During the procession the choir sings the canticle of Simeon, the Nunc Dimittis. Its antiphon, "a light for revelation to the gentiles and the glory of your people Israel," is repeated after every verse of the canticle, according to the medieval custom of singing antiphons. The solemn procession represents the entry of Christ, who is the light of the world, into the temple of Jerusalem. Today the procession is held inside the church building, especially in northern climates where it is still cold outside on February 2.

Palm Sunday and Holy Week

Egeria gives us the earliest description of the Palm Sunday procession as it took place in late fourth-century Jerusalem. The people assembled in the afternoon of the Sunday at the beginning of Holy Week on the Mount of Olives at the Church of Eleona and processed to the Imbomon (where Jesus ascended into heaven). From there, carrying branches of palm or olive, they processed back to the city repeating Ps. 118:26: "Blessed is he who comes in the name of the Lord."

The Palm Sunday procession provides an opportunity for the whole congregation to gather outside of the church building for the reading of the processional Gospel, the blessing of palms, and the procession carrying palms, perhaps through the neighborhood or around the block (weather permitting) and into the church. The hymn "All Glory, Laud, and Honor" is sung during the procession and into the church building. Note that this hymn has a repeating refrain typical of processional songs, so it is not necessary for people to sing the

---

13. See Frank C. Senn, *Introduction to Christian Liturgy* (Minneapolis: Fortress Press, 2012), 200–204.

complete text while they walk; the stanzas can be sung by the choir (accompanied by brass instruments to retain pitch and tempo). This is an opportunity for liturgical evangelism in the neighborhood around the church.

Many European countries have processions during Holy Week that are expressions of popular piety. The most spectacular of these processions occur in Spain (Holy Week in Spanish is called *Semana Santa*). The processions are organized by brotherhoods or fraternities, most of which originated in the late Middle Age, though a number of them were created during the baroque period, inspired by the Counter Reformation. In each case the processions are responses to the triumphs of Catholicism—after the Moors and Jews were driven out of Spain, during the resurgence of Catholicism following the Reformation, and in the resurgence of religious life after the Spanish Civil War in the twentieth century. The membership is usually open to any Catholic person, and family tradition is an important element in becoming a member or "brother" (*hermano*). The processions differ from one region to another, but a common feature is the general usage of the *nazareno*, or penitential robe, for some of the participants in the brotherhood. This garment consists of a tunic, a hood with conical tip (*capirote*) used to conceal the face of the wearer, and sometimes a cloak. The exact colors and forms of these robes depend on the particular procession. The robes were widely used in the medieval period for penitents, who could demonstrate their penance while masking their identity. These *nazarenos* carry processional candles or rough-hewn wooden crosses, sometimes walk the city streets barefoot, and, in some places wear shackles and chains as a sign of their penitence. The other common feature is that every brotherhood carries magnificent *pasos*—floats with sculptures that depict different scenes from the Gospels related to the Passion of Christ or the Sorrows of the Virgin Mary. Many of the floats are created by Spanish artists, and in some cases the brotherhoods have owned and preserved these *pasos* for centuries. Usually, the *pasos* are accompanied by marching bands that play the *Marchas procesionales*, although in northern Spain the processions are more solemn.

Good Friday is another day for outdoor processions. Pilgrims to Jerusalem still walk the *via cruces*, following the path Jesus took from Pontius Pilate's judgment seat to the place of execution on Golgotha. The late medieval popular devotion of the Stations of the Cross became a way for individuals or groups to make a local pilgrimage procession through fourteen stations commemorating the passion of Christ. The Stations of the Cross were not confined to church buildings; sometimes they extended for miles down a country road, as in some places in Europe. In Hispanic communities today the entire community joins in a Good Friday *via crucis* through a neighborhood, processing through the fourteen Stations, singing hymns and songs and psalms along the way and stopping at each station for a meditation on the event. The Stations are usually acted out and end with a crucifixion in which three actors, one playing Christ, are affixed to a cross and hoisted up. The reenactment of the crucifixion of Jesus also takes place in other Christian communities around the world—in the Philippines, India, Indonesia, Lebanon, and other places where Christians sometimes suffer for the faith.

The Good Friday liturgy includes the reading of the St. John Passion, followed by the Bidding Prayers. After the prayers a procession takes place using an old rugged cross. The procession stops at three stations, and at each one the minister sings the invitatory—"Behold the life-giving cross, on which was hung the Savior of the whole world"—with the people responding, "Come, let us worship." This is followed by the Reproaches and the Veneration of the cross.

The Easter Vigil also begins as a kind of stational liturgy. The congregation gathers outside the church building around the new fire for the lighting of the paschal candle and then processes with handheld lighted candles into the darkened church building proclaiming, "The light of Christ." Continuing the practice reported by Egeria in Jerusalem, the Orthodox Church lights candles within the sanctuary, and the bishop or priest emerges proclaiming, "Christ is risen.

Alleluia." A procession then occurs around the outside of the church building, with the worshipers carrying lighted candles and singing Easter hymns.

The Easter Vigil as it is practiced in the West continues in semidarkness through Old Testament readings that rehearse the history of salvation, each one followed by a psalm or canticle, silent reflection, and a prayer. A procession to the baptismal font for baptisms and renewal of baptism follows. In Catholic practice the litany of the saints is sung. Lutherans use the canticle *Benedicite opera Omnia* (All you works of the Lord bless the Lord), known as the "song of the three children." In my former parish practice, three girls or women sang the verses, and the congregation repeated the refrain, "Praise him and magnify him forever" as they left their seats and gathered around the font.

Rogationtide

Days of prayer at the time of the spring planting asking for God's blessing of a bountiful harvest probably predate Christianity in Europe. These days became especially popular in England and Germany. The Rogation days were so popular in England that their celebration continued even to the thirteenth year of the reign of the Protestant Queen Elizabeth, in 1571. The Rogation days in the Western calendar occur on the Monday, Tuesday, and Wednesday before Ascension Thursday. In his ascension Christ is our effective mediator and advocate before the Father in heaven. The Sunday before the Ascension was called *Rogate*. As with all stational processions, psalms and litanies are sung. In the Roman Rite the litany of the saints is chanted. In Anglican use the Great Litany is sung. Historically, the purpose of the Rogation processions was to walk and mark out the parish boundaries, often repairing boundary markers as they went. The boys had a grand time beating away the undergrowth as the procession made its way; hence it was also called "beating the bounds" (boundaries). Sometimes Rogation processions bumped into each other. The procession terminates in the parish church, where the Mass is celebrated. The color used in the procession and Mass is violet, reflecting the penitential character of the procession.

In this day of environmental awareness and renewed concern for the stewardship of the earth, Rogation processions might acquire a new relevance, not only in rural places but in city neighborhoods where the procession could make stational stops at local parks or community gardens, with appropriate prayers for the care of the environment, and conclude with a eucharistic celebration, using propers for the stewardship of creation. I once led a Rogation procession marking the boundaries of a church camp in rural Illinois, singing the Great Litany and blessing the fields.

Corpus Christi

If Rogation processions reflect an agricultural and rural origin, the Corpus Christi procession reflects an urban origin. The Feast of Corpus Christi emerged at a time when rural populations were being displaced from the land and were moving into the growing cities. In this climate of social unrest, as political structures threatened to disintegrate, Corpus Christi celebrated the sacrament of the body of Christ as the glue that bonded society together.[14] Its celebration brought together the whole town. At the instigation of religious women in Liege, Belgium, the Feast of Corpus Christi was promulgated by Pope Urban IV in 1264 as a universal feast in the Catholic Church. It was assigned to the Thursday after Trinity Sunday as the delayed octave of Maundy Thursday.

The main feature of the Corpus Christi celebration became the great procession with the Blessed Sacrament after the Mass. The Blessed Sacrament was held by the bishop or celebrant of the Mass in a monstrance as he walked under a canopy, and all of the clergy and religious orders processed. The trade guilds of the town provided decorated floats and often jockeyed for a position in the parade close to the canopy of the Blessed Sacrament. Like the Rogationtide

---

14. See John Bossy, "The Mass as a Social Institution, 1200–1700," *Past and Present* 100 (1983): 29–61.

processions, the Corpus Christi procession attained great popularity because local communities could invest it with their local concerns and customs. Fairs were part of the Corpus Christi celebrations, which occurred in early summer, as well as the performance of mystery plays, of which several English cycles survive.[15] Corpus Christi remains a major festive celebration in many Catholic countries.

Finally, I should note that processions were always a part of weddings and funerals. In both of these liturgies some kind of procession took place—from the house of the bride or the deceased to the place of the service, a procession into the church, and a procession out of the church and on to the place of the wedding celebration or interment. Traditionally, songs and psalms accompanied these processions. In weddings an additional procession sometimes took place to the new home of the bride and groom for the blessing of the marriage bed. These processions continue today, although the participants usually ride in automobiles to the various stations (church, banquet hall, cemetery) rather than walking on foot.

Figure 17. Ugandan youth dance at a cultural celebration of peace.

15. See Mervyn James, "Ritual, Drama and Social Body in the Late Medieval English Town," *Past and Present* 98 (1983): 3–29.

B. Liturgical Drama and Plays

There is already drama involved in some liturgical actions such as the celebration of the Lord's Supper. We are doing what Jesus did in the upper room on the night before his death when we take bread and a cup of wine, give thanks over them, break the bread, and share these elements with the communicants. In these acts, we need to distinguish between two Greek terms that refer to memorial or remembering. *Anamnesis* means to remember in the sense of reactualizing the original event. When Jesus said, "Do this for the remembrance (*anamnesis*) of me," he was referring to his promise to be present in the bread and wine according to his word—"This is my body given for you. This is my blood of the new covenant shed for you for the forgiven of sins." By this memorial Christ is truly present among us when we celebrate his supper. But there is also memorial or remembrance in the sense of *mimesis*, which refers to mimicking what Jesus did in the original institution. The mimetic action can put us in mind of what Jesus did and of his sacrifice for sins. But without the sense of *anamnesis, mimesis* is only affective play-acting, not effective presence.

Traditions differ in their approach to enacting the celebration of the Lord's Supper. The Reformed tradition has sometimes tried to reenact the last supper by gathering around an actual table. The Catholic and Lutheran traditions have resisted this kind of dramatic reenactment out of concern that it undermines confidence in the objectivity of the real presence of Christ; they insist that Christ is present because of his word, "This is my body"—that is, "This is me." We should note that the Eucharist is not without its dramatic elements. It is apparent that someone takes on the role of Christ and those who come to the table are his disciples. On the other hand, we cannot exactly replicate the last supper of Jesus and his disciples; there are no photographs to show the arrangement in the upper room. We can only suggest a connection, with the help of a few dramatic strokes and props—table covered with linen, loaf of bread and chalice of wine, candlelight. And while we may gather around a table, we don't recline at table as people would have done in the first century. Even those Reformed congregations that physically sit at the table are not doing exactly what was (likely) done in the upper room at Jesus' last supper.

Liturgical Drama

We have seen dramatic actions in some of the processions we have looked at, especially the processions and liturgical actions of Holy Week. In fourth-century Jerusalem, the Palm Sunday procession was already a dramatic reenactment of Jesus' triumphant entry into the city. The foot washing in the Maundy Thursday liturgy is an exact reenactment of the dramatic action of Jesus in that upper room symposium, as well as a literal response to his command that "you also ought to wash one another's feet. For I have set you an example, that you also should do as I have done to you" (John 13:14–15, NRSV). The Armenian Orthodox Church has performed this rite down through the centuries. As in the Catholic Church, the highest cleric—such as the pope or a bishop or the parish pastor—washes the feet of twelve selected persons. But in the Mennonite church the members of the congregation actually wash one another's feet, since they are all disciples of Jesus doing what he told them to do. This practice of a congregational foot washing is spreading to other Protestant congregations and Catholic parishes, although the case has been made that a substitute action is needed to make this servant act more culturally relevant. Some have tried washing one another's hands, but this gesture seems feeble in comparison.

The chanting of the passion narratives as Gospels during Holy Week—St. Matthew on Palm Sunday, St. Mark on Tuesday, St. Luke on Wednesday, and St. John on Good Friday—opened the door for music drama in the liturgy. Because the passion narratives are long, the text was broken up between three cantors: a tenor singing the words of the evangelist, a bass singing the words of Jesus, and a baritone singing the other parts (called *turbae*). After the Reformation, chorales and hymns were added as congregational responses after each section of the passion, and the chanting tones became recitatives in the style of the emerging baroque operas. Eventually arias were added as solo reflections on the events in the passion. The end result was the passion-oratorio in Lutheran and Roman Catholic churches. The high points of this development were the St. John and St. Matthew Passions of Johann Sebastian Bach.

Little music dramas were also sung in the medieval church at Matins on Easter and Christmas mornings. The earliest of these little music dramas used the Latin question *Quem quaeritis?* (Whom do you seek?), which was sung/enacted after the third responsory, before the canticle *Te Deum laudamus.* It refers to four lines of chant in the medieval Easter liturgy that later formed the kernel of the large body of medieval liturgical drama. It was introduced into the liturgy as an Introit trope in the tenth century as a new genre of liturgical ceremony:

> *Interrogatio. Quem quaeritis in sepulchro, o Christicolae?*
> *Responsio. Jesum Nazarenum crucifixum, o caelicolae.*
> *Angeli. Non est hic; surrexit, sicut praedixerat. Ite, nuntiate quia surrexit de sepulchro.*

Translation:

> Question [by the Angels]: Whom do ye seek in the sepulcher, O followers of Christ?
> Answer [by the three Marys]: Jesus of Nazareth, the Crucified, O heavenly ones.
> The Angels: He is not here; he is risen, just as he foretold. Go, announce that he is risen from the sepulchre.[16]

These lines were sung by four clerics, who were vested in albs and copes. Then followed a chorus of Alleluias, sung by the choir. The text excerpted above later snowballed into an immense body of medieval religious plays, such as liturgical drama and mystery plays. The plays that trace their genealogy to the *Quem Quaeritis* lasted for about six hundred and fifty years, until the end of the Protestant Reformation.

From this relatively simple trope sprang a series of *visitatio*

---

16. John Cassner, ed. and with Introduction, *Medieval and Tudor Drama* (New York: Applause Theatre Book Publishers, 1963, 1987), 35.

(visitation) plays, which are variations on the visit to the tomb and the discovery that Jesus has risen. In one, the disciples Peter and John race to the tomb to see if what they've heard is true; John gets there first but allows Peter to enter the tomb before him. Two monks or cathedral clergy might have run the length of a cathedral's nave to enact this version. Later, a secular figure is added to the action: a merchant selling ointments to the three Marys (Mary Magdalene, Mary mother of James, and Mary Salome) so that they can anoint the body of Christ. In the earliest versions the merchant is silent, but in later variations he haggles with the women over the price! In time, another plot was added. Pontius Pilate sends guards to watch the tomb; the angel strikes them with a thunderbolt (props are needed!); the Marys enter, buy oils from the merchant; the question is asked—*Quem quaeritis?* In the meantime the soldiers report to Pilate, Mary Magdelene laments, Christ appears to her, Christ appears to the apostles, the disciples gather at the tomb, and all sing a final *Te Deum.*

A comparable music drama, sung within Christmas morning Matins, was *Quem queritis in presepe, pastores?* (Whom do you seek in the manger, shepherds?) A carol based on the late medieval music of the *Quem pastores* is still provided in some hymnals (see *Lutheran Book of Worship,* hymn 68). This drama is the basis for countless Christmas pageants performed by church school children in later times.

While there are many conjectural answers to the question of how these medieval liturgical dramas were staged, only two elements were necessary: a mansion and a platea. A mansion is a simple scenic element that represents the location of a scene. For example, a chair can represent the throne of Pontius Pilate; a bush can represent the Garden of Gethsemane; or a cross can represent Golgotha. It was simple staging. The platea is the space around the mansion that becomes the playing area as actors move into the space and so define it by being in it.

As liturgical drama became more complex, more staging was required. Just before Easter, passion plays were performed, which included different events that led to the crucifixion, death, and resurrection of Christ. Different mansions were set up throughout the nave, and the participants in the passion plays moved from mansion to mansion to act out the different scenes. Each time they move they set up a platea around the appropriate mansion and defined the playing space with their bodies.

I noted above that the popular devotion known as the Stations of the Cross traditionally includes fourteen mansions and plateas spaced at intervals either on the walls of the nave, outside around the church building, or down a road, with a procession of worshipers moving from one station to the next. Pope John Paul II added a fifteenth station so that the Way of the Cross ended with the resurrection.

Mystery Plays

These little liturgical dramas expanded beyond the bounds of liturgical propriety. It's not surprising that by the high Middle Ages the plays were performed outside the church in the vernacular—the everyday language of the local area—not in church Latin. Liturgical drama continued, had more freedom in that it wasn't confined to the liturgy.

The first play of this kind that survives today is *The Play of Adam* (twelfth century), two-thirds of which is written in French. As the stage directions strongly imply, it was performed on the steps in front of the church. Here are some of the stage directions:

> Let Paradise be set up in a somewhat lofty place; let there be about it curtains and silken hangings, at such an height that those persons who shall be in Paradise can be seen from the shoulders upward—let there be planted sweet-smelling flowers and foliage; let divers trees be therein and fruits hanging on them, so that it may seem a most delectable place.

> Then let the Savior come, clothed in a dalmatic, and let Adam and Eve be set before him. Let Adam be clothed in a red tunic; Eve, however, in a woman's garment of white, and a white silken wimple; and let them both stand before the Figura (God); but let Adam a little nearer, with composed countenance; Eve, however, with a countenance more subdued . . . whoever shall speak the name of Paradise, let him look back at it and point it out with his hand.

> Then a serpent, cunningly put together, shall ascend along the trunk

of the forbidden tree, unto which Eve shall approach her ear, as if hearkening unto its counsel.[17]

This play belongs to a category known as mystery plays. Mystery plays were reenactments of biblical stories that were performed on the feast days or days of devotion that commemorated the event. Over the course of time, whole cycles of mystery plays were developed. On the Feast of Corpus Christi, the community could go through the whole cycle of plays, ending with the Doomsday play, the enactment of the last judgment. The mystery plays provided an occasion for the release of social tensions since the actor playing Christ the Judge could consign even the pope to hell. Many things can happen on the stage that are not politically possible in real life, although that hasn't stopped the censors serving repressive regimes in modern times.

Passion Plays

The biggest mystery play of all was the passion play. We have seen that the chanting of the passion narratives led to liturgical music dramas, which eventually reached the monumental proportions of Bach's passion-oratorios. Good Friday processions with the cross became a reenactment of the journey of Christ to Golgotha. Some of the Hispanic passion processions are actually a living enactment of the fourteen Stations of the Cross. But there were also more elaborate passion plays that weren't performed only on Good Friday.

As passion plays moved outside the church building, they could utilize the whole town for casting and space. By the fourteenth century passion plays, particularly in Germany, reached a stage of development which required repeated performances since people from surrounding districts were drawn to them. As scripts were developed and stages erected they were repeated each year. From this period came the Vienna Passion, the St. Gall Passion, the oldest Frankfort Passion, and the Maestricht Passion. All four plays are written in German rhymed

---

17. Michal Kobialka, *This Is My Body: Representational Practices in the Early Middle Ages* (Ann Arbor: University of Michigan Press, 1999), 183.

verse. The plays became more secularized as "entertainment value" was value was added and the Church lost interest in supporting them.

Passion plays continued after the Reformation in Germany, but theological polemics were added to the scripts, especially between Jesuits and Lutherans. Eventually the plays died out, except in the small towns of Bavaria and Austria. In the late eighteenth century and Age of Enlightenment passion plays were generally abolished. But there was a revival of interest in them in the nineteenth-century age of romanticism and nationalism, and some plays were started up again, not only in Germany but also in other parts of the world.

The chief survivor of former times is the Oberammergau Passion Play. It was first performed in 1634 to fulfill a vow undertaken by the citizens of Oberammergau during an outbreak of bubonic plague that killed about fifteen thousand people in nearby Munich. After a hiatus of nearly forty years it was staged again in 1810. It is now performed every ten years in a large theater on a huge stage. In 2010 about half of the inhabitants of Oberammergau took part in the once-a-decade passion play. This means that over two thousand villagers brought the story of Jesus of Nazareth to life for the audiences that attended from around the world. The play starts with Jesus entering Jerusalem, continues with his death on the cross, and finishes with the resurrection. The play is an extraordinary community enterprise. Over the years, the script has been periodically updated, particularly in 2000 to erase implications that the Jews killed Jesus. Trumpet solos now announce the presence of Herodias and Pontius Pilate, and meditative choruses add a contemplative quality.

Jumping to the twentieth century, perhaps it is not too big a stretch to see the rock musical *Jesus Christ, Superstar!* as a kind of passion play since it focuses on the events of Holy Week. With a script by Tim Rice and music by Andrew Lloyd Webber, it changed the face of musical theater when it opened on Broadway in New York City in 1971. *Time* magazine hailed *Jesus Christ Superstar* as a modern passion play that might anger the devout but might intrigue and perhaps inspire the agnostic young.

Miracle Plays

Going back to the Middle Ages, we find another genre similar to the mystery plays. The miracle plays present real or fictitious accounts of the miracles or martyrdoms of a saint. Like the mystery plays, this genre evolved from liturgical offices developed during the tenth and eleventh centuries to enhance festivals in the sanctoral cycle (the saints' days). By the thirteenth century they had become vernacularized and replete with unliturgical elements. Divorced from church services, they were performed at public festivals. Almost all surviving miracle plays concern either the Virgin Mary or St. Nicholas, the fourth-century bishop of Myra in Asia Minor. Both Mary and Nicholas had active cults (a system of religious beliefs and rituals) during the Middle Ages, when belief in the healing powers of saintly relics was widespread. Miracle plays flourished in this culture and contributed to the legends of the saints, which the Protestant reformers found objectionable.

Morality Plays

The other genre of plays that emerged in the late Middle Ages were the morality plays. These plays centered on virtues and vices. They were allegories in which the protagonist is met by personifications of various moral attributes who try to prompt him to choose a godly life over an evil life. The plays were most popular in Europe during the fifteenth and sixteenth centuries. They reflect the dominant belief of the time that humans had a certain amount of control over their post-death fate while they were on earth.

The most archetypal morality play is *Everyman*. The characters take on the common pattern of these plays in which they represent broader ideas, including God, Death, Everyman, Good-Deeds, Angel, Knowledge, Beauty, Discretion, and Strength. The personified meanings of these characters are hardly hidden. The premise of *Everyman* is that God, believing that the people on earth are too focused on wealth and worldly possessions, sends Death to Everyman to remind him of God's power and the importance of upholding values.[18] The emphasis put on morality, the seemingly vast difference between good and evil, and the strong presence of God makes *Everyman* one of the most concrete examples of a morality play. At the same time, most morality plays focus more on evil while *Everyman* focuses more on good, highlighting sin in contrast. Evil is usually more interesting, even more fun, than good.

Morality plays continued in the Reformation and post-Reformation period, but in this case the vices and virtues tended to be theological rather than moral. Protestant plays discredited Catholic teachings, and Catholic plays discredited Protestant teachings. Following wrong teachings, of course, could have eternal consequences. If the common people who watched the plays were unsure about doctrine, they could be kept in line with the right practices. In Protestant plays the good person read the Bible; in Catholic plays the good person went to communion.

The twentieth-century rock musical *Godspell* could perhaps be regarded as a modern religious morality play. With music by Stephen Schwartz and a book by John-Michael Tebelak, it started as a college project performed by students at Carnegie Mellon University and moved to La MaMa Experimental Theatre Club in Greenwich Village. It was then rescored for an off-Broadway production that opened on May 17, 1971, and became a long-running success. The musical's structure consists of a series of parables mostly based on the Gospel of Matthew (three of the featured parables are recorded only in the Gospel of Luke). The parables are interspersed with a variety of modern music set primarily to lyrics from traditional hymns, with the passion of Christ treated briefly near the end of the performance. It was criticized because the resurrection is only hinted at, but *Godspell* is really about the persistence and triumph of Love. In that sense it is more like a morality play.

We have seen how liturgical drama spawned religious plays and

18. Stanley Appelbaum and Candace Ward, eds., *Everyman and Other Miracle and Morality Plays* (New York: Dover, 1995), 36–59.

made a contribution to Western drama. There has been a tenuous partnership between Christianity and the arts. The church has needed artists with their particular sensibilities to help spread the gospel. On the other hand, theater has needed texts with dramatic potential, and the Bible has provided them.

Music, dance, and drama are among the most effective ways of striking an emotional chord in people. These arts can shed new light on the interpretation of biblical stories, but they should do so in conversation with theology. To the extent that the liturgy employs music, dance, and drama, we should remember that its purpose is to worship God the Holy Trinity—and that requires a theological critique of the media.

Figure 18. Corpus Christi procession in Sanok, Poland 2011.

12

———

Performing Bodies

A. Liturgical Performance

In her book *Natural Symbols*, anthropologist Mary Douglas deals with
the aversion to ritual in modern Western life. Writing in the late 1960s
she said: "Ritual has become a bad word signifying empty conformity.
We are witnessing a revolt against formalism, even against form." This
wasn't a new critique in the Age of Aquarius. Both the Puritans and
the revivalists held a long-standing criticism of ritualism. In their view,
wrote Douglas, the ritualist is "one who performs external gestures
which imply commitment to a particular set of values, but he is
inwardly withdrawn, dried out and uncommitted."[1]

Hopefully, the bias against ritualism has diminished over the last
fifty years. But I think that many Protestants still harbor negative
views toward ritual and ritualistic worship. Douglas implies that the
critics of ritualism regard the ritualist as insincere. But then what word
do we use, she asks, to describe a person who performs rituals and is
sincerely committed to the values and beliefs they enact? For example,

---

1. Mary Douglas, *Natural Symbols: Explorations in Cosmology* (New York: Random House, 1973), 19-20.

I don't treat the consecrated bread and wine of the Eucharist with reverence only because that's what the ritual tradition taught me to do; I treat the consecrated elements with reverence because I believe they are the bearers of the body and blood of Christ. Theological commitments are embodied in the ritual acts.

Everyone performs rituals and is ritualistic in some way, so the term must be treated in a neutral way to signify habitual actions and behavior. That's what ritual is about. As Catherine Bell points out in her book *Ritual,* ritual and ritual-like activities include these characteristics which I summarize as follows:[2]

- Formalism. There is a form.

- Traditionalism. The practice continues to be done.

- Invariance. The practices are repeated basically the same way every time.

- Rule governance. There are ways of doing something which should be observed.

- Sacred symbolism.The practices have symbolic significance.

- Performance. The performer of ritual self-consciously does highly symbolic actions in public.

I hope we have become sophisticated enough in our understanding of human ritual to realize that free church worship is as ritualistic as the worship of the liturgical churches. Just as traditional worship (however understood) is ordered by ritual, so-called contemporary worship also maintains a ritual pattern. Contemporary worship has all the characteristics of ritual-like activities: a form, an established tradition (it's been around since the 1960s), an invariable routine, guidelines for performance, symbolic significance, and performance standards.

In matters of worship the same criticism about "ritualism" also arises in terms of "performance." It is not just the evangelical free

---

2. Catherine Bell, *Ritual: Perspectives and Dimensions* (New York: Oxford University Press, 1997), 138–69.

church revivalist complaining about the "ritualism" of the high church liturgy, but the accusation that one or another liturgical style is "too much like a performance." The worshiper who is used to high church liturgy attends a contemporary service, experiences the praise band, and says, "It is too much like a performance," as if the highly skilled organist in his or her own church is not putting on a performance. Or the free church worshiper attends the liturgy at an Anglo-Catholic parish and criticizes the careful choreography around the altar as being "too much like a performance," as if the carefully timed message in his or her contemporary service, complete with teleprompters for the preacher whose body is projected on a giant screen, is not giving attention to performance.

What is needed is a more neutral understanding of "performance," just as cultural anthropology and its subdivision of ritual studies gave us a more neutral understanding of ritual. We are well aware that the term is used without prejudice in describing performance in the performing arts of music, dance, and theater. Critics analyze and evaluate performances based on the technical accomplishments and interpretations of the performers. They would never say that a performance was "too much like a performance." They would say it was a good performance or a bad performance.

The term "performance style" refers to a way in which a performance is presented. For example, early music ensembles present a Baroque or Classical period composition differently than a modern symphony orchestra. I expect to hear Handel's *Water Music* performed differently by the Chicago Music of the Baroque than by the Chicago Symphony Orchestra. Both are world-class ensembles; the difference involves not only the smaller forces used by the Baroque band but even the instruments and tunings. Handel sounds quite differently if performed by a symphony orchestra that employs larger forces and modern instruments and that probably performs at a slower tempo than does an early music ensemble. Those who grew up listening to the Robert Shaw Chorale perform Bach's *Mass in B minor* would be shocked to hear a so-called "original performance" of one voice to a part, with boys and countertenors singing the soprano and alto lines. While we may prefer one way of performing a piece over another, we can't fault an ensemble for performing it in their chosen style. We can only critique their technique and interpretation on the basis of what they intend to convey. Was it well done? Did it convince us of the value of this particular performance style?

A field of performance studies is emerging that is similar to ritual studies.[3] This field investigates the relationship between the performer and the environment in a social event. For example, how would one give a presentation to a small group in a small room in comparison with a large group in a large room? Would that not depend on the nature of the presentation as much as on the number of people present? Normally, one would speak more informally in a small room than in a large hall, but if one is presenting a doctoral dissertation defense, a certain formality will be expected even if only half a dozen professors make up audience. There is, after all, an academic tradition to be maintained. A dissertation defense is a ritual.

Catherine Bell insists that from a performance point of view ritual must be understood to be an embodied action that functions on its own terms. In a ritual people replay actions that have been performed many times before. Their bodies perform this history. By their bodily presentation they convey the nature of the event and, in the case of the dissertation defense example, its meaning and solemnity.[4] Conversely, at the annual Gridiron Dinner in Washington, DC, which is held in a large hall and attended by leading political figures and members of the news media, the nature of the event is to "roast" (make fun of) one another. Even the president of the United States must shed his formality and solemnity as he responds to the jokes that have been told about him.

Let's see if we can develop some criteria for evaluating liturgical performances using some of these principles gained from the theories of performance study.

3. See Richard Schechner, *Performance Studies: An Introduction* (London: Routledge, 2002).
4. Catherine Bell, *Ritual Theory, Ritual Practice* (Oxford: Oxford University Press, 1992), 81.

Let's begin by developing some useful definitions of "contemporary worship" and "traditional worship." Matthew Pierce suggests the following characteristics.[5]

Traditional worship:

- Tradition—what has been "handed down" (that's what the word *tradition* means)—justifies the content of the service.

- Architecture, clothing, music, and other accoutrements arose during earlier periods in history and, at times, within other cultures (e.g., a gothic building with altar, cross, and candles).

- The order of service follows an explicit, often printed, outline.

Contemporary worship:

- It might openly flout tradition, using biblicism or pragmatics to determine the form and content of worship.

- It employs architecture, clothing, music, and other accoutrements from the surrounding culture (e.g., an auditorium with a stage, lighting, and sound system).

- It uses a less explicit structure.

Now let's see if we can develop some categories that account for the diversity of styles of Christian worship in the world today. In an older book on *Protestant Worship*, James F. White categorizes worship traditions according to denominations. In an historical chronology based on origin, he lists Lutheran, Reformed/Presbyterian, Anabaptist, Anglican, Free Church (Puritan, Congregationalist, Baptist), Quaker, Methodist, Frontier Revival, and Pentecostal.[6] If we add Roman Catholic, Orthodox, and Oriental churches to this list, we cover all of the Christian traditions.

But the limitation of White's differentiations is that styles of worship

5. Matthew Lawrence Pierce, "Redeeming Performance? The Question of Liturgical Audience," *Liturgy* 28, no. 1 (January–March 2013), 55–56.
6. James F. White, *Protestant Worship: Traditions in Transition* (Louisville: Westminster John Knox, 1989).

don't stay contained in one denominational tradition. In his list only the Frontier Revival form is trans-denominational. Some denominations share similar styles of worship with one another, and some denominations embrace different styles of worship among their congregations or parishes. Some congregations have multiple styles of worship within their own community, such as traditional and contemporary. When we're talking about performance we're more interested in style than in orders, and styles cross denominational boundaries.

L. Edward Phillips suggests seven patterns of worship, each with a distinct historical foundation, that account for the diversity of America Protestant worship:[7]

1. Catholic (small c)
2. Liturgical renewal
3. Protestant aesthetic
4. Protestant revival/seeker
5. Pentecostal/praise and worship
6. Bible camp/Sunday school assembly
7. House church/prayer meeting

I would like to build on Phillips's analysis and propose six styles of worship that are evident in global Christianity, leaving out the informal camp meeting and house church patterns and adding another category:

1. Byzantine/Oriental
2. Catholic traditional
3. Liturgical renewal
4. Protestant aesthetic
5. Protestant revival/seeker service
6. Pentecostal/praise and worship

7. L. Edward Phillips, *The Character of Christian Worship: Pattern and Diversity in Contemporary Practice* (Nashville: Abingdon, 2012).

These styles of worship cross denominational lines.

The Byzantine/Oriental style is encountered in Eastern Orthodox churches, Eastern Rite Catholic churches, and churches of the East. Among the latter are Armenian, Assyrian, Coptic, Ethiopic, and branches of the Syro-Malabar churches of India that are variously in union with the Syrian Orthodox Church, the Roman Catholic Church, and the Protestant churches of South India and Northern India. Elements of the Byzantine style may also be seen in Taizé prayer and in some emerging churches.

The Catholic traditional style is seen in the celebration of the Roman Catholic Tridentine Mass but also in some Anglo-Catholic and high Lutheran liturgies.

The liturgical renewal style is practiced in congregations that have embraced the modern liturgical movement. This would include the majority of Roman Catholic parishes around the world as well as many Anglican/Episcopal and Lutheran congregations and also some Methodist and Presbyterian churches.

The Protestant aesthetic style is manifested in mainline Protestant congregations that place a high premium on expressions of high culture in worship. However, some Catholic parishes might also place a high value on art and classical church music.

The Protestant revival style is evident in contemporary seeker services, which is provided in many different Protestant denominations and Evangelical congregations.

The Pentecostal style is present in the many different Pentecostal churches around the world but also in those Protestant congregations that have moved to a praise-and-worship format for worship. Elements of the Pentecostal style may also be evident in churches that have embraced the charismatic movement. For example, I was told that the rite of confirmation in the Anglican cathedral in Singapore sees youth "slain in the Spirit" when the bishop lays hands on their heads.

In addition, there are also congregations in the historic denominations that use the traditional orders and observe the traditional practices of their denomination.

Next, I need to give a description of the uses of each of the six styles I have identified and consider what the purpose of each might be. Since this is a book about embodied liturgy, I also should say something about bodily participation in each of these styles of service. On the basis of this analysis we will have some sense of what to expect when we encounter each of these styles, and we may then judge each according to its own intentions.

Byzantine/Oriental

The Eastern Orthodox and Eastern Rite Catholic churches use the Divine Liturgies of St. John Chrysostom and St. Basil. The Oriental churches use liturgies that also trace back to ancient Christian liturgies (such as the East Syrian Liturgy Addai and Mari, the West Syrian Liturgy of St. James, and the Coptic Liturgy of St. Mark).

The Orthodox prefer a Byzantine-type building, which is a dome placed on a rectangular basilica-style structure. Yet even if they are worshiping in a former Protestant church or a warehouse, an icon screen (called the iconostasis) separates the people from the altar (or holy table) in the sanctuary. In an Orthodox church there is only one eucharistic service (Divine Liturgy) per Sunday, but it is preceded by an hour-long service of Matins (or Orthros) and several short preparatory services before that. The priest or bishop is assisted by a deacon and acolytes. The liturgies are chanted throughout with the help of a cantor and a choir, and the people often join in, especially on the litanies and the hymns they know. The chants and hymns are primarily from a particular ethnic tradition (e.g., Greek, Slavic, Syrian, etc.). There is much use of incense.

Purpose: The earthly liturgy participates in the eternal glorification in heaven of the Holy Trinity. There is little concern for time constraints. The liturgy may seem to go on and on, although it's really one service following another.

Embodiment: The body is consistently engaged in the liturgy. During the early part of the service the church may seem to be in a hubbub, with people walking up to the front of the church, praying in front of the iconostasis (the standing icons in front of the altar), kissing icons, and lighting candles, even though the service has already begun. There is no break between the services—one begins as soon as the previous one ends—and posted starting times are educated guesses. As a result of this continuous worship a continuous flow of people enter the church. There may not be pews—perhaps just some chairs or stalls along the sides for the elderly. The pews aren't needed much anyway because in the Orthodox tradition the faithful stand up for nearly the entire service. They visit the icons of the saints (like saying hello to old family members), light candles, and make the sign of the cross whenever the Trinity is invoked (which is constantly). The Orthodox make the sign of the cross from right shoulder to left, not from left to right, as Western Christians do. They sometimes make the sign of the cross three times in a row and sometimes finish by sweeping the right hand to the floor. Some may even prostrate themselves. Nobody is bothered by any of this individual activity; it's like a village going about its business, coming together at pivotal moments—when the Gospel is read and Communion is served. Not everyone receives Communion because there are fasting and confessional requirements for those who have reached an age of discretion. Children receive Communion, but it is not offered to non-Orthodox, even if they are Christian believers. Everyone is welcome to receive blessed bread at the end as an expression of hospitality. It is food for the journey home.

Catholic Traditional

The neo-Gothic or baroque styles of architecture are preferred. Roman Catholic traditionalists use a version of the Latin Mass of Pope Pius V (1570) or the Latin Mass of Pope John XXIII (1962). There are Anglo-Catholic versions of the Book of Common Prayer such as the English Missal and the American Missal. High church Lutherans tend to use their church's worship book with a few additions, especially in the Church of Sweden. Traditional vestments are worn by the priests and servers. In a High Mass a deacon and subdeacon assist the celebrant, as well as acolytes. There is a high altar (eastward orientation) with candles and the crucifix, and the celebrant presides at the Eucharist with his back to the people. The music is often Gregorian chant with organ and choral leadership. Incense is used.

Purpose: This liturgical style conveys a sense of the *mysterium tremendum;* it is an encounter with the sacred. It has a more sacrificial character than the renewed liturgy in the sense that it is understood as worship offered to God. It is part of a tradition of worship that is centuries old and provides a sense of continuity with the Catholic Church down through the ages.

Embodiment: While the Tridentine Mass has a limited role for the verbal participation of the people, there is actually a lot of bodily participation. Worshipers dip hands in holy water and make the sign of the cross when entering the nave. They genuflect toward the altar before going into their pew. They kneel several times on pew rails or cushions (e.g., at the confession of sins and during the Canon). They come forward to the chancel rail and kneel to receive Communion. Typically the Anglican and Lutheran high liturgies include hymns for the congregation, and people may join in singing the responses.

Liturgical Renewal

This style of celebration emerged in several churches in the 1960s. It was influenced by the scholarship and practices promoted by the liturgical movement of the earlier twentieth century. Elements of liturgical renewal are shared ecumenically among several denominational traditions. To the extent possible, especially in older buildings, the altar is free standing, and the congregational seating is arranged at an angle or around it. The structure of the liturgy includes gathering, hearing, and responding to the word of God, celebrating the eucharistic meal, and being sent into the world in mission. Common features include the use of some form of a common lectionary with an Old Testament reading, responsorial psalm, New Testament reading, and Gospel. The homily may be delivered away from an ambo or pulpit. Intercessions are open to the free interjections of the worshipers. A eucharistic prayer is chosen from several options. A common loaf of bread and a common communion cup are used. The musical forces lead the singing of the people; they do not replace the people's song. The musical style is either traditional or contemporary or a blending of both.

Purpose: Liturgical renewal aims to recover the liturgy as "the public work of the people" performed before God and the world. The verbal participation of the people is a primary feature; they join in singing hymns and psalms and responses. Laypersons have liturgical roles as readers, leaders of prayer, and communion ministers. The worshipers bring their worldly concerns before the Lord in prayer and are strengthened through word and sacrament to go back into the world to engage in the mission of the gospel in their daily lives. Much of the focus of liturgical renewal is on the assembly itself and its response to the needs of the world.

Embodiment: There is a relaxed character to the gathering. People greet one another as they take their seats. Later they exchange the greeting of peace with an appropriate gesture, such as a handshake or a hug or a bow. People stand and sit and perhaps kneel at various points in the order of service. Typically, people move forward to receive Communion, proceeding to a communion station. Several options may be provided to accommodate various needs, such as gluten allergies or alcoholism. Announcements are made before, during, or after the service, and laypeople share in communicating information about parish events and mission projects.

Protestant Aesthetic

During the course of the nineteenth century, high culture became accessible to the emerging middle class in Europe and North America. People attended concerts and lectures and visited museums and libraries. Increased wealth made possible the construction of impressive neo-Gothic, neo-baroque, or neo-Byzantine church buildings. Pipe organs were installed (even in congregations of the Reformed tradition, which had dismantled organs as a matter of principle in the Reformation period), and congregations paid to have trained organists and choir directors. The wealthier congregations even sometimes paid choirs or soloists. The order of service follows denominational patterns but includes several opportunities for the choir to sing and the organist to play. The sermon is usually the high point of the service, and the pastor as preacher is expected to deliver a polished oration studded with references to current events and literary citations. Holy Communion is celebrated according to the tradition of the denomination.

Purpose: This liturgy is understood to be rendered to the glory of God, offering the best we have; but it also serves to edify and inspire the people. There is an apologetic aspect to aesthetic liturgy in that it could draw in the cultured people of society (and those who could pay for it, because high culture is expensive). The churches that could afford it tended to be the so-called "big steeple" churches in the downtown sections of large cities. But many other congregations imitated the aesthetic approach to liturgy, although to a lesser effect.

Embodiment: People are rather passive in this style of worship. They enter the nave with hushed tones so as not to disturb those who are listening to the organist's well-practiced prelude. There is some standing—for example, to sing hymns—but there is much more sitting and seldom any kneeling. Communion is administered according to the practices of the particular denomination, which variously means standing, sitting, or kneeling.

Protestant Revival/Seeker Service

Great revivals occurred from the eighteenth century through the twentieth century in Protestant Europe and North America. In 1835 the American lawyer-turned-preacher, Presbyterian-turned-Congregationalist Charges G. Finney wrote his *Lectures on the Revival of Religion*. He experimented with taking the experience and knowledge gained from the frontier camp meetings into urban churches, even in the heart of New York City in his Broadway Tabernacle. His basic principle maintains that Christ and his apostles laid down no form of worship in the New Testament; therefore we are free to do what it takes to save souls. The revival form of worship that became common in many Protestant churches, not only in evangelism rallies but also on Sunday morning, was a three-fold pattern that included "preliminaries" (often with singing and testimonies), the preaching of the word, and a response to the word. Evangelists were always willing to use whatever technology was available. Billy Graham's crusades used television for the first time to reach millions of people. Robert Schuller began his ministry and worship in a drive-in movie theater in California (known both for movies and cars); in time he built the Crystal Cathedral in Garden Grove, California (which is now a Catholic cathedral). The "cathedral" was the first of the evangelical megachurches. Other megachurches followed Schuller in his desire to reach unchurched people without alienating them with the trappings of a traditional church. Both the setting and the services of the megachurches were designed to reach seekers: auditoriums were built, and popular music was presented as entertainment, followed by a message that featured practical advice on how to deal with the issues of our lives. Any specific Christian worship service with sacraments was held during the week for the core members of the church, but not on Sundays. The seeker service, however, continues to follow the structure of the revival service: "preliminaries" with a band and some testimonies, which is followed by the message and then a response.

Purpose: The purpose of the revival or seeker service is to make an impact on people in order to get them to make a conscious act of commitment. Worship is evangelism.

Embodiment: In the old revival services there was an "altar call" during which those who were making a "decision for Christ" came forward to be prayed over and given spiritual counsel. In the typical modern seeker service the body is passive. The people attending listen to the band and the message, watching both musicians and preacher on the giant projection screens. The response to the message and whole experience may signing up for small group meetings and ministry activities in the vestibule.

Pentecostal/Praise and Worship

Pentecostalism is a twentieth-century development with roots in earlier holiness movements. It began with the Azusa Street revival in Los Angeles in 1906 and spread like wildfire across America and around the world, embracing all races and classes of people. Pentecostal worship is characterizes by the exercise of spiritual gifts in the assembly—such as speaking in tongues, interpretation of tongues, prophesying, healing, or exorcizing evil spirits. While there may be an order of service, it can be interrupted by any outbreak of these charismatic manifestations. In African-American worship there are powerful outbursts of emotion, especially during the sermon; the people encourage the preacher with their "Amens" and vocal responses. Worship in the Vineyard Christian Fellowship, which appeals to young adults, may include Communion toward the end of the praise medley, in an intimate moment before the message. The praise-and-worship style, while similar to the seeker style, intends to engage the worshiper in the singing.

Purpose: Pentecostal worship is an uninhibited worship of God the Father in Jesus Christ through the Holy Spirit. In this it is not unlike Orthodox worship. But it also shares the concern of the revivalists to save souls.

Embodiment: The body is fully engaged in Pentecostal worship. People are on their feet, waving their arms, singing, shouting out, speaking in tongues, extending their hands to lay them on others, or receiving the hand-laying prayers of others. In the praise-and-worship style the worshipers also join in singing and raise their arms in praise, sometimes speaking in tongues.

Mix and Match

In this exercise I have tried to differentiate between different performance styles in worship, indicating what the perceived purpose of each style is and how it bodily engages the worshipers. The leadership of worship in any tradition has a responsibility to reflect and promote the character of worship in that tradition with bodily behavior that reflects the style of that service. In some styles formality is expected; in other styles informality, and even a sense of improvisation, is desired. Style is about consistency of expression. In congregations that offer more than one style of worship, the organ is used, and vestments are worn for the traditional service; but a praise band leads worship in the contemporary service, and the minister might wear no vestments at all, wearing casual attire.

An interesting question is whether there can be a mix and match of liturgical styles. It has been known to happen, as in the example of the charismatic Anglican cathedral in Singapore that I mentioned above, or in a liturgical renewal church that uses contemporary music. But there will be tensions in a mix-and-match style. The Anglican tradition will not want to deny the efficacy of the rite of confirmation if those who receive the bishop's laying on of hands are not "slain in the Spirit." In a liturgical renewal church the music must serve the liturgy; the music must be the people's song (and not the performers'), and it must also be selected according to what role each piece plays within the liturgical order. Catholic traditional parishes might place as a high a premium on quality traditional church music as the Protestant aesthetic congregations do. But, again, the music must fit into the order of Mass, just as in the Protestant aesthetic service the music selections should relate to the lectionary "themes."

All churches, no matter what worship style they use, can learn from other performance styles without denying their own. For example, many churches have profited from the attention given to hospitality in the megachurch seeker services, particularly in terms of how they present themselves to the public. I hope this kind of analysis helps us not only to appreciate the various styles of worship in the Christian traditions but also to be respectful of our differences.[8]

---

8. When I asked the students and pastors which of the styles best reflected the worship in their own churches, almost all of them said the Protestant aesthetic style, with the exception that there aren't many pipe organs in Indonesia because of climate conditions. Pianos, keyboards, and guitars are typical instruments used in their churches.

Figure 19. A Pentecostal youth service.

B. What, Then, Shall We Say about the Body?

In this book we have looked at the spectrum of Christian liturgy from the perspective of the body engaged in worship. We began with the theological recognition that we are created as bodies, the phenomenological view that we don't just have a boy, we are a body, and the affirmation of cognitive science that the mind is part of the body (the "knowing body"). When it comes to worship, we have nothing else with which to worship God than our bodies. When it comes to mission we have nothing else with which to serve our neighbor than our bodies, which I called attention to in chapter 7 in Christian medical missions and the social and physical education programs of the YMCA and YWCA.

An implication of this is that the body is needed to worship God the Father, Son, and Holy Spirit and to serve the neighbor in need. The Christian belief in everlasting life does not mean that our earthly life has no meaning or that it can be neglected—on the contrary. The eternal life promised in Holy Baptism ("One who believes and is baptized shall be saved," Mark 16:16, NRSV) begins with our earthly life. In the Divine Liturgy we are already engaged in the eternal worship of the Father through the Son in the Holy Spirit, along "with angels and archangels and all the company of heaven," as we sing in the Eucharistic prefaces. The offering as a part of worship is a symbolic reminder that the needs of the neighbor are not removed from worship. The collection for the poor goes back to the earliest days of the church. The earthly life of a Christian is the workshop of his or her future life. The most important thing we can do in this life is to glorify God in both our liturgical service to God and in our diaconal service to our neighbor.

Taking Care of Our Bodies

Because we need our bodies to carry out these responsibilities to God and our neighbor the Christian should take care of his or her body in addition to nourishing his or her soul. I have suggested that the soul (*psyche*) is what makes each of us unique. The soul is nourished by hearing the word of God and by receiving the sacraments of Christ, by engaging in prayer and serving others, and by being a part of a community of faith. But the soul is not disembodied. It is affected by our experiences of life in the body. So the body must also be nourished by love, be kept strong and healthy, and engage in morally appropriate behavior. It is an error when the Christian does not maintain in theory and practice the coexistence of the body and soul in unity. The body without the soul is a biological machine. The soul without the body has no concrete reality. The Christian believes in the unity of soul and body. Christian spiritual writers have given much attention to the conditions of the soul but too often have neglected the body in Christian teaching. But according to the Bible, the human body is a direct creation of God. Without the body the soul of the human being—who we essentially are—cannot fulfill the purpose that God has prepared for us.

Moreover, the importance of the body is evident by the fact that Jesus Christ rose from the dead. Christ's resurrected body was a glorified or transfigured body, but it was still a body that could be recognized by his disciples and that could share meals with them. The apostle Paul stresses the point that without the resurrection of the body of Jesus Christ, both the gospel and faith are in vain: "But if there is no resurrection of the dead, then Christ has not been raised; if Christ has not been raised, then our preaching is in vain and your faith is in vain" (1 Cor. 15:13-14, NRSV).

The human body was honored at the time of its creation by being created in the image of God. Even after the fall of humanity, the divine image was restored in the incarnation of the eternal Son of God, who became truly human and physically experienced everything that human beings experience from birth to death.

Most important of all, "the Word became flesh and dwelt among us" (John 1:14, NRSV). God bestowed high dignity on the human body by assuming a human body in the incarnation of the Son of God in the historical figure of Jesus of Nazareth. This body ascended into heaven and was assumed into the Godhead. In Christ, God has a body and continues to relate to us in bodily ways.

The gospel of Jesus Christ was brought to humankind through chosen personalities, that is, through men and women who devoted their bodies and souls to the mission of God's rule and will among human beings. They often made the ultimate witness by suffering bodily as martyrs. Christians then wanted pieces of the bodies of the martyrs to be entombed in the altars on which they celebrated the Eucharist if their churches couldn't be built over the graves of the martyrs. The bodies as well as the acts of the martyrs are honored.

The Healthy Body

God has greatly honored the human body, and we as God's creatures should respect God's will by protecting our bodies and by doing those things that promote the wellbeing of the whole creation and the betterment of human society of which we are a part. A healthy body is an obligation to its Creator. The prolonging of human life is not only a law of our nature but also an obligation for the purpose of fulfilling the new commandment to love one another, which the God who became man has asked us to observe.

Certainly a healthy body is an indispensable instrument for the fulfillment of the love commandment. Therefore, the nourishing and safeguarding of our body is not only our wish or desire; it is also an obligation to the Creator. This is why the church in its mission has given so much attention to the bodies of hurt and broken human beings—to the healing ministry and to the ministries of feeding the hungry, clothing the naked, and sheltering exposed bodies. The healthy life is a gift from God and as such must be used to give glory to God in acts of worship and service, in *leitourgia* and *diakonia*.

The baptized body is the temple of the Holy Spirit and therefore a sacred place that is to be accorded honor and reverence.[9] Two things are important in keeping our body in good health. First, we must nourish it properly, not only with what we eat but also with a spiritual direction, because the physical well-being of our bodies is connected with our spiritual well-being. In an embodied spirituality we need to reflect on how we are using our bodies to the glory of God in the worship of God and service to our neighbor. This might involve activities such as serving as a communion minister and serving in soup kitchens.

Second, to safeguard our body from physical ills, we need to be concerned with the prevention of disease, proper nutrition, and physical exercise. The human body is a complicated mechanism, and it is important not only to consult the special ministers of the body—that is, the medical doctors—but also to make use of other ministers of the body, such as physical trainers and massage therapists who can help us keep our bodies in good shape. It is erroneous to think that physicians, physical fitness trainers, and bodyworkers have no place in our faith, that the pains and ills of the body are merely a state of mind, or that we should simply bear pain and suffering because Christ did. While there is a role for martyrs and confessors who bear in their

9. See Carl E. and LaVonne Braaten, *The Living Temple: A Practical Theology of the Body and the Foods of the Earth* (New York: Harper & Row, 1976).

bodies the afflictions intended for Christ, ordinary aches and pains that can be relieved are not expressions of martyrdom. Among their parish programs, some congregations in America have established health-and-wellness ministries that provide parish nurses, opportunities to test blood pressure, nutritional guidance, and even yoga classes.

We need to be aware when promoting fitness and health that some people suffer from debilitating physical conditions over which they have little control. These conditions may be temporary or lifelong. But exercise is a key factor in maintaining and improving overall health, even for people with physical disabilities. In 1996, the National Center for Chronic Disease Prevention and Health Promotion reported that "significant health benefits can be obtained with a moderate amount of physical activity, preferably daily."[10] More recently, the *Physical Activity Guidelines for Americans* (2008) provides science-based guidance to help individuals with disabilities aged six and older improve their health through appropriate physical activity. These benefits are even more important for people with disabilities, since people with disabilities tend to lead less active lifestyles.

In promoting health and fitness we also need to be aware that many people suffer from poor or negative body image—that is, how people see themselves. They may have an unrealistic view of how they regard their body, which is exacerbated, if not caused, by media-driven images of ideal bodies. This often produces eating disorders, most commonly in women, as people try to maintain what they see as ideal standards of thinness. But men may also suffer from this disorder. Those with poor body image begin forming their perceptions of their body's attractiveness, health, acceptability, and functionality in early childhood. This body image continues to form as they age and receive feedback from peers, family member, coaches, and so forth. Personality traits such as perfectionism and self-criticism can also influence the development of a negative body image. Professional fitness trainers stress that not all bodies are alike; therefore we need to do what is appropriate for our own bodies.

10. http://www.cdc.gov/nccdphp/sgr/disab.htm.

With these caveats, I must nevertheless stress the need of Christians, and especially of clergy, to keep their bodies healthy. Too often the ministers of the church, like those in other "helping professions," do not take proper care of their bodies. Clergy give leadership to a community that includes the physical wellbeing of people in its mission and ministries. Pastors routinely visit the sick as a major part of their ministry, and they often see the unfortunate consequences of lifestyle choices in the illnesses of those they visit. Yet they themselves may lead a sedentary lifestyle, get insufficient exercise, make poor food choices, consume too much alcohol, smoke cigarettes, and foster other unhealthy habits that increase the chances of becoming overweight and developing a number of chronic diseases. These behaviors reduce their ability to lead the people of God in worship and other forms of mission. Liturgical leaders need healthy bodies.

Healthy bodies help us feel better about ourselves, and that's important for those who communicate with their bodies before the public. In all Christian traditions, no matter what the liturgical style, the ministers (priests, pastors, deacons, musicians) lead the worshiping congregations, the liturgical assemblies, with their bodies. As Amy Schifrin writes:

> Our bodies (and that includes the tonal quality of our voices) communicate to others the meaning of our words. Our bodies tell what we feel (or don't feel) about what we're saying. Our bodies betray any and all incongruences, because unlike flat text on page, we are multidimensional beings who often communicate far more than we are aware of. As pastors and theologians we spend a great deal of time learning the importance of precision and accuracy in words for communicating truth, but our whole bodies were made to tell the truth of God.[11]

What does our sheer physical presence communicate about what we are saying or celebrating? When used for God's glory our bodies are among the best tools we have for conveying God's incarnational love to humankind. Without denying that the Holy Spirit works faith when

---

11. Amy C. Schifrin, "A Primer for Presiders: Your Body in Worship," January 28, 2015, in *Let's Talk: Honoring the Body* 18, no. 2 (Easter 2013): http://mcsletstalk.org/honoring-the-body/primer-presiders-body-worship/.

and where the Spirit pleases, the Spirit also works through the body of the minister—the spoken or sung word, the tone of voice, body posture and gestures, even grooming and attention to personal presentation (how we are dressed)—to communicate God's healing word. When the whole body of the minister is employed in communicating God's truth there is a far greater chance that those who assemble to receive the gifts of life and salvation (healing) from God's word and the sacraments of Christ (Baptism, Eucharist) will go out into the world to serve God by loving their neighbor and acting as good stewards of creation.

Personal Testimony

We become more aware of our bodies by paying attention to them. We often don't pay attention to our bodies until something goes wrong with them. I paid little attention to my body before my bout with colon cancer. After a year of chemotherapy my weight was down and my muscles were atrophied. I had to begin the painstaking process of going through a physical fitness regimen with a trainer to build up muscles. But as I had noticed the deterioration of my body, so I noticed its rehabilitation. I also learned some valuable lessons in fitness. For example, I learned that strengthening the core is one of the most important things to work on—and a strong core does not mean six-pack abs. In fact, strengthening only abdominal muscles tends to pull our bodies in, whereas our real need, as those who spend many hours each day sitting behind a computer screen or an automobile wheel know, is to stand tall and open the chest. Standing tall also requires a sense of balance. Good physical training works on balance as well as strength. I found myself becoming more aware of my physical presence as a liturgical minister as I began physical training and then began to practice yoga. The difference between yoga and other forms of physical exercise is yoga's focus on the use of the breath.

About a year after I finished chemotherapy I fell and shattered my left elbow, which required me to get an elbow implant. When physical therapy went as far as it could to straighten my left arm, the physical therapist suggested massage therapy. I began to receive massages regularly. As the massage therapist worked on different muscles and joints I could sense from his or her probes or strokes what was beneath the surface of the skin. Through the ministrations of the hands of others I began feeling what my body was about, and I began to learn things about my body that I never knew before. I also became used to the gift of touch in massage. All too often, we tend to be afraid of touching one another, especially in American culture. Yet research is showing the amazing effectiveness of touch, as I indicated in chapter 3. Touch also has its place in liturgical interaction, especially at the greeting of peace.

As a colon cancer survivor it was also important for me to change my diet. My wife Mary was ahead of the curve on this because she had been studying matters of food and nutrition and the relationship between food and mood for years. She even attended a couple of national medical conferences on food as medicine. Needless to say, we changed our diet and began to eat more fruits and vegetables (locally produced if possible) and less red meat (but from grass-fed cattle when we did have it). We also started buying organic milk, in addition to other organic products, and eggs from free-range chickens.

The Value of Yoga

I have included references to yoga practice and philosophy throughout this book, and along these lines it is worth pointing out that the yoga tradition also has a great interest in diet and digestion. For yogins (male yogis and female yoginis) everything that we eat is food for our souls as well as our bodies. Yogins believe that food is the creator of the *prana* (life force) that sustains our bodies and brings us vitality and health. The discipline of yoga suggests an ethically pure vegetarian diet, which facilitates the development of *sattva*. *Sattva* is a quality of love, awareness, connection, and peace with all sentient beings. Yogins believe that food is our first interaction with the world around us, and if we do not eat with a sense of love, awareness, connection, and peace with nature, all other facets of our lives are inclined to suffer. Since the basis of *sattva* is the concept of *ahimsa* (non-harming), a sattvic diet avoids any foods that involve killing or harming of animals. Sattvic diets also encourage foods grown harmoniously with nature, that is, foods that are ripened and grown naturally. In addition, the foods that we eat should be prepared with love, received with gratitude, and eaten with appreciation.[12] As I noted in chapter 5, ancient peoples tended to eat meat only when it was offered in sacrifice to God. It was available for feasts but not as part of the daily diet.

My purpose in drawing on yoga in the course I taught on which this book is based was not to get the students or you, the readers, into the practice of this discipline (although I wouldn't discourage it either). However, the practice of yoga is not only an all-around good workout; it also reminds us of important aspects of our faith that we tend to forget. Breathing exercises (*pranayama*) can remind us of the life-giving Holy Spirit's work in our bodies. Attention to postures (*asanas*), supported by the energy of the breath, can influence a Christian's self-understanding as a body created in the image of God and an object of unutterable dignity redeemed by the blood of Christ. Postural yoga, with its well-documented physical and mental benefits, might help one better exercise the stewardship of his or her own body as well as the rest of God's creation. Meditation supported by the breath and by solid posture can put us in mind of our relationship with God and our place in God's world.

Incarnational Spirituality

Many people today are interested in spirituality. For Christians, spirituality cannot be divorced from our incarnational faith. One of the greatest dangers to authentic Christian spirituality is a "spiritualism" by which people disembody their call to holiness. Spirituality is often not seen as having anything to do with bodily functions or sexual morality. Even marriage is commonly viewed today as an emotional

---

12. See Dr. Swami Shankardevandanda, *Yoga for the Digestive System* (Monghy: Bihar School of Yoga, 2006).

bond of intimacy[13] rather than as a conjugal union designed, as a reflection of the Holy Trinity, to produce a third person.[14]

Authentic Christian spirituality is always an embodied spirituality. It gives attention to matters of food and sex as well as fasting and abstinence. It is expressed in art, music, dance, and drama that utilize the body as the means of communication. The very "logic" of Christianity is that God communicates his life and love to us in and through the body—the Word made flesh. The spirit that denies this "incarnational reality" is the Antichrist (see 1 John 4:2-3). Incarnational spirituality uses the body in the service of God and neighbor.

As I have studied Tantric philosophy[15] and the late Pope John Paul II's theology of the body, I have been intrigued by the parallels. While both systems are about more than sex, neither fails to take sexuality seriously. In both systems the human body is the incarnation of the supreme Reality (Shiva/Shakti in the yogic body; the divine Word in the human Jesus and the Holy Spirit dwelling in the body united with Jesus Christ). In both systems it is through the body that we enter into union with the divine. Dialogue would certainly establish differences between these systems, not the least of which is theological—the identity of the divine—but they need not be seen as completely contrary *spiritualities*. I think that a profitable theological dialogue can be achieved between Tantra/Hatha Yoga and Christianity.

I don't know whether Christian theology gives more or less thought to the body than the yoga traditions do, but I know that the body is absolutely essential to Christian theology. Christians could learn from yoga to honor and respect our bodies, especially in terms of maintaining health and vitality in a way that is consistent with our theology of the goodness of the creation and our stewardship of it. Honor and respect for the body can also help Christians focus on their

13. See Stephanie Coontz, *Marriage, a HistoryL from Obedience to Intimacy or How Love Conquered Marriage* (New York: Viking Penguin, 2005).
14. This is the view promoted by Pope John Paul II, *Man and Woman He Created Them.*
15. See Georg Feuerstein, *Tantra: The Path of Ecstasy* (Boston and London: Shambhala, 1998) and David Gordon White, *Kiss of the Yogini: "Tantric Sex" in its South Asian Contexts* (Chicago and London: University of Chicago Press, 2003).

own beliefs concerning the dignity of humankind created in the image of God, the incarnation of the Son of God in the body of Jesus, the body as the temple of the Holy Spirit, and the resurrection of the body to new and eternal life.

Still, the fact that yoga comes out of a different religious and spiritual tradition requires Christians who practice this discipline to decide what content to invest in their practice. No yoga class will be entirely without spiritual content, no matter how minimal. Some classes will be more heavily invested in Eastern religious and spiritual content than others. Christian yoga has emerged to provide an alternative to these influences; but the real value of the practice is the practice. In the practice of yoga, experience is more important than theory.

One need not Christianize yoga in order to practice it as a Christian. Indeed, the actual techniques of yoga, developed over the millennia, will be the same in all uses. The Buddhist does not practice different yoga techniques than the Hindu, even though the Buddha was opposed both to Brahmanic ritualism and to exaggerated asceticism and metaphysical speculation. According to the Buddha, saving truth must be experienced. But with this proviso Buddhists employ traditional yoga based on the *Yoga Sutras* and other classic texts. It is the same when Christians practice yoga. We do not bring new techniques to yoga practice, but the Christian liturgical tradition gives us rituals and texts that can be brought to our yoga practice. For example, one could begin the practice with the sign of the cross. I suggested in chapter 4 that the twelve poses of the sun salutation could be an enacted *Gloria Patri* (perhaps even chanted, although that would require a lot of *prana*!). One might even place an icon of Christ at the head of the yoga mat and focus on it in meditation.

Theosis

Moreover, what is esoteric in the Yoga tradition is readily available to all Christians in the sacraments: the union of the human and the divine. This wasn't a foregone conclusion in early Christianity. Early

Christianity entered into mortal combat with Gnosticism, a religious movement that regarded matter as evil. *Gnosis* means "knowledge," but it is a spiritual, even an esoteric, knowledge. Gnostics regarded this esoteric knowledge taught by their teachers as saving knowledge. Gnostics could not accept God becoming flesh in a human being. In his great work against the heresies, *The Refutation and Overthrow of the Knowledge Falsely So Called* (ca. 185), Irenaeus, bishop of Lyons, sought to demonstrate that God's creation is good, the human body is good, that God could not redeem human flesh without entering into it, and that we receive the benefits of Christ's saving acts in earthly elements.

> So, then, since the Lord redeemed us by his own blood, and gave his soul for our souls, and his flesh for our bodies, and poured out the Spirit of the Father to bring about the union and communion of God and man—bringing God down to men by [the working of] the Spirit, and again raising man to God by his incarnation—and by his coming firmly and truly giving us incorruption by our communion with God, all the teachings of the heretics are destroyed.[16]

This positive teaching of what Christ did in the flesh "for us and form our salvation" (as the Nicene Creed would put it) passed into Eastern Christianity, which developed the doctrine of *theosis* (deification).[17] What was the point of the incarnation of the Son of God in human flesh? St. Athanasius of Alexandria famously answered in *On the Incarnation*, "[The Word of God] assumed humanity that we might become God. He manifested Himself by means of a body in order that we might perceive the Mind of God. He endured shame from men that we might inherit immortality."[18]

Second Peter 1:4 says that we have become "partakers of divine nature." This is *theosis*—the idea that we can become one with God to such an extent that we share in God's nature. A classic Christmas collect prays

---

16. "Irenaeus' Against Heresies," in *The Library of Christian Classics,* Vol. 1: *Early Christian Fathers,* Newly translated and edited by Cyril C. Richardson (Philadelphia: Westminster Press, 1953), 386.

17. See Norman Russell, *The Doctrine of Deificatiuon in the Greek Patristic Tradition* (Oxford and New York: Oxford University Press, 2004).

18. Athanasius, *On the Incarnation,* trans. Penelope Lawson (Crestwood, NY: St. Vladimir's Seminary Press, 1953), chaps. 54, 93.

O God, who didst wonderfully create, and yet more wonderfully restored, the dignity of human nature: Grant that we may share the divine life of him who humbled himself to share our humanity, thy Son Jesus Christ...[19]

As St. Athanasius insists, this is only possible because the Word of God, the divine Logos, was made manifest in a human body and has shared our human nature. "He has not assumed a body as proper to his own nature, far from it, for as the Word He is without a body. He has been manifested in a human body for this reason only, out of the love and goodness of His Father, for the salvation of us men."[20]

When we want to know the mind of God, says Athanasius, we should not strain toward heaven but look to the works performed by Christ in his body.[21] These are the works enumerated in the Nicene and Apostles' Creeds—Christ's birth, crucifixion, death, resurrection, and ascension. Indeed, the central proclamation of the Nicene Creed is that the one who was of the same stuff as God the Father became the same stuff as humans for the sake of our salvation. And how did Christ win salvation for us? By enduring the shame of the cross, bodily and mental suffering, and the death that we endure, and overcoming it in his resurrection on the third day and glorification at the right hand of the Father.

This is Christian orthodoxy, and it is incomprehensible apart from the actual, incarnate body of Christ. But Christians keep returning to Gnosticism again and again, refusing to deal with material reality. In whatever way we can we must avoid the gnostic mindset; we need to affirm that matter *matters*. God's creation is good. The human body is good. Its goodness is restored in the incarnation—the embodiment—of the Word of God who made all things in the very beginning. As St. Athanasius says, if you want to know the mind of God for us, look to the body of the Christ.

Christ descended bodily into the life and death of the flesh and rose bodily to new life. By our baptism into Christ our bodies become temples of the Holy Spirit that will be raised by the Spirit when Christ

19. The Book of Common Prayer (1977), 162.
20. Athanasius, *On the Incarnation,* chapter 1: 26.
21. Ibid., chapter 54: 93.

comes again in glory. In the Holy Eucharist we receive the body and blood of Christ into our bodies and are nourished in our life in him. Christian mystics have sought "union with Christ" through contemplative prayer. But we all become one with Christ through the sacraments of Christ that are received on and in our bodies, by which we become members of the body of Christ in the world. With our bodies we offer worldy stuff back to God in a sacrifice of love and praise. In our bodies we raise our arms in praise and bow down in supplication, as the Holy Spirit within this living temple prompts us. This is embodied liturgy—Christ's saving work in his body offered to us in the divine liturgy of word and sacrament and our bodily response as a living sacrifice acceptable to God.

The Body in Worship

If this is the theology, there must be the corresponding liturgical practice. In part A of this chapter we looked at various liturgical styles and how each one generally engages the body. I conclude this book with a maximal description of the Christian at worship in his or her body. Clergy, in several Christian traditions, have instructions and rubrical manuals to guide them in conducting the service or presiding in liturgy, which direct them on what to do with their bodies. I will list some of these manuals in the bibliography. What follows here is a description of the involvement of the lay worshiper.

As Alexander Schmemann wrote, "The liturgy of the Eucharist is best understood as a journey or procession. It is the journey of the Church into the dimension of the Kingdom. . . . The journey begins when Christians leave their homes and beds."[22] The first bodily act of Christian liturgy is to get out of bed on Sunday morning and make one's way to the place where one's Christian community is gathering, to constitute the church as the assembly of word and sacrament.

One enters the building, greets people, receives worship aid material, and finds a place to sit in the worship space. During the

---

22. Alexander Schmemann, *For the Life of the World: Sacraments and Orthodoxy* (Crestwood, NY: St. Vladimir's Seminary Press, 1973), 26, 27.

entrance hymn, song, or psalm if there is a procession led by a cross the worshiper stands and faces toward the cross as it enters the worship space (which may mean facing the rear of the nave where the procession is forming). Bowing toward the cross as it passes by is comparable to standing and placing one's hand on one's heart (or saluting if one is in uniform) when the nation's flag passes by in a parade. The cross is the ensign of Christianity as the flag is the ensign of the nation. The cross may be flanked by acolytes carrying torches.

There are bodily actions and motions in worship. At invocations of and blessings with the name of the Trinity one may make the sign of the cross. If the presiding minister extends hands in greeting (The Lord be with you), the worshiper gestures back (And also with you). At the mention of the name of Jesus in hymns and prayers, one inclines one's head. At words of praise of the Holy Trinity (doxologies), one bows from the waist.

One sits for the readings and the psalm but stands for the announcement and reading of the gospel. If the gospel book is carried in procession to the midst of the nave, worshipers turn their body to face the minister at the place where the gospel is being proclaimed. One always faces in the direction from which someone is speaking. It would seem more natural and obvious to do this if our bodies weren't hemmed in by pews or chairs. We sit up and listen intently to the homily.

In the Creed one makes the sign of the cross at the phrase "(I believe) in the resurrection of the dead" (applying this promise to oneself). In some churches one kneels for prayers of intercession and thanksgiving, and also for prayers of confession of sins (which may take place before the entrance song or before the greeting of peace). At the greeting of peace worshipers shake hands with or embrace with a slight hug the people within reach. It is important to look a person in the eyes when you wish them "The peace of the Lord." Otherwise your greeting may seem perfunctory and insincere.

At the offering one places a gift in the receptacles passed through the assembly by ushers. In the Great Thanksgiving one bows at the

"Holy, holy, holy, Lord God of power and might. Heaven and earth are full of your glory" of the Sanctus and makes the sign of the cross at "Blessed is he who comes in the name of the Lord" (as if saying, come also to me, Lord). At the Lord's Prayer one might raise one's hands with open palms. In some places (especially in Catholic churches) the worshipers hold hands during the Our Father.

There are various options for receiving Holy Communion depending on one's tradition. In Reformed traditions the sacramental elements may be passed through the pews. Some Anglicans and Lutherans come forward and kneel at the chancel or communion rail to receive the elements. The most common practice today in several traditions is to walk forward to a communion station to receive the bread and cup. One makes the sign of the cross and says "Amen" as each element is presented and received. One receives the bread humbly in one's hands that are formed into a cup to receive the body of Christ. Don't grab for it. One takes hold of the cup and guides it to one's lips. In some Protestant churches individual glasses are used and the communicant will be guided as to how to receive and return the little glass. When one returns to one's place after receiving communion it is appropriate to kneel or sit for a personal prayer of thanksgiving and then join in singing the hymns or songs accompanying the administration of Holy Communion.

If there is a concluding hymn or song, one follows the cross as it leads the procession out and turns to face the back of the nave for the dismissal.

There may be other actions, including processions. Entrance and sending processions often involve a lot of bodies if the choir is included. There are also occasional processions that can involve the whole congregation, such as on Palm Sunday (in which one carries palm branches) and at the Easter Vigil (in which one carries candles). In some congregations worshipers may be invited to gather around the font for a baptism or to renew one's baptismal covenant.

These actions and gestures indicate that liturgy is a participatory and interactive event. It is even more so in Orthodox churches that have not installed pews or chairs. Seating, installed for listening to long sermons, hampers the movement of the body in worship and makes worship less engaging both physically and mentally. It goes without saying that processions involving the congregation require easily-learned repetitive responses so that worshipers in motion don't have to be looking at a book or a screen.

Some modern worshipers, especially visitors or those who attend church irregularly, might not like having to do something when they come to worship beyond standing and sitting with the rest of the congregation. They don't like a lot of movement or having to interact with people at the sharing of the peace. One value of older Gothic churches is that there are pillars and posts and darkened side aisles where those who prefer to "take in" what is going on rather than "participate" in it can have some relative isolation and anonymity from the main body of worshipers. On the other hand, the enthusiastic participation of worshipers in their liturgy can make a positive impact on visitors. If visitors begin to return more frequently, they'll catch on to the action and begin to participate. This has been my observation over a period of forty years of pastoral ministry. It also helps if worshipers themselves are willing to extend themselves bodily to strangers by greeting them, finding out a thing or two about them, and welcoming them back. Even those who lurk along the sidelines or in the back pews really like to the noticed.

Liturgy is not a spectator event. One does not come to public worship to be left alone with one's thoughts. That's what one does in private meditation and prayer. One comes to public worship to be as bodily engaged as one might be as a fan at the Sunday afternoon football game after the service.

If there is to be an opportunity for quiet meditation (before, during, or after the service), the time for meditation must be specified and jealously guarded. That means there should not be music during the time of silent meditation. The time of meditation can be started and concluded with the ringing of a small bell or the striking of a meditation bowl as in yoga classes. I have attended liturgies in which ten minutes of silent reflection followed the readings, and the room was quiet. Taizé services are known for their extended periods of silent meditation during which hundreds of people are capable of sitting quietly. (It's an awesome experience!) It takes time for the body to become still enough to focus on something. We need to consider that the quieted body is also the body at worship.

As in yogic meditation, one can still the restless body and calm the active mind by focusing on the breath—breathing in and out evenly and then letting it go. Let the mind focus on one thing—a word or an object—as we experienced in the meditation on bread and wine in chapter 5. Let the Spirit fill the body and guide the mind until the word or object is absorbed and some insight is gained. Then, as the time of meditation ends, let the Spirit raise up the body to engage in the act of worship or be dismissed to serve the Lord in the world. The peace of the Lord be with you. Go in peace.

Figure 20. Warrior 1 yoga pose.

Selected Bibliography

The academic course on which this book is based was originally aimed at undergraduate students of performing arts studying church music, but also pastors from Indonesian churches who participated in the class sessions. I hope this book will also be accessible to the general reader. I have kept the bibliography basic. By limiting myself to a half dozen works, more or less, in each category, I chose the titles that seem to me most pertinent to the ideas in this book. For other references see the footnotes for each chapter. The order of the bibliographic categories begins with philosophy, theology, and ritual (foundational studies); then moves to liturgical theory and practice (liturgical studies); and concludes with this book's interest in the biological body, yoga, and massage (ancillary studies). Thus:

Philosophy
Theology
Ritual
Introductions to Liturgy: General and Historical
Liturgical Rites
Liturgy and Culture
Liturgy and Music
Liturgical Arts
Liturgical Practice
Yoga
The Biological Body and Human Culture
Massage

Philosophy

Abrams, David. *The Spell of the Sensuous.* New York: Vintage Books, 1996.

Damasio, Antonio R. *Descartes' Error: Emotion, Reason, and the Human Brain.* New York: Putnam's Sons, 1994.

Johnson, Mark. *The Body in the Mind: The Bodily Basis of Meaning, Imagination, and Reason.* Chicago: University of Chicago Press, 1987.

Lakoff, George and Mark Johnson. *Philosophy in the Flesh: The Embodied Mind and Its Challenge to Western Thought.* New York: Basic Books, 1999.

Merleau-Ponty, Maurice. *Phenomenology of Perception.* Translated by Colin Smith. London: Routledge and Kegan Paul, 1962.

Pieper, Josef. *In Tune with the World: A Theory of Festivity.* Translated by Richard and Clara Winston. Chicago: Franciscan Herald, 1965.

Theology

Athanasius. *On the Incarnation.* Translated by Penelope Lawson. Crestwood, NY: St. Vladimir's Seminary Press, 1953.

Braaten, Carl E. and LaVonne Braaten. *The Living Temple: A Practical Theology of the Body and the Foods of the Earth.* New York: Harper & Row, 1976.

Cox, Harvey. *The Feast of Fools: A Theological Essay on Festivity and Fantasy.* New York: Harper & Row, 1969.

Jenson, Robert W. *Visible Words: The Interpretation and Practice of Christian Sacraments.* Philadelphia: Fortress Press, 1976.

John Paul II. *Man and Woman He Created Them: A Theology of the Body.* Translated by Michael Waldstein. Boston: Pauline Books and Media, 2006.

Lathrop, Gordon W. *Holy Ground: A Liturgical Cosmology.* Minneapolis: Fortress Press, 2003.

Ritual

Bell, Catherine. *Ritual: Perspectives and Dimensions*. New York: Oxford University Press, 1997.

Douglas, Mary. *Natural Symbols: Explorations in Cosmology*. New York: Vintage Books, 1973.

Eliade, Mircea. *Rites and Symbols of Initiation: The Mysteries of Birth and Rebirth*. Translated by Willard R. Trask. New York: Harper & Row, 1958.

Rappaport, Roy A. *Ritual and Religion in the Making of Humanity*. Cambridge: Cambridge University Press, 1999.

Turner, Victor. *The Ritual Process: Structure and Anti-Structure*. Chicago: Aldine, 1969.

Van Gennep, Arnold. *The Rites of Passage*. Translated by Monika B. Vizedom and Gabrielle L. Caffee. Chicago: University of Chicago Press, 1969.

Introductions to Liturgy: General and Historical

Chan, Simon. *Liturgical Theology: The Church as Worshiping Community*. Downers Grove, IL: InterVarsity, 2006.

McGowan, Andrew B. *Ancient Christian Worship: Early Church Practice in Social, Historical, and Theological Perspective*. Grand Rapids: Baker Academic, 2014.

Ramshaw, Gail. *Christian Worship: 100,000 Sundays of Symbols and Rituals*. Minneapolis: Fortress Press, 2009.

Senn, Frank C. *Introduction to Christian Liturgy*. Minneapolis: Fortress Press, 2012.

Truscott, Jeffrey A. *Worship: A Practical Guide*. Singapore: Genesis Books, 2011.

White, James F. *A Brief History of Christian Worship*. Nashville: Abingdon, 1993.

White, James F. *Introduction to Christian Worship*. 3rd ed. Nashville: Abingdon, 2000.

Liturgical Rites

Bradshaw, Paul F. and Maxwell E. Johnson. *The Eucharistic Liturgies: Their Evolution and Interpretation.* Collegeville, MN: Liturgical Press, 2012.

Connell, Martin. *Eternity Today: On the Liturgical Year.* Vol. 1, *On God and Time, Advent, Christmas, Epiphany, Candlemas.* New York: Continuum, 2006.

Connell, Martin. *Eternity Today: On the Liturgical Year.* Vol. 2, *Sunday, Lent, The Three Days, The Easter Season, Ordinary Time.* New York: Continuum, 2006.

Johnson, Maxwell E. *The Rites of Christian Initiation: Their Evolution and Interpretation.* Collegeville, MN: Liturgical Press, 1999.

Rutherford, Richard. *The Death of a Christian: The Order of Christian Funerals.* With the assistance of Tony Barr. Rev. ed. Collegeville, MN: Liturgical Press, 1990.

Stevenson, Kenneth W. *To Join Together: The Rite of Marriage.* New York: Pueblo, 1987.

Taft, Robert. *The Liturgy of the Hours in East and West: The Origins of the Divine Office and Its Meaning for Today.* Collegeville, MN: Liturgical Press, 1986.

Truscott, Jeffrey A. *The Sacraments: A Practical Guide.* New Delhi: Christian World Imprints, 2016.

Liturgy and Culture

Amaladoss, Michael. *The Asian Jesus.* New York: Orbis Books, 2006.

Chupungco, Anscar J. *Liturgical Inculturation: Sacramentals, Religiosity, and Catechesis.* Collegeville, MN: Liturgical Press, 1992.

Power, David N. *Unsearchable Riches: The Symbolic Nature of Liturgy.* New York: Pueblo Publishing Company, 1984.

Senn, Frank C. *Christian Worship and Its Cultural Setting.* Philadelphia: Fortress Press, 1983.

Uzukwu, Elochukwu E. *Worship as Body Language: Introduction to Christian*

Worship—An African Orientation. Collegeville, MN: Liturgical Press, 1997.

Wilkey, Glaucia Vasconcelos, ed. *Worship and Culture: Foreign Country or Homeland?* Grand Rapids: Eerdmans, 2014. [Brings together in one volume the three Lutheran World Federation study books on worship and culture from 1994, 1996, and 1998, with additional essays and reflections.]

Worship and Music

Foley, Edward. *Ritual Music: Studies in Liturgical Musicology.* Washington, DC: Pastoral Press, 1995.

Leaver, Robin A. and Joyce Ann Zimmerman, eds. *Liturgy and Music: Lifetime Learning.* Collegeville, MN: Liturgical Press, 1998.

Levitin, Daniel J. *This Is Your Brain on Music: The Science of a Human Obsession.* New York: Penguin, 2006.

Lucarini, Dan. *Why I Left the Contemporary Music Movement: Confessions of a Former Worship Leader.* Webster, NY: Evangelical Press, 2002.

Mitchell, Tony. "World Music and the Popular Music Industry." *Ethnomusicology* 37 (1993): 309–38.

Redman, Robb. *The Great Worship Awakening: Singing a New Song in the Postmodern Church.* San Francisco: Jossey-Bass, 2002.

Webber, Robert E. Editor. *The Complete Library of Christian Worship.* Volume 4, *Music and the Arts in Christian Worship*, Book 1. Nashville: Nashville: Star Song Publishing Group, 1994. [This volume is devoted to music in worship.]

Liturgical Arts

Daniels, Marilyn. *The Dance in Christianity.* New York: Paulist Press, 1981.

Davies, J. G. *Liturgical Dance.* London: SCM, 1984.

Kennel, LeRoy. *Visual Arts and Worship.* Scottsdale, PA: Mennonite Publishing House, 1983.

Vosko, Richard. *Through the Eye of a Rose Window: A Perspective on the*

Environment for Worship. Saratoga, CA: Resource Publications, 1981.

Webber, Robert E. Editor. *The Complete Library of Christian Worship.* Volume 4, *Music and the Arts in Christian Worship*, Book 2. Nashville: Nashville: Star Song Publishing Group, 1994. [This volume is devoted to the visual arts, drama and dance, and language.]

White, James F. and Susan J. White. *Church Architecture: Building and Renovating for Christian Worship*. Nashville: Abingdon, 1988.

Liturgical Practice

Brugh, Lorraine S. and Gordon W. Lathrop. *The Sunday Assembly. Using Evangelical Lutheran Worship*, Volume 1. Minneapolis: Augsburg Fortress, 2008. [While this volume is a manual for a particular denominational worship book, the ecumenical nature of the four-action shape of the liturgy makes this volume ecumenically useful.]

Cherry, Constance M. *The Worship Architect: A Blueprint for Designing Culturally Relevant and Biblically Faithful Services.* Grand Rapids: Baker Academic, 2010.

Deitering, Carolyn. *Actions, Gestures, and Body Attitudes.* Saratoga, CA: Resource Publications, 1980.

Fischer, Balthasar. *Signs, Words, and Gestures.* New York: Pueblo Publishing Company, 1981.

Hovda, Robert. *Strong, Loving, and Wise: Presiding in Liturgy.* Collegeville: The Liturgical Press, 1983.

Moon, Hwarang. *Engraved Upon the Heart: Children, the Cognitively Challenged, and Liturgy's Influence on Faith Formation.* (Eugene, OR: Wipf and Stock, 2015.

Vanderwell, Howard. Editor. *The Church of All Ages: Generations Worshiping Together.* Herndon, VA: The Alban Institute, 2008.

Yoga

Eliade, Mircea. *Yoga: Immortality and Freedom.* Translated by Willard R. Trask. Princeton: Princeton University Press, 2009. [This was originally Eliade's doctoral dissertation, published in 1936 and revised in 1958. It was the first Western scholarly study of the yoga traditons of India.]

Feuerstein, Georg. *The Yoga Tradition: Its History, Literature, Philosophy, and Practice.* 3rd ed. Prescottt, AZ: Hohm, 2008.

Freeman, Richard. *The Mirror of Yoga: Awakening the Intelligence of Body and Mind.* Boston: Shambhala, 2012.

Miller, Barbara Stoler. *Yoga: Discipline of Freedom. The Yoga Sutra Attributed to Patanjali.* Translation with Commentary. New York: Bantam Books, 1998.

Singleton, Mark. *Yoga Body: The Origins of Modern Posture Practice.* Oxford: Oxford University Press, 2010.

White, David Gordon. *Sinister Yogis.* Chicago and London: University of Chicago Press, 2009. [This is a scholarly book that draws a picture of what yogis were like before the advent of modern yoga.]

The Biological Body and Human Culture

Berman, Morris. *Coming to Our Senses: Body and Spirit in the Hidden History of the West.* New York: Simon & Schuster, 1989. [The second volume of a trilogy devoted to the evolution of human consciousness. This volume focuses on the relationship between culture and the human body and the somatic basis of Western religious experience.]

Capra, Fritjof. *The Web of Life: A New Scientific Understanding of Living Systems.* New York: Anchor Books, 1996. [A post-Darwinian description of the interrelationships and interdependence of psychological, biological, physical, social, and cultural phenomena.]

Johnson, Don Hanlon. *Body: Recovering Our Sensual Wisdom.* Berkeley:

North Atlantic Books, 1992. [Explores how the mind/body split coaxes us to distrust what our senses tell us and argues that individual awareness of the consequences must be joined with social efforts to alter the shapes of our social body, its institutions and practices.]

Sagan, Dorian and Tyler Volk. *Sex/Death*. White River Junction, VT: Chelsea Green Publishing Company, 2009. [This is two separate books in one volume by two popular science writers. Dorian deals with sex as a natural phenomenon and Volk treats death as a part of life.]

Spretnak, Charlene. *The Resurgence of the Real: Body, Nature, and Place in a Hypermodern World*. Reading, MA: Addison-Wesley, 1997. [Spretnak sees the modern view of the human body as a machine, with the mind as a separate entity, being replaced by a postmodern view that sees not only the brain but also the immune system, the bodily tissues, and even each cell as living cognitive systems. The healthy body connects with the natural cycles of sun and moon, days and nights, and interacts with its biosphere or environment.]

Massage

Calvert, Robert Noah. *The History of Message: An Illustrated Hisrory from Around the World*. Rochester, VT: Healing Arts Press, 2002.

Juhan, Deane. *Job's Body: A Handbook for Bodywork*. Barrytown, NY: Station Hill, 1987. [A comprehensive and detailed study of human anatomy for bodyworkers. A classic bodywork textbook.]

Lindell, Lucinda. *The Book of Massage: The Complete Step-by-Step Guide to Eastern and Western Techniques*. New York: Simon & Schuster, 2001. [A basic approach to the techniques of massage, shiatsu, and reflexology, with ample pictures and drawings.]

Appendix: Questions and Answers

The material for this book originated in classroom lectures, so of course there were questions. Gathered here are questions actually asked and answers actually given (edited after the fact). The questions asked by the students and pastors in the course might be similar to questions in the minds of the readers, and are therefore included here as a resource. I will identify the chapters to which the questions are related.

Chapter 1

Question: Much of our Reformed worship is singing songs and listening to the sermon. We don't use all the body actions that you demonstrated. Should we be moving (no pun intended) to include more of the senses and physical postures in our worship?

Answer: I'm convinced that many people today (at least in Western culture) are more focused on the body than they used to be. They run. They bike. They go to health clubs. They even try out yoga classes. Their kids are in youth sports. To some extent this is to compensate for the fact that our lifestyles have become more sedentary. We spent too much time in awkward physical positions at our computers and driving cars—and people know it. People are looking for ways to get exercise and move their bodies. I think the more embodied our worship is, the more it will engage the worshipers. It is difficult to change from one style of worship to another, but you could prepare people for more embodied experiences of worship by pointing out that singing and listening are also bodily activities.

Question: I appreciate your emphasis on the body. But we have been brought up thinking that we are bodies and souls. Can you say more about the soul?

Answer: There isn't much about the soul in the Bible. Certainly not as much as there is about the body. There is no article of faith concerning the immortal soul in the way that there is about the resurrection of the body. So we are left to speculate, and it is important to disentangle biblical evidence and from the Platonism that influenced ancient Christian thought. I think of the "soul" as our essential self; it is who we are. But the soul cannot be abstracted from the body—or from our life experiences either. Maybe that's why the Western Christian tradition developed a view of the soul's need for purification in a post-death purgatory before it could come into the divine presence. I think that in death our souls are held in God's keeping until the resurrection. That's the sense in which we can speak of our souls being in heaven, because that's where God is. Heaven is like a storehouse. At the resurrection the soul will be restored to the body to give our new bodies their personal identifying characteristics, but purified. In speculating on our resurrected bodies, we have something to go on: the risen body of Jesus. The risen Jesus was both in continuity and in discontinuity with his predeceased body. He could be recognized and not recognized.

Question: Much of our evangelical worship is, as you said, focused on Christ. Should all hymns and songs selected for worship be Trinitarian?

Answer: Not necessarily. There are a lot of hymns in the Christian tradition addressed to Christ alone. One thinks of "Beautiful Savior." The issue is that the worship of the Holy Trinity should be reflected in the totality of the order of worship. When the "script" of worship is prepared, someone should ask: Will a person participating in this liturgy realize that the Christian God is Father, Son, and Holy Spirit? I would note that many of the classical hymns in the tradition conclude with Trinitarian doxologies. There are traditions of standing for these doxological final stanzas if the congregation has been sitting, or bowing at the name of the Trinity in these stanzas. These postures call attention to the worship of the Trinity.

Chapter 2

Question: I'm struck by the similarity between the early Christians praying the Lord's Prayer five times a day and the Muslims praying five times a day. Is there any relationship between these two practices?

Answer: Christians were praying the Lord's Prayer five times a day at least since the end of the first century. I don't know if this Christian practice influenced Muslim practice. But in Muslim countries when the calls to prayer are chanted over loudspeakers from the mosques, there's no reason Christians can't pray at least the Lord's Prayer at those times.

Question: You practice yoga in a predominantly Christian society. In Asian countries many Christians might be converts from Eastern religions like Hinduism. Do you think that Christians should practice yoga if it is associated with non-Christian religion? Would this fall into the category of not offending weaker brothers and sisters?

Answer: In this situation, a different decision might have to be made. We do not want to offend the weaker brothers and sisters. But such considerations are always balanced by the need to expand people's horizons. In terms of practices that are associated with other religions, almost all of our bodily postures and use of natural symbols have corollaries in other religions. Human ritual and symbolic language draws on a limited repertoire of bodily actions. Ancient church fathers like Justin Martyr recognized that the pagan mystery cults also had rites of washing and eating meals and he regarded them as diabolical imitations of Christian sacraments. We know today that rites of washing and sacred meals are common in many religions. Let's take an example of a posture that is practiced in yoga: child pose. Several religions practice prostrations—Eastern Orthodox Christians, Muslims, Hindus, and Buddhists. How many different ways are there to kneel down on the floor with your head touching the ground? The issue is, to whom are you rendering adoration? Another example is incense, which is used in many religions. Mar-Thoma Christians in India use incense. So do Hindus. And they live and worship side by side. The issue here is, what God is being honored by this offering?

Question: Christians have had much disagreement over the earthly elements in the sacraments—for example, the amount of water used in baptism or the kind of food and drink used in Holy Communion. Do you have any comments on this?

Answer: If the earthly elements are "visible words," the concern should be what these words are communicating. What is communicated in the way the sacraments are performed? I think we should begin discussions about the sacraments by remembering that baptism is about taking a bath and Holy Communion is about sharing a meal. These basic facts should be taken into account in sacramental theology. Sacramental theology would then suggest using more water in bigger fonts or pools rather than little bowls on a pedestal and using real loaves of bread rather than wafers and goblets of wine rather than individual, pre-filled containers.

Question: You seem to downplay the role of hospitality in Holy Communion in favor of bonding. Some pastors and churches open the table to all people on the basis of hospitality. Could you comment on this?

Answer: I don't think any meal is only about hospitality. That's a means to the end. The end of serving street people in a soup kitchen is to nourish hungry bodies. We practice hospitality because we want guests to feel comfortable. The purpose of Holy Communion is nourishing the relationship between Christ and his disciples, the church. It is about union with Christ. The Eucharist has been called the liturgy of the faithful. But we want even the faithful to know that Christ welcomes repentant sinners into his fellowship and offers them the forgiveness of sins through this means.

Chapter 3

Question: Have you ever performed a nude baptism?

Answer: No, but I would if the conditions were right. If the candidate is a child the parents would have to agree to it if this is not the usual practice. And if the candidate is an adult or an older youth he or she would have to agree to it. Since baptisms are now usually performed in the open worship space there would have to be appropriate provision for modesty. I understand that some adult candidates for baptism in the Greek Orthodox Church wear a bathing suit. There would also have to be a font or pool big enough so that the candidate could actually go into the water. There would have to be a changing room nearby in which the newly baptized dry off and are dressed in their baptismal clothing, with an alb over the clothing for older neophytes.

Question: In the yoga chakra sequence you asked what sensations we felt. What sensations should we have felt?

Answer: Yoga resists right or wrong when it comes to what one experiences in a practice. Some people are more prepared to tune into feelings, emotions, or thoughts than other people. Some people claim to feel throbbing at each chakra. I'm sure this only happens after a lot of practice, in addition to applying more focus to each chakra than we did in this sample practice. For example, there are sounds that accompany work on each chakra: lam, vam, ram, yom, ham, and om. There is no sound for the crown chakra. In a course I took on experiential yoga philosophy we chanted through each of these sounds many times. The sheer chanting of these sounds can send vibrations through the body. One also needs to focus in meditation on the place where each chakra is located: the root chakra at a spot between the genitals and the anus; the sacral chakra is on the sacral bone at the lower back; the solar plexus chakra is a bit above the level of the navel; the heart chakra is at the level of the heart; the throat chakra is at the base of the throat; the third eye chakra is at a point slightly above the spot between your eyebrows; the crown chakra is at the top of your head. It is considered crucial to open the root chakra before opening any of the others because this holds the possibility of releasing creative energy, the kundalini, to move up he central axis of the body through the other chakras.

Question: Why would one want to activate or open the chakras?

Answer: According to Buddhist/Hindu teaching all of the chakras should contribute to a human's well-being. When our chakras are activated or open our instincts join forces with our feelings and thinking. Some of our chakras are usually not open all the way; some may be overactive. If the chakras are not balanced, peace with oneself cannot be achieved. This simply means that lower and higher capacities, our physical and spiritual selves, should be in balance. The heart chakra balances all of these realities in our lives, and the issues of the heart are devotion, worship, and service. I think we Christians would agree that that's where our heart should be: loving and serving God and loving and serving our neighbor.

Question: Pastors in the Reformed churches in Indonesia usually wear a black gown or a dark suit when leading traditional worship. How would you get them to wear an alb?

Answer: The Reformed tradition wanted to abolish vestments, so the ministers wore their ordinary street dress. At the time of the Reformation that meant wearing a cassock and gown. But today the so-called Geneva gown has become a vestment because it is only worn for worship. Likewise, the dark suit itself becomes a vestment if it is only worn for worship. It is an anthropological principle that leaders wear special clothing for public liturgical worship. Even if the pastor wears khaki pants and a Hawaiian shirt in a contemporary service, that choice has been deliberately made since there are other options. Albs enjoy an ecumenical use today, along with the stole in the proper liturgical color. I would think that a lightweight linen white robe is a lot more comfortable to wear in a tropical climate than a black gown or a dark suit, but your churches are air-conditioned. Nevertheless, the idea that the alb is the baptismal garment also commends its use by all liturgical ministers—acolytes, readers, and communion ministers as well as ordained ministers. Ordained ministers are designated by wearing the stole. The presiding minister at the Eucharist might also wear a chasuble with a matching stole—perhaps in Indonesia one made of batik.

Question: Do you have any suggestions concerning what to wear if one wants to practice yoga?

Answer: The main objective in choosing the right yoga wear is being able to ignore it during yoga practice. The original yogis were ascetics who sought liberation from the limitations of the world and wore nothing, or next to nothing. I'm told that there were also traditions of naked yoginis. When modern gurus brought yoga traditions to the West in the early twentieth century they exchanged a simple loincloth for Western-style briefs, which are now made of spandex. In the West, yoga came to be practiced more by women than by men—the opposite of India—and athletic stores today provide much suitable yoga attire for women, but not so much for men. So I address men's needs here.

You need yoga attire that goes where the body goes without getting in the way. Most women in yoga classes wear tight-fitting tops and bottoms that cling to the body. Women's tops usually allow for bare arms and shoulders, which means that they receive the cooling and energizing benefits of the evaporation of sweat. Loose-fitting T-shirts favored by men get in your face during inversions and become heavy when wet with sweat. In my observation men are always fussing with their T-shirts. My suggestion to men is to practice shirtless, if that is allowed in the studio. It provides for freedom of movement, and the evaporation of sweat is energizing. If you wear a shirt it should be tight fitting and should wick away sweat. Yoga pants for men should be very flexible. Gym shorts, running shorts, and sweat pants all work. I find that a drawstring on the front can be uncomfortable when lying on your stomach. You can buy expensive yoga pants. I prefer inexpensive, but very flexible, Thai fishermen's pants. Ties are on the side rather than in the front. The wide legs can be pulled up for some poses—for example, if you want to place your foot on a bare leg for traction in tree pose.

Yoga is practiced barefoot. It is good to have a blanket or a pullover for final relaxation, because the body cools down quickly. A yoga mat is also helpful.

Comment from a student: It's hard to find a yoga studio here in central Java.

Response: Maybe your university should include yoga instruction in its Physical Education Faculty.

Chapter 4

Question: How do you get people who grew up in a staid Protestant tradition to use their bodies in worship?

Answer: By modeling the use of your body as a worship leader and by doing so in a natural, rather than a self-conscious, way. It helps to have lay worshipers who model the use of their bodies in worship for other worshipers. They make the sign of the cross at invocations of the Trinitarian name. They bow to the cross when it passes down the aisle at the head of a procession. They turn to face the action or the speaker, wherever that may be, which may not be "up front." By doing things consistently, not much needs to be said, and people begin to catch on. Of course, it helps to give some directions orally or printed in the worship folder, like "Please stand and face the back of the church" When someone is speaking or some action is taking place there.

Question: Has liturgy been too solemn? Should we make worship more playful?

Answer: There is a place for solemnity also in play. Sometimes children can be very solemn. Worship is a very serious activity, but that doesn't mean it should lack joy. Someone once said that the worst accusation made against Christians is that they had no joy. If we consider what we are celebrating, our worship should be a joyful event, even if it is solemn.

Chapter 5

Question: You have addressed the issue of the open table previously. But in Asia the issue is that converts to Christianity are alienated from their families if they are baptized. Some churches are allowing the unbaptized to receive Communion so that they can consider themselves as Christians but not alienate their families. Can you comment?

Answer: If non-Christians regard baptism as the mark of conversion and becoming a Christian, then the church has been successful in communicating its beliefs to the rest of the world. But if the issue is to not be identified as a Christian, then being a communicant member of the church doesn't help. Church membership has been defined historically in terms of receiving Communion. First Communion is the goal of Christian initiation, and table fellowship defines the core membership of the church. So communing without being baptized is no solution to the disruption of family relationships that is caused by conversion, and it gives the impression that baptism is not necessary. Jesus said that his coming into the world would set family members against one another, and unfortunately it is true, even in places like America that have a Christian majority.

Comment from a student: I came from a Muslim family, and I converted to Christianity. I expected to be beaten by my friends. The hardest part was to be beaten by my family.

Response: The ancient church would honor you as a confessor of the faith.

Question: I've been thinking that our Reformed celebration of the Lord's Supper has been too mournful, too lacking in joy. What can we do to make Holy Communion a more joyous celebration like the banquets in the early church must have been?

Answer: I can't judge how mournful your Reformed communion services are, and I don't know how joyful those ancient Christian symposia were either. We need to be careful about romanticizing the early church. But the Reformed tradition is not the only church lacking a sense that the Eucharist (the thanksgiving meal) is a joyful celebration. Of course, you can't force people to be joyful. But the music selected can have a great impact on our emotions. Even so, you want the music to evoke a wide range of emotions, without relying too much on what we call "happy clappy" songs.

Question: As a church musician I find it difficult to find a unifying theme on the Sundays after Pentecost because of the semi-continuous first and second readings. If I focus on the Gospel, which is the principal reading, I feel that I am ignoring the other readings. But there's often little or no connection between the three readings. Do you have any suggestions?

Answer: As a preacher, I share your pain. At least with the typological track it is easier in sermons to deal with the Old Testament reading when focusing on the Gospel. If your congregation has a choice, I would urge that it follow the typological track for the Old Testament rather than the continuous reading track. There are other times and ways to get at the portions of Scripture that the lectionary misses, such as in Bible study during the week—in which it is possible to go through the Bible chapter by chapter, verse by verse, in some detail—or in weekday services when the daily lectionary might be used. If your purpose is to expose people to more of the Bible, the classroom works better than the liturgy. (I realize, of course, the preference in the Reformed tradition for continuous reading and commentary on biblical books as opposed to a periscope system.) Beyond that, I would say that you can focus on any of the readings as well as the responsorial psalm in selecting hymns, songs, and choir music. In the ordinary time of the year there are no "themes" such as there are during Advent, Christmas, Lent, and Easter.

Chapter 6

Question: I was struck by how important fasting has been in Christian practice, and yet in the Protestant churches we don't emphasize fasting. How does one begin a practice of fasting?

Answer: By reaching into the tradition. When you want to restore something that has been lost, don't make it up. Go back to the historic tradition. The Friday fast is well attested in Christian history. You can begin there. The tradition also focused on not eating meat. I would also begin there. Then embrace the Lenten fast. Again, meats are the objects of the fast (and if you really want to get serious, meat products). A long fast like the six weeks of Lent requires advance menu planning, just like the Muslims do for Ramadan. After that, you can get creative. Someone has suggested that since fasting is a non-consumerist activity, you could give up buying any unnecessary consumer goods on a fast day. But you should always combine fasting with almsgiving.

Question: In your second session today you talked about a lot of excessive piety that is offensive to modern sensibilities, especially in the flagellant processions and crucifixions that still go on in the Philippines. We have a bit of it here in Java among the Catholics. Can any sense be made of this kind of piety?

Answer: As I said, the purpose of the flagellant movements was to make reparation for the sins or the lukewarm commitment of other Christians and the sins of the church against Christ. This found new expression in the seventeenth century, above all in the devotion to the Sacred Heart of Jesus. We should understand that this was not an attempt to atone for sins, as if Christ's atonement for the sins of the world was insufficient. Rather, the flagellants were doing penance because the church, the body of Christendom, had failed in its love of the Lord who has given himself for his church. Self-flogging has a long career as a penitential exercise in the religious orders, so this was a means by which groups of pious penitents could undertake penance on behalf of the whole church. Like many forms of popular piety (Protestant as well as Catholic), it had an emotional appeal that doesn't square well with a more rational approach to religion. It is certainly a unified expression of body and mind. Unfortunately, in an age of iPhones and YouTube videos, the bloody processions and crucifixions have a certain entertainment value, and the Catholic hierarchy has tried to dissuade people from participating in them, especially in the Philippines. But people will not be dissuaded. It's not a pious practice I would want to undertake. But I admire the piety of those who do.

Chapter 7

Chapter 7 was not presented as a classroom lecture, but the following question came up in another context.

Question: I've read that some Catholic bishops are lowering the age of confirmation to seven, but others raised the age to the late teens. Could you comment on this divergence of practices?

Answer: In recent years, confirmation has come to be seen as a rite of passage that is better administered in adolescence, similar to what Protestants do. The Catholic Church wants to give young people opportunities to participate in a pastoral and educational ministry that will help them make a mature profession of the Christian faith. Some Catholics have even taken to calling confirmation a renewal of baptism, like Protestants do. However, confirmation in the Catholic Church is administered after first communion. Traditional Catholics argue that the sequence of the sacramental economy has been broken. Their desire to restore the sequence of baptism, first communion, and then confirmation is for reasons of both theology and identity. Theologically, one should be "born again of water and the Spirit" (John 3:5) before receiving the body of Christ in the Eucharist. In terms of identity, confirmation at age seven is an outward mark of traditional Catholicism.

Chapter 8

This chapter was not presented as a classroom lecture, but I gave the students an assignment to present an Indonesian ritual to instruct me. They presented one part of the extended ritual process of getting married in Indonesia—the visit of the bride and groom after the wedding to the homes of the parents. In this case I asked the questions and the participants answered from their own experience. What struck me most was how elongated the rites surrounding marriage are in Indonesia when compared with American practices, and also how elaborate. One sees heaps of flowers and ribbons outside the building in which the wedding reception is taking place that are placed there by the families and the wedding guests. Where in America the concern may be to cut the guest list for the reception, in Indonesia there is concern not to eliminate anyone. Wedding receptions accommodate hundreds, even thousands, of guests.

Chapter 9

Question: You said that dialogue on the relationship between worship and culture must take place within each congregation. How do we know when a decision has been reached?

Answer: It should not be by majority vote. In fact, I don't think any liturgical decisions should be made by majority vote. The congregation must try to achieve consensus on matters that affect its life and mission over which it has some control. The church needs to be able to say, as in Acts 15:28:, "It has seemed good to the Holy Spirit and to us." The Spirit is at work in the prayerful deliberations of the assembly. Consensus requires a lot of dialogue and does not mean complete agreement. It means that the group senses the direction in which discussion is moving and has agreed to live with that direction. If there remains a strong vocal minority opposed to that direction, consensus has not been reached, and more discussion is needed to achieve a consensus.

Question: What criteria do you use for selecting art for the worship space?

Answer: The first thing is to have persons with artistic critical ability help to select art that will adorn the space for public worship. We need to respect people's gifts. Their judgment should be balanced by the judgment of other worshipers. The second thing you have to consider is durability. You can change the hymns and the sermon every week, but you're stuck with the art week after week. Art pieces can become dated. Icons have staying power because they are more representational than realistic and more objective than subjective in style. I think folk art can also have this enduring character.

Chapter 10

Question: Do you think it is practically possible to include all six of Levitin's types of song in every worship service?

Answer: I don't know if it is practically possible, but if we select hymns and songs according to the mood of the liturgy at different moments in the liturgy, we will cover several bases. For example, we have songs of praise, which are usually joyful, at the entrance, teaching songs around the sermon, songs of love at the offertory, and songs of friendship and comfort during communion. The psalter expresses all of these moods. Of course, we also select hymns and songs for how their content relates to the liturgical days and seasons as well as to the lectionary readings. That's a lot to balance in the weekly task of hymn selection.

Question: Many of our churches have praise bands. What do you think about contemporary Christian music? Is there a way it can be used while maintaining liturgical integrity?

Answer: Contemporary Christian music was a tidal wave originating in Nashville that apparently can't be resisted. The issue is to make CCM serve the word and the liturgical order just like every other kind of worship music. The songs should be spread throughout the liturgy and chosen for their suitability to their place in the order, the seasons of the church year, and their relationship to the scripture readings for the day; they should not clumped together like a concert. If the hymns and songs are spread throughout the order there is also no problem with blending worship music from different times and places because the pieces are not performed next to each other. You might have a traditional hymn at entrance or sending, chanted psalmody for the responsorial psalm, and spiritual songs at the offertory and during communion. There is no reason why liturgies should use only one kind of music.

Chapter 11

Question: Where in the liturgy do you think dance might be most effectively used?

Answer: Wherever there is a procession. The procession itself is like a very formal dance. But it could also involve more rhythmic swaying and stepping. So the entrance procession, the gospel procession, and the offertory procession could be more dance-like. But I would see this kind of motion more likely occurring in African and Asian contexts than in European and North American—and to better effect.

Question: Isn't it difficult to provide musical leadership in processions? Processions can get spaced out. If people are singing, how do they stay together?

Answer: This can be a problem. So it is important to have instruments that people can easily hear. Brass works well—trumpets and trombones. The instrumentalists do not need to be at the head of a procession. In fact, they could be placed in the middle or even at a stationary place. When we had Palm Sunday processions in my parish, the brass were stationary so that their playing could be heard outside and inside the building. When the procession began to enter the building it was then easy for the organ to pick up leadership of the hymn, "All Glory, Laud, and Honor." Even so, the last people to enter were always lagging in tempo.

Question: Do you think that plays can be performed in church services, perhaps in place of a sermon?

Answer: A play could take the place of the sermon if there is a clear gospel proclamation. I enjoyed writing plays for the youth of my congregation. One or two were, in fact, performed in place of the sermon. Sermons could also be a dramatic monologue, with the pastor as the solo actor. I once wrote a monologue given by the devil on the First Sunday in Lent, to give the devil's view of the temptations of Christ. Hopefully the gospel message came through, even in this C. S. Lewis-type inversion of perspectives.

Chapter 12

There were no questions after my lecture on liturgical performance, but several students and pastors expressed appreciation for it. They said the model I presented helped to open their minds about the practices of other Christian denominations than their own, and not be so judgmental. Some also thanked me for introducing yoga practices in connection with the lectures because it also helped them to open their minds about these techniques, and to see yoga as not just Hindu practice.

In the conversations during the oral examinations of the students, all of them expressed appreciation for the value of giving more attention to the role of the body in worship, especially in their Reformed traditions. Several quoted the dictum—"I don't have a body, I am a body"—as something they had never considered before.

Index